D0679497

Commonsense Grammar and Style

Commonsense Grammar and Style *by Robert E. Morsberger*

based on Commonsense Grammar
by Janet Aiken

Thomas Y. Crowell Company
New York
Established 1834

¶ Copyright © 1965 by Robert E. Morsberger

All rights reserved. No part of this book may
be reproduced in any form, except by a reviewer,
without the permission of the publisher.

Designed by Judith Woracek Barry

Manufactured in the United States of America
by Vail-Ballou Press, Inc., Binghamton, New York

Library of Congress Catalog Card No. 65-18700

First Printing

√ Acknowledgments

Quotations in this volume include copyright material, used with
permission from the following sources:

Lines from Robert Bolt, *A Man for All Seasons*, © Copyright, 1960,
1962, by Robert Bolt; from Truman Capote, *Breakfast at Tiffany's*,
Copyright © 1958 by Truman Capote; and from Alfred Duggan, *The
Cunning of the Dove*, © 1960 by Alfred Duggan, reprinted by permission
of Random House, Inc.

Quotations from the Edgar Rice Burroughs Tarzan stories by permission
of Edgar Rice Burroughs, Inc., Tarzana, California.

Lines by Robert Frost from *Complete Poems of Robert Frost*, Copyright
1923 by Holt, Rinehart and Winston, Inc., Copyright 1942 by Robert
Frost. Copyright renewed 1951 by Robert Frost. Reprinted by permission
of Holt, Rinehart and Winston, Inc.

Harcourt, Brace & World, Inc., for permission to quote lines from George
Orwell, "Politics and the English Language," in *Shooting an Elephant
and Other Essays;* from Vernon L. Parrington, *Main Currents in American
Thought;* from Charles Carpenter Fries, *The Structure of English;* and
from E. E. Cummings, *Poems 1923–1954.*

Lines from *To Kill a Mockingbird* by Harper Lee. Copyright © 1960 by
Harper Lee. Published by J. B. Lippincott Company.

Lines from *Sincerely, Willis Wayde* by John P. Marquand, Copyright
1954, 1955 by The Curtis Publishing Company, Copyright 1955 by John
P. Marquand, reprinted by permission of Little, Brown and Company,
Publishers.

DEFIANCE PUBLIC LIBRARY

428 M   MAR 23 '67   C. 1

Lines from *My Fair Lady, A Musical Play in Two Acts,* Based on *Pygmalion* by Bernard Shaw, Adaptation and Lyrics by Alan Jay Lerner, Music by Frederick Loewe, Copyright © 1956 by Alan Jay Lerner and Frederick Loewe, by permission of the publisher, Coward-McCann, Inc.

Nineteen Eighty-Four by George Orwell, Harcourt, Brace and Company, Inc. Copyright, 1949 by Harcourt, Brace and Company, Inc. Reprinted by permission of Brandt & Brandt.

Quotations from John Osborne, *Luther,* are used by permission of Criterion Books, Inc.

Rembar and Zolotar for permission to quote from the writings of Norman Mailer.

A passage from *I Wanted to Write* by Kenneth Roberts. Copyright 1949 by Kenneth Roberts and Anna M. Roberts. Reprinted by permission of Doubleday & Company, Inc.

Lillian Ross for permission to use quotations of Ernest Hemingway from the "Profile of Ernest Hemingway" in *Reporting* by Lillian Ross, Simon and Schuster, Inc., 1964.

Charles Scribner's Sons for permission to quote from Ernest Hemingway, "In Another Country," in *Men Without Women* and *The Fifth Column and the First Forty-Nine Stories;* and from Edith Wharton, *A Backward Glance.*

Extracts from *Pygmalion* by Bernard Shaw © 1962 by The Public Trustee as Executor of the Estate of George Bernard Shaw, reprinted by permission of The Public Trustee and the Society of Authors.

Simon and Schuster, Inc., for permission to use quotations from Joseph Heller, *Catch-22,* Copyright © 1955, 1961 by Joseph Heller.

The passages from the writings of James Thurber are quoted by permission of Mrs. James Thurber and are copyrighted © 1931, 1933, 1937, 1953, 1955, 1959, 1960, 1961 by James Thurber. Copyright © 1962 by Helen Thurber.

A passage from Lionel Trilling's Introduction to *The Adventures of Huckleberry Finn,* Rinehart Editions. Copyright © by Lionel Trilling. Reprinted by permission of the publisher, Holt, Rinehart and Winston, Inc.

The Viking Press, Inc., for quotations from John Steinbeck, *In Dubious Battle,* Copyright © 1936 by John Steinbeck, and *The Grapes of Wrath,* Copyright © 1939 by John Steinbeck.

"Ode to Cow" was contributed by Evelyn Wood to *Thought* of Delhi, was reprinted in the United States in *Atlas* magazine, June, 1962, and is reprinted by permission of Mr. Wood and *Atlas.*

My work on this book was assisted by a research grant from Michigan State University.

For *Grace, Wendy,* and *Robbie*

√ Foreword

This book derives from *Commonsense Grammar* by Janet Ranken Aiken of Columbia University. First published in 1936, *Commonsense Grammar* went through five editions and seemed to answer a need of the time. At a period when much teaching of grammar was still Latinate and prescriptive, *Commonsense Grammar* was a welcome and refreshing change, dealing in a sensible and tolerant manner with actual usage rather than absolute "rules." Written with warmth and wit, it was a pioneering work in examining the way people use words in practical situations.

A generation later, the publisher wanted to reissue the book but found it somewhat dated. There have been many changes both in linguistic use and attitudes since the 1930's, and a new edition would have required extensive revision.

The present book is a new work almost altogether. Its general approach is indebted to Mrs. Aiken's, but most of the text is original. Chapters 2 and 19 borrow heavily from Mrs. Aiken, and a few sentences and examples have been incorporated into Chapters 5, 8, 12, and 14. The rest of the book is entirely new. In writing a book for the 1960's, I have tried to create a descriptive grammar on historical principles, with many illustrative examples of actual usage from Chaucer to *Catch-22*, including contemporary literature, journalism, politics, and advertising. My approach is liberal and often uses satire to examine the relation of style and sense, language and logic. I am happy to follow in Mrs. Aiken's footsteps, especially because she once walked down Broadway in her bare feet to protest some issue in the 1930's.

Contents

Commonsense Grammar and Style

I √ Common Sense and the Psychology of Grammar

We are divided by a common language.
WINSTON S. CHURCHILL

An Englishman's way of speaking absolutely classifies him.
The moment he talks he makes some other Englishman despise him.[1]
ALAN JAY LERNER, *My Fair Lady*

Most secondary school students when asked their least favorite subject name English. They seem particularly to resent and resist grammar. Their groans may be the result of twelve years of repetitive exercises in the same "rules," so that the grammarian appears as a drillmaster and grammar as a rather meaningless manual of arms that they must somehow perform if they are to get good grades and be eligible for college. Though students use some form of grammar with every thought they have, they do not think about grammar; they express themselves well enough to get along with their companions, and grammar seems an external and arbitrary discipline threatening their independence and natural expression.

The trouble is that most students and some teachers have a mistaken concept of the nature of grammar and the role of the grammarian. Grammar is not an external order to be compulsorily superimposed upon the speech habits of the hapless student and citizen. It is instead a description of those habits and to some extent a classification of them. Habit is the key word here. Since language is our basic means of expression, it is not merely an academic matter but is essential to our fundamental concept of ourselves. To criticize a person's language is to challenge his background, his family, his social status, his intelligence, and to a very real degree his sense of personal integrity. What a person thinks is reflected in

1

what he says and this, in turn, is inseparable from the way he says it. His speech habits are formed before he enters school; and if those habits are unacceptable in educated circles, then it may be a traumatic experience for him to try to alter them, since to do so is to break from his linguistic background. Thus grammar is a social and psychological, even an economic and political matter; and it is no wonder that the subject provokes prejudices and creates antagonisms and resentment.

In a broad sense, there is no such thing as ungrammatical English. Everyone speaking the English language must use grammar, though some uses are more unconventional than others and a few are highly idiosyncratic. It is not even so much that ungrammatical speakers are unconventional as that they follow different conventions from those approved in educated circles and that there is more individuality within the conventions they follow. This "unacceptable" grammar has its own patterns; and Mark Twain, William Faulkner, John Steinbeck, Ring Lardner, Sinclair Lewis, and a host of other authors with an ear attuned to the vernacular have created with its aid quite recognizably realistic and sometimes eloquent dialogue and first-person narrative. If it were presented as their own grammar, it would rarely receive a passing grade from an English teacher. In fact, *Huckleberry Finn* when it first appeared was banned in many communities, partly because critics complained of Huck's "uncouth" grammar, which they considered an affront to cultivated gentility. But Mark Twain observed, in "The Stolen White Elephant," that "a nation's language is a very large matter. It is not simply a matter of speech obtaining among the educated handful; the manner obtaining among the vast uneducated multitude must be considered also."

The die-hard purist is something of a reactionary. He fears that language is in constant danger of being corrupted and that about nine tenths of the people already speak a debased, ungrammatical version of English. (Noah Webster condemned "the well-nigh universal misuses of English," but if everyone misuses the language, how can there be a right use?) Since language is developed by the people rather than revealed from God on high, these are curious statistics reminiscent of the old Puritan concepts of election and depravity by which nine tenths of the human race were predestined for hell. But, if English is being corrupted, what is it being corrupted from? Probably the oldest surviving scrap of English writing is the Anglo-Saxon poem *Widsith,* which begins:

2

Wīdsīð maðolade, wordhord onlēac,
sē þe [monna] mæst mægþa ofer eorþan,
folca geondfērde . . . .

But then about seven hundred years later than the "pure" language of *Widsith,* we find the language corrupted into the more modern (hence debased) English of Layamon:

An preost wes on leoden, Laȝamon wes i-hoten;
He wes Leovenaðes sone: liðe him beo Drihten!

Two hundred years later, we find English further corrupted and modernized in *The Second Shepherd's Play:*

Lord, what these weders ar cold! and I am yll happyd;
I am nere-hande dold, so long have I nappyd.

But all is not lost. As we go down to the year 1702 and examine the writings of Cotton Mather, we seem to have a return from the "depraved" simplicity of *The Second Shepherd's Play* to something more remote and hence more pure:

Reader! I have done the part of an *Impartial Historian,* albeit not without all occasion perhaps, for the Rule which a worthy Writer, in his Historica, gives to every Reader, *Historici Legantur cum Moderations & venia, & cogitetur fieri non posse ut in omnibus circumstantiis sint Lyncei. Polybius* complains of those *Historians,* who always made either the *Carthagenians* brave, and the Romans base, or *è contra,* in all their Actions, as their Affection for their own *Party* led them.

Yet, alas, when we remove the Latin and the italics, we find that the Reverend Mather has corrupted the language by changing it yet further from the primitive purity of *Widsith.* Finally we come to the mid-twentieth century, where we encounter such debased prose as "Snoopy's out there stranded on top of his doghouse! He needs help!"[2] Certainly Widsith would find this unintelligible, and the Second Shepherd would doubtless find it difficult.

Obviously there is no "well of English undefiled." If we are no longer using precisely the language of Shakespeare and Spenser, Shakespeare and Spenser did not use the language of Chaucer, and Chaucer did not use that of *Beowulf.* What some pedants mean when they say that English is corrupted is that it is a corruption from Latin. A Germanic language, English was never based on Latin, so it is hard to see how it could be a corruption of it. But from the Middle Ages (when Latin was already dead as a vernacular language) down into the nineteenth century, Latin was the language of Western scholarship. Its advocates praised the logic of its structure (forgetting that the actual Romans never spoke the pure classical Latin of Cicero and that even St. Jerome wrote in the vulgate) and insisted that it should be the model for all language. Some people have said that they never really understood English grammar until they studied Latin; but they say this in English, not in Latin, grammar. The only thing the study of Latin grammar can do is to make the student conscious that words have formal inflections and functional relationships, if he hasn't already bothered to discover this in English. Certainly both form and function are un-English, as in the Latin *Assurgentem regem resupinat* and its translation, "As the king was trying to rise, he threw him down." It is true that classical Latin has the abstract logic of mathematical equations, but a living language is not abstract; it is spoken by individual throats, tongues, and teeth in an infinite variety of specific contexts and situations. Thus it is impossible for grammarians to enforce any linguistic laws, even if such laws were logical, as often they are not. It is not the grammarian's province to police the language.

Yet there are penalties for not using the grammar and vocabulary approved in dominant and more highly educated social circles. Your own educational opportunities and future—the sort of job you can get (and therefore your standard of living and the neighborhood in which you can afford to live), the sort of close friends you will have, the person you will marry, and even the future of your children are to a considerable extent determined by your use of language. If your grammar and diction are considered vulgar or illiterate you will be so classified by the more cultivated.

"You see this creature with her kerbstone English; the English that will keep her in the gutter to the end of her days," says Henry Higgins in Bernard Shaw's *Pygmalion*. In this play and its musical version *My Fair Lady*, Higgins, a professor of phonetics and elocution, takes a penniless flower girl and turns her into a lady by teaching her upper-class grammar, pronunciation, and manners. For grammar and pronunciation are a species of manners, a socially relative matter rather than a sign of intrinsic merit. Neither grammar nor pronunciation by itself is enough. If Eliza had precise grammar and a slum accent, she would be an anomaly indeed. As it is, she learns elocution first and makes a trial appearance at a

4

tea party where, with the most impeccable accent, she tells in guttersnipe grammar a story about her aunt's being murdered in gin row: "But it's my belief they done the old woman in." The incongruity is ludicrous, and Higgins quickly explains that Eliza is merely entertaining them with the new small talk. A young man present finds it vastly amusing; but Eliza, bewildered, demands, "If I was doing it proper, what was you laughing at?" So Eliza must proceed to learn to speak grammatically, though she complains, "I don't want to talk grammar. I want to talk like a lady."

In the sentimental and genteel American novels of the first half of the nineteenth century, social status was extremely important; rarely could anyone qualify as hero or heroine who did not come from an upper-class background and independent wealth. Thus, frontiersmen like Leatherstocking and his many imitations were ineligible because of their crudeness and particularly because of their backwoods dialect. Since an aristocrat might outwardly disguise himself as a hunter or trapper, dialect became the ultimate test of status. Historian Henry Nash Smith, who made an extensive study of such novels, observed, "The belief that no one is suitable to conduct a sentimental courtship unless he speaks a pure English is very strong."[3] Smith further noted that if a person from a lowly background became involved in a love affair, his English almost immediately became free of dialect, regardless of his earlier usage or that of his parents. However, this aristocratic speech was stilted rhetoric fossilized by literary convention and infinitely less vital than the socially unacceptable language of Huck Finn. Some of Mark Twain's contemporaries (like the "proper" element in Huck's own town of St. Petersburg) condemned Huck as worthless and immoral trash, a social outcast. Actually, Huck, though ragged around the edges, is a profoundly moral and decent person, far more so than the slaveowners in his society. As for his language, there is no such thing as correct or incorrect, good or bad English grammar in any moral sense, though these labels have been used to embarrass and to color the values of generations of schoolchildren. Language can indeed be used immorally, as a vehicle of illogical persuasion, thought control, hate-mongering, or euphemistic diction to conceal the true names of political atrocities. But a person who uses nonstandard grammar is not thereby morally inferior ("I'm a good girl, I am," Eliza keeps telling Henry Higgins), whereas Shakespeare's villains often speak an exalted rhetoric. If one grammatical usage is preferable to another, there must be

5

some concrete reason, not simply the abstract concept of what is good and bad.

As you can see in the quotations from *Widsith* to *Peanuts*, language changes. As it does so, standard practices may become nonstandard, while other nonstandard ones may become standard. For instance, the multiple negative, now unacceptable, was customary in the time of King Alfred and was common in Chaucer. *Thou* and *thee* and their accompanying verb endings have disappeared from ordinary usage. *Right* as an adverb (*right good, right soon*), which is now frowned upon, was common in Elizabethan English. Principal parts of many verbs have changed. Even in isolated communities, language changes, though it may do so in different ways than the main stream. In one Tarzan book, the apeman discovers a lost city inhabited by descendants of the Crusaders. Their costumes, customs, and language are supposed to be unchanged from the Middle Ages. But the dialogue Edgar Rice Burroughs gives them is not early Middle English; instead it is imitative of Sir Walter Scott's medieval romances—nineteenth-century prose with a sprinkling of archaic diction and word order and a few *thees* and *thous*:

"Whence comest thou," he asked, "and what doest thou in the Valley of the Sepulcher, varlet?"

Blake, the American, mistakes the latter-day Crusader for a movie extra and asks to see the director:

"Director? Forsooth. I know not what thou meanest."
"Yes, you don't!" snapped Blake, with fine sarcasm. "But let me tell you right off the bat that no seven-fifty a day extra can pull anything like that with me!"

"Od's blud, fellow! I ken not the meaning of all the words, but I mislike thy tone."[4]

The actual English Crusaders would have spoken Norman French or else a form of English largely unintelligible in pronunciation, grammar, and vocabulary to the modern Englishman. The real Robin Hood, if there was one, did not speak like Errol Flynn; his language would have been something like "Biþinne castelwalle,/ per i was atte ʒate;/ Nolde hi me in late./ Modi i-hote hadde/ To bure þat me hire ladde."

Some misinformed people claim that pure Elizabethan is still spoken in the more isolated communities of the Southern Appalachians, but this is no more true of those living there than it is of Tarzan's Crusaders. Try this for a sample of Appalachian mountain dialect and see if it is pure Elizabethan: "Hit didn't happen me that I wushed to contrary the revenoors, but hit turns my stomach over-fair to think how them thar shammuckin' revenoors has mommocked up an' well-nigh ruinated things fer the blockaders an' pore ailin' bodies."[5]

It would be outside the province of this book to discuss the detailed development of the language from Old to Modern English, but the lesson is plain that there are no absolute rules or authorities, nor any fixed, ideal standard of English grammar. Instead, there are, subject to change, certain linguistic forms and practices accepted in each generation by the majority of well-educated people. (These can, if you like, for the time being, be considered rules, though *conventions* is the more accurate word.) Language conforming with these forms is known as standard English, and departures from them are termed nonstandard or—if really illiterate—substandard.

Thus, standard English is really a sort of class dialect, and that is the reason for the prejudices, antagonisms, and resentments that grammar and diction arouse. One of Steinbeck's characters explains, "You know, Doc, men are suspicious of a man who doesn't talk their way. You can insult a man pretty badly by using a word he doesn't understand. Maybe he won't say anything, but he'll hate you for it."[6]

This reaction operates not only among Steinbeck's migrant farm workers; the "upper" levels of society also harbor resentment against the so-called lower ones. Many native-born Americans looked down upon non-British immigrants because of their dialect and broken grammar; and for several generations during the height of immigration, we had programs of compulsory Americanization. The prejudice extended to unfamiliar-sounding foreign names. In 1919, when an Armenian, Bagdasar Baghdigian, went to register at a Kansas City night school, the teacher winced at his name and said, "Oh, give that up and change your name to Smith, Jones, or some name like that and become Americanized. Give up everything you brought with you from the Old Country. You did not bring anything worthwhile anyway." Baghdigian reacted angrily, but many others did change their names, as part of their climb to so-called respectability. Nevertheless, some new immigrants, even when handicapped by a limited knowledge of English grammar, managed to be more eloquent than most native-born Americans. In

7

James Thurber's and Elliott Nugent's play *The Male Animal,* a bigoted trustee attacks a university professor who wants to read to his class a passage from Bartolomeo Vanzetti, the Italian fish-peddler who many believe was unjustly convicted of murder. When the trustee belligerently asks why Professor Turner can't read from some American instead—Herbert Hoover, perhaps—Turner replies that Hoover can't write as well as Vanzetti.

For several generations after the Civil War, dialect humor was much in vogue, and the source of such humor is partly a snobbish amusement towards those whose pronunciation is different and therefore felt to be inferior. The minstrel show laughed condescendingly at a stereotype of Negro dialect. For a long time, Hollywood movies portrayed Negroes mostly as amiable oafs speaking a "Yassuh, sho-nuff, boss" type of dialogue, and there are still derogatory jokes told in allegedly Negro and Jewish dialects. Actually there is no specifically Jewish dialect, and many Negroes speak English undistinguishable from that of other Americans. Such dialect as there is, is regional (i.e., Brooklynese, Deep Southern), rather than religious or racial.

All Americans are immigrants, and our language as well as our population rightly reflects this inheritance. Thus, for well over a century and a quarter after the United States won its independence, many British men of letters sneered at the English used by all Americans, even that of Jefferson, John Marshall, and John Quincy Adams, terming it vulgar and uncouth. Some Anglophilic Americans agreed with them; as late as 1893, one went so far as to describe it as "an inferior dialect of the English." In 1908, a British writer in *Blackwood's Magazine* stated that America still acknowledged the sovereignty of English letters: "American is heard at the street corner. It is still English that is written in the study." Thus Alexis de Tocqueville, the French critic who examined American democracy in the 1830's, observed, "It is not then to the written but to the spoken language that attention must be paid, if we would detect the modifications which the idiom of an aristocratic people may undergo when it becomes the language of a democracy." The more class barriers a nation has, the deeper are its linguistic divisions; and Britain still contains more numerous and divergent dialects than does the entire United States. American social change enriched and vitalized the language, whereas the British status quo has made modern British literature much more linguistically conservative, except for the work of some Welsh and Irish rebels.

8

Today the younger British writers from working-class backgrounds and provincial universities, people from outside the Establishment, are producing some of the most vigorous and unorthodox poetry and prose.

The "English that is written in the study" was never that of the majority of Britons any more than of Americans; it belonged wholly to the educated literary caste. But what is the language of English literature? Does it not include the language of Thomas Hardy's peasants and of William Faulkner's sharecroppers? Robert Burns wrote far better in Scot dialect than in academic English. Many distinguished American writers (including Benjamin Franklin, Herman Melville, Abraham Lincoln, Mark Twain, Walt Whitman, Sherwood Anderson, Theodore Dreiser, Jack London, Ernest Hemingway, and William Faulkner) have had a limited formal education. James Fenimore Cooper was among the most militantly aristocratic of our authors, yet Mark Twain became a vastly superior stylist and wrote several essays satirizing and improving Cooper's prose. Though for a long time, as we mentioned earlier, Mark Twain was not considered entirely respectable in established literary circles (both because of his background and his use of the vernacular), Oxford University eventually recognized his merit and awarded him an honorary doctorate of letters. On the other hand, many "proper" writers, praised at the time, have been forgotten by all but the most specialized literary historians.

Still, language remains a sign of class distinction. The incongruous mixture of a snobbish attitude with nonstandard grammar is a reliable source of humor. Helen Hokinson's first captioned cartoon (1925) has a salesgirl tell a customer of a perfume: "It's *N'Aimez Que Moi*, madam—don't love nobody but me." And in the *Thurber Carnival* revue, a woman boasts, "So I gave him a haughty look and I said, 'Whom do you think you are, anyways?' " Her *whom* is the result of overcompensation, the nonstandard speaker being so anxious to appear superior that she rejects the natural *who* for the incorrect case. It is more pathetic than amusing when people are so distrustful of their speech that they suspect any natural expressions and believe the proper ones must be the opposite of their own usage.

Bergen Evans, a leading spokesman for the liberal linguists, says that scholars "do not believe that anyone who is a native speaker of a standard language will get into any linguistic trouble unless he is misled by snobbishness or timidity or vanity." [7] This is perhaps too

9

utopian; *will* should be changed to *should,* for it is still possible to get into trouble. Should you speak as your neighbor speaks? This depends partly on your neighbor and partly on your own ambitions. If Lincoln had known only the frontier speech of New Salem, Illinois, he would not have been asked to run for President. On the other hand, politicians sometimes cultivate a fake folksy speech in order to win votes. In June 1962, the Salem, Indiana, *Democrat* noted, "The word 'ain't' has been declared respectable, and we candidates for office must develop something else to show that no one is more ordinary than we are." Apparently some politicians are indifferent to St. Augustine's advice that one should never smite an opponent in bad grammar. In 1952 and 1956, Adlai Stevenson spoke a clear and polished prose while Dwight Eisenhower's grammar was often garbled, yet Stevenson's speech showed so much education that many people reacted against it, while Eisenhower's occasional incoherencies apparently didn't bother the public. In fact, Eisenhower's grammar was standard but sometimes sufficiently awkward to make his style sometimes seem like a self-parody.

In a democratic society, the signs of class distinction are not always visible. Americans have always been uneasy about democracy; we claim to believe in equality, but we really feel that some are more equal than others. The newly rich may be uncultured clods, while the underpaid professor represents one sort of elite despite his dearth of conspicuous consumption. Since a goon in a three-hundred-dollar suit is still a goon, while a Barrymore in rags is obviously a gentleman, people insecure socially are particularly uneasy about their use of English. They can relax with friends, but in unfamiliar company, they may become apologetic about their pronunciation, grammar, or vocabulary. Even the well-educated are sometimes embarrassed by their educated usage.

The English teacher is too often thought of (and perhaps considers himself) a linguistic traffic cop, but this is not his function. The usual comment people make when introduced to an English teacher is, "Oh, oh! I'll have to watch my language." Apparently they think of the English teacher as a prissy, fastidious character, like the Puritan God outraged at the least offense. Actually, no English teacher with any sense goes around "correcting" the language of others. In fact, the professional student of language is likely to be far more broad-minded than the person who exclaims, "I'll have to watch my language." Far from being disturbed, he is apt to be intrigued with linguistic idiosyncracies. For the true func-

10

tion of the linguist is to observe and describe how language is used, rather than to prescribe how it should be used. He is a historian, instead of a lawgiver, and he realizes the futility of trying to legislate language for millions and to enforce such legislation. The Italians in 1582 and the French in 1635 established an academy to stand guard over their national tongue, to purge it of any impurities, and to prevent any change (hence decay) from setting in. Some English men of letters, like Dryden and Defoe in the late seventeenth century and Swift and a host of lesser figures in the eighteenth, urged the founding of an English academy to perform a similar function. Had they succeeded, Huck Finn would have had one more reason for running away from the restrictions of "siviliza-tion."

Language should not be a rigid set of rules to be followed but a supple and flexible instrument to be used. The authoritarian uses grammar like the Articles of War; but language is a vehicle of communication, not commandment. The literary artist employs it to create the effects he wants; he is its master, not its prisoner. Thus Lionel Trilling writes of *Huckleberry Finn:* "As for the style of the book, it is not less than definitive in American literature. The prose of *Huckleberry Finn* established for written prose the virtues of American colloquial speech. This has nothing to do with pronunciation or grammar. It has something to do with ease and freedom in the use of the language. Most of all it has to do with the structure of the sentence, which is simple, direct, and fluent, maintaining the rhythm of the word-groups of speech and the intonations of the speaking voice." [8] Actually, style does have something to do with grammar, for a writer who straitjackets himself by rigidly following prescriptive and artificial rules too far removed from actual usage will not get the fluent freedom of Mark Twain.

Lionel Trilling stresses Twain's awareness of the cadences of oral speech; and it is important to remember that essentially language is spoken, not written. Only within the last two centuries has there been a wide reading public for English; and in the world at large a great majority is still illiterate. Written English is usually more careful and precise than casual speech, but it must be based upon spoken usage, or it becomes increasingly separate and ultimately dead—the written language of a particular caste or class, like classical Sanskrit. As if in recognition of this, we speak of languages as *tongues,* not as *pens, presses,* or *typewriters.* Only Tarzan learned to read and write English before he could speak it. He grew

11

up speaking the "language" of the great apes but discovered his parents' books in their cabin on the edge of the jungle; and there, sitting by his parents' skeletons, he taught himself to read and write by the "look-see" method, beginning with the pictures and words in children's primers (D-O-G matches the picture of a dog) and progressing to adult books with abstract words that he could have never learned by such a method or any other, since they then had no context or significance to him. When he did discover human speech, he learned French before he learned English. This could happen only in science fiction.

Unlike Tarzan, most people speak English better than they write it. Some who are fluent and vigorous in conversation become incoherent and atrocious stylists when they try to express themselves on paper. Despite the linguists' stress on spoken language, a person who writes English poorly is usually a poor reader and therefore reads little. We usually connect grammar and literacy. So grammar is involved in reading as well as in writing and speaking, and few people write well who do not read extensively in the work of superior authors. Business firms complain of poor writing and advertise, "Send me a man who reads." According to a survey made in the late 1950's, only about 17 percent of Americans were then reading a book, as compared to 34 percent of the Australians and 55 percent of the British. Over a century ago, Thoreau complained: "We are underbred and low-lived and illiterate; and in this respect I confess I do not make any very broad distinction between the illiterateness of my townsman who cannot read at all and the illiterateness of him who has learned to read only what is for children and feeble intellects." He went on to complain, "The best books are not read even by those who are called good readers," and observed, "Most men have learned to read to serve a paltry convenience, as they have learned to cipher in order to keep accounts and not be cheated in trade. . . ." Yet, "To read well, that is, to read true books in a true spirit, is a noble exercise, and one that will task the reader more than any exercise which the customs of the day esteem. It requires a training such as the athletes underwent. . . ." Benjamin Franklin had a much more utilitarian view of literature than Thoreau, but he related that being very ambitious to write well, he studied and imitated the best authors of his time until he developed his own workmanlike style; and towards the end of his career, he claimed that he owed much of his success to his writing ability.

12

By contrast, many a college student confesses that he never reads a book that is not assigned and cannot comprehend how anyone can read for pleasure. Just as the musically uneducated may find serious music painful, the poorly read student usually has a tin ear for language (which is, after all, a sort of music, as poets realize) and is incapable of revising his own written work or developing an effective style. Thoreau urged that the classics and other important works of the past be read, whereas there is some tendency today for high school students to be assigned easy, modern popular books or versions of the classics rewritten in simpler (and undistinguished) language with most of the intellectual content removed. (On the other hand, some high school reading lists sound like those for a master's degree.) But a badly written, though intellectually easy, book is slower and more difficult to read than a well-written one; hack writing is like poor, unoiled machinery, with a jerky rather than a forward movement and rhythm.

Thus there is grammar in a broad as well as a narrow sense, yet too often only the latter is taught. Many students and apparently some teachers do not see the connection between grammar and style and clear, perceptive thinking. Instead, they concentrate on the mere mechanics of grammar—exercises on agreement, antecedents, verb forms, and writing complete sentences, without considering whether the examples themselves have any grace, style, or wit. As a result, some students give up in frustration and boredom, while others turn out prose that is grammatically correct but hopelessly awkward. On the other hand, skilled stylists often violate "correct" grammar to achieve gracefulness or emphasis. James Thurber frequently attacked modern manglings of grammar, but he also satirized his old English composition teacher, Miss Groby, who loved to torture the life out of sentences by parsing them on the blackboard and who saw literature only as a hunting ground for figures of speech that could be picked out and labeled. Probably she would have agreed with Thomas Wentworth Higginson, who wanted to "correct" some of the grammar in Emily Dickinson's poetry. Yet Higginson confessed that "When a thought takes one's breath away, a lesson on grammar seems an impertinence."

Does teacher know best? Even if there were a definitive "best," as there is not in many cases, not all English teachers would be able to recognize it—let alone teach their students to do so. According to a bulletin published by the National Education Association, about one third of those teaching high school English did not themselves major in English or in any related field while at college. Ninety percent of the teachers interviewed said they thought they were not qualified to teach reading, over half considered themselves inadequately prepared to teach composition, and about half felt they were not prepared to teach literature and language. Though elementary school teachers spend more time on English than on any other subject, fewer than 10 percent of them had majored in English; only one in three had been required to study literature; and less than one in five had been required to take more than a freshman course in composition. In the light of these statistics, the average teacher's "authority" is not too reliable. William Morris reported in the *Washington Post* that an English teacher in a highly rated Connecticut school maintained that "Have you become accustom to the noise?" was correct and "accustomed" incorrect. (Can you imagine Rex Harrison singing, "I've been accustom to her face"?) And three teachers told a student that of the sentences (1) "You are suppose to do your schoolwork" and (2) "You are supposed to do your schoolwork," only the first is acceptable. Four confused teachers are not, of course, enough to indicate a trend; and there are many others who, underpaid and overworked, do a fine job in recognizing and encouraging effective writing.

The effective teacher will be a guide, rather than a lawgiver; he will have some knowledge of the history and evolution of English, and he will recognize that usage, the only real authority, is both changing and relative. However, the principle of relativity can be carried to impractical extremes. Some liberal, descriptive grammarians bend so far over backwards to avoid anything that can be construed as a value judgment that they may end by making no judgments at all. One professor maintained that if he were teaching secondary school and had students who used the kind of grammar represented by "I knowed we was suppose to hand in our papers, but them assignments wasn't no easy ones to do," he would ask the students what they planned to do after they graduated. If they expected to work in a garage or on an assembly line, he would tell them not to worry about their language, because it would be appropriate to that environment. But if they hoped to have a white-collar job or become an executive, then they should elevate their grammar to a standard acceptable in higher social and occupational circles. This would be an adequate explanation if language were merely a matter of adjustment or adaptation. Some timid souls even suggest that you should alter your diction and grammar to conform to the company in which you find yourself, so you won't be rejected as different. Thus if you are in basic training, you should adopt nonstandard grammar and employ the omnipresent obscenity of the troops. But this approach is both dishonest and unnecessary. Nobody objects to standard grammar or demands obscenities; as long as you use relaxed colloquial English and avoid snobbish affectations, you will get along anywhere. You might, as Steinbeck observed, be resented if you use a learned vocabulary beyond your listener's level of understanding; but this is a question of manners, not of grammar. Assuredly you will be resented if you lecture people on the unacceptability of their language. Lawrence of Arabia confessed, "I became . . . quite intolerable to the Staff on the Canal. I took every opportunity to rub into them their comparative ignorance and inefficiency in the department of intelligence and irritated them yet further by literary airs, correcting Shavian split infinitives and tautologies in their reports." [9] In *To Kill a Mockingbird*, the children Jem and Scout criticize their housekeeper Calpurnia for using different levels of language at home and at work. She explains, ". . . folks don't like to have somebody around knowin' more than they do. It aggravates 'em. You're not gonna change any of them by talking right, they've got to want to learn themselves, and when they don't want to learn there's nothing you can do but keep your mouth shut or talk their language." [10]

Obviously, not everyone is going to become a skilled grammarian and stylist, and it is pointless to bemoan this fact. But this does not mean that the grammarian should give up his job or that there is no advantage in standard English. Though standards change, there is a decided advantage in using grammar and diction that is clearer, more precise, more effective in expressing complex ideas and subtle distinctions of meaning. Though some moving passages in literature are written in the vernacular (e.g., much of Scott, Dickens, Hardy, Twain, Steinbeck, and J. D. Salinger), nonstandard tends to lapse into clichés (as is apparent in the work of Salinger), to be far more monotonous and limited than educated usage. Paradoxically, standard English is more flexible, and the very limitations of nonstandard tend to standardize thought. This is particularly true of the dialogue in television Western, hillbilly, and crime shows that grind out standardized nonstandard speech and thereby kill the colorful diversity of genuine regionalisms.

Of course, many regionalisms are perfectly acceptable. In a broad sense, everybody's English is the product of some sort of regionalism. Pronunciation is the most obvious regional distinction, but diction and grammar also change somewhat from area to area. As for pronunciation, no particular dialect is intrinsically superior to any other. Most Americans share a broad-gauge common pronunciation, but this does not make a Bostonian or Southern accent any less valid. If the New Englander wants to call his region *Noon Gland,* if the Missourian wants to call his state *Missourah,* and the Nevadan to flatten the *a* in the name of his, that is their privilege. Dialects are a weakness only if they are so thick and so localized as to be a barrier to broad communication. Thus the characters in the British movie *Sparrows Can't Sing* spoke such an impenetrable East End Londonese that it was necessary to provide subtitles for the American audiences—and possibly for some British ones as well. Certainly there is no need for anyone to apologize for an accent, though snobbery may try to raise social and professional barriers against people whose accents are unfashionable. Some writers use phony spelling like *sed, sez, luv, trubble, wuz, pore,* and *likker,* to suggest regional ignorance or illiteracy, though this is the way these words are actually pronounced. Actors and public speakers may find it advisable to overcome the limitations of accent, and mush-mouths and nasal twangs may not be euphonious, but there is no genuine basis for disparaging anyone's accent. This is not to say that there aren't mispronunciations; for example, it is nowhere acceptable to say *heenious* for *heinous, inviduous* for *invidious, peotry* for *poetry,* or *liberry* for *library.* Thus, *sho nuff* is accepted as a regionalism, whereas *nucular* (for *nuclear*) is non-standard even when used by President Eisenhower.

As for diction and grammar, some regionalisms are all right in their cultural context. Some words are standard in one region and not in another; the distinction is geographical, not moral, though pedants try to make it so. Henry Higgins even tells Eliza, "You will get much further with the Lord if you learn not to offend His ears." [11] Within different regionalisms, there is standard and non-standard usage, just as there are social distinctions within regions. Nancy Mitford wrote a satiric book distinguishing between the vocabulary used by upper-class and non-upper-class Britons, whereupon social snobs became quite alarmed lest they be caught using Non-U instead of U terminology. Which is U—*sofa* or *couch*—and does it matter? George Bernard Shaw wrote in *Pygmalion* that "an honest and natural slum dialect is more tolerable than the attempt

16

DEFIANCE PUBLIC LIBRARY
428 M
c. 1

of a phonetically untaught person to imitate the vulgar dialect of the golf club. . . ." In America, so-called provincial speech is not necessarily inferior to that of the urban areas. It is simply that some regionalisms are "in" and others are "out"; thus Pennsylvania Dutch is considered provincial but Bostonian is not. Why should *might could* be frowned upon as shibboleth and the ubiquitous suffix *-wise* be accepted as "sophisticated"? Merely because every little "in" group has a jargon all its own.

Carrying relativism to extremes, researchers at University College, London, wrote that when comparing the language of the King James and New English versions of the Bible, "No one has good grounds for supposing that one of these styles is necessarily better than the other; nor, for that matter, does one have evidence for thinking that either of these styles is better than the style of advertising. . . ." For the versions of the Bible, they are correct in general but perhaps wrong in particular. That is, seventeenth-century prose is not necessarily superior to that of the twentieth-century. Certainly Hemingway wrote better than Gabriel Harvey. Yet styles are not abstract; you must look at particular works, and it may well be that in many specific passages the King James translation is more eloquent and poetic than the New English Version. Freed from archaisms, the latter is undoubtedly clearer to modern readers, but clarity is not everything. *Better* has several meanings, and you must ask, "Better in what way?" The style used in advertising may be appropriate for advertising; but when applied to religion, it produces billboards demanding that you "Get Right with God!" When scholars insist that there is only one acceptable style, they produce a dead "literary" language with the stereotyped rhetoric of the old Shakespearean actor in the movies and comic strips. On the other hand, it is doubtful that the London researchers would concede that the style of *Hamlet* in *Classic Comics* is as good as that in Shakespeare's play. In speaking of style, they should amend "better" to "appropriate"; for if no style is better, then all distinctions vanish: Mickey Spillane and Edgar Guest are the equal of James Joyce and Robert Frost.

However, this does not mean that there is one "right" style. Robert Frost, T. S. Eliot, E. E. Cummings, Dylan Thomas, Wallace Stevens, and Robert Lowell are all great twentieth-century poets, yet each has his own distinctive voice. In fact, many writers have several styles for different occasions. Style, of course, is more than grammar, but it includes grammar. Usually, literary artists em-

17

ploy standard usage except in some dialogue, but there is considerable leeway between relaxed colloquial and highly formal grammar. Even colloquial grammar has a rather formal control in Hemingway's concise prose—including his dialogue, nonstandard though some of it is. For Hemingway's prose shows the discipline of the artist, not of the authoritarian. Literature uses the unregimented language of the imagination. Thus James Thurber, though irritated at much modern grammar, protested because too much advertising, bureaucratic, and journalistic prose is slovenly, rather than because it breaks absolute rules. Thurber's style, like Hemingway's, was disciplined, but he wanted to do his own disciplining. When editor Harold Ross of *The New Yorker* red-penciled a writer's work too rigidly, in accordance with Fowler's *Modern English Usage,* Thurber protested, "I was increasingly disturbed by Ross's insistence on super-clarity, over-punctuation, and strict rules of grammar and syntax and parsing. I knew that if McNulty became a prisoner of pattern, something warm and unique would go out of his writing." [12] For language is not a ritual incantation but a personal voice. It should be exciting rather than inhibiting. Just as the modern composer makes use of the twelve-tone scale, jazz, and hitherto unorthodox instruments, such as the saxophone or exotic percussion, so the modern creative writer should be able to exploit all the resources of the language.

This does not mean that anything goes and that standard grammar is obsolete. Nor does it mean that any nonstandard habit can be justified on grounds of widespread usage. When mangled grammar interferes with clarity and logic, when it produces prose as graceless as a spavined mule, as shabby as a sharecropper's cabin, and as precise as a politician's promises, then it certainly needs revision. The remedy is functional, rather than formal, grammar. The grammatical equivalent of five-finger exercises may help at first, but later you must be free to relax and to experiment. For, let me repeat, there is no single, abstract standard for correct or good writing. There is only effective writing. This requires contextual grammar; the question is not whether it is abstractly right, but whether it works in context. If you break grammatical conventions, you must do so effectively, not ignorantly and carelessly. There is a world of difference between E. E. Cummings's "what if a much of a which of a wind/gives the truth to summer's lie" and "Us Tareyton smokers would rather fight than switch"; between Cummings's "my father moved through dooms of love/ through sames of am through haves of give" and "We don't want none of them eggheads in politics."

In short, you should be a stylist, rather than a pedant. Much writing that is grammatically "correct" is dull and clumsy. It is relatively easy to achieve academic correctness; but really effective writing, far from practicing the idea that anything goes, requires far more sensitivity and self-discipline than the schoolmarm dreams of. Thus without being imitative, you should follow the practice of effective authors, rather than the precepts of linguistic legislators. This is a pragmatic approach in which clarity is more important than purity.

If there are laws, they must be enforced, and some critics think English teachers should have the job of policing the language. Thus Louis B. Salomon, writing in the *Bulletin of the American Association of University Professors,* insists that "If English teachers don't want to be traffic cops . . . then they might as well turn in their badges." [13] But to police traffic is dull stuff; to go on exploring expeditions is more exciting, and the teacher can be a guide. Expeditions, of course, need careful planning and the right equipment. So what of the rules of grammar? If these are merely analogous to marching in rank, then they are expendable; but if they embody some common sense, like scouting the terrain and knowing the location of waterholes, then they are invaluable. The issue should be one of common sense. If a grammar rule is merely arbitrary (like the distinction between *shall* and *will* or *like* and *as,* the use of the apostrophe, or the injunction against ending a sentence with a preposition), then it is apt to be violated and eventually discarded. But most grammar is not just a set of arbitrary edicts; it has a commonsense foundation. Clarity demands that subjects agree with their verbs, that most pronouns have antecedents and that they clearly agree with these antecedents, that modifiers not dangle or be misplaced, that parallel constructions be in the same grammatical form, in short, that the relation between sentence elements be unambiguous. Why should grammatical conventions have developed at all? The enduring ones have a built-in logic, lacking in the distinction between *shall* and *will.*

As for such formal problems as the plurals of nouns or the principal parts of verbs, language needs some stability as well as growth; despite linguistic change and relativity, we need a common core for communication. "All right," you may argue, "but nonstandard English can communicate clearly. 'Who done it?' is as

19

clear as 'Who did it?' " True. In this case the answer is merely that discriminating usage prefers the latter. The descriptive grammarian will avoid branding someone's speech as vulgar or bad, but he should have the honesty to indicate where stigmas and shibboleths do exist (whether they should or not) and point out the perils of breaking standard conventions. When the publisher Henry Holt carefully wrote a letter in reformed, i.e., simplified, spelling to his new mother-in-law (a Beacon Hill dowager), the lady was not converted but exclaimed in dismay, "Florence has married a man who doesn't know how to spell!" The grammatical nonconformist runs the same risk.

Thus usage itself acts as a powerful control against both change (let alone the idea that anything goes) and the enforcement of obsolete (and perhaps unjustifiable) rules. Try to teach a child some usage conflicting with that of his (ugh) peer group and see how far you get. Likewise, one well-read lady, aware of the proscriptions of pedants, said, "I try not to use *contact* as a verb, but I can't help it." Her worry is pointless; *contact* in its verbal sense has been established by widespread usage for at least forty years. It is perfectly legitimate and rarely meets with objections. As for more questionable practices, such as the use of *irregardless* (for *regardless*) and *where is it at?* these are undesirable not for moral or social reasons (despite the stigma of the latter example) but because the *ir-* and *at* are irritating dead wood, as useless and unnecessary as a sixth toe.

The fact that grammar is an intellectual and emotional habit is not enough. Writing can be an art, and art requires consciousness and control. Even the slovenly writer watches his grammar more carefully on the page than in his speech; people who say *ain't* and *you was* are not apt to write them. Since the writer can revise, there is less excuse for the wordy, imprecise, bumbling, and grammatically dubious prose that sometimes slips by in careless conversation. But the prose used in conversation can also be an art. In Hemingway's story "In Another Country," an American soldier hospitalized in Milan tells an Italian major that he had difficulty taking an interest in Italian because it seemed too easy. " 'Ah, yes,' the major said. 'Why, then, do you not take up the use of grammar?' So we took up the use of grammar, and soon Italian was such a difficult language that I was afraid to talk to him until I had the grammar straight in my mind." [14]

On this encouraging note, let us begin.

2 √ Grammar down the Ages

Formal grammar has been traditionally used to impart a dead language to a living people. Our word *grammar* is derived from *grammatikē* (γραμμᾶτική), from *gramma* or "something engraved," hence a letter. In the early Christian era, grammatical studies at Alexandria and Pergamum dealt with the elucidation of texts, textual criticism, and rhetoric. Gradually the name was transferred to the study we now call grammar.* As long as language is thought of as divinely inspired, the problems involved with it are philosophical rather than philological. Did language come from the gods? Was there a supernatural sanction for certain words and a prohibition against others? Were there some words so sacred or so dreadful that they should never be uttered? Is there a necessary connection between words and the visible world? The Greeks and Hebrews were both concerned with the origin of language and the significance of names, and their approach was speculative rather than scientific.

¶ THE FIRST GRAMMARIANS

The first formal grammar antedates Christianity by about a thousand years. It developed in India and consisted of a few short stanzas to be recited or sung as an aid to memorizing and understanding the Vedas—the sacred hymns, rules, and stories of the ancient Hindu religion. Originally composed in Sanskrit, the Vedas were handed down by word of mouth (for when they were composed, there was no alphabet); and as the vernacular speech of the people altered, there was increasing danger of error being introduced into the sacred texts. So priests and scholars began to analyze

---

* An odd offshoot of the term is *gramarye,* a medieval word for magic; an even more surprising one is *glamour,* derived from *gramarye* in the sense of "bewitch or allure."

21

and systematize words, sounds, and syllables in a remarkable system designed to help both memory and comprehension. They developed the six branches of Vedic linguistic science—phonetics, meter, grammar, etymology, astronomy, and ceremonial—all necessary to the proper use and perpetuation of the Vedas.

For some centuries Vedic grammatical science grew and developed. Grammars were memorized, superseded, and forgotten. This oral transmission was a surprisingly accurate system, so that today our texts of the Vedas are better preserved than those of the Hebrews, who wrote on rolls of parchment. The first and the greatest Sanskrit grammar to survive is the work of Panini, who is to Sanskrit what Euclid is to geometry. Panini was born at Shalatura in the Punjab. Tradition says he was so wayward and stupid in his youth that his Brahman teacher expelled him. Stung by shame, Panini did so many acts of penance that he touched the heart of the god Siva, who became his guide and graciously revealed more grammar to him than was known by all his teachers. Legend says he was killed by a lion.

Panini's grammar is composed in the traditional mnemonic style, although by this time (variously estimated as from 700 to 200 B.C.) the Hindus had probably developed their alphabet and could commit their books to writing. Panini's grammar is not altogether original (he mentions some sixty-four predecessors), but it is unique in its arrangement and analysis. It consists of eight parts of four chapters each, comprising 3,996 sutras or aphorisms—brief rules in the form of stanzas to be recited. Panini's central theory was that nouns grew out of verbal ideas. He classified inflections according to the sounds composing them. Phonetic changes were his chief concern, and he largely disregarded syntax. His work is still used as the standard grammar for the study of the Vedas, the *Mahabharata,* and the *Ramayana* in the Brahmanic schools of India, but it did not become known to Western scholars until the early nineteenth century.

¶ HEBREW GRAMMAR

The early Hebrew grammar was speculative and philosophical rather than religious. For example, men asked themselves why it was that the earth held so many and such different tongues, and some one gave an answer in the story of the tower of Babel. The Hebrews were also intrigued to discover or invent the origins of proper names and developed a practice of composing etymological stories to account for them. They were not then concerned with the accurate elucidation and preservation of their sacred texts, many of which are contemporary with Homer.

¶ WHEN GREEK MEETS GREEK

The Greek approach to language centered around a question. Are words developed through a positive connection with the things or ideas they name, or are they arbitrary symbols that became conventional? The Analogists saw a necessary connection (analogy) between words and ideas; the Anomalists denied it. This may seem like a mere quibble until you examine the issue carefully. Then you realize that questions on the origins of language are related to the origin of man, religion, god, law, and the nature of authority— more urgent matters than whether or not an infinitive should be split or a sentence ended with a preposition. The problem is as old as Plato and as current as *Webster's Third New International Dictionary.* Protagoras and Socrates, two of the most famous teachers in Greece's golden age, both pursued these questions; and although they opposed each other's philosophical views, both were accused of impiety, of atheism, and of corrupting youth. Protagoras died at sea as he was fleeing into exile, Socrates was tried and executed, during a period of civil instability.

Socrates was concerned with the search for absolutes, the Platonic ideals of beauty and truth. In the *Cratylus,* he advanced the idea of language as something revealed by a divine lawgiver and also the opposite position that custom and convention play a part in the development of language. He discussed the view (still widely though erroneously held) that the language was debased from its ideal state in an original golden age or Garden of Eden, a common belief in ancient times. The concept of progress is quite recent. Socrates was not sure of his theory of linguistic origin, but neither could he accept the notion of Heraclitus that all is in a state of continual change:

Whether there is this eternal nature in things, or whether the truth is what Heraclitus and his followers and many others say, is a question hard to determine; and no man of sense will like to put himself or the education of his mind in the power of names; neither will he so far trust names or the givers of names as to be confident in any knowledge which con-

23

demns himself and other existences to an unhealthy state of unreality; he will not believe that all things leak like a pot, or that the whole external world is afflicted with rheum and catarrh.

Protagoras was more inclined to the relative view: "For he says that man is the measure of all things, and that things are to me as they appear to me, and that they are to you as they appear to you." (Plato, *Cratylus*.) In the *Protagoras,* he and Socrates debate whether virtue (in the sense of the classic virtues: wisdom, courage, temperance, justice) can be taught. The extreme relativist position can make these terms meaningless; on the other hand, Protagoras revealed the weakness of the absolutist position by this line of argument:

I know plenty of things—foods, drinks, drugs, and many others—which are harmful to men, and others which are beneficial, and others again which, so far as men are concerned, are neither, but are harmful or beneficial to horses, and others only to cattle or dogs. . . . Manure, for instance, is good for all plants when applied to their roots, but utterly destructive if put on the shoots of young branches. Or take olive oil. It is very bad for plants, and most inimical to the hair of all animals except man, whereas men find it of service both to the hair and to the rest of the body. So diverse and multiform is goodness that even with us the same thing is good when applied externally but deadly when taken internally.

One point upon which they were agreed was that "the most important part of a man's education is to become an authority on poetry." By this they meant the ability to read carefully, to organize one's thoughts, and to give a carefully reasoned opinion when called upon. Thus the relation of poetry to politics becomes more apparent. Our technical civilization has somewhat obscured the basic issue which, however, is still very much with us: What does a man need to know to govern himself? And the answers are still, in large part, connected with the use of language, basic to all communication and knowledge.

Aristotle, whose life spans approximately the same period in the fourth century B.C., as Protagoras' life does in the fifth, was interested in the detail as well as in the philosophy of grammar. Aristotle distinguished cases in the Greek noun, differentiated the parts of speech, and classified nouns as simple and compound. Scattered throughout his writings are bits of grammar which, taken together, form a fairly extensive body of knowledge. It was not until two centuries later, however, that the first formal Greek grammar was written by Crates of Mallus, about 150 B.C. This Crates founded a famous school of grammar at Pergamum and made numerous written contributions to the scholarship of his time.

Greek culture and the Greek language were widespread over the civilized world. In Palestine the earliest surviving manuscripts of the New Testament were written in Greek. In Rome, about 50 B.C., Dionysius Thrax wrote a Greek grammar for Roman schoolboys that had an extraordinary longevity; it was still in use in England until the end of the eighteenth century as a textbook at Winchester. At Alexandria there was endless debate in the schools between the analogists and the anomalists; on the whole, scholarly opinion seemed inclined toward the analogist view. But besides such philosophical speculation, there was philological progress, such as the work done in the second century by Apollonius Dyscolus and his still more celebrated son Herodian, who wrote treatises on syntax and the parts of speech. Greek was then becoming the accepted language of Western scholarship, and it was necessary to establish texts. Herodian, who flourished in Alexandria and Rome, dedicated his grammar to the emperor Marcus Aurelius. He was dignified with the title *maximus auctor artis grammaticae*—the greatest shaper of the grammatical art. By this time the Romans ruled the Mediterranean.

¶ WHEN IN ROME

Just as the conquering Romans appropriated the world they conquered, so they appropriated scholarship wherever it was found. But they were far from being experts on the Greek grammar they sought to adapt as Latin grammar, and they made some curious mistranslations, some of which still confuse grammatical terminology. For example, the word *accusative* was translated into Latin as though it came from a Greek verb meaning *accuse*, whereas the Greek term meant simply "the case of object," a meaning restored in *objective*, which has replaced *accusative* in most English grammars. The Latin *genitivus* means mistakenly "the case of origin," whereas the Greek term in fact meant "the case of kind or species." Here again the term *possessive* has been substituted, though it does not entirely clear up matters because the possessive case is used for situations ("a day's work") that do not involve any actual possession.

Once again, the Latin language went through the same process as Sanskrit, from spoken to written to sacred or scholarly texts, while a new vernacular developed and the former Roman Empire spoke the Romance languages—Italian, French, Spanish, Portuguese, and Rumanian—or else outlandish tongues like Slavic, Celtic, and Anglo-Saxon. By the Middle Ages, Latin had become the language of religion and of scholarship. Despite the dominance of Aristotle (read in Latin translation), Greek literature lapsed into relative obscurity, to be rediscovered in the Renaissance. Latin grammar throughout the Middle Ages was dominated by the work of two scholars. The first is Aelius Donatus, a Roman of the fourth century, who is noted as the teacher of St. Jerome. His grammatical writings are in three books, which concern respectively letters, syllables, feet, and tones; the eight parts of speech; and barbarisms and solecisms. So popular were these treatises of Donatus that in everyday speech a *donat* or *donet* came to be a term for any sort of textbook. The word is still to be found in the second edition of *Webster's New International Dictionary,* though it has been dropped from the third. Prescian, the other outstanding Latin grammarian, lived and wrote about two centuries after Donatus. The eighteen books he called *Commentariorum Grammaticorum Libri XVIII* were dedicated to the consul Julianus of Constantinople, where Prescian taught at court on a government salary. For centuries his and Donatus's books were the grammatical authority for churchmen and scholars.

¶ VENI, VIDI, VICI

Probably the first English grammarian was Alcuin of York (735–804), an early exchange professor who became adviser to Charlemagne and wrote his grammar (a Latin grammar, of course) in the form of a dialog between the emperor and himself. Later, about the year 1000, Aelfric surnamed the Grammarian wrote of Latin declensions and conjugations for the benefit of small Saxon chieftains and perhaps for the family of King Canute the Dane as well. After the Norman Conquest, French was for several centuries the language of the court; and with Latin for scholarship, the church, and the law, English became the language of the lower classes. Chaucer (like Dante with Italian) was the first major figure to write in the English vernacular; his contemporary Gower wrote three books, the first in Latin, the second in French, and only with the last dared use his native tongue. Latin grammars for English pupils continued in use. The most famous by William Lily or Lyly (grandfather of the poet and playwright) monopolized the Tudor textbook trade and continued in use for centuries.

The story of this celebrated grammar is remarkable. Its author, born in 1468, learned his Latin, Greek, and Hebrew at first hand on extensive journeys to Jerusalem, Rhodes, and Rome, after his graduation from Oxford. By 1512, he had been appointed high master of St. Paul's Cathedral School, and his biographers have ever since been busy asserting or refuting stories of his "cruel and inhuman severity" toward his pupils. His famous book first appeared some time after 1509, but only as a part of Colet's *Grammatices Rudimenta*. It was a brief statement of Latin syntax, the rules being given in English. Later, about 1513, this same syntax, with rules in Latin instead of English, was published anonymously as the *Absolutissimus de Octo Orationis Partium Constructione*. The lack of an author's name was probably due to the fact that Erasmus had a large share in the work.

About 1540, both versions were merged into one, and later a special copy on vellum was made for Edward VI. The grammar did not reach its final form until the revision of 1574, over half a century after Lily's death, when it was called in plain English *A Short Introduction of Grammar*. Bills were more than once introduced into Parliament to make it the official textbook for all schools, but it was so in fact even if it never became so by law. That Shakespeare learned Latin from it can be demonstrated by tags in *Love's Labour's Lost* and other plays.

Grammar to the Elizabethans was, of course, Latin grammar; if English had a grammar, it was thought scarcely worth study. (In fact, not until 1857 did a professor of poetry at Oxford University [Matthew Arnold] lecture in English rather than in Latin.) British scholars of the sixteenth century were concerned with two problems about the English language: the regularization of its chaotic spelling and the extent to which foreign, particularly Latin, words should be allowed to enter the native tongue. Ben Jonson (1573–1637) and John Milton (1608–1674) both wrote brief treatises on English grammar. These, as well as other early English grammars, were little more than Latin terms and classifications applied to native words. From five to seven cases were ascribed to the English noun; even though it had no dative, ablative, locative or vocative, Latin had these cases so English should have them too. In 1653 John Wallis in his *Grammatica Linguae Anglicanae* ventured to protest that English was a language different from Latin (though Wallis wrote

27

his protest in Latin) and that it therefore required different treatment, but his argument went largely unheeded. It was not so much that scholars consciously idealized Latin language patterns as that these were so much an ingrained part of their mental equipment that English naturally took form in their image. John Dryden, in fact, confessed that he often framed his thoughts in Latin before expressing them in English.

Still the mass of Englishmen knew nothing of Latin and continued, as the mass of people always do, speaking their native tongue according to hereditary and environmental habits. English, in its oldest form, came to the British Isles about the time of the fall of the Roman Empire. Previously the Britons spoke Celtic, with a smattering of words borrowed from the Roman overlords who governed after the legions of Claudius began to subjugate the more accessible parts of the island in A.D. 43. Continued barbarian invasions and onslaughts weakened the frontiers of the empire, and in the middle of the fifth century, successive waves of Teutonic invaders (Angles, Saxons, and Jutes) ravaged the eastern coast of Britain and drove the Celts (those who survived the slaughter) into the Highland marches of Scotland, Wales, and Cornwall or over the sea to Ireland, where Celtic (Gaelic) can still be heard today. The Anglo-Saxons became the English and their language the oldest form of English. The first invaders were heathen; but by the beginning of the seventh century, missionaries from Rome and Ireland made considerable headway in restoring Christianity and with it the Latin of the church, from which the English borrowed about 450 words during the Old English period. From the middle of the eighth to the early eleventh century, the Vikings (Norse, Danish, and other Scandinavian sea rovers) harassed, plundered, and sometimes settled along the east coast. Those who stayed intermarried with the inhabitants and adopted their language but in so doing, brought about nine hundred Old Norse words into English as well as about fourteen hundred Scandinavian place names. Despite Latin and Danish borrowings, Old English grammar was Germanic, a highly inflected synthetic grammar far more difficult than ours today.

Old English remained the vernacular for about six hundred years —longer than any subsequent period in the history of the language. It was violently interrupted by the Norman Conquest of 1066. With the triumph of William the Conqueror, Norman French became the language of the ruling class. The common people continued to speak English, but their tongue began to be modified by that of their conquerors. By the time of Chaucer (1340?–1400), English was once more the paramount language of the land, but an English greatly changed by interaction with French. The basic vocabulary and grammar remained English, but many inflectional endings were leveled. Eighty-five percent of the Old English vocabulary was lost, while over ten thousand words were borrowed from French as well as more Latin vocabulary from the church and the law. The language from about 1100 to 1500 is known as Middle English, a transitional period in which the vernacular became simplified from that of Alfred the Great (now unintelligible except to translators) to a version not too difficult for the modern reader. (See *Le Morte d'Arthur*: "For this book was ended the ninth yere of the reygne of King Edward the Fourth, by Syr Thomas Maleoré, Knight, as Jesu helpe hym for Hys grete myght, as he is the servaunt of Jesu bothe day and nyght.") Modern English emerged at the beginning of the sixteenth century, without any help from grammarians, who had contempt for any speech but cloistered Latin. The great flexibility of our language, its natural gender, few inflections, reasonable and logical word order, versatile vocabulary and rich hoard of synonyms were all developed in the Old and Middle periods when English had no formalized grammar and was scorned as a vernacular for illiterates.

And then, paradoxically, just as Englishmen began to esteem their native speech and scholars to use it for treatises and dissertations, the bars began to be raised. Modern English has been conditioned by two powerfully conservative forces: the printing press and the schoolhouse. Both have tended to fix English and to lessen the rate of linguistic change, with the result that English has achieved less simplification during the four and a half centuries since 1500 than in the two centuries previous. Considering the chaotic nature of Middle English, in which grammar, dialect, and spelling were each man for himself, this stabilization has been a great gain to communication, but it can be too rigid. Where Chaucer might spell a word in a score of different ways, about the best the sixteenth century could do is illustrated by a pamphlet of Robert Greene's of 1591, where the word *cony* (meaning "dupe" or "gull") appears in nine forms: *cony, conye, conie, coni, conny, cuny, cunny, connie,* and *cunnie.* A like approach to restraint is observed in grammar.

Such "native woodnotes wild" flourished even more weakly in the first half of the seventeenth century and were pretty well clipped into regularity by the time of the Restoration (1660) and the

Latinate language of John Dryden. As early as Shakespeare's time, education was beginning to draw English into the cloister. "Free" grammar schools were found in most English villages, where children were forced to undergo the rigors of the language of culture and scholarship, namely Latin. Even though English was not taught in such schools and it was Latin verses that must be "just" or "correct," the schools were spreading the general notion of grammatical regulation. That inveterate Latinist Ben Jonson—bricklayer, swordsman, poet, playwright, and graduate of the Westminster school—charged Shakespeare with having "small Latin and less Greek"; and this was perhaps fortunate, for in Shakespeare's work we see the greatest expression of a free diction largely unbound by the shackles of rule and dogma.

What sort of English did Shakespeare use? How would his voice sound to us today? No doubt his speech was, or became, that of the cultivated people of his time; it is not probable that an actor who performed before monarch and court would fail to alter his Warwickshire argot where necessary to harmonize with more aristocratic accents.

These aristocratic accents were certainly different from ours in some aspects, such as the value given to final *s* in certain common words. *His* was *hiss* instead of *hiz*, and *was* was *wass* instead of *wuz*. Thus *is* and *this* are good rhymes for Shakespeare, also *his* and *bliss*. When Iago tells Desdemona and Emilia that they are ". . . players in your housewifery, and housewives in your beds," *house* is pronounced *huss* as in *hussy*, with the implication of that word as well.

Shakespeare, no doubt, used with fair consistency the pronunciation which is now rustic dialect in such a phrase as "Consarn ye!" The vowel before *r* plus consonant, that vowel which we spell so variously in *curt, word, bird,* and *heard,* was *ah. Servant* was *sarvent, concern* was *consarn,* and *clerk* was *clark*—the last still thus pronouncing the vowel sound in modern British usage. Some tags and remnants of this fashion still persist in Scottish dialect and in words like *heart, hearth,* and *sergeant,* while the spelling though not the sound has come down to us in *Southwark* (pronounced *Sutherk*).

For Shakespeare, *work* rhymed with *dark,* and *word* with *guard.* As late as the 1800's, Noah Webster had to warn the users of his famous blue-backed speller not to pronounce *mercy* "marcy" or *perfect* "parfect."

But probably the most noticeable feature of Shakespeare's pro-

30

nunciation would be what would sound to us like an Irish brogue. A considerable group of words, mainly those we spell with *ea* and pronounce with *ee*, such as *sea, east, leap, heat, speak,* and *steal,* were pronounced by the careful, cultivated Elizabethan with the vowel of *hay: say, ayst, lape, spake,* and so on. For Shakespeare, *gape* and *leap, pail* and *steal* were good rhymes.

The inflections Shakespeare used were somewhat different from ours. For one thing, he enjoyed greater freedom in his choice of third-person verb forms. Notice in Portia's celebrated mercy speech, how the *-eth* ending—*blesseth, droppeth, doth*—alternates with the *-s* ending—*gives, takes, becomes, shows.* For the poet this alteration must have been a boon, for a syllable might be added or subtracted in any verb by the simple device of changing the ending. But freedom was passing; the *-s* form, already dominant, drove out the *-eth* completely.

Like his contemporaries, Shakespeare retained the distinction between *thou* and *you* in the singular. The former was used incongruously enough to indicate either affectionate intimacy or blighting contempt; the latter, distance and respect. Most of the changes are rung in the first scene of *Othello*; where the Venetian senator Brabantio, not recognizing Roderigo, addresses him with the conventional *you*; but discerning his daughter's unsuccessful suitor and being enraged at his own rude awakening, he turns to the *thou* of scorn and contempt. At the end of the scene, overcome by the humiliation of Desdemona's elopement with a Moor, he falters, "Oh, that you had her!"

Elizabethan inflectional forms included many *-en* plurals now lost —*eyen* for *eyes, shoon* for *shoes, housen* for *houses.* On the other hand, some innovations have appeared since 1600. For instance, *its,* as the neuter possessive pronoun, is almost unknown in Shakespeare; the cultivated Elizabethan might use instead *his, the, it, thereof,* or some circumlocution.

As for syntax, probably the most sweeping change we have made since Shakespeare's time is our use of the auxiliary *do* in questions and negative statements. Rosalind says, "What talk we of fathers?" where her modern cousin would say, "Why do we talk of fathers?" Falstaff says, "I hear not of Master Brook," where "I do not hear" would be the contemporary usage. Page says, "I do invite you to breakfast," where we would omit the *do.* And Brabantio asks, "What said she to you?" instead of "What did she say to you?"

Shakespeare and his contemporaries use certain other construc-

31

tions since outlawed, such as the double comparative, the adverb lacking *-ly,* and the double negative. To Shakespeare a point could be *more higher* or *most highest,* and a thing could be *done noble,* or *noble done.* In general, however, Elizabethan syntax is not too far removed from modern syntax; the conventions have not, from then to now, altered greatly.

It is different with idioms and with word meanings, where much change has taken place, shifts often so complete as to confuse the modern reader. Shakespeare could speak of *hitting of* (i.e., "hitting on," "recalling") a man's name; he could use *censure* and *notorious* with good intent, while *companion* usually meant "low companion." To Shakespeare, *nowadays* was probably a vulgar word; he gives it only to Bottom in *A Midsummer Night's Dream,* to the gravedigger in *Hamlet,* and to a fisherman in *Pericles. Charm* to Shakespeare was always connected with magic; *bonnets* were worn by men as well as by babies. A *blue-eyed* person was not attractive but ugly, with bluish circles around sunken eyes. One's *favor* was one's face or general appearance, and *wretch* was a term of endearment.

Shakespeare's attitude toward certain words can be shown to have changed with his development as a playwright. He uses *beautify* in several of his earlier works, but later, in *Hamlet,* he permits Polonius to say, "That's a vile phrase! Beautified is a vile phrase!" and afterwards he excludes it from his vocabulary. The word *wood,* in its Middle English meaning of *insane,* he uses also in his earlier plays but not the later ones. By the year 1600 this use of *wood* was probably a provincialism.

The famous linguist Otto Jespersen gives figures which throw some light on the Shakespeare-Bacon controversy. Where Shakespeare uses *also* only twenty-two times and those nearly always in vulgar or affected speech, Bacon uses the word freely and indiscriminately. Where Bacon has both *might* and *mought,* Shakespeare prefers *might* with one solitary exceptional *mought.* Bacon uses only *amongst,* while Shakespeare frequently has *among.* Bacon confines himself to *scarce,* while Shakespeare uses both *scarce* and *scarcely.* And finally, Bacon makes fairly frequent use of *whereas,* whereas the word is entirely absent from the works of Shakespeare.

Shakespeare's vocabulary has been variously estimated at from 15,000 to 24,000 words, which is not more than are known to the average intelligent high school boy or girl of today. But to know a word and to use it are wholly separate things; few writers have actually used so great a vocabulary. Several experts estimate that one quarter of our speech is covered by just nine words—*and, be, have, it, of, the, to, will,* and *you*—and we do not usually show any great ingenuity or variety in selecting the other three quarters. To Shakespeare, disdain is "sour-eyed"; hate is "barren"; murder is "withered"; a traitor is "toad-spotted"; about to rape Lucrece, Tarquin has a "ravishing stride"; a flea sticking upon Bardolph's nose is "a black soul burning in hell-fire," and as for "mincing poetry, 'Tis like the forc'd gait of a shuffling nag." No writer ever had a greater gift for the sharp, surprising, but precise word or employed metaphor with more inventive vitality.

Curious misunderstandings have grown up around some of Shakespeare's lines, which have had their original meaning distorted by later quotation. A double instance occurs in *Hamlet,* Act I, scene 4, lines 13–16:

> But to my mind—though I am native here
> And to the manner born—it is a custom
> More honoured in the breach than the observance.

Hamlet is referring to the drunken wassail kept by the king his uncle to celebrate his marriage to Gertrude, Hamlet's mother. Hamlet admits that such revelry is a custom of the country, but adds that though he is born into this custom, or manner, he feels that it is more honorable when omitted than when observed. There is no *manor*—that is a misquotation introduced by later speakers in place of *manner*—and Hamlet does not say that this custom has actually fallen into disuse, but that it should do so.

A predominant feature of Shakespeare's diction is his reliance on functional shift. *Stranger, nose, lip, mutiny, villain, ruffian* (". . . it hath ruffian'd so upon the sea"), *paragon* (". . . he hath achieved a maid/ That paragons description and wild fame"), *weapon* ("though you do see me weapon'd"), and practically any unlikely noun can also be a verb. *Both-sides* and *flood-gate* ("my particular grief/ Is of so flood-gate and o'erbearing nature") are adjectives; *backward* can be a noun, and Antony can be *unqualitied* for shame. Normally an adjective, *soft* can be a reflexive verb ("Soft you; a word or two before you go."). This freedom to use words out of their ordinary functions contributes more than a little to the fresh and startling effect of the dialog. No barriers are put up, for instance, against using *contact* as anything but a noun. As for Shakespeare's nouns, they often have an unorthodox shape, like

33

"the importancy of Cyprus to the Turk," "for every minute is expectancy of more arrivance."

And then we come to those passages in Shakespeare which would certainly be blue-penciled if found in any theme in high school or college composition. One such is in *All's Well That Ends Well*, Act I, scene 3, lines 173–174:

> Can't no other
> But I your daughter, he must be my brother?

This passage is so packed overful with its statement that the words burst and crack. To paraphrase it requires nearly twice as many words.

The infrequency of *whom* in Shakespeare has already been mentioned, if not illustrated. Rosalind says, as any modern girl might, "Who do you speak to," and Corin tells her of the shepherd, "Who you saw sitting by me on the turf." These are both ordinary usage in Shakespeare, but a choice instance is Cassio's response when Iago states, "He's married." "To who?" says Cassio. Likewise, in *Much Ado About Nothing*, Benedick says of Claudio, "He is in love. With who?"

One odd thing about Shakespeare's grammatical originalities is that they are not too easily perceived, not glaring to the casual eye. How many times, for example, one might read over *The Merchant of Venice*, Act IV, scene 1, lines 75–76, and see nothing curious:

> You may as well forbid the mountain pines
> To wag their high tops and to make no noise.

Yet if we press the dull business of analysis, we are startled to find the pines being forbidden first to move and next to be silent—which is certainly not what Shakespeare intended. Editors explain the thing on the basis of ellipsis: the real meaning is "forbid them to make noise when they walk." In the same play (Act II, scene 1, lines 32–33) we hear the Prince of Morocco saying:

> If Hercules and Lichas play at dice
> Which is the better man . . .

Here no question is intended in the second line. The sense will be plain if we put *to determine* after *dice*.

Ellipsis appears either for rhythm and meter or for conciseness. Sometimes Shakespeare was guilty of indulging in meandering word play too intricate to be followed by the audience and too tedious to move the action; perhaps there was a touch of autobiography in Polonius, who after all once acted Caesar on the stage. But when Shakespeare wanted action, he could cut out words as a cavalryman might lop off heads at a gallop. "Myself will straight abroad," says Lodovico at the end of *Othello*; had he said, "I myself will immediately go abroad," he might have missed the ship.

Any high school student desirous of emulating Shakespeare in this sort of phrasing would receive short shrift from his English instructor. He could not leave out *who*, as does Launcelot Gobbo:

> There will come a Christian by,
> Will be worth a Jewess' eye.

The Merchant of Venice is full of such passages as must fairly shriek to the consistently minded: How can a thing be wrong in the composition class and great literature in the Shakespeare class? How can students be blamed for doing what the greatest master of English commonly did? Is it possible that high school teachers would do well to encourage writing a little more along the lines Shakespeare marked out?

Here is yet another sample (from *King John*, Act II, scene 1, line 65): "With them a bastard of the king's deceased." It is safe to say that out of its context this line could never be understood, and even within its context there is nothing to show plainly whether the bastard or the king is dead. As every one in the audience knows the bastard is alive and well, why should Shakespeare labor to make clarity doubly clear? The meaning of the line is: "With them came a bastard of the deceased king."

A verbal puzzle occurs in *Pericles*, Act IV, scene 1, line 5, where the wicked Dionyza is warning her henchman Leonine not to falter in the task of killing the princess, Marina. Says Dionyza, "Let not conscience, which is but cold, inflaming thy love bosom, inflame too nicely." Editors, recognizing that something or someone—poet, transcriber, or compositor—is askew here, emend this line to "inflaming love in thy bosom." But is it conscience which inflames love? And can a cold thing inflame? The idea is, "Let neither cold conscience nor inflaming love come too near thy bosom." Here the grammar is an obstacle to understanding.

Another tangle needs untying in *Love's Labour's Lost*, Act II, scene 1, line 238, describing the King of Navarre as having, "His tongue all impatient to speak and not see" the Princess of France. For *to* read "because it could only," and you have the generally accepted solution. This is by no means writing that cannot be misunderstood, or even writing that can be readily understood. We know the general effect (of admiration) Shakespeare wanted to convey, but again the words seem to be secondary in importance.

It was Shakespeare's aim ever to create an effect. He was a linguistic impressionist. So long as the whole speech did what he wanted, he cared little about the detailed means by which the effect was gained. That ancient precept, "Write not so that you can be understood, but so that you cannot be misunderstood," was not Shakespeare's guiding principle.

Many of Shakespeare's grammatical experiments can be explained by the demands of versification, but they occur in his prose as well. It is often overlooked that much of Shakespeare's finest dialogue is prose; both Falstaff and Iago customarily speak in it, and Benedick and Beatrice in *Much Ado About Nothing* wage a good deal of their duel of wits in it. In an age of intricate baroque prose, Shakespeare's seems remarkably natural and modern. Yet both poetry and prose often present elaborate conceits (prolonged metaphors) and complex cadences sometimes more majestic than immediately meaningful.

To Shakespeare the whole was more than the parts, the line than the words, the speech than the lines. If he wished to show men being incited to fury, torn by uncertainty, overcome by love, he made those emotions live in the broad sweep of language; he did not niggle and twist among single words. If he wanted to show a young girl being put to sleep by the prosy, involved recitation of long-past events, this is how he went to work (*The Tempest,* Act I, scene 2, lines 66–74):

> My brother and thy uncle, call'd Antonio—
> I pray thee, mark me—that a brother should
> Be so perfidious!—he whom next thyself,
> Of all the world I lov'd, and to him put
> The manage of my state; as at that time,
> Through all the signiories it was the first,
> And Prospero the prime duke; being so reputed
> In dignity, and for the liberal arts,
> Without a parallel . . .

The grammar may be bad, but it is masterly for the purpose; it is precisely suited to Prospero.

Ambiguity is dangerous where a single sentence is your unit. If a sentence is all you have, you had better make it clear. But clarity as a principle may apply to either larger or smaller effects, and if the large ones are clear, as they are so magnificently in Shakespeare, there is less need to worry about the small. Shakespeare might throw a word to the dogs, as he would toss a penny to a beggar; his larger reaches, the coins of his main fortune, are pure gold.

As seventeenth-century England evolved from the baroque to the neoclassic period, its literary language became increasingly formalized. It was handled not so much from the scientific as from the moralistic or regulatory angle. English was like a garden whose luxuriant growth had never been pruned. Now it must be clipped into classic patterns. English must be inventoried, stabilized, and standardized, so as to separate the good from the bad, the correct from the incorrect.

Failing to establish an official body to regulate and codify English, eighteenth-century purists published a succession of prescriptive grammars, legislating on hundreds of expressions, most of them minute and unimportant. Of these the most popular were Robert Lowth's *Short Introduction to English Grammar* (1762) in England and Noah Webster's *A Grammatical Institute of the English Language* (1784) in America. By contrast, Joseph Priestley's sensible and progressive *The Rudiments of English Grammar* (1761) was largely ignored.

While Priestley, a scientist, recognized that English must and should grow, change, and develop as any living language does, Lowth and his many successors and imitators sought not to describe but to stabilize or fix English, setting up a body of rules as final authorities to govern the language for all time to come. These rules were not determined by any great scientific knowledge of the character and history of English. Many of them were conscious or unconscious analogies from Latin; others were based on observation of actual cultivated usage; and too many others were mere matters of personal prejudice.

In 1710, Jonathan Swift had published a paper in *The Tatler* in which he vented a long series of personal antipathies to certain words, such as *sham, banter, bubble, shuffling*; against abbreviated words, such as *mob* (instead of *mobile vulgus*), *rep* (*reputation*) and *incog*; and against contractions, such as *shan't, he's, disturb'd, rebuk'd,* the last two of which he would have pronounced with three syllables (*dis-turb-ed*). None of Swift's prejudices seem to have actually succeeded in modifying the course of English,

37

but Lowth is probably responsible for the present use of *have written,* rather than *have writ* (the form used by Shakespeare) or *have wrote* (a form popular in the sixteenth century).

Lindley Murray's immensely popular textbooks typify the general temper of nineteenth-century grammar. Of Quaker stock, Lindley Murray early moved from Pennsylvania to New York. A lawyer and merchant, Murray amassed a small fortune and retired, first to Long Island and thence to Yorkshire, England. As a diversion, he occupied himself in teaching at a nearby school, for which he produced his famous *English Grammar,* followed by *English Exercises,* the *English Reader,* the *Spelling Book,* and other authoritarian and absolutist textbooks. Following down the path marked out by Lowth, Murray's was a grammar of dogmatic rules with no exceptions, of prejudices magnified into edicts. If anything could have fixed the English language, it would have been such widely used books as those of Lowth and Murray.

But a rival grammar, based on the historical and scientific study of English, as well as on the comparative study of Indo-European and other languages, beginning in the late eighteenth century and growing in the nineteenth, was eventually to undermine the authority of dogma. Scandinavian and German philologists like Rasmus Rask, Jacob Grimm, and Karl Verner demonstrated relationships between Germanic and non-Germanic branches of the Indo-European family of languages, of which English is one. The study of Old English began to flourish. In 1864, the Early English Text Society was established to edit and publish medieval texts hitherto preserved only in manuscript. Work was begun on *A New English Dictionary Based on Historical Principles,* with quotations illustrating changing usage; this finally became the great *Oxford English Dictionary,* or *OED.* Linguists like Sweet, Ellis, Max Muller, and Whitney began to study grammar from the point of view of explorer, rather than legislator. It was not until the twentieth century that this new science of linguistics began to come into actual conflict with the legislative grammarians. Today the conflict between descriptive and prescriptive grammarians has erupted into open warfare.

3 √ You Name It

Grammars traditionally begin with an account of the parts of speech:

1. *Nouns* are names of persons ("W. C. Fields"), places ("Jamaica"), things ("crossbow"), actions ("battle," "execution"), abstract qualities ("fortitude"), collective groups ("a herd," "cattle").

2. *Pronouns* substitute for nouns ("Homer smote *his* lyre").

3. *Adjectives* describe or modify nouns and pronouns ("the *yellow* book").

4. *Verbs* convey action ("Dracula *entered* his coffin"), state ("I *feel* faint"), or being ("Gibraltar *is* a rock").

5. *Adverbs* modify verbs ("fight *fiercely*"), adjectives ("*incredibly* dull"), or other adverbs ("she sings *quite* badly").

6. *Prepositions* show the relationship between a noun or pronoun and some other element in the sentence ("fell *to* the ground," "sat *on* the table," "live *in* Albuquerque").

7. *Conjunctions* or *connectives* connect word ("Laurel *and* Hardy"), phrases ("to go *or* to stay later"), and clauses ("She won't go *because* it's raining").

8. *Interjections* are words or phrases used as an exclamation without grammatical connection (Yeech!).

¶ FORM VERSUS FUNCTION

The trouble is that a great many words cannot be confined to one part of speech but function in several capacities. *Dog,* for instance, though conventionally labeled a noun, can be used as an adjective ("dog biscuit"), an adverbial prefix ("dog-tired"), a transitive verb ("dog his footsteps"), or an interjection ("hot dog!"). Similarly, *water* can be a noun, a transitive verb ("water the grass"), an intransitive verb ("his mouth watered"), an adjective ("water buffalo"), or an adverbial prefix ("watertight"). *Wine* can be a noun or an adverbial prefix ("the wine-dark sea"); *box* can be a noun, a verb ("to *box* something in") or an adjective ("*box* kite"). A few prepositions can be nouns ("an *in* with the director"). "A record high" has a noun used as an adjective and an adjective used as a noun.

Dictionaries still label words as particular parts of speech, but this is only one way of examining them. Words have both form and function. Formally, nouns and pronouns have number and case; adjectives and adverbs have forms for the positive, comparative, and superlative degrees; and verbs can be conjugated. Grammar involves function as well as form, and errors can occur in both. When you give nouns and pronouns the wrong number or the wrong case, when you use a faulty comparative or superlative, when you use the wrong past tense or past participle of a verb, you have made an error in form. But equally or even more important is function. On this score, you can make errors in agreement or reference, make modification unclear, upset parallel phrasing, use dead wood and faulty diction, and write sentences mangled in structure and style.

Dictionaries contain more nouns than any other kind of word; they are the most frequent element in English expression. But *noun* is an inadequate label in that it describes only form and not function. Traditional definitions say that a noun is a naming word, but nouns have no monopoly here; verbs certainly name actions or conditions; prepositions name directions or time sequences (*over, under, behind, before, after*); adjectives name qualities (*hard, green, hot*) and in fact most nouns can double as adjectives (e.g., "*passenger* pigeon," "*disaster* area," "*sword* blade"). Furthermore, nouns can have various grammatical functions. They can be used as the subject of a verb ("*Koala bears* eat eucalyptus leaves"), as the object of a verb ("We saw the *Koala bears* eating eucalyptus leaves"), as the object of a preposition ("Give the eucalyptus leaves to the *koala bears*"), as predicate noun ("My daughter was made an honorary *koala bear*"), as appositive noun ("Those animals, *koala bears,* live in New Zealand"), as adjectival modifier ("*koala* bear," "*eucalyptus* leaves," "*giant* auk," "*symphony* orchestra"), and as adverbial modifier ("I like to loaf *weekends,*" "I stayed home *yesterday*").

Thus it is often more helpful to talk about sentence relationships (subject, complement, verb, modifier, connective) than about parts of speech per se. Professor Fries would use a new terminology and distinguish words by four classes, each with several frames and by

40

groups *A* through *O*. James Sledd would use *nominal* instead of *noun,* and define nominal as "a word or larger form which occupies a position typically occupied by nouns." For subjects and complements can be participles ("I enjoy *swimming*"), phrases ("*The blade of the sword* snapped in two." "*To believe in racial superiority* is a sign of ignorance"), and clauses ("People thought *that the play was over*"). Some nominal phrases cause problems with the possessive case, so that you seem to have to put the apostrophe *-s* on a preposition or participle: "The girl he was dancing with's name was Natasha," "The dog I was feeding's tail wagged," "The man she was talking to's teeth were bad." To get around this, use the periphrastic, "The name of the girl he was dancing with was Ysolde."

In informal speech, one often hears nominal constructions like "I liked *when they put the watch in the geyser*." But *when, where,* and *because* are not acceptable as nouns; and students are corrected if they write "An example is when . . ." "An example is where Huck talks about kings," or "The reason is because . . ." These are frequent errors both in form and function. "Because some Indians were crude was no reason for the whites to treat them as animals" should be changed to "The fact that some Indians were crude was no reason . . ." "One bad thing about freedom of speech is when a citizen can't think of anything to say he says it anyway" also needs a *that* before the *when*.

You must be able to recognize the subject of a sentence if you are to avoid errors in case, number, or forming grammatically incomplete sentences. There are a number of situations where fragmentary sentences may be effective, but every complete sentence and clause must have a subject and verb. First, find the verb; then see if it has a subject. If not, or if the subject is unclear, you need to rewrite the sentence. Second-person imperative verbs (so-called commands, though they may not be very commanding) are the only ones that do not require that their subject be expressed: *Open* the window; Please *pass* the salt. Once you have found the subject, make sure it is in the subjective case. Then see if the subject is singular or plural and make sure that the verb is in the same number. In nominal phrases, you have to single out the particular word that governs the number of the verb. This may prove confusing if a singular noun is followed by a plural modifier. For example, in the sentence, "A pair of swords is on the wall," the subject is *pair,* not *swords,* and so, "A pair of swords are on the wall" has an error

41

in subject-verb agreement. Similarly, "The highwayman, together with his gang, were captured" is wrong, because the subject is the singular *highwayman,* which requires a singular verb, *was.* These matters will be treated in detail in the chapters on case, agreement, and sentence structure. Nouns used as objects pose fewer difficulties; the only problem is to put them in the proper (i.e., objective) case.

¶ TYPES OF NOUNS

But we still have not adequately defined nouns. The term comes from the Latin word *nomen* ("name"), and traditional descriptions say that a noun is the name of a person, place, thing, abstract quality, collective group, or action. Nouns have several categories: (1) Proper nouns are the names of specific persons, places, or things (*Alfred E. Neuman, Utah, Magna Charta*); the first letter of each important word is capitalized. (2) Common nouns are all that are not proper nouns. (3) Abstract nouns name qualities (*honor, courage, weight, joy, sorrow, dignity*) and include many gerunds (present participles used as nouns: *thinking, creating, dreaming*). Often these abstract terms have to be made more specific: *Happiness Is a Warm Puppy, Misery Is a Cold Hot Dog.* (4) Collective nouns are words like *congregation, team, audience, militia, navy, fleet, family.* There may be those who are uncertain as to whether *backs* and *ends* are collective nouns in the sentence, "And Navy came onto the field with orange phosphorescent helmets on their backs and ends"; but if they are not, the picture is pretty ludicrous.

¶ DECLENSION

Since, as we have seen, many nouns can also function as other parts of speech, how can we tell whether, or rather when, a given word is a noun? In context, *when* is more important than *whether*; the way a word is used, as subject, object, or modifier, is more significant than its grammatical name. If we consider words out of context, we can say that they are nouns if they can be preceded by the article *the* (not necessarily by *a* or *an*; we never encounter *a milk, a wheat, a tea, a sugar, a flour,* or similar words). Considering form rather than function, we find that nouns have the characteristics of case, number, and gender. The form of the English noun has been greatly simplified from Old to Modern English. Like Latin and German, Old English was a highly inflected language that used different endings to indicate whether a noun was nominative, singular or plural; masculine, feminine, or neuter. These various endings are called a noun's declension. There were several declensions of Old English nouns, all with different inflectional endings for case, number, and gender. For example, *fugol* ("bird") was masculine and was declined as follows:

	SINGULAR	PLURAL
NOMINATIVE AND ACCUSATIVE	fugol	fuglas
GENITIVE	fugles	fugla
DATIVE AND INSTRUMENTAL	fugle	fuglum

Today, English nouns remain the same in the subjective (nominative) and objective (accusative) cases and inflect only for the possessive (genitive) case and for the plural. (For the possessive, see Chapter VIII on case and the apostrophe.)

¶ PLURALS OF NOUNS

About ninety-five percent of all English nouns form the plural simply by adding *-s* or *-es* to the singular, but there are a number of categories in which problems arise:

1. Nouns ending in *-s, -x, -z, -ch,* or *-sh* add *-es* to avoid a double sibilant (*hisses, taxes, quizzes, researches, dishes*). Sometimes little children mistake an *-s* ending for the singular and form faulty plurals by analogy: *birdses, pigses, wormses.*

2. Nouns ending in *-o* preceded by a vowel add *-s* (*rodeos, radios*). Most nouns ending in *-o* preceded by a consonant add *-es* (*heroes, Negroes, tomatoes*); but some, mostly of Italian or Spanish origin, add *-s* only (*albinos, falsettos, gauchos, pianos, virtuosos*). A few words ending in *-o* take either *-s* or *-es* (*buffalos—buffaloes; cargos—cargoes*).

3. Nouns ending in *-y* preceded by a consonant change the *-y* to *i* and add *-es* (*duty—duties, navy—navies*) unless they are proper names ("Last night there were four Marys"). Nouns ending in *-y* preceded by a vowel retain the *-y* (*donkey—donkeys, joy—joys, tray—trays*).

4. Some nouns ending in *-f, -fe,* or *-ff* change the *f* to a *v* and add *-es* (*calf—calves, knife—knives, leaf—leaves, life—lives, shelf—shelves*). The British sometimes use *beeves* as a plural for *beef,* but

43

Americans no longer do so. Be careful not to make an error with a word that retains the *f*, particularly common when there is a verb ending in *-ves* in the third person singular: *belief—beliefs* (NOT *believes*).

5. A few words, keeping the Old English umlaut form, change the vowel: *foot—feet, goose—geese, louse—lice, man—men, mouse —mice, tooth—teeth, woman—women*. (Sometimes you encounter a faulty analogous plural for humorous effect: *house—hice, grouse— grice, spouse—spice,* and Jinks the cat's "I hate meeces to pieces.") *Children, brethren,* and *oxen* are also survivals from the Old English form.

6. Some nouns, usually names of animals, keep the same form in the singular and the plural: *deer, fish* (but *fishes* for more than one kind or species of fish), *sheep, swine, species.* Others have a singular meaning but appear only in the plural form: *athletics, barracks, gallows, mathematics, mumps, news, pants, trousers* (*trousers* always has a plural form as a noun, but it can be singular as an adjective "up his trouser leg").

7. The largest group of irregular plurals occurs in nouns borrowed from foreign languages. In some instances, popular usage is now giving them Anglicized plurals; and there is no reason why it should not do so, since English has done so with thousands of other borrowings. Usage is the determining factor, and some words still retain the foreign practice:

(*a*) Latin nouns ending in *-a* use *-ae* in the plural (*alumna— alumnae, lacuna—lacunae*).

(*b*) Latin nouns ending in *-us* use *-i* in the plural (*alumnus— alumni, nucleus—nuclei*).

(*c*) Latin nouns ending in *-um* use *-a* in the plural (*agendum— agenda, curriculum—curricula, medium—media*).

(*d*) Greek nouns ending in *-is* use *-es* in the plural (*crisis—crises, parenthesis—parentheses*).

(*e*) Greek nouns ending in *-on* use *-a* in the plural (*criterion— criteria, phenomenon—phenomena*).

(*f*) French nouns ending in *-eau* add *-x* for the plural (*beau— beaux, tableau—tableaux*).

Some words that occasionally appear in one of the forms above use as often or more often an Anglicized plural: *formulas, vertebras, funguses, millenniums, beaus.* In practice, some foreign borrowings appear usually or always in the plural, which is often given a singular meaning, as in *data, agenda, insignia. Media,* originally the plural of *medium,* is so often used as a singular that we have now given the word a new plural, *medias,* though this does not yet have academic approval. There are no hard and fast rules for foreign plurals; the best way to settle any doubts is to consult the dictionary. If you don't, you may commit errors like the faulty plural of *cherubim* in the sentence attributed to a "youth leader": "Cherubims aren't particularly impressive to a generation that has become used to astronauts."

8. Compound words form their plurals in several ways. Most simply use the plural of the last and most significant unit: *motorboats, raincoats, church workers, piano players.* If the most significant word comes first, it usually takes the plural: *mothers-in-law* and other in-law relatives (but *in-laws* by itself), *passers-by, attorneys at law, justices of the peace, crèpes suzette.* The significant word remains plural when preceded by *assistant* or *deputy* (assistant chiefs of staff). When both words are equally significant, both are made plural (*men students, women doctors*). A few compounds go either way: *attorney generals* or *attorneys general, court-martials* or *courts-martial, poet laureates* or *poets laureate.* Compounds ending in *-ful* as a unit of measure add *-s* to the last unit: *bucketfuls, cupfuls, spoonfuls.* If the stress is on the container rather than the measurement, then we say "two buckets full of sand."

Nonstandard American-English speech sometimes uses a singular form for a plural with numbers: "He's six foot tall," "It's three year old," "The garage is ten mile from here," "Gimme three gallon of whiskey." This practice is actually a vestigial medieval partitive genitive plural after numbers (which you can immediately forget) and is older than current standard English.

¶ GENDER

One great advantage of English grammar is that it uses a natural rather than an artificial gender. In German and Latin, nouns are ascribed to the masculine, feminine, or neuter gender; and in Romance languages they are ordained masculine or feminine by grammatical rule rather than through any actual sexual attributes. A word for the same object can be masculine in one language, feminine in another, and neuter in a third. There is no logic, and the poor student has to memorize the gender of each noun, so that he will be able to use the proper article, pronoun, and adjective endings with it. Thus French has *le crayon* ("pencil") but *la plume* ("pen"); "il est cassé," but *elle est pleine d'encre."* Old English had grammatical gender, but it gradually disappeared during the centuries after the Norman Conquest, and good riddance. Probably no other feature is so troublesome to a language, since it involves agreement in all articles, adjectives, pronouns, past participles and even requires that these have different sets of endings. In Old English, *woman (wif-mann)* was masculine, but *wife (wif)* was neuter, as it is today in German. *Goat, goose, louse,* and *mouse* were feminine; *bird* and *horse* were masculine; *cattle* was neuter. *Hand* and *tongue* were feminine; *eye,* neuter. Medieval monks might find it appropriate that *temptation, sin,* and *hell* were feminine, but why should *coat of mail, battle,* and *tomb* be so, and why should *weapon* be neuter?

Except for a few nouns that have a different form in the masculine and the feminine (*actor—actress, czar—czarina, earl—countess, fox—vixen, hero—heroine, maharaja—maharani, marquis—marquise, master—mistress*), gender is now a problem only when pronoun reference is involved. Today some feminine words have a slightly derogatory connotation in activities shared by both sexes. We have several feminine suffixes: *-ess, -ette, -trix, -ine.* These are connotatively neutral in *countess, heiress, actress, majorette, executrix,* and *heroine.* But *-ette* can also mean diminutive (*cigarette, dinette*) or commercially even imitation or synthetic (*leatherette*). Sometimes *-ette* and *-ess* are not merely grammatical suffixes but convey status as well. *Suffragette* is still a bit derogatory, and nobody thinks of a *farmerette* as doing any real work. *Jewess* and *Negress* convey a distinct flavor of derogation and prejudice which is not present in *Jew* and *Negro.* When women do the same work as men, the feminine suffix can be condescending; *authoress, directress, mayoress, lawyeress, poetess, sculptress* are slighting and suggest dilettante or amateur standing. Why not simply *author, director, mayor, poet, sculptor?* Sometimes a distinction is necessary, as in *ballerina;* but *woman* or *lady doctor, lady author, woman scientist,* etc., seem condescending and discriminatory. One artist wrote to *Esquire,* "It was very thoughtful of you to refer to me as a 'lady painter'. . . . Due to the huge numbers of man painters named Anita running about, there might have been considerable misunderstanding—and your foresight, I'm certain, saved us the humiliation of mistaken identity." [1] Certainly *male nurse* and *male dancer* give an undesirable image, and men teaching in elementary and junior high school would hardly like to be called *male teachers.*

Sometimes gender presents amusing problems. Is the person conducting the meeting of a woman's club a chairman or a chairwoman? It seems ridiculous to speak of a girl busboy, but have you ever heard of a busgirl? What about a freshman woman? And is the plural *freshman women* or *freshmen women*? The ultimate absurdity is the scene in the movie *Mr. Roberts*: when the chief Navy nurse commands her sexy subordinates, "Carry on, men," Jack Lemmon as Ensign Pulver does a double take and repeats ironically, "Yeah, carry on . . . men."

¶ BLENDS

Hundreds of thousands of new words have entered the language in the last two centuries, most of them nouns from science and technology, with many others from politics, sociology, and psychology. Linguistic growth is healthy, but there are always some blighted growths, and some neologistic nouns are both weird and wonderful. Advertisers and journalists, as well as scientists, are particularly fond of coining blends; that is, combining parts from two or more words into one, supposedly to achieve a clever or striking result. Blends go back quite a ways, with long-established terms like *cablegram, newscast, motel,* and *urinalysis* for *cable telegram, news broadcast, motorist's hotel,* and *urine analysis.* As a form of simplification, the blend can be useful; *paratrooper* is better than *parachute trooper,* and *cortisone* is certainly preferable to *17-hydroxy 11-dehydrocorticosterone hormone.*

But merchandising blends are often no more than coy puns, like *funderwear, lapkin, broasted* ("broiled and roasted" or "baked and roasted"?), *play-jama, scardigan* ("scarf and cardigan"), *Fabricadabra!, angel-abra* (angel and candelabra), *leisurals* (leisure and casual shoes), *funderful, flexagons* ("flexible hexagons"), *sportraits,* and similar slanguage. Many blends are culinary and gastronomical, from *groceteria* to *vegamato* to raisin-bran *brunchwiches* ("breakfast-lunch sandwiches") to *fishkabob.* Macaroni is often dehydrated into *-roni* in such blends as *Beef-a-roni, Elbo-Roni, Noodle Roni, Rice-a-Roni, Saladroni, Scallop-a-Roni, Tenderoni,* and (urp!) *Twist-a-Roni.* It would be as valid to use *Mac-a-beef* or *Mac-a-noodle,* but the suffix has prevailed. Hamburgers were originally named after the German town of Hamburg, but Americans apparently think that they are made of ham, instead of beef, and so blend the suffix *-burger* with everything from fish to pizza until you encounter such toothsome morsels (crunch!) as *rampburgers*. No doubt, a *foodaholic* washes them down with *Nectaroma*; and if he fails to survive the ordeal, his ashes can be preserved as *cremains*.

¶ ACRONYMS

Closely related to blends are acronyms, words made up of the initial letters or first syllables of the words in a phrase. Government and science have produced so many of these that they have been called alphabet soup, but they can be useful abbreviations. *Laser,* which is an acronym of the italicized letters in "*l*ight *a*mplification by *s*timulated *e*mission of *r*adiation" is certainly handier than the original. Often organizations pick a name that will form a convenient and easily remembered acronym: SHAPE (*S*upreme *H*eadquarters *A*llied *P*owers in *E*urope), CORE (*C*ongress of *R*acial *E*quality), CARE (*C*ooperative for *A*merican *R*emittances to *E*verywhere). In the latter example, the acronym is used exclusively except for some technical documents. Some acronyms have almost entirely replaced the original in common speech; e.g., ANZAC, WACS, WAVES, NATO, UNESCO, UNICEF. Some in fact, have become so universal that the original is all but forgotten: *Jeep* (*gp*—general purpose vehicle), *GI* (Government Issue), *Seabees* (*CB*—Construction Battalion). Some, like *awol* ("absent without leave") and *radar* are usually written lower-case as a word. Others like QUINK (quick-drying ink) remain merely brand names. Some remain essentially spoken slang, as *Veep* for Vice President, a term that John Adams would have scorned when he held that office. On the other hand, *VIP* is widely spoken and printed, but you rarely if ever encounter "very important person." Show biz has its own special acronyms complete with feminine forms: A disc jockey has become a *deejay*; and a woman disc jockey, a *deejane*. A master of ceremonies is an *emcee*, so the woman is a *femcee*. Some acronyms are deliberately humorous, like NUTS (Northwestern University Trail Society); others unintentionally so, like "Eliott is retained as EMU head" (Eastern Michigan University). Most are harmless, and some are helpful.

George Orwell found sinister possibilities in political acronyms and noted that the tendency to use them "was most marked in totalitarian countries and totalitarian organizations." As examples, he gave *Nazi* ("National Socialist"), *Gestapo* ("*Geheime Staatspolizei*"), *Comintern* ("Communist International"), *Inprecorr,* and *Agitprop* ("Ministry of Agitation and Propaganda"); and one might

48

add the changing name of the Soviet secret police. The acronym is intentionally sinister in SPECTRE ("SPecial Executive for Counterintelligence, Terrorism, Revenge and Extortion"). Orwell wrote that "In the beginning the practice had been adopted as it were instinctively, but in Newspeak it was used with a conscious purpose. It was perceived that in thus abbreviating a name one narrowed and subtly altered its meaning, by cutting out most of the associations that would otherwise cling to it." The connotations are removed, leaving a rather abstract bureaucracy and dogma." "Agitation and propaganda" suggests violence and conspiracy, whereas *Agitprop* sounds efficient and antiseptic. "Communist International" might suggest the heretical idea of human brotherhood. "The word Comintern, on the other hand, suggests merely a closely knit organization and a well-defined body of doctrine." [2] Whereas the individual words suggest a picture and require at least a minimum of thought, the abstract acronym can be automatic, thoughtless jargon.

¶ RAMATHON RIDES AGAIN

Equally thoughtless are the proliferating words ending in *-rama, -thon,* and *-ness,* that I have elsewhere called "Ramathon and the ness monster." [3] As a Greek suffix, *-rama* (actually a clipped form of *-horama*) means "a view"; in this sense it is used legitimately in *panorama, cinerama, cyclorama,* and even in the *Futurama* of the 1939 World's Fair. *Silverama* TV may be O.K., too, but we are getting into loose territory with the British *Striperama* ("Take it off"), though it certainly gives a view. But *-rama* has spread like a mindless fungus until it has become simply advertising jargon in *Educator Crackerama, ham-o-rama* (Dogpatch hams?), *freeze-a-rama* (Brrr!), *bowlerama* (Strike!), *playorama* toys, *launderama* ("Lady, youse is usin' de wrong detergent"), *cleanorama, garagearama* (three-car family?), *trailorama, camporama, confedorama* (Hoo-hah!), *gorgarama, pearlorama, tint-o-rama* (sunglasses), *souparama, tacorama, bananarama, gagerama,* and other *pun-o-ramas.* If you try to get a close view of *spinnorama* 45 r.p.m. records, you may become bug-eyed. *Sniff-o-rama* perfume and *Scent-a-rama* (British whiskey sniffers) are as patently absurd as the short-lived *Aromarama* movie; etymologically, all three mean a view of a smell. Show biz has also provided *Wonderama* (Captain Jolly on TV), *horrorama, nervorama* ("2 Fiendish Features in a New Horror Show!—*Werewolf in*

49

a *Girl's Dormitory* [The Ghoul in School] and *Corridors of Blood*"),
and even pictures filmed in *sin-a-rama* ("I always knew I shouldn't
have taken her to that hotel room"). Usually *-rama* suggests merely
an indiscriminate superlative (though *slendorama* lunch shouldn't
make you a living skeleton), and *rumorama* has it that *-rama* is best
translated as "big deal." It becomes ghoulish in *death-a-rama* (Dis-
count Funeral Parlor) and sacrilegious when a store in Quebec that
sells religious items advertises *Christorama*.

Amputated from *marathon*, *-thon* seems to be losing the race
with *-rama*, but it is used loosely in such blends as *saleathon*,
pushathon, *telethon*, *phoneathon*, *laffathon*, and even *rock-a-thon*
(around the clock, naturally).

The trouble with "ramathon" is that such nouns show an impoverished verbal imagination that simply plays follow-the-leader
instead of finding a way to describe precise words. This is even
truer of the cancerous growth of *-ness*, which is devouring other
suffixes or adding superfluous ones and reducing nouns to a monotonous uniformity. As *Vogue* says, "Appetizingness is no skin off
anyone's nose." [4] Thus students turn *safety* into *safeness*, *youth* into
youngness, *waste* into *wastefulness*, *hunger* into *hungriness*, *election*
(in the Calvinist sense) into *electness*, *treason* into *treasonness*,
hatred into *hateness*, and show their *inadequateness* (inadequacy)
by turning *wisdom* into *wiseness*. Is it *naïveness* or *stupidness* that
creates *greatestness* as a superlative? At any rate, democracy is safe
as long as we have *freeness* and *equalness*. Let freeness ring! Liberty,
equalness, and fraternity!

¶ NOW YOU SEE IT, NOW YOU DON'T

There are many curious examples of nouns used for other parts of
speech and other parts of speech pressed into service as nouns. In
the Great Smoky Mountains this interchange is particularly colorful. Verbs serve as nouns in "The mountain people have a *lavish*
of pride," "You can git you one more *gittin'* of wood out of that
pile," "I didn't hyear no *give-out* about hit," and "Listen, all you
settin' rounders." Nouns double as verbs in "I didn't *fault* him for
hit," "That b'ar'll *meat* me for a month," and "*Chair-bottomin'* is
easy settin' down work." [5] Adjectives function as nouns in "Them
Yankee soldiers stole a right *smart* of horses" and "It's a better kind
of *different*." An adverb becomes a noun in "A person has a *rather*
about what he drinks." The mountain people often use redundant

compound nouns like *rifle gun, tooth dentist, sulphur match, ham meat, cow critter,* and *preacher man.*

But these are tame examples compared to current journalistic and advertising practices, where we find *two for* used as a noun (i.e., two theatre tickets for the price of one) and *7-Up* used as a verb ("7-Up your thirst away"). You can also "*rainbow* your 7-Up floats." If you buy a *two for* (or *toofer*), *The New York Times* says that "Seated is how to look at Lincoln Center." You can *holiday* in Majorca and *porpoise* about in the water, or you can *splendor* at a French château. If you have a *yearn* for home, you can *garage* your car, but it's better to take to the open road, for as Texans say, American cars are "hell for *stout.*" When you go *supermarketing,* you'll find that "There's more to a ham than its *lean.*" But the best shopping is for ladies' fashions, where, as *Vogue* announces, you can buy pajamas "All sinuous *slink* to a voluminous *swell* of trousers." "Gone: the *little-girlisms.* Arrived! . . . the intriguery of fabrics with demeanor and dimension." Among Hollywood columnists, it has become semiofficial jargon to use certain nouns for verbs. Film stars never entertain anyone or give anyone a gift or have a romance; instead they *guest, gift,* or *romance* someone. It is doubtful that F. Scott Fitzgerald would have approved Sheilah Graham's diction when she wrote that "Columbia gifted Carl Foreman with an expensive 1962 limousine. . . ."

¶ A SHREWDNESS OF APES

While some new nouns seem witless and expendable, there are certain obsolete ones with sufficient character or charm that they deserve to be rescued from antiquity, notably the medieval collective nouns, or "company terms" for groups of animals and birds in farming, hunting, and falconry. Today we use *herd* and *flock* or more loosely *bunch* or *group* to cover most cases, but knights and squires were not so casual. *Flock* was appropriate for sheep and *herd* for cattle, but cattle could also be a *drove.* One spoke of a *harras* of horses, a *rag* of colts, a *pack* of hounds, a *cowardice* of curs, a *kennel* of raches, a *route* of wolves, a *skulk* of foxes, a *kindle* of kittens, a *down* of hares, a *swarm* of bees, a *bundling* of ducks, a *gaggle* of geese, a *group* of ganders, a *sord* of mallards, a *rafter* of turkeys, a *plump* of wild fowl, a *company* of widgeon, a *wisp* of snipe, a *fall* of woodcock, a *nye* of pheasants, a *covey* of partridges or quail, a *bevy* of quail, a *stand* of plovers, a *cast* of hawks, a *herd* of cranes, a *sedge* of herons, a *watch* of nightingales, a *muster* of peacocks, a *brood* of grouse, a *flight* of swallows, a *building* of rooks, a *murmuration* of starlings, a *dule* of turtledoves, an *exaltation* of larks, and a *murder* of crows. Any knight that spoke of a *wisp* of pheasants was apt to have his spurs hacked off. There were a *cete* of badgers, a *doylt* of tame swine, a *sounder* of wild swine, a *singular* of boars (an odd—or singular—choice for a collective noun), a *bevy* of roebucks, a *gang* of elk, a *pace* of asses, and a *bale* of turtles. In the water, one found a *shoal* of fish, a *hover* of trout, a *stand* of salmon, a *gam* of whales, a *trip* of seals, and a *pod* of walruses. To go farther afield, there were a *sloth* of bears, a *troop* of buffaloes, a *pride* of lions, a *leap* of leopards, a *crash* of rhinoceroses, a *troop* of monkeys, and a *shrewdness of apes*. Unfortunately, there is not much demand for these terms; but some of them vividly characterize the birds or beasts they apply to, and the language would be enriched by their return. Instead, *quail* has become a slang term for sexy wenches (cf. *Kiss Me, Kate*), and so we speak of a bevy of girls. *Life* recently made a new "company term" when it wrote of "an orgy of Barrymores." Who could ask for anything more?

Exercise 1: Replace the following *-ness* monster words with more precise suffixes. For instance, *braveness* should be *bravery*.

1. scholarness	. . . .	11. spectacularness	. . . . . .
2. beautifulness	. . . . . .	12. feminineness	. . . .
3. savageness	. . . .	13. expensiveness	. . . . . .
4. angriness	. . . .	14. suppressiveness	. . . . . .
5. futileness	. . . .	15. cowardness	. . . .
6. vandalness	. . . .	16. courageousness	. . . . . .
7. hostileness	. . . .	17. confusingness	. . . . . .
8. curiousness	. . . .	18. miserableness	. . . . . .
9. honestness	. . . .	19. euphoniousness	. . . . . .
10. aggressiveness	. . . . . .	20. illiterateness	. . . .

4 √ The Perplexing Pronoun

The noun—like Lon Chaney, Alec Guinness, or Peter Sellers—can appear in many guises and perform in many roles, sometimes in one and the same sentence. Much the same characteristic is true of the pronoun. It has not one grammatical function but four. No two grammars include the same words in their lists of pronouns; and it is, as we shall see, very difficult to define a pronoun adequately. It might be simpler to drop the pronoun classification altogether, but for the fact that there are six words set apart by using special forms in the subjective and objective cases. These six words (*I, we, he, she, they,* and *who*) require some separate category. Technically, they are case survivals, but they are customarily called pronouns.

The pronoun is usually defined as a noun substitute, but this explanation is inadequate. A pronoun functions grammatically exactly as a noun does; it may be subject, complement, modifier; in addition, it may be used as a connective. And if we are to have both nouns and pro-nouns, why not have verbs and pro-verbs, adjectives and pro-adjectives, adverbs and pro-adverbs? If a pronoun stands for a noun, as we are told, so are there words which stand for verbs, like *did* in "He learned and so did I"; words that stand for adjectives, like *the same* in "You are lazy and I am the same"; words that stand for adverbs, like *so* in "He worked quickly but she less so." All these are word-substitutes, pro-words, and they might reasonably be so named.

True, there are more noun substitutes than verb, adjective, or adverb substitutes, and this fact might seem to justify making a special pro-noun group. But then there should be good clear distinctions between nouns and pronouns, whereas few grammarians agree altogether on what a pronoun is. Nearly any common noun may be a pro-noun, as *book* may stand for *Ivanhoe* or *man* for *F. Frothingham Smith.* According to the usual definition of pronoun,

53

the word *thing* is pronominal in practically every one of its uses, since it nearly always stands for something more specific than itself. Indeed, *something* and *anything* are commonly classified as pronouns, although they do not stand for another noun so clearly as does *thing* itself, a word always classified as a noun. Any number can be used pronominally ("*Two* were present," "I saw *hundreds*"), as can words like *dozen, pair, couple, several, few.*

All the numbers can also serve as adjectives, and any comparative or superlative adjective can be used pronominally: "I have three sons; the *youngest* is in kindergarten, and the *oldest* is at Harvard." Color words can be pronouns, as well as nouns or adjectives: He chose the *yellow*." "I bet my money on the bobtail nag; somebody bet on the *bay*." Dictionaries label *former* and *latter* as adjectives, but they usually function pronominally to stand for a noun in a preceding sentence or clause. *Here* and *there,* usually called adverbs, take the place of nouns in phrases like "from here to Denver" and "from there to Santa Fe."

And not all pronouns are substitutes for any noun. Look at *none* and *nothing*—pronouns by classification but not standing for any person or thing. And as for the pronoun *I,* you might say that in conversation the use of your individual name would be a substitute for the pronoun, rather than the other way around. For the individual speaking of himself, the use of any word but *I* and *me,* is so rare that by no show of reason can this be taken for anything but normal standard practice.

Evidently the noun-substitute test is not sufficient for pronouns. Perhaps we recognize pronouns not so much by word of textbook as by some inner light, some grammatical intuition or instinct possessed by the fortunate. These objections to the definition and delimitation of the pronoun are not new; they are well known to students of grammar. And they appear as obvious facts when we cease merely repeating grammatical rules and begin thinking about grammatical ideas.

If we try to find some real distinction that sets apart nouns and pronouns, we shall have to consider first the "case-survival" words already mentioned. Those six subjectives (*I, we, he, she, they,* and *who*) together with their objective forms (*me, us, him, her, them,* and *whom*) make up the twelve words about whose use there is more uncertainty than any others in the English language. They present special problems even to the native speaker and are seldom fully mastered by the foreign one. They must be studied and handled separately. We cannot even say with complete accuracy that the subjectives are subjects and the others complements:

> It might have been (I, me).
> I expected it to be (she, her).
> (Who, Whom) do you think he was looking for?
> (Who, Whom) do you think he was?

The traditionally correct choices are *I, her, whom,* and *who;* but such choices are likely to trick all who use English. From Shakespeare to Mark Twain to James Thurber, there are innumerable instances of reputable writers departing from conservative practice on pronoun case. Broadly speaking, there's no English-speaking person who knows absolutely how to use *who* and *whom, I* and *me, he* and *him* in rapid or unguarded speech. Apparently grammarians only make the situation worse. Studies have shown that when it comes to using pronouns more mistakes are made by students in the higher grades than in the lower ones. It seems that teachers' efforts to make their pupils conscious of grammar have largely served only to confuse the issue, causing students by overconcern to make additional errors.

Pronouns have a number of categories, but this terminology is largely irrelevant to their effective use grammatically. No speaker or writer thinks consciously, "Now I want a demonstrative pronoun"; these things come instinctively. Yet although pronoun classification is, for the most part, not a matter of communication but of terminology, you may find the labels used below helpful in discussing grammar.

¶ PERSONAL PRONOUNS

These are inflected by person, number, case, and (in the third person singular) gender. The *first person* is used for the speaker or writer (*I, my, me, we, our, us*); the *second person* is used for the person addressed (*you, your*); the *third person* is used for someone or something written or spoken about (*he, his, him, it, its, she, her, they, their, them*). In addition we have the possessive predicative forms (*mine, yours, hers, ours, theirs*) that are really adjectives and peculiar survivals of an otherwise outmoded grammar. In older English (and today in what we might term imitative King James Biblical style), *mine* and *thine* could be interchanged with the personal possessive pronoun ("Mine eyes have seen the glory of the coming of the Lord," "It is thine adversary"). By analogy to *mine* and *thine,* American frontiersmen (and some of their isolated descendants) coined *yourn, hisn, hern, ourn,* and *theirn;* but these were used only after the verb *to be* or in absolute form ("The hat is *hern,*" "My life or *hisn*") and never as an adjective before a noun (*"hern hat," "hisn rifle"*).

Old English had dual pronouns for *we two* (*wit, uncer, unc, uncit*) and *you two* (*git, incer, inc, incit*), and we can be thankful for their disappearance. Medieval and Elizabethan English distinguished between the second person singular and plural by using *thou, thy,* and *thee* in the singular and *ye* or *you* and *your* in the plural, but we now have no way except the context to know whether *you* is being used for one person or a group. (Accordingly Southerners resort to *all of you, you all, youse,* and even *you-uns.* Sometimes Yankees use *you all* for the singular as well, but no one who has grown up with the phrase ever does so.) The only thing gained by dropping the second person singular is the removal of subjective and objective case endings. These still bother ministers who improvise prayers in ersatz Elizabethan. If you expect to conduct prayer meetings, you should know that God is addressed in the subjective case as *thou* (with *art* or with verb forms ending in *-st* or *-est*—"thou dost," "thou goest") and in the objective as *thee* ("We supplicate thee").

There is no reason why God cannot be addressed as *you;* it certainly carries no disrespect. Actually, during the Elizabethan period English used both *thou* and *you* in the second person singular, as French uses *vous,* Spanish *Usted,* and German *Sie* for either singular or plural, the choice being dependent not only on number but also upon one's relationship to the person addressed. When we had *thou* as a second person singular, it was used to address either inferiors or intimates and loved ones; in the latter sense, it is used for the Deity. In Shakespeare's *Richard III,* Richard wooing Princess Anne first addresses her courteously as *you,* while she spurns him contemptuously with *thou.* By the end of the scene, Richard has so far won her that she speaks to him respectfully as *you,* and he calls her intimately *thou* and *thee.* Shakespeare was not always so careful nor are many historical novelists. Even in *Quentin Durward,* Scott has the Duke of Burgundy tell Durward, "But if you falter or double in your answers, I will have thee hung alive in an iron chain from the steeple of the market-house, where thou shalt wish for death for many an hour ere he come to you." The Quakers insisted on using only the second person singular, as a symbol of universal equality, just as they refused to remove their hats before monarchs and judges. Thus there is a joke that a Quaker mother, angered at her troublesome child, said, "Oh, thou little *you*, thee." George Fox, founder of the Quakers, wrote:

Do not they speak false English, false Latine, false Greek . . . and false to the other Tongues, . . . that doth not speak *thou* to *one,* what ever he be, Father, Mother, King, or Judge is he not a Novice and Unmannerly, and an Ideot and a Fool, that speaks *You* to *one,* which is not to be spoken to a *singular,* but to many? O Vulgar Professors and Teachers, that speaks Plural when they should Singular.

But O, George Fox, that uses a singular verb (*doth* and *speaks*) with plural subjects (*they, Professors and Teachers*). Eventually the Quakers discarded *thou* and used the objective *thee* for the wrong case and with the wrong verb; "*Thee are* (or *is*) a good whaler." [1] In Europe young men do not address girls with *tu* or *du* until they are on kissing terms. Such distinctions are social, rather than grammatical, but they can be useful.

Some personal pronouns are confused with their homonyms; thus people mistakenly interchange *its* with *it's, their* with *there* and *they're,* and *your* with *you're. It's* is a contraction of *it is; there* is an adverb or an expletive; *they're* is a contraction of *they are;* and *you're* is a contraction of *you are.* Confusion is a sign either of carelessness or semiliteracy; careful proofreading should eliminate sentences like "The beetles were brought in from Kansas, where there use in cleaning skeletons for the museum was discovered by accident."

In isolated backwoods communities, you sometimes encounter the plural pronoun followed by *-uns* (*we-uns, us-uns, you-uns, they-uns*). This is probably a slurring of *ones* rather than a carry over of the German *uns* (*us*). At any rate, *-uns* is a dialect form that is best discarded from standard usage. *Hit* (for *it*) lingers in the Southern Appalachians as a vestigial survivor of standard Chaucerian speech.

¶ DEMONSTRATIVE PRONOUNS

This and *that,* with their plurals *these* and *those* are called demonstrative pronouns when they are used to indicate or point out something close at hand. ("*This* is my toy; *those* are yours.") Actually they function more often as adjectives ("*These* men have scurvy," "The rats are leaving *this* ship"). The main error is that

57

nonstandard English speech often uses the personal pronoun *them* instead of the plural demonstrative. ("Can I have another of *them* brochures on the tropical fish?" "Where do I find *them* ice caves?") This nonstandard use of *them* often appears in folk songs ("I've been in the Bend/ With *them* rough and rowdy men") and in fiction dialogue, but in other contexts it should be avoided. The error is doubled when *them* is used for the subjective case (*Them* is graceful birds in the water. *Them* chigger bites itches), and it is tripled when it is used with a singular verb ("*Them* is mighty good corn squeezings"). Perhaps "God damn them bugs"² is more expressive than "God damn those bugs," but it lacks the proper credentials.

Another common error is using *this* and *these* to refer to something that is vague and unfamiliar to the reader or listener: "There was *this* girl," "I sat on *this* bench," "*This* bird sat on my hat." What girl, what bench, what bird? In these cases, what should be used is simply the indefinite article *a*: "*a girl*," "*a bench*," "*a bird*." Suppose Thomas Wolfe had written "This stone, this leaf, this door"? The reader wouldn't know what he meant. J. D. Salinger's Holden Caulfield is addicted to the vague use of demonstratives. It is a hallmark of teen-age jargon. ("There was *this* mother in the zoo standing before *this* hippopotamus and telling *this* kid not to stick his hand in too far because he should remember what happened when *this* monkey got hold of him.")

¶ RELATIVE PRONOUNS

Who, whose, whom, which, what, and *that,* with their compounds *whoever, whosoever, whomever, whichever, whatever,* and *whatsoever,* are termed relative pronouns when they are used to connect, or relate, a subordinate clause to the rest of the sentence ("Moby Dick was the whale *that* took off Ahab's leg"). In this capacity they act as a subordinate connective, but they also still function as a subject or object:

> Lohengrin is the knight *who came* in the swan boat.
> Polyphemus is the Cyclops *whom* Odysseus *blinded.*
> This is the house *that* Jack *built.*

Actually it is their function of relating the dependent clause to the main clause that distinguishes relative pronouns. The italicized words are not relative pronouns at all in the following sentences:

58

Let's have no nonsense *whatsoever*.
Whoever cooked the soup should be drowned in it.
I'll eat *whatever* is on the menu.
Whosoever finds Mycenean relics must turn them over to the
Greek government.

¶ INTERROGATIVE PRONOUNS

Most relative pronouns (*who, which, what,* and their compounds)
double as interrogative pronouns, which are used to begin direct or
indirect questions. More significant is the fact that every interrogative pronoun is always a subject ("Who is it?"), a complement
("What do you mean?"), or a modifier ("Which book did you
buy?" "Where did he go?").

¶ REFLEXIVE PRONOUNS

In such sentences as "I celebrate myself," "He cut himself," "You
will make yourself ridiculous," "They fell over themselves," the
words *myself, himself, yourself, themselves* are termed reflexive
pronouns, because they reflect back the action of the verb upon
the subject:

	SINGULAR	PLURAL
1ST PERSON	myself	ourselves
2ND PERSON	yourself	yourselves
3RD PERSON	himself, herself, itself	themselves

In nonstandard speech you sometimes hear *hisself, theirself, their-
selfs* and *theirselves,* by analogy to the possessive form in *myself,
ourselves,* and *yourself.* Having used a plural pronoun in faulty
agreement with a singular subject, Holden Caulfield once com-
promised with a reflexive *themself,* half singular and half plural,
as in "a guy that's crazy about themself." Medieval and Elizabethan
English often used the personal pronoun reflexively in forms that
are now obsolete: "It likes me" (meaning "I liked"), *"I doubt me
whether . . . ," "I think me."* The latter lingers in the archaic form
methinks.

¶ INTENSIVE PRONOUNS

These are the same in form as reflexive pronouns and are used to
emphasize or intensify the antecedent ("I'll do it *myself.*" "Give it

to the king *himself.*" "Penelope *herself* failed to recognize Odysseus."). In Irish dialect, one sometimes finds the intensive pronoun used alone, as subject or object: "*Myself* will give you a whipping." "Pass *himself* the whiskey." The same nonstandard forms used for reflexives turn up again as intensives (e.g., Huckleberry Finn's "There set Pap, his own self!").

¶ INDEFINITE PRONOUNS

All, any, both, each, every, few, many, much, no one, one other, several, and *some* act as modifiers before a noun ("Is there *any* peanut butter?") but function as pronouns when they appear alone as subjects or complements (*All* is ready). Since they have no specific antecedent, they are called indefinite. These pronouns include *none* and compound forms with *body, one,* and *thing—anybody, anyone, anything. One* can take a plural form ("one of the good *ones*"). For practical purposes, *they* has also become an indefinite plural ("*They* don't build houses the way *they* used to").

It is not important to remember the categories of pronouns so long as you know how to use them. Some of the problems connected with their use are dealt with in the next two chapters.

Exercise 2: Correct any errors in unclear pronoun reference.

1. Many times the cars and trucks would break down, and with the little money saved they bought spare parts at an exorbitant price.
2. In gun-running they pay off handsomely.
3. We tried to inflate the air mattresses without a pump, which was an exhausting procedure.
4. John Carradine killed Tyrone Power in *Jesse James,* and he was killed in *Stagecoach, The Grapes of Wrath, The House of Frankenstein, Mary of Scotland,* and *Captain Fury.*
5. Sociologists observe that a person often votes for the same party your family voted for.
6. During his experiences at sea, Melville observed a great deal of man's inhumanity to man; and this made him skeptical of the Transcendentalist concept that there is really no evil.
7. One park visitor pushed a bear into the front seat of his car next to his wife to photograph them together, which was an incredibly foolish thing to do.
8. In New York they wouldn't even pay attention if an octopus reached out of the sewer to drag down a pedestrian.

60

9. On the sign at the park entrance it says that feeding the bears is unlawful.

10. When the Lone Ranger jumped off the roof, he missed his horse, which made him fall flat on his face.

11. Many of the Cherokees were quite civilized in the 1820's, which made President Monroe suggest that they should be made citizens.

12. But in the late 1820's, gold was discovered on Cherokee land in North Georgia, and this made the squatters and speculators try to dispossess the Indians.

13. The eleven white missionaries to the Cherokees were sentenced to four years apiece at hard labor for speaking in the Indians' defence, which Chief Justice John Marshall said was unconstitutional.

14. It does not say in the Preamble to the Constitution that all men are created equal; it says so in the Declaration of Independence.

15. Porkypine's Uncle Baldwin kissed Miss Hepzibah, which made her blush.

16. On the night before exams, it is better to go to the movies and not worry about it than to stay up all night studying.

17. I don't enjoy drive-in movies when you have to run the windshield wiper.

18. In trial by ordeal, a person accused of witchcraft might be tied and thrown into a river. If he sank, he was innocent (but drowned); but if he floated, he was guilty, and they put him to death.

19. In Mark Twain's later writings, he often discussed "the damned human race."

20. Puritans believed that most men would be damned because they deserved it.

21. Just because a state passes a law, this doesn't mean the law is legitimate.

22. During the Fourth of July weekend, there was a great deal of vandalism, many of them adults who should have known better.

23. In Walt Kelly's *Pogo* he deliberately writes in nonstandard grammar for humorous effect.

24. Ruth pointed out Martin Eden's nonstandard grammar, which embarrassed him and made him try to improve himself.

25. Some people call reactionaries conservatives, but they don't really want to conserve anything.

5 √ Who's on First? Riddles of Reference

"If you've been chigger-bit, you ought to put nail polish on them." This is good advice, but it is ambiguous, since the pronoun *them* does not refer clearly to any other word in the sentence. What you ought to do, of course, is to put nail polish on the chigger bites. If you hear someone saying, "I hardly ever drink myself, but I keep some on hand for visitors," you assume that *some* refers to liquor, but there is no clear grammatical reference. Sometimes such faulty reference is no problem; sometimes, it is awkward; and occasionally it is downright confusing, as in "The driver of the 45-foot tank truck nonchalantly lighted a big cigar and expertly maneuvered it through Boston traffic, en route to central Massachusetts." [1] Here *it* seems to refer to the cigar, creating an intriguing but inaccurate mental picture. When you encounter the ad, "Ann Landers will be glad to help you with your parents. Send them to her in care of this newspaper enclosing a stamped self-addressed envelope," you might wonder what the postage will be and whether Miss Landers knows what she's doing. At least, you might consider marking the envelope "Fragile" and sending it "Special Handling."

Harassed by such statements as "T. S. Eliot's poems are full of bald-headed men who worry about it," English teachers sometimes declare that every pronoun must have a clear and definite antecedent. However, it is not true that a pronoun always must, should, or even can, have an antecedent. A good proportion of such words —*what, whoever, anyone, none, they, I,* even *who* and *he*—may be used correctly without any antecedent whatever. What is the antecedent of *He* in "He who hesitates is lost," or of *Who* in "Who strives succeeds"? What is the antecedent of *I* in any of its uses?

And furthermore, it is often just as important for a noun to have an antecedent as for a pronoun to have one; the absence of the

62

antecedent leads to ambiguity just as surely. Take, for example, the sentence "On the table lay *David Copperfield, Macbeth,* and *Rob Roy;* I picked up the book and began to read." The meaning is ambiguous because we don't know the antecedent of the noun *book.* If the sentence stated that the titles were *David Copperfield, Macbeth,* and *A Golden Trashery of Mad* and that I picked up the non-book, then there would be no question.

I, of course, does not need a direct antecedent; the speaker or writer is understood. But, since the repetition of *I* may become immodest and overly intrusive, some writers bend over backwards to avoid using it at all, especially in impersonal, technical, or other specialized professional fields. Likewise, the language of business and bureaucracy prefers to efface the individual in favor of the corporate or departmental image. The result is an excessive and cumbersome use of the passive voice, which gives sentence structure the motion of two steps forward to one step back. Unless you are writing a first-person narrative, you should not bother the reader with chatty first-person observations or reactions; many students spoil the interest inherent in any objective opinion by saying more about themselves than about their topic. ("When I first read *Walden,* I thought Thoreau was some kind of a kook, but then I thought the matter over, and I decided that maybe he had something to say to me. I don't dig a lot of Thoreau, but I think I know what I should get out of his ideas.") But you should not be afraid of using *I* or *me* when they are appropriate, when for instance you are expressing a personal judgment, wish, or opinion. "I think" and "I hope" are infinitely preferable to "It is the opinion of the author that . . ." and "It is hoped that . . ."; "I am grateful to . . ." is more gracious than "Gratitude is due to . . ."

The clinical or editorial *we* can be both irritating and ludicrous. When a nurse says, "Now it's time for us to take our nap," the patient may either invite her to join him or tell her to go and take her own nap—depending on the state of the patient's recovery and the attractiveness of the nurse. If she says, "Let's take our medicine like a good boy," the patient is justified in demanding that she take her half of the prescribed dose. The editorial *we* is an annoying mannerism, especially if the reader disagrees with the editor. Perhaps editors use it to surround themselves with imaginary collaborators lest a frail editorial *I* seem exposed too naked to the world. But unless you (as the author) and the reader are mutually involved, you should avoid the editorial *we* and stand by your own

63

guns. The only *we* acceptable in the singular is the royal *we* ("We [*King Henry*] do hereby decree . . ."), theoretically because the king speaks for the kingdom but actually because he can command, "Off with his head," if someone challenges him—at least, he could in the old days.

As an indefinite pronoun, *one* is academic and stuffy ("One often finds one's conventional views challenged in college"). It is best to minimize such constructions. If one insists on using *one,* one can at least improve the example by replacing the second *one* with *his,* can't you? This garbled sentence illustrates another point: once you have used a pronoun, be consistent in maintaining it in the same person throughout, and do not switch from *I* to *you* to *one* or vice versa. (E.g., "One doesn't enjoy movies when people are talking behind *you,*" "Football is no fun for *me* when *you* have to sit in the rain." Besides, the use of different pronouns makes the meaning of the last sentence unclear; perhaps the speaker doesn't mind the rain himself but is concerned only for his companion.)

You is more relaxed and less abstract than *one* and seems to speak more intimately and directly to the reader. But beware of using either pronoun in inappropriate or ludicrous situations. Analyzing the work of J. D. Salinger, one student felt so much empathy for the characters that he wrote, "One wants to get in the tub with Zooey." The student can speak for himself, but the reader may not wish to share this sudsy experience. Keep your audience in mind. When coeds write themes telling you how you iron your lingerie or put your hair in curlers, a male reader may reply, "Who, me?" Hemingway writes what it's like when you shoot a kudu, or when you kill a man for the first time, or when you order absinthe, or when you have the moment of truth in the bull ring, as if the reader has done these things or should have done them if he's to belong to the club. Bad imitators of Hemingway write things like, "When you want to smash somebody's teeth in, you should use brass knuckles so you don't cut your hand."

In the case of *they,* grammarians can be too rigid in insisting on an antecedent. Technically, English has no plural indefinite pronoun, but *they* has pretty much come to fill this function. For example in the sentence, "In London they have lots of fog," it is pedantic to insist that *they* is unclear and that the sentence should be revised. The French use *on* and the Germans *man* to mean *they, you, people* (*on dit* and *man sagt,* "people say"); and there is no reason why English cannot use *they* in the same way, as long as

64

there is no ambiguity. Certainly Thurber's "I wandered into Stoeger's famous gun house in Fifth Avenue the other morning to see if they could repair my derringer" poses no difficulty, whereas any revision, e.g., "to see if the employees could repair," would be clumsy without any gain in clarity.[2]

It is only when *they* is used as a nameless pressure to conformity that you had better be on guard. Thoreau complained:

When I ask for a garment of a particular form, my tailoress tells me gravely, "They do not make them so now," not emphasizing the "They" at all, as if she quoted an authority as impersonal as the Fates, and I find it difficult to get made what I want, simply because she cannot believe that I mean what I say, that I am so rash. When I hear this oracular sentence, I am for a moment absorbed in thought, emphasizing to myself each word separately that I may come at the meaning of it, that I may find out by what degree of consanguinity *They* are related to *me,* and what authority they may have in an affair which affects me so nearly; and, finally, I am inclined to answer her with equal mystery, and without any more emphasis of the "they,"—"It is true, they did not make them so recently, but they do now."

That is one way to beat the system. *They* is more difficult to put down when it is the voice of rumor: "They say that so-and-so is up to such-and-such unsavory activity." If you ask, Who says so? you are apt to be told, "They all do," one advantage of this sort of vague reply being that it begs the question of responsibility and reliable evidence. In political purges, *they* can be sinister in its shapelessness: *they* accuse you; *they* say that you are guilty; *they* condemn you; and you never learn who *they* are that you must answer and oppose.

When *they* or *them* does have an antecedent, the reference must be clear. In the movie *Them,* when scientists in the New Mexico desert find a child in a state of shock screaming "Them!" over and over, they have to discover what "Them" refers to; "them," or rather *they,* are in fact, giant predatory ants caused by atomic mutation. In the sentence, "If Proctor had really been a witch, they would have given him their forgiveness and his life," it is not clear who "they" are. The sentence, "Bundles of wood were placed about the witch's feet, and a torch ignited them," is equally open to question. What was ignited, the feet or the bundles? There is even more confusion in an ad for "Playskool Puzzles": "After each of the individual puzzles has been accomplished—or if yours is an exceptional child—it is recommended that they be mixed to offer a more difficult challenge of a 12-piece puzzle." Here the interjected comment makes it appear that children, rather than puzzles, should be mixed. Students are frequently guilty of using a construction in which *they* refers to some idea or *ism*, rather than to its followers: "These are a few basic principles of deism. By reason they felt they could better understand God and their role in life." Here the noun must be substituted: "By reason, deists felt . . ." Sometimes it is clear enough what the pronoun stands for, yet the reference is grammatically unbalanced, as in "Annixter professes that he is a woman hater. The real problem is that he doesn't know how to act in their presence." *Their* referring to *women,* not to *woman hater,* the first sentence needs to be rewritten. Truman Capote writes, "Within the next quarter-hour a stag party had taken over the apartment, several of them in uniform." [3] Here *them* stands for party-goers, not for party; but the meaning is clear enough and perhaps conciseness and style excuse the grammar, since a revision (e.g., ". . . a stag party had taken over the apartment; several of its members in uniform") would be longer and more formal.

Whenever a pronoun's meaning depends upon reference to a particular noun or another pronoun, the antecedent should be specific. Another common and clumsy construction in student writing is, "In Griffin's book he states a problem of which I was unaware." Here, once again, the third-person pronoun has no clear antecedent, though the reader probably assumes that *he* stands for Griffin. But *he* could refer to someone else contributing to Griffin's book, in which case the meaning should be made clear. The solution is, "In his book Griffin states a problem of which I was unaware." Sometimes when there are two names to which a pronoun could refer, you have to include explanatory nouns in apposition: e.g., "Captain Flume had obtained this idea from Chief White Halfoat himself, who did tiptoe up to his cot one night as he was dozing off, to hiss portentously that one night when he, Captain Flume, was sound asleep, he, Chief White Halfoat, was going to slit his throat open from ear to ear." [4] If the pronoun seems to refer to the wrong noun (usually one closer to it than the actual antecedent) or to no noun at all, the meaning may be confused or nonsensical. (E.g., "Many times the cars and trucks would break down, and with the little money saved they bought spare parts at an exorbitant price.") Such errors occur particularly often in the use of the *it*: "He was very sick and died of it." Of what? "In Franklin, God should be worshiped because he deserved it." This should be revised to read,

"Franklin believed God deserved to be worshiped." In the sentence, "I wasn't being very entertaining, but I didn't feel up to it," *it* doesn't sum up the previous clause but implies a contradictory idea. Sometimes dialogue (as, for example, Holden Caulfield's in *The Catcher in the Rye*) is deliberately nonstandard (Holden explains that he is quite illiterate but reads a lot); but sometimes in informal conversation *it, that, this,* or *which* can refer to the idea of an entire preceding clause, though such vague reference is avoided in a formal style:

INFORMAL. The penguins were diving into the water, which was an amusing sight.

FORMAL. It was amusing to see the penguins diving into the water.

INFORMAL. The St. Bernard wasn't satisfied with dog biscuits for supper and made no bones about it.

FORMAL. The dean was not satisfied with tenure policy and was quite specific in his criticism.

But even careful stylists sometimes use vague pronominal reference. Mark Twain wrote, "I never was so scared before and survived it," and James Thurber wrote of Harold Ross, "He was a horse player, completely addicted to it, and a steady loser." [5] If Thurber's grammar were smoothed to "He was completely addicted to horse playing and was a steady loser," the sentence would lose flavor and stress. On the other hand, Alfred Duggan's "All summer the fleet remained at Sandwich, which was very expensive" gives the reader a double take.[6] Rather than rules, the careful writer should consider clarity and style. There is some grammatical awkwardness in the sentence "Proctor is essentially a strong-willed man, which is shown in his actions with the court," but the revision "Proctor is essentially a strong-willed man, a fact which is shown . . ." is even worse; the proper formal style would be "The fact that Proctor is a strong-willed man is shown . . ." "Although it is not a common practice to frost pound cake, it can make a pleasant convenience for autumn and winter dining," is unclear. Does *it* refer to practice, to the act of frosting, or to the pound cake itself? Particularly objectionable in both grammar and style are constructions like "Just because society says something is evil, this doesn't mean that it is evil." "The fact that society says something is evil doesn't necessarily make it so" is clearer and more concise.

Despite the various grammatical hazards involved, you shouldn't be afraid to use pronouns. Often they are necessary to avoid repetition and create more fluid transitions:

Before he went to Hollywood, Errol Flynn had a number of exotic adventures in the South Pacific. Errol Flynn was a sailor, a plantation boss, and a sheep-gelder. Errol Flynn was even a slave trader. Once Errol Flynn bought a cargo of slaves and paid for them in San Francisco exposition tokens, which Errol Flynn told the chief were more valuable than money. Later the chief vowed he would kill Errol Flynn if he could ever get his hands on Errol Flynn.

This paragraph has the jerky movement of a car driven for the first time by a learner who can't handle the clutch. The substitution of *he* and *him* for most of the repetitions of the name *Errol Flynn* would unify the paragraph and connect the sentences more smoothly.

Any useless pronoun should be cut. A frequent and annoying construction is "In the Bible it says . . . ," "In *Hamlet* it says . . . ," "In algebra it says . . ." *It* is nothing but dead wood; "The Bible says . . ." is sufficient. Many students are addicted to "In such and such it says," and careless writers use this construction automatically. One *Life* editorial used it twice in successive sentences: "It says in the U. N. Universal Declaration of Human Rights that 'Everyone has the right to leave any country, including his own . . .' But it says in the U. S. State Department rulebook that the U. S. disapproves of the principle of asylum." [7] *Commonsense Grammar and Style* says *it* would never be missed.

Exercise 3: Put in the blank the correct substitute for any error in the case of a noun or pronoun.

1. One circus performer had a friend whom, he said, could flap his arms and fly off like an eagle. . . . .
2. The rabbit wasn't hers; it was her brother. . . . .
3. At the door, the princess saw the frog, whom she had quite forgotten. . . . .
4. "Whom did it?" Snoop asked Blabber. . . . .
5. That evening Dad took Mom and I to see *Frankenstein Meets the Wolf Man*. . . . .
6. The girls who were making accusations as to whom the witches were, did so to escape being accused themselves. . . . .
7. It seemed as if his fate were controlled by he himself. . . . .
8. Martin states that certain traits show whom is a barbarian. . . . .
9. They invited his wife and him to the beach party. . . . .
10. This turtle may be symbolic of the Joad family, around who Steinbeck centers his story. . . . .

68

11. What will you do in the event of Arnold leaving? · · · ·
12. We are set back, but have no fear that us will rally. · · · ·
13. I hope you don't mind me interrupting. · · · ·
14. Us Star Plug chewers would rather bite than spit. · · · ·
15. May and she went to the Museum of Natural History. · · · ·
16. "Quick," hissed the hunchback; "run the current through it's electrodes." · · · ·
17. A large bat fluttered by Helen and I. · · · ·
18. Jean Valjean was sentenced to five years imprisonment for stealing a loaf of bread. · · · ·
19. As a prisoner, Jean Valjean spent nineteen years in the galley's. · · · ·
20. Two members—Eugene and me—were initiated into the Abner Bibberman fan club. · · · ·
21. Whose playing a transistor radio during the concert? · · · ·
22. Fenimore took an instructors position in the Arizona Veterinary College. · · · ·
23. The ranger didn't like them cutting the rhododendrons. · · · ·
24. Kathy admires Julian Breams adaptation of Ravels "Pavane for a Dead Princess." · · · ·
25. Presley has more old volume's of *National Geographic* than most doctors offices do. · · · ·

Exercise 4: In the following sentences, choose the appropriate pronoun case.

1. One of the most important things in schools is the opportunity to talk to those who know more than (I, me). · · · ·
2. You don't have perforating fingernails like (I, me). · · · ·
3. The dispossessed farmers wanted to fight somebody, but (who, whom) could they fight? · · · ·
4. "Junior, (who, whom) are you playing with in there?" said the mother kangaroo. · · · ·
5. He was seen with a girl (who, whom) he said was his cousin. · · · ·
6. I like music according to (whom, who) is performing. · · · ·
7. Bring your friend, (whoever, whomever) she is. · · · ·
8. I like to know (who, whom) I'm talking to. · · · ·
9. We observe the failure of individual initiative in the face of (he, him) who is bigger. · · · ·
10. Ivan the Terrible, (who, whom) everybody thought was dying, rose wrathfully from his bed. Moral: Never think dead of the ill. · · · ·
11. The person who picked the rattlesnake orchids should be ashamed, (whosoever, whomsoever) he may be. · · · ·
12. I want to make certain of (who, whom) I'm dating. · · · ·

13. Here are two perfectly good cups of coffee for (whoever, whomever) wants them. . . . .

14. This is a perfect day for Don and (I, me) to climb Mt. LeConte. . . . .

15. After H. G. Wells's attack, there was no chance for a reconciliation between Henry James and (he, him) . . . . .

16. The personnel director ruled that all seasonal employees except (we, us) experienced ones must be available from June 1 to Labor Day. . . . .

17. (Who, whom) do you think was killed in more movies—John Carradine or Basil Rathbone? . . . .

18. Does it come in anything except pressurized cans? I get nervous about (them, their) exploding. . . . .

19. Was it (they, them) (who, whom) the skunk had sprayed? . . . .

20. The buffet was prepared by two members—Mrs. Cooper and (I, me) . . . . .

21. Do you know (who, whom) invented the Franklin stove? . . . .

22. Julie gives a kiss to (whoever, whomever) buys a bond. . . . .

23. The boat needs caulking, and (it's, its) bottom should be scraped. . . . .

24. The doctor told Boris and (I, me) to meet him at the deserted mill. . . . .

25. The burgomeister told (we, us) men to take torches and search the woods. . . . .

6 √ Pronoun - Antecedent Agreement

"A person in there looks just like they did in life, only with a nice tan, like you have right now," said the coffin salesman.[1] Here death's sting is in the forked tongue of the salesman. This unctiously commercial pitch is dubious in taste, misleading in theology, false in comfort, and wretched in grammar. The coffin is also expensive; but then the salesman can justify the cost by saying that it's large enough for two—at least, it had better be if "they" are to look right in it. Is this a case of "When a body meets a body?" Or has the salesman had too much rye? Or is this the first recorded case of posthumous schizophrenia? Obviously, there is only one body, and it should have a singular pronoun.

A pronoun must agree with its antecedent in person, gender, and number—but not in case. The case of a pronoun depends upon its use in its own clause. Thus if you are to use pronouns correctly you must be aware of grammatical construction and the relationship of words. First find the pronoun; then see if it has an antecedent. If it does not, or if the antecedent is unclear, you have an error in reference, unless the pronoun can stand alone. When you have found the antecedent, see what its person, gender, and number are. Then look at the person, gender, and number of the pronoun. Are they the same? If not, there is an error in agreement; and you must change either the pronoun or the antecedent to make their person, gender, and number the same. This sounds like a painstaking process, but you need to follow it only if you are addicted to error in this area. Most experienced writers don't have to think twice about agreement but handle it by conditioned reflex. Unfortunately, many people habitually use the wrong pronoun, so their grammatical reflexes need reconditioning by practice in conscious sentence analysis.

71

EXAMPLE	EXPLANATION
I comb *my* hair with greasy kid stuff.	*My* is first person singular to agree with *I*.
The *girl* had *her* purse stolen.	*Her* is feminine third person singular to agree with *girl*.
The *gnu* scratched *its* nose.	*Its* is neuter third person singular to agree with *gnu*.
The *tigers* sharpened *their* teeth.	*Their* is third person plural to agree with *tigers*.

¶ PERSON

Disagreements in person occur almost exclusively with vague or impersonal pronouns. The sentence "One should watch your step" has a second-person pronoun, *your,* and a third-person antecedent, *one.* It is necessary to be consistent and to avoid errors, such as, "On Zenith one was forced to conform to conservative politics and live your life the way the group wanted you to." A particularly choice example occurred in an article entitled "Blowing Rock, N.C.": "Years ago they could tell a stranger was 'an outsider by the cut of your pants.' But education and business has seeped up from the big cities and universities to the hills, and they have changed somewhat the cut of their own pants."[2] Here we have a third-person singular antecedent *stranger* mismatched with a second-person singular pronoun *your*—an error in both number and person. The second sentence is a real hodgepodge: *education and business* require a plural verb. It is not clear whether *they* refers to *education and business, hills,* or something else. And if the hills change the cut of their pants, then the metaphor is ludicrous.

Another amusing shift in person appears in a young actress's statement, "*My* figure's all right—*I* don't mind it. Sometimes it gets a little out of hand after *you've* had a three months' vacation when *you* just sit around the pool getting tan and fat . . . then *I* have to go on a crash diet. . . . *I* have such an investment in a whole lot of stretch pants and they all fit within an eighth of an inch and if *you* gain more than a half ounce *you've* had it. *You* can't wear them." (Italics mine.) This becomes doubly deranged if the reader imagines that *you* refers to himself.

¶ GENDER

The gender of a pronoun should be the same as that of its antecedent. This seems obvious, and the reader is not likely to make errors like "Mr. Lummox got tired of commuting every morning with twenty-five pounds of bread in *her* lap." Most errors occur with relative pronouns. *Who* should be used to refer to persons; *which,* to refer to things; and *that,* to refer to persons, animals, or things. In an assignment on *The Grapes of Wrath,* students wrote of "the tractors who," "the farmers which," "the turtle who," "the ant who," "the car who," "the migrants which." In each of these the gender is wrong; *who* is masculine or feminine, *which* is neuter, and *that* can be used without regard to gender. Sometimes the choice should depend on euphony: *the sandwich that* is obviously preferable to *the sandwich which.* In the possessive, *whose,* though masculine or feminine, is sometimes used for things as well as persons, to avoid the awkward *of which.* "The ship whose side was rammed" is better than "The ship the side of which was rammed." Thus abstract rules have to surrender to concrete problems of style.

Because English uses natural gender, there is little problem with personal pronoun reference; most nouns take *it.* Even an animal with a specific sex, like cow, bull, and sow, can be referred to as *it.* Usually we reserve specific gender for persons. But in casual practice we assign *it* to many things. All ships are feminine, even *The Great Harry* or *The General Hahn.* Melville wrote of *The Pequod,* "She was a ship of the old school, rather small if anything; with an old fashioned claw-footed look about her." But often when the specific word *ship* is used as an antecedent, the pronoun that follows is *it*: "The ship changed its course." Cars are customarily feminine, so much so that Faulkner wrote in *Intruder in the Dust* that "the automobile has become our national sex symbol." Yet Faulkner referred to the car as *it.* Most people say, "She needs a grease job," "Fill her up," or "She has only 35,000 miles." A very few may say, "Fill it up," but you never hear, "Fill him up." Axles, bushings, brakes, and other parts of the car are usually neuter, though almost any machine or tool can be feminine: "Hand her here," "She has a good cutting edge," "She has a lot of power," "Set her down carefully." Even weapons are often referred to as feminine, from the huge Scottish cannon Maun's Meg to the Old Betsy. "What's her range?" an artilleryman might ask. Despite Burt Lancaster in the movie *From Here to Eternity,* instructors for the .30 caliber machine gun warn, "Never hold the barrel in your bare hand if you fire from the hip; she gets red hot, and she'll roast your hand."

Except for mares, cows, and dogs that have just become mothers,

the gender of most animals, when not referred to as *it* is masculine.
Whitman wrote, "The spotted hawk swoops by and accuses me;
he complains of my gab and my loitering." In *The Old Man and
the Sea,* Santiago's giant marlin and the sharks that devour him
are spoken of as masculine, though, in fact, they could equally well
be feminine. The first man to have seen bacteria is reported to have
said, "I can't make out his shape. But he is alive!"

Finally, semantic change has altered the gender of some words.
Harlot was once masculine and meant simply "young fellow," as in
Chaucer's description of the Summoner as "a gentil harlot and a
kynde." And *girl* once meant a young person of either sex and could
take a masculine pronoun.

After an antecedent of mixed or indeterminate gender, the masculine pronoun is conventionally used:

> *Every child* should put away *his* toys.
> *Everyone* is to bring *his* own camping equipment.

The men and women were told that *everybody* must contribute
his share. "Everybody must contribute his or her share" is long-
winded and pedantic. When the antecedent is specifically feminine,
then it is followed by a feminine pronoun: "The ladies' bridge club
decided *everyone* should bring *her* own cards."

¶ NUMBER

Most errors in agreement occur in number, usually because a
singular antecedent is erroneously followed by a plural pronoun.
There are several constructions that may create difficulties.

1. The pronoun should be plural when it has two or more antecedents connected by *and*:

> My wife and I took *our* vacation in Grundy Center.
> Fitzgerald and Hemingway had some rifts in *their* friendship.
> Brutus and Cassius killed *themselves.*

2. When a collective noun is considered as a unit, it takes a
singular pronoun:

> *Congress* adjourned *its* eighty-first session.
> The *congregation* supported *its* minister.
> The Slippery Rock football *team* had *its* forty-fourth
> consecutive undefeated season.
> The *enemy* issued *its* ultimatum.

74

3. When a collective noun is considered as a number of separate individuals, it takes a plural pronoun. Thus you would write, "The audience applauded *its* speaker," but "The audience *were* cheering, hissing, and booing *their* speaker"; "The jury followed *its* instructions," but "The jury were divided in *their* verdict."

> *Wildlife* are at *their* best in backcountry.
> *Congress are* divided on *their* views of foreign aid.
> The *congregation* were sufficiently divided about *their*
>   minister to drive Jonathan Edwards from his parish.
> The Slippery Rock *team* got permission to postpone *their* exams.
> The *enemy* were both resisting and running away from *their* attackers.

Sometimes an unexpected word appears as a collective plural noun. Thus, Thomas Hutchinson wrote in the eighteenth century, "New Hampshire, by *their* convenient situation were induced to become *their* own importers." *Importers* is the key word here that makes New Hampshire plural.

Other errors occur when a collective noun followed by a plural pronoun is given a singular verb:

> "The public only *thinks they* are saving money." [3]
> Apparently the Student Government mimeograph service *has* been
>   derelict in performing *their* duties.
> In *The Grapes of Wrath* the bank *moves* in with *their* tractors.
> "I wonder if the Army's generous with *their* peanut butter"
>   [italics mine]—Truman Capote, *Breakfast at Tiffany's* [4]

The first two examples require a plural verb: *think* and *have*. The last two should keep the verb singular and change the pronoun: "*its* tractors," "*its* peanut butter." Actually the last example being part of the dialogue in a novel is in the original entirely appropriate in character.

4. Traditionally the possessive personal pronoun is put in the singular when its antecedent is *each, either,* or *neither,* even if it is followed by a plural object:

> *Each* of the queens lost *her* head.
> *Either* of the candidates could alienate *his* followers
>   by an unpopular stand.
> *Neither* of the magicians would reveal *his* tricks.

Often colloquial speech uses a plural verb and pronoun: "Neither of them were willing to stop their quarrel." But in the preceding examples, logic and grammar combined require the singular pronoun. Sometimes, however, logic is on the other side, especially if the plural modifier precedes *each, either,* or *neither*: "The three little pigs each built themselves a house" is more fluent than "The three little pigs each built himself a house." An ad for glue says of its ingredients, "*Each . . . has his* contribution ready. But E-Pox-E Glue sticks to iron, steel, brass, copper, bronze and bonds *them* to *each* other." Here *each* is singular as a subject but plural as an object following *them.* In "The principal stands behind each of his students when they accept a job," common sense requires the plural; "when he accepts a job" would seem both illogical and vague in reference.

5. Conservative grammar requires the use of a singular pronoun when there is a numerically indefinite antecedent, such as *anyone, anybody, each, either, every, everybody, everyone, neither, no one,* and *nobody*:

> "What if *everyone* in the whole world suddenly decided to run away from his problems?"[5]
> "Let *everyone* carry out *his* own corpse," Jim Fisk told the investigators.
> "You mean *anyone* can have a giant in *her* washing machine?"—detergent ad.

But in general practice, these indefinite antecedents are often followed by a plural pronoun: "Everybody has their lunch," "Nobody got their dessert." This is a particularly sore spot with many grammarians. The controversy is caused by the difference between a formal and a colloquial style of grammar. Formal, conservative grammar requires that the number of a pronoun be governed by its form, regardless of meaning, whereas colloquial usage is usually concerned solely with conveying meaning. Each of these numerically indefinite antecedents has a plural meaning but a singular form; and since meaning generally carries the day, the formalists are losing ground. In Thurber's "The Interview," an irascible writer tells a reporter: "Everybody replies to my questions the way they think I want them to reply. You can say that I say 'everybody-they'; I hate 'everybody-he.' 'Has everybody brought his or her slate?' a teacher of mine, a great goat of a woman, used to ask us. There is no other tongue in the world as clumsy as ours is—with its back to certain corners." [6]

Certainly many able writers sometimes agree in practice with Thurber's author. Hemingway, Steinbeck, Mary McCarthy, Edmund Wilson, John P. Marquand are a few of them. ". . . everybody no matter what superficial annoyance they might show, liked to be recognized and noticed." [7] Norman Mailer regularly uses such constructions:

"Nobody minds if they read in the papers that they were thrown in a swimming pool when in fact they did not go near a glass of water." [8]

". . . everybody else in the book is connected by their skin to another character who is connected to still another." [9]

On the political scene we find Governor Scranton of Pennsylvania saying, "I feel very strongly that one of the mistakes that we have made in the past is to try to tell everybody how they should vote at a national convention." [10] And General LeMay has stated, ". . . no one is going to start a war unless they think they are going to win." [11]

Of course, politicians are not necessarily dependable guides in grammar; some are quite the reverse. But there are situations where *everybody* and the other indefinite antecedents require a plural pronoun if a sentence is to make any sense; e.g., "He talks to everyone as if they matter." "He talks to everyone as if he matters" completely reverses the meaning. "Practically everybody in Congress would like to get the budget down; sometimes they form up in assault squads to do it." [12] If "he forms up in assault squads," he is certainly fragmenting his personality. "Had *everyone* felt and acted as Proctor did, or had *they* been free to do so, the mass hysteria of the witch trials never could have controlled Salem," requires *they* for the plural meaning. So does Edmund Wilson's observation, "And, as seems to have been natural in the nineteenth century so much more than it is in our own, *everybody* speaks in character in such a way that one can often almost hear *their* voices." [13] (Italics mine.) In "*Neither* driver knew *he* was leading until *they* reached the Morogoro checkpoint," clarity requires that the first pronoun be singular and the second plural. "Everybody was very courteous; they gave me hay to sit on," requires *they* for meaning, though the situation remains curious.

On the other hand, meaning as well as form often requires a singular pronoun. "Everybody thinks their own child is remarkable" is awkward. Does everybody have the same child, and how many parents does the child have? "Everyone calls everyone Richard or whatever their name is, if they don't call them darling," is a double dose of grammatical schizophrenia.[14] Common sense says

77

that specific situations, rather than abstract rules, should determine whether an antecedent like *everybody* takes a singular or plural pronoun. As the parents sing in *The Fantasticks,* "No one can hear with beans in their ears." "*Every* wine has *its* proper glass—it's imperative to know *them* all" has faulty agreement in form but makes sense in context, while "Everybody is writing their auto-biography" is confused, mainly because a plural possessive pronoun is coupled with a singular object.

Another reason for confusion, and one that more legitimately bothers formalists, is that *anyone, everyone, no one,* etc., always take a singular verb, whether or not they are followed by a plural pronoun. You never hear, "Everybody are coming home," "No one were raking their leaves," or similar constructions. Presumably, if words like *everybody* have a plural meaning, they could take a plural verb, but the *-body* and *-one* endings make a singular verb habitual. Accordingly, unless the meaning requires a plural pro-noun, it is better to stick to the traditional form and use the singular. There is no reason for defending "Nobody brushes their teeth in the bathtub." In conversation it is usually not necessary to worry about pronoun-antecedent agreement, but any lack of agreement, such as in "Anyone in good physical condition can climb Mount Rainier if they have the desire," needs to be revised for careful writing. How, then, do you know when the rule is flexible? "Every daisy in the dell seems to know but they won't tell—Mary Ann." You have to use your own judgment. Look at the following exam-ples and see if you would revise them or let them stand:

If you make a quality product, you can't make enough of them.

The Cuban crisis really shook everyone up in their fear of an all-out nuclear war.

"You ask anybody from around Chun King. They'll tell you Aunt Jenny's the best cook in town."

He sees everyone sitting around town waiting for Friday night so that they might start their parties.

Of course, not all sentences can be taken out of context. "Everyone helped when they hatched aboard ship in the Arctic" sounds like science fiction, but the meaning becomes clear when it is preceded by "His Excellency took a great interest in my butterflies." [15]

Unfortunately, many people—perhaps proceeding by analogy with *everybody . . . they*—use *they* with any third person singular antecedent. *Anyone . . . they* can sometimes make sense, but *a person . . . they* does not. "Can they be a nurse?" asks an ad. They can't if they're schizophrenic, but maybe they can if they're Siamese twins. This indiscriminate use of *they* has become so widespread that some people seem to have forgotten the use of *he, she,* or *it.* One minister used *they* so regularly ("One should get on their knees and ask God to forgive them") that he barely avoided saying *God . . . they.* "Whoever invented radiators should have their head examined." Yes, and his grammar revised. "The minimum time any *clerk* can work in this Hi-Fi department is 3 days! After that, we send *them* to a boiler factory for a week, to relax *their* nerves!" we read in *Mad.*[16] (italics mine). The pronoun-antecedent agreement is mad, too. Sometimes it is the antecedent that should be changed, rather than the pronoun: in "Mark Twain was impressed with the Negro and regarded them as fellow human beings," *them* is the right pronoun, but the antecedent should be *Negroes.* Conceivably *Negro* might be considered a collective noun that could take a plural, as in Norman Mailer's ". . . and the Negro had already demonstrated to the collective psyche of America that they had the greatest potential for violence of any political body in our American world; now, on this afternoon, they chose to show that they also possessed the finest capacity for order and discipline in the nation." [17] But Mailer is too obviously violating agreement when he writes, "Once inserted into politics a lady betrays the difference between a person and their project." [18] Or are *they, their,* and *them* to replace the third-person singular, as *you* did *thou?* This may come to pass, but in the meantime, you should use a singular pronoun with a singular antecedent and avoid such careless prose as Stony Burke's "It's too bad somebody can't make themselves a few bucks helping me," or "If there was a real-life prototype of a part she was about to portray, Ingrid hunted them out, examined and absorbed their uniqueness." [19] Miss Bergman did play in *Dr. Jekyll and Mr. Hyde,* but it was Spencer Tracy who portrayed the double character.

"In Puritan New England, breaking the law would show disfavor in the eyes of God, since they were set up by those considered under His divine influence." The faulty agreement here creates ambiguity; unless *law* is changed to *laws, they* seems to refer to "the eyes of God." Again, the antecedent rather than the pronoun needs changing in "From the Calvinist point of view, *man* is so wretched that the only true justice would be everlasting fire for all of *them.*"

Finally, when a subordinate clause comes first, the pronoun may be the antecedent for the noun, with occasionally such attendant confusion as, "Through his preoccupation with his work, teachers often neglect their families." Some teachers even write grammar books.

Exercise 5: Select from the words in parentheses those that will agree with their antecedents.

1. Once more the soldier saw the gnome, (which, whom) he had quite forgotten.
2. Thoreau disliked seeing everybody hurry around wasting (their, his) lives.
3. Mississippi has (its, their) top unit in there right now.
4. Professor Dibdin received his M.A. and Ph.D. degrees from Southeastern University and has been a professor in (its, their) English Department since 1938.
5. Nobody's ever told that joke (has he, have they)?
6. When a person grows up in the city, (one, you, he) goes wild over trees.
7. Doesn't everybody have a TV set in (his, their) Rolls-Royce?
8. You and every other American own Cape Hatteras National Seashore, as (you, he, they) should know.
9. One should not go shopping with curlers in (their, your, his, her) hair.
10. If someone in your neighborhood has seen this movie, don't let (them, him, one) tell you the ending in which the butler is revealed as the killer.
11. One can always identify a logger by the way (you, they, he) (stir, stirs) coffee with (your, their, his) thumb.
12. The actor (which, that) has been seen by the largest audience is Charlton Heston.
13. The cast (was, were) celebrating (their, its) one hundredth performance of *Mr. Limberlost, or The Kind Keeper.*
14. Does the Prohibitionist Party really think (their, its, it's) candidate has a chance?
15. How many officers use Top Brass to condition (one's, your, their, there) hair?
16. The audience appalled Henry James by (its, their) vulgarity at the opening of *Guy Domville.*
17. The Army is penny-wise with (its, their) pencils and paper and pound-foolish with expenses for (its, their) top brass.
18. Only two of Henry VIII's wives lost (her, their) (head, heads).
19. Ruritania thinks (their, its) king is Rudolph V, but Rudolph Rassendyl of England was crowned at Strelsau in (its, their) cathedral.

20. Neither Henry James nor H. G. Wells would patch up (his, their) friendship.
21. Pythagoras discovered the relationship between the length of a string and (their, its) pitch.
22. Neither John Carter nor Thuvan Dihn know where (he, they) were until (he, they) reached the Carrion Caves.
23. Everybody was very considerate; (he, they) let me sit next to the fire.
24. Whoever invented daylight saving should have (his, their) head examined.
25. Shakespeare often borrowed a plot from some previous author but transformed (it, them) into an original work of art.

Exercise 6: Some of the pronouns in the following sentences fail to agree with their antecedents in person, number, or gender. If the pronoun does not agree, put the correct form in the blank.

1. If the student returns to you the next term for enrollment, they must first come to me for their folder. . . . .
2. The United States has a government who represents the people. . . . .
3. Everybody in the bakery looked like they had a big question mark over their heads. . . . .
4. When we wanted to reward someone, we would give them five or six cartridges. . . . .
5. When a person is climbing mountains, one should watch your step. . . . .
6. At the Jinja golf course, any player may lift their ball out of a hippopotamus footprint without penalty. . . . .
7. If nobody has a toy elephant, I can give them one. . . . .
8. One man which was bitten by a rattlesnake used the snake for a tourniquet. . . . .
9. The book is written in plain language by a University of Michigan scientist which really knows his mushrooms. . . . .
10. Somebody who would take their mother-in-law for a drive in a small foreign car is asking for trouble. . . . .
11. We need a candidate what can speak for the people. . . . .
12. Does anybody want a banana on their cereal? . . . .
13. Often a person working overseas cannot adjust to unfamiliar ways that cause him cultural shock. . . . .
14. Bats vary to a degree what hardly seems possible. . . . .
15. The Scruff family is holding their annual reunion at Huggins Hell. . . . .
16. Nobody in their right mind wants a python for a house pet. . . . .
17. Amaryllis and she won first prize for her rhododendrons. . . . .

18. When you take polaroid pictures, one should be careful to throw their negatives in a proper receptacle and not on the ground.

. . . .

19. The big dog which followed father home belongs to Mr. Schildkraut and their boys.

. . . .

20. The way you tell a black widow spider is that they have a red spot on their underneath.

. . . .

7 √ Case and Its Curiosities

EVANS.	What is your genitive case plural, William?
WILLIAM.	Genitive—horum, harum, horum.
QUICKLY.	Vengeance of Jenny's case! Fie on her! Never name her, child, if she be a whore.
EVANS.	For shame, 'oman.
QUICKLY.	You do ill to teach the child such words: he teaches him to hick and to hack—which they'll do fast enough of themselves, and to call "horum"; fie upon you!
EVANS.	'Oman, art thu lunatics? Hast thou no understanding of thy cases, and the number of the genders?

WILLIAM SHAKESPEARE, The Merry Wives of Windsor

Finno-Ugrian has sixteen cases. This is of no concern to anyone except philologists and Finno-Ugrians. For the latter, it is quite a headache. Modern English has only three cases; it is on this score one of the simplest languages in the world, yet the case of our nouns and pronouns causes a great many difficulties and controversies. Arguments over *who* and *whom, I* or *me, we* or *us* have ruined marriages, made children rebel from their parents, and caused grammarians to denounce each other as prissy schoolmarms or dangerous subversives.

Actually, case in English was once a great deal more complicated than it is at present; the language has become increasingly streamlined, and the issue at hand is (partly) whether it should be simplified further. In a highly synthetic language like Latin or German, case is indicated by inflection (that is, by changing the ending), and students must suffer the ordeal of learning various laborious declensions. In Latin there are five main cases with forms in the singular and plural, and the problem is further confounded by artificial gender. Thus the Latin word for *farmer* (*agricola*), belongs to the first declension and is feminine in gender:

	SINGULAR	PLURAL
NOMINATIVE	agricola	agricolae
GENITIVE	agricolae	agricolārum
DATIVE	agricolae	agricolīs
ACCUSATIVE	agricolam	agricolās
ABLATIVE	agricolā	agricolīs

And there are four other declensions in Latin, each with characteristically different endings, making a total of fifty possible case endings, though some of these duplicate each other. This should be evidence enough that English does not have Latin grammar and is infinitely better off without it. In German not only the nouns, pronouns, and adjectives but also the articles (*the, a, an*) must be inflected according to number, gender, and case. Old English was similarly complex; it had four cases (nominative, genitive, dative, accusative, and sometimes a fifth—the instrumental), each with different endings in the singular and plural. There were five major declensions, four minor ones, and variations on all of them. The adjective had a strong and weak declension and had to agree in case, number, and gender with the noun it modified. As in German, the definite article was fully inflected.

But in modern English one can forget all this. Our articles and adjectives do not inflect at all (except for the comparative and superlative forms), and our nouns do so only for the plural or in the possessive case. The only problems with nouns are some irregular plurals, the use of the apostrophe (not really a grammatical issue), and the use of the possessive case for nouns modifying gerunds. The three cases used in modern English are the subjective, possessive, and objective. Sometimes these are given the Latinate names nominative, genitive, and accusative; but we shall use the English terms. Latinist grammarians used to insist that English had five cases, but instead of dative and ablative inflections, we use word order or prepositions. Case endings are essential in Latin to indicate a noun's function; instead we rely upon word order to distinguish subject from object. Thus "Nero interfecit Agrippinam" and "Agrippinam interfecit Nero" both make Nero the murderer and Agrippina the corpse, but there is considerable difference in English between "Booth killed Lincoln" and "Lincoln killed Booth."

Only the personal and relative pronouns are still inflected in English, and it is with them that most problems arise:

PERSONAL PRONOUNS

	SUBJECTIVE CASE	POSSESSIVE CASE	OBJECTIVE CASE
		Singular	
1ST PERSON	I	my, mine	me
2ND PERSON	you	your, yours	you
3RD PERSON	he, she, it	his, her, hers, its	him, her, it
		Plural	
1ST PERSON	we	our, ours	us
2ND PERSON	you	your, yours	you
3RD PERSON	they	their, theirs	them

RELATIVE

Singular and Plural

who	whose	whom

A pronoun's case depends upon its use in its own clause and not upon the case of its antecedent. Formal grammar employs the following conventions:

1. The subjective case is used for pronouns that are
    (*a*) Subjects of verbs (*"He told* her *he loved* her, but oh, how *he lied"*).
    (*b*) Pronouns in apposition to subjects ("Three winners—Susy, Ermentrude, and *I*—shared the prize").
    (*c*) Complements of the verb *to be* ("The accused confessed it was *he* who operated the still").
2. The objective case is used for pronouns that are
    (*a*) Objects of verbs ("The moose frightened *us*").
    (*b*) Objects of prepositions ("The moose charged at *us*").
    (*c*) Pronouns in apposition to objects ("The moose chased *us* —Edgar and *me*—into the lake").
    (*d*) Subjects or objects of infinitives ("I told *him* to drop dead." "I pretended to be *him*").
3. The possessive case is used for pronouns that
    (*a*) Modify a noun or another pronoun ("The vampire climbed into *his* coffin." "These are *my jewels*").
    (*b*) Modify a gerund ("She didn't like the *toucan's eating* her African violets." "*His seeing* the abominable snowman was the most exciting part of the trip").

85

There are several situations in which these conventions are changing. Though formal grammar requires the subjective case for the complement of the verb *to be,* colloquial usage usually takes the objective. Some die-hard purists protest, but nowadays practically no one says "It is I," or "It was she."

> " 'You don't have to talk as though you were addressing a meeting any longer, Willis,' Bess said. 'It's only me.'
> " 'Only I, Bess,' Willis said, 'only I.'
> " 'Oh, my God,' Bess said, 'I bet you clipped a coupon and bought one of those courses in proper speech.' "[1]

Bess's "It's me" is perfectly acceptable; she does not say "you was addressing" or "them courses," which would have made her English substandard. Very much on the make, Willis is a social climber and a snob, and his self-conscious grammar here reflects his phoniness. As Ensign Pulver says nervously in *Mr. Roberts,* "Captain, it's me. It is I, Ensign Pulver."

For most people, "It's me" is habitual and needs no apology. The French have always said, *"C'est moi."* "It's me" has been used by distinguished writers from Shakespeare to Hemingway and has been generally colloquial since Elizabethan times. Teachers who insist dogmatically upon "It is I" usually succeed only in causing their students to write, "Between you and I . . . ," or, "Serve the pizza to Irving and I." "It's him," "It's her," "It's them," "It's us" are likewise common colloquial forms and are so recognized by the *Oxford Dictionary.*

If a pronoun after the verb *to be* is followed by a relative pronoun introducing a clause, then both pronouns are in the subjective case ("It's I who am to be married." "It's we who are to blame"). Colloquial speech usually avoids such constructions. As an answer to such a question as "What do you say [or see or think or like]?" one ordinarily says, "Who, me?" or "Who, us?" though the rule calls for *I* or *we* along with the subjective *who.* But "Who, me?" has become idiomatic, like the French *"Qui, moi?"* Nobody ever heard a Frenchman say, *"Qui, je?"* Yet for some reason (perhaps from hearing too many Indians in Hollywood movies say, "Me gottum firewater"), many people unconsciously feel that *I* is more aristocratic than *me,* regardless of its grammatical function. Notice the different connotations of *The King and I* and *Me and the Colonel.*

Nobody but little children and aborigines in the movies ever uses *me* in a subject ("Me want play outside." "Me want Dorothy La-mour"). Nor does *us* ever appear directly preceding the verb ("Us are playing poker"). But a frequent nonstandard practice is to use *us* for the subject if there is an appositive intervening between it and the verb. Thus Huckleberry Hound says, "Us jungle boys are real swinging types," though not even Huck would say, "Us are real swinging types." Apparently the intervening noun causes con-fusion. This seems to be equally true of a compound subject, where the error is often doubled by using a singular verb): "Me and her was at the dance," "Him and me is hungry." But no one would say "me was," "her was," "him is," or "me is." Grammarians have com-plained of the cigarette ad, "Us Tareyton smokers would rather fight than switch." The admen replied that "We Tareyton smokers" would sound sissified to the working stiffs at whom the ad was aimed.

Similarly a compound object often seems to cause confusion and result in the wrong case being used: "I once went dancing with she and Princess Margaret" and "Thangbrand took Phil and I to see John Gielgud in *King Lear*." Holden Caulfield often makes this sort of error. But one would never say, "I once went dancing with she" or "Thangbrand took I." You shouldn't let compounds disconcert you, for doubling the subject or object doesn't change the case of the pronoun. "Show it to Sally and I" or "He loves both you and I" are not only nonstandard; they are particularly annoy-ing to careful grammarians.

¶ PRONOUNS AFTER THAN, AS, LIKE

Than and *as* are conjunctions used in comparison, and formal English grammar requires a pronoun following them to be in the same case as the noun to which it is compared.

> Subjective: John Carradine is thinner than *I*.
> She is as good a fencer as *they*.
> Objective: The dinosaur impressed them no less than *me*.
> The code puzzled us as well as *him*.

The first two constructions are clumsy and appear mostly in gram-mar textbooks. In casual speech many literate people now say, "John Carradine is thinner than me"—unless they are thinner than John Carradine. Conventionally, *than* is supposed to connect two clauses, with the pronoun following as the subject of a verb under-stood ("John Carradine is thinner than I am"), but many people think of *than* as a preposition that should be followed by an object. There is no innate reason why *than* cannot be a preposition; it is for usage to decide; and the reader can be cautious or relaxed, suiting his grammar to the occasion.

Traditionally, *like* is a preposition and not a conjunction. Today it often appears as the latter ("Let's all sing like the birdies sing"); but when it is more correctly used as a preposition, it is followed by the objective case. ("He doesn't look a bit like me.") Here an obsession with grammatical correctness often leads the half-educated to confuse *like* with the conjunction *as* and say, "He looks like I," which merely sounds affected:

> So be like I,
> Hold your head up high,
> You will find the bluebird of happiness.

All you really find is an awkward rhyme.

¶ TO WHOM IT MAY CONCERN

In a Washington phone booth, under the sign, "Who Shall I call First?" someone wrote, "An English teacher." Traditional grammar calls for *whom* as the object of the verb, but this tradition is rapidly breaking down. When an interrogative pronoun appears as the opening word of a question, *who* has become the customary form to use in extremely formal occasions. Not even the most fastidious grammarian, if his daughter shouted that she saw a weird face peering in the kitchen window, would answer, "Whom did you see?" Bergen Evans claims there is a basic vulgarity to "Whom are you talking about?" In such a situation *whom* sounds too calculated and betrays an affected snobbishness, like the false elegance in a modest backyard of cast-iron dogs and flamingos. The semi-literate snob is apt to think that *whom* is invariably preferable and to use it indiscriminately or when he wishes to make an impression. "So I gave him a haughty look and I said, 'Whom do you think you are, anyways?'"[2] This sort of speech is about as aristocratic as Mamie Mullins in the comic strip. As its author, James Thurber, wrote satirically, "'Whom' should be used in the nominative case only when a note of dignity or austerity is desired. . . . To address a person one knows by a 'Whom are you?' is a mark either of incredible lapse of memory or inexcusable arrogance."[3]

Who has become practically universal as an interrogative pronoun, even when it is the object of a verb or preposition. Thus if

88

someone said, "We're going to stake the vampires next," his companion might ask, "The who?" "The whom?" sounds comically affected. When someone asks, "Tell who off?" the pronoun seems the right choice. "So who do they get to be the baby sitter? Me, that's who." In this colloquial context *whom* would be so unnatural as to call attention to itself. Henry James's "whom the deuce I did know" is incongruous, with the grammatically fastidious "*whom*" being followed by the slang the deuce.

In common usage, then, *whom* is weakening except after prepositions ("He is the man *to whom* I was talking." "Stanley, a brown, black, and white basset hound, is the mascot of the Betas, *with whom* he has resided for the past two and a half years"). In conversation one is likely to avoid such constructions. ("He is the man I was talking to.") Even after *to, whom* is barely holding its own. In *Catch-22,* when Yossarian explained that he gave away all the fruit juice and dried fruit he got from the mess hall, "'To who?' cried Milo, in a voice cracking with dismay." [4] Elizabethan English was rather freewheeling in its use of *who* and *whom.* Shakespeare could write "To who?" and the translators of the King James Bible have Jesus say, "Whom say ye that I am?" Today the English language shows some disposition to get rid of *whom* altogether, and unquestionably it would be a better language without it. French has gotten along for centuries with *qui* for both cases (*Qui va là? A qui avez-vous donné le chat noir?*).

As it is, *whom* causes only confusion. Norman Mailer has fun with it when he writes: "But there is a tool of investigation for political mysteries. It is Lenin's formula: 'Whom?' Whom does this benefit? Who prospers from a particular act? Well, whom? . . . Whom? asked Lenin, who benefits?" [5] You frequently hear someone say, "What are the choices for dessert, and what would whom like?" You read in the paper, "Major Gagarin, whom the Soviets say has orbited the globe safely, is shown with his wife." But in both of these examples *whom* should be changed to *who,* for it is the subject of a verb and though *who* is becoming acceptable for *whom,* the reverse is not true.

"Whom should he meet but Mr. MacGregor," sounds neatly old-fashioned; and when you see Charlton Heston as El Cid, battered and bloody after hand-to-hand combat, gasping, "To whom does the city belong now?" you know you are hearing the stilted dialogue of a Hollywood epic. "Who's shooting who?" Thurber asked in one of his final stories.[6] "Who do you love, I hope?" sings Annie

Oakley in *Annie Get Your Gun*. "Who would you vote for?" asks a UPI wire. "Haley Mills is very particular about who she goes out with," one reads. "Who do you call at General Tel?" asks an ad. "Amateur genealogist wonders who he'll find in his family tree," appears in *Life*.[7] "Historically, in the West, who has taken advantage of who?" asks Glendon Swarthout. "Tracking would be easier if the Comrade General would explain exactly who he is after," says a character in Mark Rascovich's *The Flight of the Dancing Bear*.[8] *Mad* prints a "What to Buy Who" questionnaire. Television programs are called *Who Do You Trust?* and *Who Do You Kill?* One might protest that these are not very literary examples, but they indicate widespread usage. Besides, grammar isn't everything. If someone asks, "Who do you kill?" you have other things to worry about than the case of the pronoun.

If a person deliberates too much about which pronoun to use in conversation, he sounds bookish and formal. In a relaxed atmosphere it is better not to worry whether a grammatical slip is showing. But for carefully written prose, you should know the established practice; you can then decide whether or not to use it as the context requires.

Most *who* and *whom* errors occur with infinitives or in parenthetical constructions, where it is not immediately clear if the pronoun is used as subject or object. There is no difficulty with "That is the doctor *who* made the monster." If a parenthetical clause like "they claim" is added, the pronoun is still the subject of the verb: "That is the man *who*, they claim, made the monster." Such parenthetical clauses do not affect the function of the pronoun, but a careless or uncertain writer is apt to become confused and alter *who* to *whom*.

WRONG CASE	EXPLANATION	CORRECTION
The man *whom* I hear is an excellent pianist also plays the flugelhorn.	Pronoun is the subject of *is* and requires the subjective case.	The man *who*, I hear, is an excellent pianist also plays the flugelhorn.
He is the teacher *whom* the students say gives the roughest exams.	Pronoun is the subject of *gives* and requires the subjective case.	He is the teacher *who*, the students say, gives the roughest exams.
Give the shakuhachi to the one *whom* you think plays it best.	Pronoun is the subject of *plays* and requires the subjective case.	Give the shakuhachi to the one *who* you think plays it best.

Whoever and *whomever* follow the same rule as *who* and *whom* but are often confused when they follow a preposition or a transitive verb and seem to be objects. In "Give it to whomever you will," the objective case is needed; but in "Read it to whoever will listen," the pronoun functions as the subject of *will listen,* rather than as the object of *to;* the complement of the preposition is the entire clause, "whoever will listen."

WRONG CASE	EXPLANATION	CORRECTION
Move *whomever* is in the way.	Pronoun is the subject of *is;* entire clause is object of *move.*	Move *whoever* is in the way.
The sergeant gives KP to *whomever* finishes last.	Pronoun is the subject of *finishes;* entire clause is object of *to.*	The sergeant gives KP to *whoever* finishes last.

Overconcern about *who* and *whom* can lead people to use *whom* when they shouldn't. This is not sanctioned by contemporary usage and is simply a grammatical flaw. Though Wilson Follett is sometimes unsound in his denunciation of *Webster's Third New International Dictionary,* he objects legitimately to its apparent approval of *whom* and *whomever* as subjects: "(a . . . recruit whom he hoped would prove to be a crack salesman) (people . . . whom you never thought would sympathize) . . . (I go out to talk to whomever it is) . . . (he attacked whomever disagreed with him)." Usage could make these forms standard; but it has not yet done so, and they remain errors to be avoided.

¶ POSSESSIVE CASE

The possessive, or genitive, case is used to indicate possession ("The wombat burrowed under *Bligh's* floor." "He put greasy kid stuff on *his* hair") and modification ("all in the *day's* work," "a *month's* rent"). The best solution would be to abolish the apostrophe altogether; but as long as it's still in operation, one should know how to use it:

A singular noun forms the possessive by adding an apostrophe and *-s: aardvark, aardvark's habitat.*

EXCEPTION: If a noun of more than one syllable already ends in *-s,* one may add an apostrophe only: *fortress, fortress' gate.*

91

WARNING: If a noun ends in -s, put the apostrophe after the -s, not before it. Correct: Henry *Adams'* (or *Adams's*) house. Incorrect: Henry *Adam's* house.

A plural noun ending in -s forms the possessive by adding an apostrophe only: *bears, bears'* den.

A plural noun not ending in -s adds an apostrophe and -s: *women, women's* hats.

These rules could be simplified into one; if a noun, singular or plural, ends in -s, then add an apostrophe only to form the possessive; if it does not end in -s, then add an apostrophe and -s. If possession is indicated by the preposition *of* (a periphrastic possessive —"*The Bride of Frankenstein,*" "a reunion of the Coopers"), the objective rather than the possessive case is used. (Wrong: "a reunion of the Coopers'"; Even more wrong: "a reunion of the Cooper's.")

Personal and relative pronouns do not use an apostrophe in the possessive case; thus *our's, her's, their's, your's, you're, it's,* and *who's* are wrong. The first four do not properly exist; *you're, it's,* and *who's* are contractions for *you are, it is,* and *who is.* Sometimes small children form faulty possessives by analogy: "Yours is the green towel, and mines is the pink one." There are also the semiliterate variants of possessive pronouns—*his'n, ourn, hisself*—and Southerners have a problem with the possessive for *you all,* which is rendered variously as *you all's, your all, your all's* ("I forgot to bring your all's desserts"). Here the solution is to drop the *all* and change "Your all's eggs are ready" to "Your eggs are ready," although if one insists on using *you all, your all's* is probably the correct possessive.

The only difficult rule is the one that requires the use of the possessive case for a noun or pronoun modifying a gerund. (A gerund is a present participle used as a noun.) Thus, "She didn't like *him* being late," calls for the possessive case. She may have liked him quite well; what she objected to was the being late. Whose being late? *His* being late. If, however, the participle is used to modify the noun or pronoun, then the latter takes the objective case.

PARTICIPLE AS A MODIFIER	PARTICIPLE AS A GERUND
Strether found Chad having tea.	Strether was disturbed by Chad's refusing to come home.
I'm glad to see you doing your homework.	I admired your speaking up.

In such instances colloquial usage is more and more gaining ascendency and usually abandons this rule, putting the modifier in the objective case. ("I don't like you working at night.") Thus Truman Capote writes, "You can love somebody without it being like that." [9] Both the possessive case before a gerund and the subjective *who* are neatly illustrated in the following sentence (italics mine): "The colonel was insecure about Milo because other colonels were trying to lure him away and Colonel Cathcart still had that lousy Big Chief White Halfoat in his group *who* that lousy, lazy, Captain Black claimed was the one really responsible for the bomb *line's* being moved during the Big Siege of Bologna." [10]

Sometimes an author may deliberately violate standard usage to create a desired effect, as in the reverse snobbery of the Tareyton ad. A better example appears in John Osborne's *Luther*:

> MARTIN: Father, why do you hate me being here?
> HANS: Eh? What do you mean? I don't hate you being here.[11]

The father is an uneducated man who has sent his son to the university at great sacrifice and resents his becoming a monk. Here Osborne uses the objective case with the gerund, to have Martin and his father speak colloquially as they would at home. In addition, Martin really feels his father may hate *him* (for) being in the monastery; and the father's answer also includes this double meaning. This example is rather far removed from the Tareyton ad but shows the difference between a commercially contrived solecism and the careful use of a nonstandard form for artistic purposes.

Occasionally an awkward situation arises, such as "The president of the university's son's wife's dog just dug up our petunias. What shall I do?" The only way out of this jumble is to rephrase the entire sentence, preferably forgetting about academic connections, or more simply to take the dog home and replant the petunias. Another puzzler occurred when a critic wanted to explain the title of Fellini's movie "8½." It couldn't have been Fellini's eight and a halfth film, so it must have been his eighth and a half.

¶ FALSE POSSESSIVES

Sometimes modifiers, especially proper names ending in -s, are mistaken for possessives and adorned with needless apostrophes:

Hjalmar Hjalmarson was naturalized a United States' citizen.
Lester Cholmondeley is a distinguished General Motors' executive.
A Henry Adams' scholar.
A Scribner Modern Standard Authors' book.

None of these examples have any idea of personal possession, and the apostrophe should be dropped. *United States, General Motors, Adams, Authors* are used as adjectives, like *news* in *news item* or *mathematics* in *mathematics professor*. Likewise there is no apostrophe needed in *Highways Department* or *Public Works Administration*; and the apostrophe is often omitted from *Lions, Odd Fellows,* and *Elks Club*.

¶ POSSESSIVES WITH TITLES

Certain royal and ecclesiastical titles are preceded by a possessive pronoun. Kings and queens are addressed as *your majesty* or *your highness,* dukes and duchesses as *your grace,* bishops and archbishops, as *your excellency,* cardinals as *your eminence,* patriarchs as *your beatitude,* the pope as *your holiness.* In the third person, they are referred to as *his highness, his holiness,* and so forth. When in 1876 the Republican politicians, through bribery and forgery, changed twelve electoral votes to give the Presidency to Rutherford B. Hayes, the Democrats referred to Hayes as "His Fraudulency."

¶ PARALLEL POSSESSIVES

"You or your family's hands cast in glowing pewter—a decorative and personal gift." A unique gift indeed; the only question is where to store you, but perhaps the delighted recipient can place you at the door as a pewter footman. To avoid such awkwardness, put both parts of the parallel construction in the same case (Your hands or your family's cast in glowing pewter . . .). Otherwise, you might end up as the missing *corpus delicti* in the perfect crime.

8 √ The Wayward Verb

No other part of speech causes so many mistakes, misunderstandings, mutterings, and such general mayhem as the verb. Even pronouns are tame by comparison. Nouns are simple; adjectives and adverbs, even simpler; but verbs, though slightly streamlined since Anglo-Saxon days, still have the most complex forms of any words. Functionally, verbs indicate the central action or essential being of their subject; they state what the subject does ("Cats *chase* rats") or what its condition is ("Achilles *is* dead." "Things *are* not what they *seem*"). They also indicate tense, person, number, mood, and voice. All of these functions have their own forms, either by inflectional endings or changed vowel stems. These various forms of a verb are called its *conjugation*. Thus innumerable errors are possible with verbs, and most of them are as widespread and stubborn as the common cold. To shift the metaphor, in an age of zippers, verbs are like the old snap fasteners or hook and eye; many of them are apt to be missed or to come undone when you are in a hurry. Of all the parts of speech, verbs are the most academic; yet English, as she is spoke in the vernacular, is a very unacademic language, governed by habit and not by learning. Habit operates with a minimum of conscious effort. With the verb there are so many variations to keep in mind, so many formalities to observe and choices to make that some people, instead of taking deliberate aim, give up altogether and fire at random: "If I would of knew verbs was so hard, I might could have give them more attention."

¶ PRESENT TENSE

Let us first look at the verb in its simplest form. The dictionary entry is the infinitive, which is usually the stem for the present tense; it may appear with or without *to*: *to laugh* or *laugh*. The present tense (except for the verb *to be*) uses the infinitive without inflection except for the third person singular. (*I laugh, you laugh, he laughs, we laugh, they laugh.*) The third person singular adds an *-s* to the stem, except for the verbs *to be* and *to have*; *haves* is awkward and *has* serves instead. There are two problems in spelling. Verbs ending in *-o* add *-es* (*go—goes*), and those ending in *-y* change the *y* to *i* and add *-es* (*cry—cries, deny—denies*). Verbs *never* form the third person singular by using an apostrophe and *-s*. Wrong: *comply, comply's*.

Older English used different endings for the second and the third person singular; the second person ended in *-st* or *-est* ("thou laughest," "thou hast") and the third person in *-th* or *-eth* ("he hath," "he knoweth"). In Middle English, the first person singular ended in *-e*, and the plurals in *-e* (*n*), but the latter forms had disappeared by the Elizabethan period. During the later Middle Ages, - (*e*)*s* began to occasionally replace the *-eth* ending in the third person singular. In the English Midlands, *-eth* remained dominant, while - (*e*)*s* developed in the northern shires. By Shakespeare's time *-eth* or - (*e*)*s* could be used interchangeably, even in the same sentence. As *Hamlet* opens, Marcellus asks, "Who *hath* reliev'd you? What, *has* this thing appear'd again tonight?" (Italics mine.) At the same time, *you* began to replace *thou* for the second person singular; as it did so, the - (*e*)*st* ending vanished. Today, - (*e*)*st* and *-eth* appear only as deliberate archaisms; ministers, seeking to imitate the prose of the King James Bible, often use them though one finds in the King James Bible the more modern forms as well. The present tense causes problems in agreement, but not in form, except for occasional errors in spelling.

¶ TENSION OVER TENSES

It is with the less uniform forms of the other tenses that the difficulties come. In the past tense (or preterit) English has both weak (regular) and strong (irregular) verbs. Most are weak, and form the past tense by adding *-d* or *-ed* to the infinitive (*blame, blamed, want, wanted*). The past tense of weak verbs also serves as the past participle. But many of our most common verbs are strong and form the past tense and past participle by changing the root vowel (*blow, blew, blown; ring, rang, rung*). There are some recurrent patterns in strong verbs; e.g., the *-ow, -ew, -own* forms (*grow, grew, grown; know, knew, known; throw, threw, thrown*) and *-ing, -ang,*

-ung; but there are a great many variants and inconsistencies. Some verbs change both vowel and consonant (*seek, sought; think, thought; will, would*). Some strong verbs are identical in their past tense and past participle (*sit, sat, sat*); others have a different form. A few are called defective, or preterit-present, verbs because they use the same form for both present and past tenses (*ought, must, can, shall, may*). The past of the latter three (*could, should, might*) are used for the conditional present. *Durst*, the older preterit-present of *dare* is now considered nonstandard: "You durst not do it." A few verbs have both strong and weak conjugation.

Obviously there are innumerable possibilities for confusion. It is impossible to rely upon analogy as a foolproof guide to the principal parts of verbs. If we have *lie, lay, lain*, why not *try, tray, train*? If the past of *bring* is *brought*, why shouldn't the past of *ring* be *rought*? In fact, some people reverse this and use *brang* as the past of *bring*. Here are a few more possible but nonexistent analogical forms: *slay, slew, slain—play, plew, plain* ("I plew lacrosse yesterday"); *stand, stood—land, lood* ("I lood the plane safely"); *sit, sat —knit, knat* ("She knat a shawl")—flit, flat ("A bug flat against the window")—quit, quat ("Herman quat his job"); *strike, struck —like, luck* ("He always luck to have a beer on the way home"); *wind, wound—blind, blound* ("The sun blound him"); *stick, stuck —nick, nuck* ("The bullet *nuck* him")—prick, pruck ("The needle pruck her"); *sink, sank, sunk—think, thank, thunk—wink, wank, wunk* ("I wunk at her"); *eat, ate, eaten—beat, bate, beaten* ("He bate her with a broom"); *draw, drew, drawn—saw, sew, sawn* ("I sew a cord of lumber"); *take, took, taken—make, mook, maken* ("She mook a doll")—bake, book, baken ("Grandma book a cake"), and so on. These errors are purely imaginary, but show the danger of analogy. People often make strong verbs weak by analogy ("I fell and hurted my knee," "The bug bites bleeded," "The no-see-ums bited me"), but rarely make weak verbs strong. Little children are particularly prone to weaken strong verbs: "My elephant drinked her snurf medicine," "I hanged onto the tree while the bear eated my food." In the Smokies you sometimes encounter a weak verb made strong. A few of these may be archaic holdovers from Elizabethan days, since language tends to make strong verbs weak (e.g., *shined* instead of *shone, dived* instead of *dove*). One North Carolina author claims that "If I'd a-knowed it was you, I'd a-flang out my arm and wove at you" sounds like Chaucer.[1] It sounds more like Snuffy Smith. There is no longer any pure Chaucerian or Elizabethan speech remaining in the hills, and this specimen of freewheeling grammar demonstrates the fact.

¶ PRINCIPAL PARTS

Here are the principal parts of the most common irregular verbs:

INFINITIVE AND PRESENT	PAST	PAST PARTICIPLE
be, am, is, are	was, were	been
bear	bore	borne
beat	beat	beaten
begin	began	begun
bite	bit	bitten
bleed	bled	bled
blow	blew	blown
break	broke	broken
bring	brought	brought
build	built	built
burst	burst	burst
cast	cast	cast
catch	caught	caught
choose	chose	chosen
come, become	came, became	come, become
deal	dealt	dealt
dig	dug	dug
dive	dove, dived	dove, dived
do	did	done
drink	drank	drunk
drive	drove	driven
eat	ate	eaten
fall	fell	fallen
find	found	found
flee	fled	fled
fly	flew	flown
forget	forgot	forgotten
forsake	forsook	forsaken
freeze	froze	frozen
get	got	got, gotten
give	gave	given
go	went	gone
grow	grew	grown
hang (suspend)	hung	hung
hang (execute)	hanged	hanged

98

INFINITIVE AND PRESENT	PAST	PAST PARTICIPLE
have	had	had
hear	heard	heard
hold, behold	held, beheld	held, beheld
know	knew	known
lay	laid	laid
lead	led	led
lend	lent	lent
let	let	let
lie	lay	lain
light	lighted, lit	lighted, lit
lose	lost	lost
prove	proved	proved, proven
ride	rode	ridden
ring	rang	rung
rise, arise	rose, arose	risen, arisen
run	ran	run
see	saw	seen
set	set	set
shake	shook	shaken
shine	shone, shined	shone, shined
show	showed	showed, shown
shrink	shrank, shrunk	shrunk
sing	sang	sung
sink	sank, sunk	sunk
sit	sat	sat
slay	slew	slain
slide	slid	slid
slink	slunk	slunk
speak	spoke	spoken
spin	spun	spun
spit	spit, spat	spit, spat
spring	sprang, sprung	sprung
stand	stood	stood
steal	stole	stolen
stink	stank, stunk	stunk
strive	strove, strived	striven, strived
swear	swore	sworn
swim	swam	swum
take	took	taken
teach	taught	taught
tear	tore	torn
throw	threw	thrown
tread	trod	trodden, trod

INFINITIVE AND PRESENT	PAST	PAST PARTICIPLE
wake	waked, woke	waked
wear	wore	worn
weave	wove	woven, wove
win	won	won
wind	wound	wound
wring	wrung	wrung
write	wrote	written

¶ EXCEPTIONS AND ERRORS

Though there are several recurrent patterns here, there are so many exceptions that no rules hold. Each set of principal parts must be learned separately, until they become habitual. The trouble is that many people have already formed habits—the wrong ones—that are all the more difficult to change because they are unconscious. No one can stop to weigh each word; if we did, conversation would be as slow as bricklaying. Errors in selecting the right principal part are among the most common and obvious yet most ineradicable examples of nonstandard usage. Perhaps for that reason, grammatical purists or those who use speech as a social measuring rod find them particularly objectionable. The use of *seen* for *saw*, or *throwed* for *threw*, for example, creates no barrier to understanding or any imprecision in meaning. These and other nonstandard inflections may well become standard in time, without in any way corrupting the language. As it is, those who use them could say (if they ever thought about the matter) that they simply have a different set of rules that are valid for them, because standard, in their environment. In the appropriate cultural context, nonstandard verb forms are perfectly acceptable. But this is not so in the world of higher education and business, or of any communication in writing more official than family correspondence or notes to the milkman. Of course, if you are writing fictional dialogue for, say—since this is a class distinction—the "proletariat," you should use the appropriate grammar. Actually some of these nonstandard forms have so much character that it is a pity to correct them. Their use accounts for much of the richness of language in *Huckleberry Finn*, *The Grapes of Wrath*, Faulkner's fiction, and other great works of American literature. Accordingly, let us examine some representative nonstandard practices, so that you can know how to use them or avoid them, as the case may be.

100

One of the simple errors with the verb *give* is the use of the present for the past tense: "I give him the money yesterday." *Come* is also misused this way ("Uncle Silas come around last Monday"), but this is more likely a result of confusing the past participle with the past tense.

As we have already seen, children and many adults tend to make strong verbs weak by using *-ed* for the past tense and past participle:

> I've teached [taught] everybody how to fight fires.
> My toenails haven't been cutted [cut] for a long time.
> He blowed [blew] his horn both loud and shrill.
> The monkey drawed [drew] my picture so it didn't look like me.
> I seed [saw] a moose a-coming down the road a little piece away.

Sometimes children add a double *-ed* to a weak verb: "I washeded my hands," "The kitten drowneded." Sometimes the strong form of the verb appears with an *-ed* tacked on, making it doubly past: "I founded the map," "I was borned and raised in Cataloochee," "Last week in the course of two hours it blewed and snowed and friz." And occasionally you encounter a weak verb used with *-ed* but with the root vowel changed: "That horse trompled [trampled] me," "It holped [helped] a man not to be beholden to nobody." And the standard instruction for weaving patterns is the archaic "Tromp as writ," instead of "Tramp as written." Though the tendency of linguistic change is to make irregular verbs regular, there are a few strong verbs that once had weak endings. Seventeenth-century authors could write, "We had builded our houses," and *The Book of Common Prayer* speaks of "language understanded of the people." One ancient form, though labeled dialect, is persistent: Articles purchased from a store (usually clothes) are always "store-boughten," never—or almost never—store-bought.

It is less common for a weak verb to be treated like a strong one, but it sometimes happens in error or in jest; e.g., "He clumb [climbed] on his horse," "It holpt [helped] to keep the varmints out," "Cal clen [cleaned] the stable," "I should have stood [stayed] in bed," and "Who thunk [thought] the skunk stunk?"

One of the most common and noticeable errors is the use of the past participle for the past tense of strong verbs. Most frequently substituted are the past participles *been, seen, done, come, gone* for the past tenses *was, saw, did, came,* and *went*. Since these verbs are five of our most necessary words, habitual errors in the use of their principal parts occur with damning regularity: Thus it is consid-

101

ered semiliterate to say, "I never seen nothing in these here hug dances," "The girls in our family done all the grinding," "They done it themselves," "I been sick," "The preacher come yesterday." Perhaps the speakers meant to use the present perfect tense and simply omitted the auxiliary—"I've been sick"—but in any event the grammar needs revising. *Whodunit,* frequently used as a slang noun for mystery novels, owes its popularity to the conscious humor of its gumshoe grammar.

Again, people sometimes mistakenly use the past tense for the past participle, particularly with the verb *go.* You hear in jest, "My get-up-and-go has got up and went" (never *gone,* the required past participle), but similar statements occur in nonstandard speech; e.g., "We should of went across that bridge," "I was shook up when I found a tarantula in my boot," "It might have fell out," "If I would of knew it was so far, I would of stayed home." Apart from other errors—especially the use of *of* for *have*—these sentences need *gone, shaken, fallen,* and *known.* Occasionally someone plays it safe (and is doubly wrong) by using both the past tense and past participle, instead of a perfect tense construction: "That crow's done gone and went." Often the final *-n* of a strong past participle is dropped in nonstandard speech: "Beef cut and froze" or the memorable "The dam has broke!" from James Thurber's *My Life and Hard Times.*

One verb has caused international friction. In American English, *get* has two past participles, *got* and *gotten,* whereas during the eighteenth century the English dropped *gotten* and have since used *got* almost exclusively, though *gotten* has occasionally reared its ugly head through the influence of American books and films. Neither side is right or wrong; each country's usage is perfectly valid at home. But temperamental and inaccurate British writers insisted for a long time that Americans never say *got,* that to use *gotten* exclusively is an identifying mark of the Yankee. Thus some British fiction writers made their American characters speak quite absurdly and inaccurately. Though we have both past participles, they are not interchangeable, even if there are no definite rules governing the choice of one over the other. The distinction is partly idiomatic and partly a matter of emphasis and rhythm. *Got* has dozens of different meanings in England; when it appears in the sense of *become,* we tend to prefer *gotten:* "I've gotten sick every January for the past ten years." When it means *have* or is used to intensify *have,* we prefer *got:* "I've got a cold," "Have you got the

102

answer?" Thus, the American in British fiction who says, "I've gotten an idea," sounds fake.

¶ PERFECT TENSES AND IMPERFECT AUXILIARIES

The past participle is combined with the appropriate form of the
auxiliary verb *have* to form the perfect tenses. The present perfect
indicates an action or condition completed past action ("I have
done the deed") or past action extending into the present time ("I
have forgotten"). The past perfect indicates action or condition
completed or existing before the time stated or implied in the sentence ("He had swallowed the drink before he realized it was
poison"). The future perfect indicates an action or condition that
will have been completed in relation to some time in the future
("We shall have traveled 10,000 miles by the end of summer"). The
auxiliaries used are *has* and *have* for the present perfect tense, *had*
for the past perfect, and *shall have* for the future perfect. This
seems simple enough, yet confusion reigns, resulting in much nonstandard practice. Because *have* is often contracted to *'ve*, pronounced *uv* with conditional verbs ("I might've," "they could've"),
many people mistakenly use *of* for the auxiliary verb. In slurred
speech it is difficult to tell whether *have* or *of* is used, but the error
is obvious when *of* is written for the verb in student themes. Fiction writers like Mark Twain or John Steinbeck deliberately use *of*
as an auxiliary in dialogue to show illiteracy. (Sometimes they prefer *a*: "You'd a thought so.") In more conventional writing, "I
might of gone," "He should of read the assignment," "I wish you
would of danced with me" stand out like flies in the soup. A cure
might be to make students guilty of this practice write a hundred
times, "I *of* eaten my spinach," and "I *of* gone."

The genuine semiliterate wastes none of his opportunities but
combines as many errors as possible in any one sentence. Thus he
will use *of* as a verb with the wrong principal part ("We could of
went to the Whipsnade Zoo, but we seen the Tate Gallery instead"). Another favorite illiteracy is the use of several auxiliaries
together, most of them wrong. A popular error is the use of *done*
for *have*, as in the folk song "Another Man Done Gone." Again,
done and *did* appear erroneously to reinforce *have* (or the substandard *of*) in such constructions as, "We've done left Grandpappy
to be et by the wolves" and "The boys have done finished the

103

work." Here *done* is useless and should be cut. *Is,* likewise, does not qualify as an acceptable auxiliary when it is used as part of the perfect tense. In the passive voice, *is* functions with the past participle to form the present tense ("He is hurt"), but *is* must be replaced by *have* in "My arches is fallen" and by *has* in "This is got to be my last game." Colloquial English sometimes uses *got* as a passive auxiliary ("I got bug-bit," "Walt got hit by a car"), but *was* or *has been* are preferable in informal and formal style alike. *Got* is superfluous, but may be defended if it makes the auxiliary emphatic.

In conditional perfect constructions, redundancies abound. *Might could* and *might would* are idiomatic in some regions: "I might could make some molasses." It seems that *might could* means *maybe I could,* as in "I thought she might could cry." In this instance, the only valid objection is that the phrase is a limited regionalism. But there are numerous other cases where multiple auxiliaries are sheer dead wood, like *had* in "You had ought to mend the fence." "You didn't ought to have let that fire out," says Piggy in William Golding's *Lord of the Flies*; the standard form is *ought not.* "They shouldn't had ought not to of done it" is riddled with errors, including redundancy; "They shouldn't have done it" is accurate and concise. Sometimes the whole construction needs to be changed: "I used to could touch my toes" requires the infinitive, "I used to be able to touch my toes." The first has a commendable brevity, but is nonstandard.

Conditional constructions seem particularly troublesome in introductory subordinate clauses. "Did I of known, I would of said something" not only misuses *of* but has an extra word; "Had I known, I would have said something" is correct. Sometimes *did* is misused for an introductory *if,* as in "Did I could, I would take the car." These examples are somewhat exaggerated but a common error in student writing is the use of *would have been* instead of the concise *had been*: "If these actions would have been [had been] done, we could have succeeded." "If I would have known [had known] it was so far, I would have stayed home." In short, be precise and never use a useless auxiliary verb.

¶ FUTURE TENSE

Most people, if asked how English expresses future time, would say that it uses the future tense, combining the appropriate form of

104

shall and *will* as an auxiliary with the infinitive: *I shall be late*; *The time will come*. Actually there are many other ways to indicate futurity. Some languages, like Latin and French, have a whole set of special verb endings for the future tense. English dispenses with these and relies upon a variety of expressions. Often we use the present tense, modified by an adverbial phrase, to show habitual action or future condition:

> I go to Washington next Monday.
> The ship sails next week.
> Christmas comes on Friday this year.

We also use the progressive present:

> I am going to propose to Sophie.
> We are vacationing in the Caribbean next summer.
> Jethro is coming next week.
> Are you going to the Hallowe'en party?

The infinitive can be used to express the future: "There is to be a church picnic." And we can even use the past tense to express futurity: "It's time we *went* home."

Many teachers ignore these devices and concentrate on *shall* and *will*. Generations of schoolchildren have puzzled over the distinction between them and have been browbeaten into believing the rule that in declarative sentences, to express simple futurity *shall* is used in the first person and *will* in the second and third persons, and to express determination these auxiliaries are reversed, with *will* used in the first person and *shall* in the second and third persons. But few people, including grammarians, follow this edict with any consistency. It is ironic that perhaps the best-known grammar rules are the three least important or valid ones: *shall* vs. *will*, and the prohibitions against splitting an infinitive and against ending a sentence with a preposition. The half-educated pedant who knows no other grammar expounds these as dogma. To him they are the hallmarks that distinguish the "cultured" person from the peasant. Actually this discrimination is moribund and was never really alive to begin with. Like the Frankenstein monster, it is an artificial creation. In Elizabethan English there was no inflexible difference, though *shall* was more common for the first person and was sometimes used for determination, as in Horatio's urging Hamlet, "You shall not go, my lord," *will* appears indiscriminately in sixteenth-

and early seventeenth-century writing. But in 1653, the British mathematician John Wallis, who wrote in Latin under the name Johannis Wallis, formulated in *Grammatica Linguae Anglicanae* the quite arbitrary edict about the use of *shall* and *will*. It was not based upon actual usage; it became a rule only because Wallis so proclaimed it. Eighteenth-century grammarians, devoted to authority, hardened this decree into dogma; and subsequent teachers and editors did their best to enforce it. The few realistic linguists, such as Joseph Priestley, who criticized Wallis's unrealistic ruling were dismissed as eccentrics. Priestley was a religious heretic anyhow, so his challenge to grammatical authority was simply a further indication of his unregenerate state. Thus argued the academicians, though they failed to follow the so-called "rule" themselves.

There is an old, apocryphal, and oft-repeated story of a Scot, thrashing around in a mill pond, who cried, "I will drown, and nobody shall save me." Because of his future auxiliaries, bystanders thought he was determined to drown and so made no attempt to rescue him. Had he said, "I shall drown, and nobody will save me," someone might have thrown him a lifeline. This is an overly subtle distinction, unjustified by actual usage. Benjamin Franklin wrote in one proverb, "He that lieth down with dogs, shall rise up with fleas"; in another, "He that falls in love with himself, will have no rivals." Today *shall* is rarely used in declarative sentences; it sounds artificial and self-conscious except when it is used for a first-person question: "Shall we dance?" "Shall I see who's at the door?" "Shall I pick you up at eight?" *Will* here would be out of place, though either *will* or *shall* can sometimes be used in first-person questions: "Will I see you tomorrow?" In general speech, *will* is used without regard to person; it sounds affected to say, "I shall take the clothes to the cleaners." *Shall* still occurs with some frequency after *we* to avoid the repetitive *w* of *we will* if the stress is on the subject: "We shall see." If the auxiliary verb is stressed, *will* is more common: " 'Be on time.' 'We *will*.' " Usually people use the contraction *'ll* ("*I'll do it*," "*He'll give it to you*"), making it impossible to tell if the verb is *shall* or *will*. *Shall* is appropriate for the fastidious Prufrock's "I shall wear white flannel trousers and walk upon the beach," but most people say, "I'll be down to getcha in a taxi, honey." Legal statements still require *shall*: "The author shall receive ten percent." As for the negative contraction *shan't*, it sounds overfastidious and outdated as if it belonged to a day when boys had their hair in ringlets and wore Lord Fauntleroy suits.

106

There is nothing wrong with *shan't* as a word, but it has the wrong connotations.

The conditional future is expressed by combining the auxiliary verb *should* or *would* with the infinitive: "I would like to visit Tahiti." Fastidious writers and speakers are fond of using *should* with the first person and of choosing the conditional tense, instead of the present, as a sign of courtesy. We might call this practice the polite oblique; instead of saying, "I want a drop of sherry," one says, "I should like a drop of sherry." It is possible to be too oblique. "Will you marry me?" is preferable to "I should like to inquire whether you should find that you can marry me." Though this is an extreme example, too many *shoulds* hedge a statement, making it sound hesitant and a bit slithery. In general speech, *should* is weakening except in the sense of *ought to*: "We should get the TV set repaired."

After this lengthy discussion, you may suddenly start to wonder whether you use *shall* and *will, should* and *would* correctly. For all practical purposes there is no reason for you to be concerned. The few real distinctions are idiomatic and come naturally; any others are artificial and nonessential.

¶ TENSE SEQUENCE

It is necessary to be consistent in using tenses; never use a different tense to express the same time. Students writing papers about some past-tense narrative often shift back and forth from the past to the historical present: "When Goodman Brown *goes* into the forest, he *met* varius figures who *reveal* to him the hypocrisy of his society. The climax *came* when Brown *realizes* that his wife Faith *is* at the witches' sabbath. He *urged* her to resist the devil, whereupon the scene *disappears*. Brown *was* so thoroughly disillusioned that he *becomes* an embittered misanthrope and *condemned* all mankind as corrupt." This shifting of tenses is quite disconcerting; either the past or the historical present might have been used successfully, but there must be no vacillation between the two.

Often a sentence requires the use of more than one tense. In the sentence, "Alfred *forgot* that the earth *is* the third planet from the sun," the second verb must be put in the present tense, *is,* to show that its subject is in a continuing or present state of existence; *was* makes it seem as if the earth were no longer the third planet from the sun. Thus whatever is true at the time of writing calls for the

107

present tense, no matter what other tenses may be used in the sentence: e.g., "Horpington *wondered* why the ninth month *is* [not *was*] called September."

Conditional constructions require a use of the conditional tense consistent with sense. "Eisenhower *said* he *will* go to Korea to end the war" is wrong. What Eisenhower said was, "I will go to Korea." The indirect statement should be "Eisenhower *said* that he *would* go. . . ."

Finally, use common sense. "We hope the New Year *will be* as kind to you as it *has been* to us" is nonsensical. Last year may have been kind, but the New Year has just begun for both you and us.

¶ THE MOODY SUBJUNCTIVE

Besides person, number, and sense, verbs have mood and voice. Verbs are most frequently used in the indicative mood: this mood indicates what occurs or take place factually. The imperative mood is used for commands ("Nay, answer me," "Stand and unfold yourself"), instructions ("Go, bid the soldiers shoot"), and requests ("Get thee to a nunnery"). In form, it is the infinitive without *to* (e.g., "Hurry! Please hurry and help him!" and may be used with or without a subject ("You come right here!" "Come here!"). It is often considered that it is used only in the second person present tense, but it can be used with the first person plural as well ("Well, sit we down, And let us hear Bernardo speak of this"). There are no grammatical difficulties connected with the imperative, so don't worry about it.

The subjunctive mood, on the other hand, does pose difficulties, partly because most people have never heard of it. Accordingly, the subjunctive is disappearing, though certain uses linger in our speech. Latin has an elaborate subjunctive—a complete conjugation that matches each tense of the indicative. Old English also had an involved subjunctive, and we are well rid of it. Today the subjunctive forms of the verb *to be* are used for all numbers and persons: *be* for the tense (*I be*) and *were* for the other tenses (*he were*). The subjunctive is still used to express possibility ("*if it be true*"), hypothesis ("*if Pogo were President*"), wish ("*if only El Kabong were there*"), improbability ("*if Marjorie Main were playing Hamlet*"), and condition contrary to fact ("*if the earth were flat*"). As you see, it is often introduced by *if* (or *though* or some other conditional word). Some liberal grammarians say that it is being too

108

fastidious to bother with the subjunctive—that it is as obsolete as the farthingale or moustache cups—and it does sound strained in the following translation given in a German auto manual: "Should trouble occur and there *be* no Borgward workshop, care must be taken when carrying out adjustments." (Fortunately the Borgward runs better than this sentence, which has also an awkward use of the passive voice and a dangling modifier.) But it is still non-standard and a mark of social inferiority to say "If I was king," instead of the subjunctive "If I were king." (Incidentally, this famous line, the most famous of the French poet François Villon, was not written by Villon at all but by Justin McCarthy in the melodramatic novel that was thus entitled.) Try to imagine Ronald Colman declaiming, "If I was king, ah, love, if I was king," and you get a line as bad as Tony Curtis's "Yonder lies duh castle of duh caliph, my fadduh."

The subjunctive also survives in some idiomatic expressions ("Be that as it may," "Be it ever so humble, there's no place like home"). It is even enshrined in the national anthem: "Thus *be* it ever when freemen shall stand . . ."

Finally, the subjunctive is still used in *that* clauses after verbs like *demand, require, insist, recommend, suggest,* or the phrase *it is necessary that.* ("I demand that *he resign* immediately." "I suggest that *she take* a nap." "It is necessary that *he go* to London.") Informal style would probably turn the latter into "It is necessary for him to go to London." Often we avoid the subjunctive either by using the infinitive (thus "It is impossible that he come" becomes "It is impossible for him to come") or a verbal phrase with *can, may, should,* and *ought* ("If it were to happen" becomes "If it should happen"). But formal parliamentary procedure still requires the subjunctive: "Fogbound moved that Dogpatch be reapportioned," "It was moved and seconded that the bill be sent to committee." You will encounter the subjunctive far more often in the works of older writers than of contemporary ones. Shakespeare's dialogue is full of it:

> If music be the food of love, play on.

> If it be now, 'tis not to come; if it be not to come, it will be
>   now; if it be not now, yet it will come: the readiness is all.

> If Hamlet give the first or second hit,
> Or quit in answer of the third exchange,
> Let all the battlements their ordnance fire. . . .

I'll cross it, though it blast me.
No spirit dare stir abroad. . . .

If this be error and upon me proved,
I never writ, nor no man ever loved.

Samuel Johnson is supposed to have said, when offered refreshment, "If this be coffee, give me tea; if this be tea, give me coffee."

Imitating Shakespeare, scriptwriters for Hollywood epics often favor a use of the subjunctive, but the result is usually stilted bombast instead of eloquence. A British critic found the film *Cleopatra* "lavish in subjunctives." James Thurber observed that the subjunctive "lends itself most easily to ranting and posturing"; but instead of the affairs of Cleopatra, he wrote a definitive analysis of the subjunctive as used by a jealous husband and a defensive wife, who employs such constructions as "Far be it from me" for indignation and hauteur. Rhetorical vacillations from the subjunctive to the indicative and back again create dangerous misunderstandings. "Husbands have come to know that a wife's 'if . . . were' usually means that what she is presenting as purely hypothetical is, in reality, a matter of fact. Thus, if a wife begins, one evening after an excellent dinner, 'Dear, what would you do, if I were the sort of woman who had, etc.,' her husband knows full well that it is going to turn out that she is the sort of woman who has. Husbands are suspicious of all subjunctives. Wives should avoid them." [2]

Today we find the indicative in many situations that formerly used the subjunctive. "If he go, I shall perish" sounds archaic; we would say, "If he goes, I shall perish," or, more likely, something less melodramatic. In practice, you need not worry about *be*; probably you use *be* habitually in idiomatic phrases; and in others, it is not essential. The main problem is whether to use *was* or *were* in conditional clauses. When the sentence states a real condition, rather than a hypothetical one, that is improbable or contrary to fact, the indicative is called for: "If he were there, he was guilty." Consider the ad for the movie *The Playgirls and the Vampire*: "She knew . . . when she felt his lips on her, that there was no other man for her . . . *if this was a man!*" This is all right because there is a real alternative, instead of a wish or condition contrary to fact. In this case, grammar is not the primary concern; the girl needs a crucifix, holy water, wolfbane, or a stake more than a subjunctive verb.

110

¶ REFLEXIVES WITHOUT REFLEXES

French and German have a number of so-called reflexive verbs—verbs that are conjugated with a reflexive pronoun as direct or indirect object, where we would use none. Whereas we say "go away," the French say *"allez-vous en"*—"go you away." Other similar French reflexive verbs are *se lever* (to get up), *se promener* (to take a walk), *se tromper* (to make a mistake). Contemporary English is fortunately free of this encumbrance, but medieval and Elizabethan English sometimes employed it, as in "Get you gone," "Get thee to a nunnery," and "It likes me well" (meaning "I like it"). Today it still lingers as an archaism in some Southern Appalachian speech, particularly with the verb *happen*:

Hit didn't happen me that I wushed to contrary the revenoors . . .

Hit happens me I don't wush any more bussin' from you.

Pap uster say when the North jumped on the South, his paw just blowed up an' yelled: "Hell is a-hootin' now, an' hit happens I'm a-jinin' up with the Confedricsy."

In very colloquial usage, we all use a reflexive occasionally, as in "I got me a bargain," or "I got me out of there."

¶ THE PERILOUS PASSIVE

Transitive verbs can be used in either the active or the passive voice. In the active voice, the subject does the action ("The painter dropped a bucket"); in the passive voice the subject is on the receiving end ("Irving was hit by the bucket"). The passive voice is formed by combining the appropriate form of the verb *to be* with the past participle of the transitive verb:

PRESENT	I am hit	PRESENT PERFECT	I have been hit
PAST	I was hit	PAST PERFECT	I had been hit
FUTURE	I shall (or will) be hit	FUTURE PERFECT	I shall have been hit.

Future Perfect Conditional: After all this, I should have been hospitalized. The passive voice can also be used with infinitives of the verb *to be*: " 'tis a consummation devoutly to be wish'd."

When newspaper headlines, in their clipped style, omit the auxiliary verb in passive constructions ("Six Senators Accused"), you cannot always tell whether the verb is active or passive. Are the

111

senators accusing or being accused? Headliners are so addicted to this practice that they make even active verbs suspect: "George Romney Crowned Webberville Firemen's Oxroast Queen"—as a headline, this causes a double take.

The passive voice is axiomatically less forceful than the active voice and therefore should be used sparingly. The last sentence illustrates an appropriate use; when the verb refers to a general rule or procedure, when the action has an indefinite rather than a specific actor, then the passive voice is suitable. For example, "It's a club rule . . . that any ball swallowed by a goat can be replaced without loss of stroke or distance." [3] The passive voice makes the object of the action into the subject; thus it can be used effectively when the object is to be emphasized at the beginning or when the action is to be emphasized at the end of the sentence. "My appendix is to be removed" is more emphatic than the active "The doctor is going to remove my appendix." "Civil liberties must be defended" is more forceful than "We must defend civil liberties," unless *we* is the word that is intentionally to be stressed. Probably the most familiar passive construction occurs in the sentence, "Dinner is served." Thus when the performer is less important than the performance, the passive may be preferable; e.g., "Let justice be done."

But the passive has a number of potential dangers. Since it reverses the direction of the action, its use in narrative makes sentences crawl backward like the crab. Thus there is a stylistic ricochet in "The rifle was aimed by the marksman who was hidden behind the fence; the trigger was squeezed; the bullet was fired; and the victim was struck in the chest and knocked from his saddle." This sort of thing is less common than the overworked use of the passive in technical and professional writing. In an attempt at objectivity, some engineers, scientists, and businessmen go to absurd lengths to avoid first-person comments; instead of writing *I* or *we,* they resort to passive constructions which often hobble them. "It was decided," "It was discovered," "It is believed," "It has been confirmed," "It is observed," and similar forms have become lifeless stock phrases. Such self-effacement is not only clumsy; it can be evasive, hiding individual thought and responsibility. In fact some of the better scientific magazines have broken the taboo against the first person and now use it when it is appropriate. Scholars in the humanities are less prone to bog their prose down with passives, but they have been frequently guilty, also.

A solitary passive now and then causes little deceleration of prose movement, but piled-up passives can be ponderous. The historian C. Vann Woodward uses passives appropriately, but barely manages to escape entanglement in a series of them: "The new Southern system was regarded as the 'final settlement,' the 'return to sanity,' the 'permanent system.' Few stopped to reflect that previous systems had also been regarded as final, sane, and permanent by their supporters. The illusion of permanency was encouraged by the complacency of a long-critical North, the propaganda of reconciliation, and the resigned compliance of the Negro. The illusion was strengthened . . ." [4]

Sometimes the passive voice with its reverse movement, creates needless obscurity: "Care should be taken in assembling the parts that the wires are not left uninsulated and that the screws are all tightened so that no loose connections are left by which malfunctioning can be caused to occur and danger of shock is permitted." Is it not clearer to write, "Insulate the wires and tighten all the screws to prevent malfunctioning or possible shock."

Another danger of the passive is the dangling modifier. "When using it to fight fires, a Pulaski should be kept sharp." In such constructions, the subject (whoever is using the Pulaski) is omitted; the object (the Pulaski) is turned into the subject, and there is no one for the participial modifier (using) to modify. Again, the passive encourages the use of bumbling prepositional phrases—"by the board of directors," "by the administration," "through the proper authorities," "by the driver"—that are better avoided.

Finally, there is sometimes simply a confusion in voice: "The pioneers were abhorred by the Indian way of fighting." An educated Indian, like the Cherokee writer Elias Boudinot, would have abhorred the paleface's prose.

¶ INTRANSITIVES IN TRANSIT

Verbs are classified as transitive or intransitive. Transitive verbs can take a direct object. (The cook made moose-meat pie.) Intransitive verbs cannot take a direct object, though they may have an indirect one or a modifier as complement. ("The lady vanished." "Don't look at the Gorgon." "I feel bilious.") Obviously, some verbs can function either transitively or intransitively. ("Lord Randall tasted the broth [transitive]; the broth tasted like eels [intransitive]." "When Isaac felt his son [transitive], Esau felt hairy [intransitive].) Verbs like *sing, think, feel, speak* can be either transitive or intransitive. Most verbs can be used without an object, particularly in the progressive form ("I am writing"), but a few require an object, e.g., *carry, bring, lug* ("I'll lug the guts into the neighboring room"). Verbs like *travel, swim, arrive, disagree, succeed, look, complain, grumble, fall* ("The sky is falling!") are always intransitive, as are the various linking verbs. If you want a test for whether a verb is transitive, try to turn it into a passive construction, in which the object becomes the subject. If there is no object, obviously you can't do this. "I clobbered him" can become "He was clobbered," but "Tarzan was swimming" cannot become "It was swum by Tarzan."

Most people couldn't care less whether a verb is transitive or intransitive, and most grammars devote little space to the distinction, except to stress the difference between *lie* and *lay, sit* and *set. Lie* (in either meaning) and *sit* are intransitive and never take an object, while *lay* and *set* are usually transitive, except in a construction like "The sun is setting." Though these pairs are frequently confused, the wrong choice is still considered nonstandard and carries a social and educational stigma, like it or not. Many fine people confuse them, but liberal linguists have not succeeded in making their usage interchangeable. *Lay* means to put or set down, and *lie* to recline. Thus you *lay* your cards on the table, but you *lie* on the bed for a nap. One idiomatic exception is with snow; snow may lie on the ground, but you frequently hear "Is the snow laying on the ground?" not "Is the snow lying?" Perhaps the confusion stems in part from the older use of *lay,* with a personal pronoun in the objective case, as in "Now I lay me down to sleep." Without the pronoun, this is unacceptable, as in the sloppy ad for a movie called *The Head:* "It just won't lay down and stay dead!" *Sit* means, in the inimitable words of *Webster's New Collegiate Dictionary,* "1. To rest upon the haunches; to occupy a seat. 2. To perch or roost with the body drawn up close, as birds. . . ." *Set* means primarily to place or to cause to sit. You *set* the chairs in place and then you *sit* on them. A setting hen sits while she sets. This is elementary stuff, but habits are hard to break. Besides the related meaning and similar sound, the words in each pair are further confused by their principal parts.

PRESENT	lie	lay	sit	set
PAST	lay	laid	sat	set
PAST PARTICIPLE	lain	laid	sat	set

114

The present of *lay* is the same as the past of *lie,* and people also confuse the past participles. Actually, although the forms of *lie* are rarely if ever used for *lay,* all forms of *lay* are frequently and mistakenly used to replace *lie.* Once when the editor of a military manual designed to teach English to Germans changed "He laid in bed" to "He lay in bed," the commander ordered him to restore the faulty original, on the grounds that ninety percent of the GI's spoke that way. If these statistics are accurate, *lay* may come to replace *lie*; meanwhile, GI language is not always the best model.

Thanks largely to advertising, there is an increasing use of intransitive verbs in transitive situations. Thought up by some Madison Avenue man with an unbuttoned button-down mind, these are not justified by actual usage; but ubiquitous commercials may brainwash us with their language as well as make us buy Big Brother's detergents and deodorants. Thus we learn that "Pall Mall travels the smoke further," though the smoke does the traveling. Hoover's portable vacuum cleaner "looks and carries like luggage"; apparently, luggage is now its own porter. "The flavor [of Calvert Extra] is rich and full—yet it swallows easy." So beware, lest the drink you are about to swallow gulps you down instead; it has already turned the adverb into an adjective. Maybe you should switch to Nestle's Quick, which "tastes best and fixes easiest." What could be easier than a drink that fixes itself? Perhaps Doom Flakes, which "tastes and eats like a cereal should." Here is one way to avoid indigestion. But then some things "cook smelly and eat good." One ad asks, "Does the bread chew as hard as it tears?" Not if it has good teeth. James Thurber was irritated by this sort of confusion between transitive and intransitive verbs, whereby cars handle and ride well, instead of being handled and ridden. Actually most of these ads use the intransitive to avoid the passive voice. Vacuum cleaners are carried; Calvert is swallowed; Nestle's is fixed; cereal is eaten; things are cooked; bread is chewed; but try converting the admen, and they answer with a masking tape that "sticks immediately, holds securely, and removes cleanly." Thurber wrote sarcastically that his radio "listens fine, and travels and limpids the sound," and that he expected to encounter, "We can sleep twenty people in this house in a pinch, but we can only eat twelve." In fact, the Pennsylvania Dutch say, "Come eat yourself, Henry; Ma's at the table, and Pa's half et." So perhaps there is some precedent. A Southern Appalachian highlander might say, "Hit grumbled the old woman some." When we read that pens load with a cartridge, instead of being loaded, we can find a precedent in muzzle-loaders and breechloaders. Yet you might wonder about a vinyl that "cuts like cloth, looks like leather . . ." Do your vinyl and cloth have a dull blade these days? Perhaps they are like the can that doesn't pour well. Then there is the garment that "walks like a culotte but sits like a skirt." You don't even have to wear it. And why waste time sleeping when you can have "the 'Play-jama' that sleeps like a little girl"? You might also try "soft sleeping foam rollers," since verbals as well as verbs can be confused. As for foam rollers, "Hair that combs is a must."

If you drive through the malodorous town of Canton, North Carolina, you might conclude that Champion Paper cooks smelly and writes good—just the thing for the student who has difficulty with assignments. Of course, the topic counts, but Bob Considine claims that "San Francisco writes pretty easy, whether you're writing about its bridges—Golden Gate and Harry—or its ball club and joints." Photographs may help; Ed Sullivan's pitchgirl Julia Meade says that "Pictures remember but words forget." The only trouble is that you may not remember where you put the pictures. Elephants are better. As for literature, it is good to learn that Joyce Cary is reprinting. Presumably his books are being reprinted too. We need some stimulating literature, since "Textbooks all look and read alike." Perhaps the textbooks are afraid of being censored and of losing their positions. If you feel by now that you're losing your mind, blame it on the advertising copy men who "swarm an idea." If "Friskies chops up easily," so do verbs. The ad that the '63 Chevrolet "rides like a limousine" may remind us of Emerson's complaint, "Things are in the saddle and ride mankind." Let the buyer beware and the writer keep his transitive and intransitive verbs in their proper compartments.

Even among transitive verbs, the correct verb choice is sometimes controversial. *Teach* and *learn* are a case in point. Here the distinction is in meaning; the instructor teaches, and the student learns. Nobody ever uses *teach* for *learn*, but *learn* often replaces *teach* in nonstandard English: "I'll learn you to keep quiet," or the fake rustic, "I'll learn ye, dern ye." Shakespeare used *learn* in this fashion; Hamlet says:

> Our indiscretion sometimes serves us well,
> When our deep plots do pall; and that should learn us
> There's a divinity that shapes our ends,
> Rough-hew them how we will—

116

In time, *learn* will probably become a synonym for *teach,* but at present its misuse is unacceptable in standard practice.

Another pair of verbs often confused are *leave* and *let.* Expressions like "Leave us go home" and "Leave us not be hasty" are all right for cartoon characters but not for standard speech. Such errors occur mostly when *leave* usurps *let's* meaning "allow" or "permit," in constructions with the infinitive. These require *let* in standard English: "Let us be." The ad "Between parties—just let it standing in the center of the dining table—you need no other centerpiece!" needs revision either to "leave it standing" or to "let it stand."

Slang often uses *bust* instead of *burst.* Purists do not consider *bust* a legitimate word, yet there are two uses where it is not only permissible but necessary. Trusts and broncos are always *busted,* never *burst.* A purist who tried *bronco-bursting* or *trust-bursting* would doubtless get clobbered in either activity.

¶ VERBS VERSUS VERBALS: INFINITIVES

Not all forms of the verb actually function as verbs. Participles and infinitives are incomplete by themselves; they cannot be combined with a subject to make an independent clause. Thus some grammarians call them verbals, or verbids, instead of verbs. It is important to recognize the distinction; students who do not, often write fragmentary sentences under the illusion that they have a verb when all they have is a verbal. "The dog barking outside" is not a sentence; "barking" is a present participle modifying "dog"; it cannot serve as a verb. We shall return to this issue in more detail when we consider sentence structure. Meanwhile, let us consider infinitives and participles. As we have seen, the infinitive is the form given in the dictionary entry. Used with or without *to*— *to sing* or *sing*—it can serve as modifier and as subject or complement of a verb. Modifier: "She felt an urge to scream." Subject: "To err is human; to forgive, divine." Complement: "Captain Vere persuaded the court to convict and sentence Billy Budd." In the last example, the first infinitive (*to convict*) is preceded by *to,* which is not repeated for the second (*sentence*). Pronoun subjects of the infinitive take the objective case: "The commander ordered *them to cease* firing."

There is little chance for error here unless you get the wrong word, such as confusing *sit* for *set* or *light* for *lighten.* Occasionally

117

a whopper turns up. One Southern mountaineer said, "The last time me and Hounddog went we only got us one coot, and hit was so pore we sot hit on a limb and let hit went." [5] *Sot* (for *set*) is pretty good, but *let hit went* (for *go*) is a masterpiece matched only by the Democratic slogan of 1844: "Times ain't now as they used to was."

Sometimes infinitives are used ambiguously. The infinitive of purpose is a troublemaker. "I do not intend to run" is clear enough; but "He hurried as much as possible only to get home late for supper" suggests that he hurried in order to be late, whereas the real meaning is that he was late in spite of hurrying. Again, "Christopher Columbus defied the skeptics to discover America" should give you pause. It sounds as if Columbus said, "Skeptics, I defy you to discover America," or that he defied the skeptics for the purpose of discovering America. The meaning, of course, is that he defied the skeptics and then went on to discover America. "Food prices have risen to frustrate the housewife" suggests purpose rather than result. Heaven knows, the housewife is frustrated enough without having food prices deliberately decide to raise themselves in order to irritate her. For a final misleading infinitive of purpose, consider "Elizabeth Barrett defied her father to marry Robert Browning." The only solution for such sentences is to rephrase them and avoid the awkward infinitive.

Sometimes infinitives suggest future action: "The convention is to be held next week." But be careful not to use such a construction unless you intend to imply futurity. "It was the most successful Tupperware convention to be held in Logan" suggests that it was the most successful one that will ever be held there. Simply omit the infinitive and the difficulty vanishes. Likewise, "This is one of three dormitories to be coed" should be changed to read, "This is one of three coed dormitories." *To be* is dead wood in "This was one of the worst droughts ever to be recorded"; "ever recorded" is enough. To avoid the implication of futurity, use a relative clause instead of the infinitive. "This is the only team to have an undefeated season" should be "Slippery Rock is the only team that has had an undefeated season." For the future, *shall* or *will* is preferable to *are to*. "I am to meet you at Waterloo Bridge" suggests passive obligation; "I shall meet you" is better. Headlines often use the infinitive for brevity: "Atomic scientists to announce startling discovery"; but "will announce is only two letters longer.

118

¶ SEX AND THE SPLIT INFINITIVE

Purists insist that the infinitive must never be split by the insertion of an adverb after the *to*: "to rapidly eat." Actually this is not a problem worth worrying about. Many competent writers split the infinitive (Arthur Miller wrote "to forever guard against his own complicity with Cain. . ."), and most all of us do so in casual conversation. If the stress is on the adverb, you may want it before the verb: "To accurately portray Melville's ideas in motion-picture dialogue is exceedingly difficult." The adverb can always be placed before the *to* (cf., Shakespeare's "gently to hear, kindly to judge our play"), but this formation may seem archaic ("Accurately to portray"), and in conversation most people are not that precise. Usually there is no good reason to split the infinitive, but your only concern should be to avoid awkwardness, such as, "The self-reliant viewpoint seems to not recognize that we are partially dependent on the resources of other nations." "The thoughts in Thoreau's writings were almost impossible to practically apply" is both clumsy and ambiguous. Obviously "I like to not got home" is substandard but on other counts than the split infinitive. Arguing against over-punctitious proofreaders, Raymond Chandler stated, "When I split an infinitive, damn it, I split it so it will stay split. . . ."

Some infinitives cannot be split because they are used without *to*, in such constructions as "We must *go*," "You'd better *hurry*," "I can't *hear* you," "I don't *know*," for example.

The infinitive we have so far been discussing is the simple present infinitive, usually termed simply the infinitive. There are also the present progressive infinitive (*to be singing*), the present passive infinitive (*to be loved*), the perfect infinitive (*to have written*), the progressive perfect (*to have been working*), and the perfect passive (*to have been kissed*).

¶ VERBS VERSUS VERBALS: PARTICIPLES

Like the infinitive, participles are verbals, or verbids, that cannot serve as the verb in a main clause. The present participle is the infinitive or present stem plus *-ing* (*know, knowing*). When the stem ends in *-e,* the *-e* is dropped before *-ing* (*come, coming*). The past participle we have already examined as one of the principal parts; it is used with auxiliary verbs to form the perfect tenses and the passive voice. Both participles can be combined: *having suf-*

119

fered, being invited, having been insulted. The present participle is used with various tenses of the verb *to be* to form the progressive tenses indicating continuing action: *I am drinking, he was drinking, we shall be drinking, she has been drinking, they had been drinking, everybody shall have been stinking.*

Present participles can function as nouns, as subjects or objects of verbs and prepositions; when they do so, they are called *gerunds,* though this term is artificial and is therefore rejected by some grammarians. Subject: "Swimming is excellent exercise." Object: "Lester dislikes hunting." Object of preposition: "I'm tired of arguing."

Participles frequently function as modifiers, and, as verbals, they can in turn be modified by adverbs: "Breathing heavily, he staggered down the stairs." Sometimes it is difficult to tell whether a past participle is used as a modifier or as part of a passive construction. "The driver was uninjured" could be either; in "The driver was uninjured but nervous" the participle is more clearly a modifier. Confusion comes when it is not clear what the participle modifies; if it dangles or is misplaced, the result is such a sentence as "The librarian ordered books appealing to children with big print" or "Drinking martinis, life seemed tolerable again." We shall return to this problem in a later chapter.

¶ TRANSPOSING

As we have seen with nouns and pronouns, there are many words that cannot be pinned down and limited to a single part of speech. Often the same stem can function as several parts of speech, though when it is, its form sometimes changes to take on the endings (for case, number, person, tense) required by that function. Many nouns and adjectives and even some prepositions ("Up the volume," "Outen the light") can be used as verbs. The noun is particularly adept at this double role; such unlikely candidates as *Fulbright, ammunition, telephone pole, billboard, gooseflesh, porpoise, rainbow, steamroller, pancake, orator, subway, ash can, hemorrhage,* and *bellyache* have appeared as verbs, and H. L. Mencken has noted that the Gideons have spoken of "Bibling a hotel." Some new verbs are back-formations, the result of a removal of the ending of a noun or adjective: *enthuse* (from *enthusiastic*), *resurrect* (from *resurrection*), *sculpt* (from *sculptor*), *chiropract* (from *chiropractor*),

120

and *frivol* (from *frivolous*). Others are formed by adding suffixes to nouns; probably the most common and controversial is *-ize,* to which few object in *glamorize, lionize, popularize, publicize,* or many similar constructions, but which draws howls of outraged protest in *finalize.* Another device is the addition of prefixes, often negative ones, to make verbs from nouns or even new verbs from old ones (e.g., *to deglamorize*). But usually the unattended noun doubles as a verb (except for person, tense, or participle endings), as Snooper says, "It's some handsome, devil-may-care guy imposturing me."

The interchange of nouns and verbs is ancient and honorable, yet some cases remain controversial. Though it is gradually becoming respectable, probably the biggest shibboleth is still the use of the noun *loan* as a verb: "Loan me five bucks." Among purists, this usage is substandard, though it is widely heard and perfectly clear. The only objection (not a very valid one) is that we already have the established verb *lend* and there is therefore no need for another one. Actually, the criticism of *loan* is merely a lingering though moribund bit of linguistic snobbery.

The Southern Appalachian highlanders often show a fluent ingenuity in transposing verbs, adjectives, and nouns; the result may be grammatically nonstandard but colorful. If *fish* can be a verb, why not *squirrel,* as in "Jethro is a-fixin' to go squirrelin'"? "I don't *confidence* them dogs," said one mountain man, as he *buttocked* down in his chair; his son didn't *contrary* him none. And many a mountaineer has seen *hants* (*haunts*) in the hills.

¶ THEME ME DEADLY

In modern usage, parts of speech are becoming increasingly interchangeable. On the credit side, this gives the language an increasing flexibility, but sometimes it entangles it in jargon. In the Southern Appalachians this transposition is part of a freewheeling grammar; there is no calculation behind it. But advertisers and journalists often make a fetish of coy or contrived diction. The mountain man will make you a *run* of corn liquor; magazines inform you that you can *julep* Bourbon or you can *highball* it. And "When you go *supermarketing,* look for plump broiler-fryers . . . for they are the buy-wise choices." *Vogue* advertises "a slouchy new polo shirt that cowls as it hoods" and informs the reader that

"The mystique of this dress is made up of equal parts of shift and slink." These examples are harmless enough. Poets and novelists often interchange parts of speech for literary effect; Robinson Jeffers even used *sarcophagus* as a verb. But artists use the language creatively, while journalists sometimes get trapped in cliché. Thus it is practically obligatory for gossip columnists to write that somebody *guested, hosted,* or *gifted* someone ("Elvis Presley gifted Ann-Margret with a huge circular bed for her new home") or is *romancing* someone. Parties are *themed* with exotic decorations. The *Christian Science Monitor* complained that nouns are being made into verbs at a madly accelerated rate. Books are no longer written; now they are *authored*. Music critics so often use *guest, solo,* and *duet* as verbs that the *Monitor* wonders if Isaac Stern will soon have symphonied Brahms's *Double Concerto*. The *Toronto Globe and Mail* glumly observed, "So now that we have Christmased and New Yeared, we shall Leap Year while faithing that however we language ourselves we have already been outsolecismed." The point is not whether English can make new verbs or nouns; obviously it can, and usage can make them acceptable. It is that the majority of these words become so routine a jargon that they numb the language instead of giving it new life. Thus the language spoken in the Smokies or by Faulkner's characters, nonstandard though it is, is often preferable to that of Madison Avenue. The first is living; the latter, synthetic.

Exercise 7: Correct any errors in verb form or function in the following:

1. The reason I put salt on it is that it were a radish.
2. If those bug bites is chiggers, you had ought to put nail polish on them.
3. Grandma used to could do a cancan kick.
4. I could of went to Portland, but I ended up in Kennebunkport.
5. Ben Gunn founded the treasure of old Captain Flint.
6. We was brung up here in the cove.
7. The minister's been setting up with the sick.
8. The women in our house done all the churning.
9. It is inefficient for cereal boxes to be shook at the factory to make them appear full upon arrival.
10. Walking in public or talking in groups of two or three was forbidded in Puritan Boston.
11. If Thoreau would have been born today, he would have gone out of his mind.
12. I axed him to fotch me my rifle.
13. I thought a little bit further ahead than you may think I have thunk.

14. I drawed a monster for Papa to color.
15. The tobacco made his breath a bit strong, but he chewn a feenamint.
16. Would stout Cortez have been thinner if he would have taken Metrecal?
17. We should of went to Ft. Lauderdale spring vacation.
18. Did you ever took a picture of a fish being fitted with contact lenses?
19. These are claw marks that bears have did.
20. Schroeder plew the piano with amazing virtuosity.
21. Where was you fotch up that you don't know about bears?
22. When I brung up marrying, I weren't thinking of myself.
23. This German book is writ in some foreign language.
24. We was thinking that we ought to of brung a spare tire.
25. Homer brang the mustard, and Ajax fotched the pickles.

Exercise 8: Correct any errors in subject-verb agreement and put the appropriate form in the blank.

1. They was not sure whether it were a wildebeest or a hartebeest. . . . .
2. Melvin don't like paprika in his deviled eggs. . . . .
3. I have backslid in my time, but it seem sin don't rise so strong in me now. . . . .
4. The people wasn't even there when the bear went through their tent. . . . .
5. Even if the couple is married, they have to walk outside their home in a discreet manner. . . . .
6. *The Seven Pillars of Wisdom* are just out in paperback. . . . .
7. Is the grownups ready for coffee? . . . .
8. If you get chigger-bit, take a bath in warm soda; it will draw the chiggers before they gets set. . . . .
9. The directions for the do-it-yourself Frankenstein is on the box. . . . .
10. There is people in the cities that has never seen a cow. . . . .
11. Some lumber companies and mining firms has opposed the establishment of various national parks. . . . .
12. There is hogs so stubborn that they'll cross hell on a rotten rail to steal a camper's dinner. . . . .
13. There are many kinds of mountain crafts that has been revived. . . . .
14. The most vivid and affectionate accounts of mules was written by William Faulkner. . . . .
15. The Joad family is not religious, but they certainly are a God-fearing family. . . . .
16. Thomas Jefferson were denounced as a dangerous radical when he ran for President. . . . .

17. Ivory, apes, and peacocks was brought by the Queen of Sheba. . . . .
18. If I lets go of the roof, I'll fall on my head bone. . . . .
19. Some twins looks so much alike that they forgets who they are. . . . .
20. Women should marry people that understands them. . . . .

Exercise 9: In the following sentences the passive voice is sometimes used effectively and sometimes not. Turn any clumsy passive constructions into the active voice.

1. Although inelegant, the pickup truck was driven by us to the country club.
2. It has been confirmed that the porcupine was the first animal to have its own short-wave radio call letters.
3. The five monkeys were seen by the guests climbing up the lace curtains.
4. It is recommended that ammonia and chlorine cleansers not be used in combination.
5. When using it for medicinal purposes, vodka should be taken in small doses.
6. In attaching the buttonholer to the machine, care must be taken that the throat plate be covered with the metal shield indicated in diagram A and that the buttonholer be securely attached to the presser bar B by tightening firmly screw C.
7. Bread is made by dissolving yeast in a warm liquid and then by mixing the liquid with flour, and by subsequent kneading, rising, and baking.
8. When the grime was removed from Eliza Doolittle, a pretty girl was seen.
9. A gazebo was built by her in the backyard into which she retired to write long novels.
10. It was decided that the filing system in the library should be changed from the Dewey decimal to the Library of Congress catalogue system.
11. It is observed that while American publications render Alfred, Lord Tennyson as Alfred Tennyson, British publications list F. Scott Fitzgerald as Scott-Fitzgerald, Francis.
12. It was discovered when the freight was unpacked that several crates of cockatoos were missing.
13. Automobiles, houses, power lines, boat moorings, and farms were obliterated by the hurricane.
14. The elephants are attacked with spears until they are succumbed through loss of blood.
15. The guitar strings are numbered by counting the smallest as the first.
16. In combining the strokes of the thumb with those of the fingers, care should be taken to play the notes one after the other from the lowest to the highest.

17. In using the third finger, the little finger must be lifted from the face of the guitar.
18. When notes of the same pitch are joined by a slur, the first note only is played, prolonging its duration for tied notes to be made.
19. The Small Bar is made with two fingers on the middle strings.
20. It was decided by the committee that a holiday should be declared.

9 √ "Is You Is or Is You Ain't My Baby?" Subject - Verb Agreement

Verbs should agree with their subjects in number and person. When the subject is singular, the verb should be in the singular form; when the subject is plural, the verb should be in the plural form. A first-, second-, or third-person subject requires a verb with first-, second-, or third-person inflectional endings.

"I is ready" is an example of faulty agreement in person; *I,* the first-person singular pronoun, requires *am,* the first-person singular verb. "We is coming" uses a first-person plural pronoun with a third-person singular verb; the verb should be changed to *are.* "He sure am lazy" has a third-person singular pronoun with a first-person singular verb; the verb should be changed to *is.* "They was going to the steak house" has a third-person plural subject with a third-person singular verb; the verb should be changed to *were.* Except for the verb *to be,* all errors in agreement occur in the formation of the present tense, since other verbs have only one form in the past tense, no matter what the number and person (e.g., *I worked, you worked, he worked, we worked, you worked, they worked*). Only in the past tense of the verb *to be* are the first and third person singular (*was*) distinguished from the second person singular and the first, second, and third persons plural (*were*). There can, of course, be faulty agreement in the present perfect tense, but only in the use of the present tense of the auxiliary verb *have.* As more errors occur with the verbs *to be* and *to have* than with any others, their present tenses follow:

126

	SINGULAR	PLURAL	SINGULAR	PLURAL
FIRST PERSON	I am	we are	I have	we have
SECOND PERSON	you are	you are	you have	you have
THIRD PERSON	he, she, it is	they are	he, she, it has	they have

One of the most obvious and widespread errors is the persistent use of *was* with *you* and *they,* when *were* is required by standard grammar. "Was you there yesterday? They said they was there, and we was coming, but the car broke down" is almost a hallmark of some regions, but it is also anathema in educated circles. Until the late eighteenth century, *you was* appeared frequently in literature for the second person singular, and Webster defended *was* for the singular and *were* for the plural, though he was overruled by Joseph Priestley and other linguists. Since the early seventeenth century, the lack of any distinction between the second person singular and plural has been a nuisance in English; and we try to get around it by using *you all, youse, yousuns,* and other forms to indicate more than one *you* to compensate for the older distinction between *thou* and *ye* (at first the subjective but later replaced by the older objective *you*). In Webster's day, it might therefore have been logical to say *you* (singular) *was* and *you* (plural) *were,* although the same reasoning could be applied to retaining *art* for the second person singular present of the verb *to be.* With this sort of logic, those who say *you was* should say *you all were;* but instead, from the ambiguous *you* that can be singular or plural, *was* has been extended to cover all the plurals; and *were* has ceased to exist as a verb for many people. In some areas, even the better-educated invariably use *was.* Any logic behind this has undoubtedly been forgotten generations ago, and today those using *was* indiscriminately speak from habit, as we all do.

A less common error but one that appears to have been characteristic of the Southern Appalachians is the use of *were* (often pronounced *war* and so spelled in dialogue) instead of *was* with the first and third person singular.

He war a moonshiner.

Hit war further to the still than I thought hit war.

"Grandpappy war plumb delighted. . . . Thar war considerable confusion."[1]

"Kaze he war all drooped-up with the milk pizen, I lick-splitted hit t'the blockader's still, which war appearantly a-bein' run successful-like aspite the revenoors, an' fotch him a jair of brandy." [2]

But this practice is inconsistent, even in the same paragraph. One Civil War veteran was quoted as saying, "I were with Ransom, in ole Virginia. . . . I were shot purty nigh the last. Hit wuz when we wuz tryin' to git out'n Petersburg afore the Yankee line lapped round us." [3] You also encounter *you was* in the Appalachians: "We didn't know you was coming, and we look a fright."

Nonstandard English speech in the Old (sometimes the New) South and in the backwoods, as can be seen in the dialogue of Mark Twain and William Faulkner, frequently uses a singular verb with a plural subject: "Them is mighty good corn squeezings," "Since they dredged out that new baptizing hole, they gets more conversions down in the valley," "Thar's two eyes a-shinin' out of the cave," "There's raccoons up there, isn't there," Huck Finn's "all kings is mostly rapscallions," and the King's "your eyes is lookin' at this very moment on the pore disappeared Dauphin, Looy the Seventeen, son of Looy the Sixteen and Marry Antonette."*Huckleberry Finn* has hundreds of such examples. These errors in number are often combined with faulty past tenses and participles ("When we fell in the creek, our britches was froze solid").

Conversely, another error widespread throughout the country, is the use in the third person singular of the plural *don't* for *doesn't* ("He don't like pepper in his buttermilk"). You also find *doesn't* used, instead of *don't*, with the first person singular ("I doesn't take kindly to having my ears scrubbed"). This indicates another characteristic of nonstandard speech (particularly in the South): the use of the third-person singular verb with *I*, as in *I is, I likes, I thinks, I says* or as in the mountain woman's explanation, "I plants cucumbers afore sunup so's the bugs won't eat 'em soon's they bust the dirt." [4] This error in person is compounded by one in number when the subject is the first-person plural pronoun *we: we is, we likes, we thinks, we says,* etc. Another error in number is the use of the plural *are* (sometimes spelled *air* in dialect) with the first or third person singular, as in "Only Babalooey knows who El Kabong really are" or the Appalachian "They look mighty peaceful like off yander, but you ought to git tangled up in them laurel slicks onct an' you'd change your mind 'bout how purty an' friendly Old Smoky air." [5]

These errors are either a matter of habit or of total grammatical unconsciousness. The problem, then, is to break such habits, to consider the relationship of the words in a sentence, and to form new habits by conscious effort. It would seem simple enough. All you have to do is find the verb, locate its subject, and ask yourself the number and person of both subject and verb. If they are not the same, make them so. In practice it is not always so easy. There are a number of constructions that may cause difficulty.

1. Two or more singular subjects connected by *and* require a plural verb:

Frankenstein's monster and the Wolf Man *are* wrecking the laboratory.
Frankie and Johnnie *were* sweethearts.
"The Walrus and the Carpenter *were* walking close at hand."
Both Knossos and Mycenae *have* been excavated.

There are three exceptions to this practice. If the multiple subjects are preceded by *each* or *every*, they are considered as acting individually and are followed by a singular verb:

Every bear and woodchuck *is* hibernating.
Each camper and picnicker *cleans* up his own area.

If two singular subjects joined by *and* refer to a unit, to the same thing or person, then they take a singular verb:

His Lord and Saviour *is* Jesus Christ.
Her pride and joy *was* the cherry orchard.
Liver and spinach *has* been the most unpopular meal in the Army.

Addition or multiplication calculations may use a singular or a plural verb:

Four times five *is* twenty.   Four times five *are* twenty.
Two and two *is* four.   Two and two *are* not five.

But in subtraction, "ten minus three *is* [not *are*] seven."

In the actual practice of their craft, many famous authors have used a singular verb with several subjects joined by *and*. Shakespeare, Joseph Addison, Thomas Carlyle, Thomas Wolfe, George Orwell, Evelyn Waugh, Aldous Huxley, J. P. Marquand, Eleanor Roosevelt, not to mention various scholars are among those who have done so. Clarence Darrow wrote, "Ignorance and fanaticism is ever busy and needs feeding." The King James Bible states, "Out of the same mouth proceedeth blessing and cursing." Hamlet says, "Your fat king and your lean beggar is but variable service." In *Othello*, Brabantio asks, "Is there not charms/ By which the property of youth and maidenhood/ May be abus'd?" And Sir Laurence Olivier says of Shakespeare, "There's too much tears and bloody sweat in it." In *Catch-22,* Joseph Heller writes, "There were too many dangers for Yossarian to keep track of. There was Hitler, Mussolini, and Tojo, for example, and they were all out to kill him. . . . There was Appleby, Havermeyer, Black and Korn. There was Nurse Cramer and Nurse Duckett. . . . There were bartenders, bricklayers and bus conductors all over the world who wanted him dead . . ." [6] In this example, one might defend Heller's use of verbs in the singular by saying that the subjects appear to be people considered as a unit; but what counts is that the writing is effective, even if the mathematics fails to add up.

2. Two or more singular subjects connected by *but, or,* or *nor* take a singular verb:

> Not Hamlet but Claudius *was* chosen king.
> Not only Bette Davis but also Flora Robson *was* cast as Queen Elizabeth.
> Dickens or Thackeray *is* to be taught in seminar.
> Neither *Tarzan* nor *The Scarlet Letter* is allowed free circulation in the Plunkville Library.

3. If a singular and a plural subject are connected by *but, or,* or *nor,* the verb agrees with the nearer one:

> Neither Polonius nor Rosencranz and Guildenstern *were* able to deceive Hamlet.
> Not only Lon Chaney but also Charles Laughton and Anthony Quinn *have* played Quasimodo, the hunchback of Notre Dame.
> Either Dickens or Tennyson and Brown *are* to be taught in seminar.
> Either the Brontës or George Eliot *is* to be taught in seminar.

4. If two subjects connected by *or* or *nor* are different in person, the verb agrees with the nearer one:

> Either you or I *am* to die.
> Either you or Melvin *has* committed the crime.
> Neither Irving nor you *are* to come home late.

Such constructions may be clumsy and require rewriting for clarity and style. "She or you are keeping a stray dog in the cellar" is better rephrased as, "Either she is keeping a stray dog in the cellar, or you are."

5. A subject in the singular followed by a plural modifier takes a singular verb:

130

One of the ships at anchor *has* broken its mooring.
The *photographer* of the mob scenes *keeps* forgetting to remove
the lens cover.
The *response* of the critics *was* gratifying.
A *volume* of Civil War photographs *is* in the reading room.

Casual speech might use *are* in the last example, but there is no justification for it in careful prose.

6. If a subject in the singular is followed by some such construction as *along with, as well as, in addition to, including,* or *together with,* the number of the verb remains singular:

The captain, along with his supporters, was set adrift in the
longboat.
The whole party, including the rangers, was caught in the down-
pour.
A mother bear, together with three cubs, lives near the Big
Locust Trail.

7. Used as pronouns, *any* and *none* can take either a singular or a plural verb. Conservative usage prefers the singular, but general usage is indifferent, though sometimes a plural modifier after the pronoun requires the verb to be plural. Thus we say, "Any of the books on the list is [or are] appropriate," but we need the plural in "Are any of you ready for dessert?" There is no real problem here; common sense and clarity select the appropriate verb.

Do any of the campgrounds have a vacancy?
Does any of the campgrounds have a vacancy?
Any of the planes *is* able to make the flight in three hours.
None of us *is* [or *are*] able to shoe a horse.
None of the officers *were* [or *was*] sober.
None of you *is* going to squeal on Rocco.

8. The indefinite pronouns *anybody, anyone, each, either, everybody, everyone, neither, nobody, no one, somebody,* and *someone* usually take a singular verb:

Each of the vampires *has* his own coffin.
Neither of the clowns *was* funny.
Somebody has been eating my porridge.
Has anybody here seen Kelly?

Since *each, either,* and *neither* are often followed by a plural modifier, they are often used with a plural verb in casual conversation: "*Neither* of them *are* of legal age," "*Each* of them *have* swatted me with a fraternity paddle." Formal style still requires the singular, but this convention is breaking down. The suffix makes us habitually use a singular verb with pronouns ending in -*body* or -*one*; nobody ever says "*Everyone are* finks," though if other words come between the subject and the verb, you may hear "*Every one* of them *are* sick." Despite the singular verb, the subject is obviously plural in "Everybody is either insulting or nuts." [7] The main trouble is that careless speakers or writers follow -*body* and -*one* words with a singular verb but then refer to them with plural pronouns: "*Everybody* is kicking up *their* heels." The reason is that words like *everyone* are singular in form but collective in meaning; form governs the verb, but meaning is apt to make us use a plural pronoun. (Cf. p. 76.) This is also true of a singular subject preceded by *any, each,* and *every:* "Every *Republican thinks they* can run for President" needs the personal pronoun changed to the singular, *he.* Though the meaning is clear enough in "*Everyone is* cleaning *their* rooms," there is an inconsistency in agreement. Such constructions are nonstandard but harmless enough; they usually pass unnoticed in casual conversation. Careful style requires more precision and would use a singular pronoun to match subject and verb: "*Everyone is* capable of letting *his* ideas become intolerant." Yet many distinguished writers have used a singular verb and plural pronoun after *everybody,* and sometimes sense requires such formal inconsistencies. (Cf. p. 78.) Clarity is preferable to dogma.

9. When a collective noun is considered as a unit, it takes a singular verb. When its component parts are each considered individually, it takes a plural verb. This practice includes words like *half, number, part, percent, rest,* and *remainder.*

SINGULAR	PLURAL
"The people is a great beast."— Alexander Hamilton	The people are divided in their reaction to the plan.
The rest of the fish and chips is yours.	The rest of the penguins are eating fish.

"The rest of the penguins is disturbed" is ambiguous; out of context, there is no way to tell whether the word *rest* means "repose" or "remainder." If the penguins are taking a nap and a helicopter lands near them, then their rest *is* disturbed; whereas if some penguins have gone for a waddle, then the rest *are* sliding and swimming. As a collective noun, "The rest is silence." An ad informs us that "Forty percent of the American population possesses hair of a lifeless color"; but since each person has his own—not his or her own, for pity's sake—hair in various lifeless colors, the plural verb *possess* should be used. "The United States have one of the best national park services" is wrong: one nation and not fifty individual states is (note the use of *is,* to go with the singular *nation*) concerned, so "The United States" *takes* a singular verb. Emerson has a curious example of a collective noun with a plural verb where most authors would use the singular: "The private poor man . . . goes to the post-office, and the *human race run* on his errands; to the book-shop, and the *human race read and write* of all that happens, for him. . . ." (Italics mine.) Yet the plural can be justified on the grounds that *human race* here consists of acting individuals, rather than an abstract collection. Another unusual plural occurs in Lawrence of Arabia's statement, "The Navy were already collecting," where "collecting" implies a plural activity.

People often use a singular verb and a plural pronoun with collective nouns and thus cause an inconsistent and erroneous disagreement in number. "Is the family satisfied with their condition?" requires either a plural verb or a singular pronoun, preferably the former. "Schumans *keeps* ten horses in *their* stables" needs a singular pronoun, since "Schumans" is a single hostelry. "The opposition feels that they can stop all the trouble by killing the leader" needs a plural verb: "The opposition feel that they . . ." The leader needs either some bodyguards or political asylum.

10. Titles of books, stories, poems, songs, magazines, newspapers, plays, and movies take a singular verb. This applies even when the main noun of the title is plural. *Mad* ridiculed the grammar of Alfred Hitchcock's movie, "*The Birds* Is Coming!" but Hitchcock was quite right. On the other hand, if a character in the film had run around saying, "Help, the birds is coming," he would have deserved to be bonked on the head by a sea gull. Varying titles with plural and collective nouns, we can make the following rundown:

> *The Birds* is coming!
> The wildlife is coming.
> *The Frogs* is coming.
> *The Alligator People* is coming!
> The enemy is [or are] coming.
> *The Misfits* is coming.
> *Them* is coming!
> The ants are coming.

Leinigen versus the Ants is coming.
The Little Foxes is coming.
The Four Horsemen of the Apocalypse is coming.
Look out! the giant squid is coming.
Look out! the giant squid are coming.
(Irregular plural, like deer)

And I'm getting out of here.

11. Nouns that are plural in form but singular in meaning (e.g., *economics, mathematics, news, physics, politics,* and the names of some products) customarily take a singular verb. Thus we hear that "Rollaids consumes 47 times its weight in excess stomach acids." Huckleberry Hound says "Kellogg's Sugar Stars is new and improved oat cereal." These statements are correct but annoying; the subject seems plural yet functions as a singular ("Friskies doesn't stick to the spoon"). We are used to hearing that the *news is* bad or that *blues is* one of the oldest forms of folk music, but we do a double take when we hear, "New Burgerbits gives your dog everything he needs at every age." When a subject is plural in both form and meaning, it cannot be used with a singular verb; the emcee who asked "Is there any other bingos?" did not have a winning verb.

12. When a relative pronoun is the subject of a verb, the verb should agree in number and person with the pronoun's antecedent. Thus "There are the carding machines that combs the wool" has faulty agreement; the antecedent, *machines,* is plural and requires a plural verb.

> This is one of the *rangers who supervise* the campground.
> This is the *mouse that smokes* cigarettes.

Difficulties often arise in "one of the . . ." constructions, where the singular pronoun *one,* is followed by a plural noun. Usually each is the subject of a separate verb, so you need a singular and a plural verb to match the respective subjects:

> One of the men who work at the factory was injured.

One is the subject of *was,* while the subject *two* refers not to *one* but to *men.* Parentheses may clarify the agreement:

> One (of the men who work at the factory) was injured.

Another problem occurs if the antecedent of the relative pronoun is a word, such as *either* or *neither,* that traditionally take a singular verb, though colloquial usage is increasingly using a plural one:

134

> Neither of the movements being discussed (have, has) been
> conducted without violence.

Movements is plural, but *neither* still requires the singular verb *has*.

Some curious examples occur in John Osborne's play *Luther*,[8] where the third-person relative pronoun, rather than its antecedent, determines the person of the verb:

> "Deign to listen to me, most holy father, to me who is like a child."[8]

> "Or was it just you who made free, you and the princes you've taken up with, and the rich burghers and—" [9]

Customarily, we would say "to me who am," though it too is awkward; and certainly "you who were" is the form required by standard usage, but the speaker here is Luther's father, an unlearned man, who would probably say "you was" if the language he spoke were English.

13. If a sentence begins with *There* or *Here*, the verb agrees with the subject following:

> There *is* an *elephant* in my back yard.
> There *are* the *daggers*.
> *Are* there any *ladies* present?
> *Is* there a *doctor* in the house?
> Here *is* a bad *case* of dandruff.
> Here *are* three *kittens*.

14. Complements of the verb *to be* do not alter the number of the verb, which always agrees with its subject:

> Ship *models* are his favorite hobby.
> His favorite *hobby is* ship models.
> One *thing* I can't stand *is* noisy neighbors.
> Noisy *neighbors* are one thing I can't stand.

It is tempting to make the verb match the number of the complement; but when tempted, you should not yield. If a sentence is too clumsy, rewrite it altogether. "The irritating thing about daytime television programs is aggressive masters of ceremonies, inane give-away shows, and treacly soap operas, all played at top volume." This is grammatically accurate but stylistically awkward, and should be revised to something approximating, "For heaven's sake, turn off the idiot box."

135

Exercise 10: Underline the verb that agrees with its subject in person and number.

1. *The Flintstones* (is, are) my favorite TV program.
2. These scissors (is, are) dull.
3. Both Tarzan and T. S. Eliot (was, were) born in 1888.
4. There (is, are) only three months until our projectile departs from planet earth.
5. Is that all the animal crackers there (is, are) ?
6. I hope none of the boys (gets, get) hurt.
7. One or four (cost, costs) no more.
8. Alabama (takes, take) over on their six-yard line.
9. The remains of Noah's ark (is, are) awaiting discovery on Mt. Ararat, according to some theories.
10. There is a dramatic pause when the last note of the arpeggios (is, are) struck.
11. The shelves (is, are) as bare as last year's mouse nest.
12. The audience (stands, stand) up for the Hallelujah Chorus.
13. The Philippines (is, are) a chief producer of copra.
14. The Bill of Rights (is, are) the first ten amendments.
15. Wufflebeepers (klong, klongs) scurfly in the norp.
16. Can you name three works of English literature that (has, have) someone's arm torn out of the socket?
17. Friskies (has, have) some of the best commercials on television.
18. Crispy Critters (is, are) made from oat flour, brown sugar, precooked corn flour and wheat starch, salt, calcium carbonate, U.S. certified color, niacin, and vitamin B1.
19. It is too bad you (were not, was not) there for the festivities.
20. Lots of people (takes, take) to marriage.
21. The Smokies (has, have) about 300 bears and 3,000,000 bugs.
22. Poe is one of the few authors that (improves, improve) in translation.
23. The music of many neglected composers of sixteenth and seventeenth century England (has, have) been revived since the advent of the LP record.
24. *The Anatomy Lesson of Dr. Nicholas Tulp* is one of those paintings that you admire but that (do, does) not go well over the dining room table.
25. The New York edition of the works of Henry James (has, have) been reprinted recently.

Exercise 11: Underline the subject in the following sentences:

1. Wandering over hills and dales, through villages and towns, striding about the city by night, alone was I.
2. It is recommended that an optimum amount of fertilizer be used on the African violets.

136

3. "Who's afraid of the big bad wolf?"
4. "After many a summer dies the swan."
5. Pink, puce, chartreuse, magenta, and olive drab are not a very happy choice for a color scheme in the new apartment.
6. Here's King Kong now.
7. To listen further was beyond his patience.
8. From Lagos to Nairobi is as far as from Seattle to New York.
9. What people will think has been a recurrent anxiety.
10. About three o'clock is the best time for the meeting.
11. Whence came the giant sea serpent?
12. What makes you tick is a mystery to me.
13. To go to the theatre in New York is too expensive for many people.
14. That Thoreau refused to pay his taxes bothers some businessmen, even though they try to find various tax dodges.
15. To see a unicorn eating a rose in one's garden is a rare and remarkable experience.
16. That the elephant's trunk weighs about 300 pounds is a little-known fact.
17. "Where are the songs of Spring? Ay, where are they?"
18. "Had we but world enough, and time,
This coyness, Lady, were no crime."
19. "Darkened so, yet shone
Above them all the Archangel...."
20. "Ten thousand saw I at a glance,
Tossing their heads in sprightly dance."

10 √ Adjectives and Adverbs

Adjectives are not really and truly interesting.
GERTRUDE STEIN

Adjectives and adverbs are words that function as modifiers; that is, they limit, qualify, or describe some other word or group of words in a sentence. According to the traditional definition, adjectives modify nouns and pronouns; and adverbs modify verbs, adjectives, and other adverbs. Actually, adjectives can also be used to modify other adjectives. Adjectives have several different classifications. The commonest type is descriptive: "a *hot* potato," "the *rainy* season," "a *Grecian* urn," "the *American* experience," "*Fearless* Fosdick," "the *laughing* man," "a *broken* promise." As in the last two examples, present and past participles are often used as adjectives. Adjectives can also limit or specify the element they modify: "*your* hat," "*her* gloves," "*this* time," "*that* place," "*another* country," "*The Second* Mrs. *Tanqueray*." They can also specify and qualify number: "*one* meatball," "*both* brothers," "*many* moons." Some adjectives, both descriptive and limiting, are made from proper nouns: "*Jacksonian* democracy," "*Spenserian* stanzas," "a *Byronic* hero," "the *Napoleonic* Wars," "*Italian* art."

Sometimes an adjective modifies a compound governing element, that is, two or more words at once: "good bread and butter," "white shoes and stockings." And sometimes two or more adjectives are joined together by words such as *and, or, but*: "a poor but honest cobbler," "red or white roses."

Very often a whole clause or group of words is used to modify a noun. In "Bring the tana leaves that the mummy needs," the words *that the mummy needs* provide the answer to the unspoken question, which leaves? and therefore serve as an adjective. Similar groups of words are *who work now and then* in "Students who work now and then don't progress very fast" and *we need* in "This is the sort of program we need." Such descriptive groups of words functioning as adjectives are called clause adjectives or adjective clauses.

Another form of a group of words used as an adjective modifier appears in "That is a mule of great stubbornness," where *of great stubbornness* tells what the kind of mule is. This is known as a prepositional adjective phrase; other instances are "the edition *of 1945*," "the cat *on the table*," "ships *at sea*," "children *at play*," "pictures *on the wall*."

Predicate adjectives are used as both complement and modifier. Usually they come after a linking verb: "That camel is *dignified*," "This toast is *burned*," "I feel *fine*." For emphasis (usually in poetry) the predicate adjective may come first: "Black is the color of my true love's hair." However, except for the predicate adjective, the adjective modifier is usually placed next to its governing word. If it is a word, it normally comes before the word it modifies; if it is a phrase or clause, it may come after. Occasionally this rule does not hold. We say "bread enough," "life everlasting," "the house beautiful." In poetry especially, adjectives often follow their governing words.

Parts of speech, as we have seen, are often inadequate labels; some words that function as adjectives serve elsewhere as nouns, pronouns, verbs, or adverbs. There are some distinguishing adjective suffixes:

-*able* (debatable)	-*ese* (Japanese)	-*ive* (constructive)
-*al* (trivial)	-*esque* (picturesque)	-*less* (hopeless)
-*an* (Martian)	-*ful* (hopeful)	-*like* (doglike)
-*ant* (hesitant)	-*ian* (Grecian)	-*ly* (lively)
-*ar* (circular)	-*ible* (digestible)	-*ory* (sensory)
-*ary* (documentary)	-*ic* (impolitic)	-*ose* (verbose)
-*ate* (passionate)	-*ile* (infantile)	-*ous* (jealous)
-*en* (golden)	-*ish* (British)	-*some* (quarrelsome)
-*ent* (persistent)	-*ite* (finite)	-*y* (tricky)

But even these are not exclusive, and we can find words with some of these endings serving as other parts of speech. *Martian* and *criminal,* for instance, can be used either as adjective or noun.

Many other nouns can double as adjectives: *monster* rally, *wolf* man, *cargo* ship, *tramp* steamer, *brick* wall, *turtle* wrapping, *Christmas* present, *Thurber* dog, *Napoleon* complex. Budd Schulberg even wrote of Hollywood actresses's "little brigittebardot bottoms." In a sense, all personal first names are adjectives, for they describe and

139

specify each member of a family, so that you can tell *Jack* from *Robert* Frost and *Ernest* from *Leicester* Hemingway. Oscar Wilde wrote a whole play about the importance of being named Ernest. Likewise, all possessive-case nouns and pronouns function as adjectives, for they describe to whom or what something belongs. All ordinal numbers (*first, second, third,* etc.) are adjectives, and so are the cardinal numbers (*one, two, three,* etc.) when they are used with nouns: "five miles," "three ships," "a hundred years." All colors can serve as both nouns and adjectives. Sometimes the use of a noun as an adjective becomes a bit strained, as in "Calvert Extra is as whiskey a whiskey as any whiskey you can buy." The current fad of *fun* as an adjective has become a pseudo-sophisticated mannerism ("a fun time," "a fun party," "a fun movie"): "Don't you find *The Scarlet Letter* a fun book to teach?" And the grammar is rudely wrenched in the ad, "It's a better kind of *different.*"

Likewise, some words that are customarily adjectives can function as nouns, as when we speak of "making the *sick* well," sing of "the land of the *free* and the home of the *brave,*" or refer to *the uprooted, the underprivileged, the innocent,* and *the guilty.* We watch a *Western* at the movies; in India, moviegoers see *mythologicals.* And, of course, television offers an occasional *special* or *spectacular.* Some country people use *smart* as a noun: "I have a right *smart* of mint in the herb-garden." And, at some time or other, you have probably been asked, "Do you want some *hot* in your coffee?"

In the Southern Appalachians, adjectives and verbs are often interchanged. Adjectives appear as verbs in "He was biggin' and biggin' the story. . . . I didn't do nary a thing to contrary her; hit benasties a man's mind. . . . He weren't no good at politing people around." Verbs turn into adjectives in "the travelin'est hosses; the talkin'est woman, the nothin' doin'dest day." [1] A word like *film* can be either a noun ("Put in the film") or a verb ("Did you film the action?").

Some words are customarily nouns or adjectives and are only rarely encountered in more than one capacity; but others serve just as well in either role. Clearly, *political* is exclusively an adjective in *political convention*; whereas *motion picture* is equally a compound noun and an adjective: *motion-picture festival.* Many words, as we have already stressed, cannot be labeled as primarily an adjective or a noun: the part of speech depends upon the context, and form follows function. When a word that can be a noun (e.g., that can

140

serve as the subject of a verb) functions as an adjective, it can in turn be modified by an adjective. Take, for example, the phrase "a grammar textbook." Here the noun *grammar* is an adjective modifying *textbook*. Yet *grammar* may be modified by an adjective, as in the phrase "an English grammar textbook," and we can even add an adjective to modify *English* as in "an Old English grammar textbook." In the same way we may say "a newspaper story" or "a Boston newspaper story." In these examples the words *old, English, grammar, Boston,* and *newspaper* are all adjectives; but *English, grammar,* and *newspaper,* being naming words as well, can be fitted with adjectives.

Adjectives answer the question of *which, whose,* or *what kind.* Thus we can add adjectives to adjectives: when *blue* modifies *dress,* we can ask what kind of blue and get *a deep blue dress.* Though it is usually not advisable, we can pile up adjectives in this way to make a phrase: "The sick old merchant's three very beautiful tall blonde daughters." What kind of daughters?—blonde. What kind of blonde daughters?—tall. What kind of tall blonde daughters?— beautiful; and so on, backwards.

Perhaps to avoid stacking adjectives in this way, or possibly because adolescent writers striving for effect depend too heavily upon adjectives, some editors and instructors advise the use of as few adjectives as possible. According to one manual of instruction, "The work of skilled writers shows that verbs and nouns contribute more than adjectives in giving a reader a vivid and real impression." Yet in this very statement, the key words are *skilled, vivid,* and *real*—all adjectives. Mark Twain wrote, "As to the Adjective: when in doubt, strike it out." Literary historians tell how the young Hemingway took his manuscripts to Ezra Pound, who crossed out most of the modifiers. Yet there are seven adjectives in the first two sentences of *A Farewell to Arms.* This denunciation of the adjective can bear examination.

Literary analysts have proved by weary counting that Walter Pater, Henry James, Edith Wharton, and their kind favor the adjective more than do Rudyard Kipling, Jack London, Robert Louis Stevenson, and their kind. The work of Kipling and his ilk presents a sense of swift action; the school of Pater does not. But the present age is an age of action. Ergo, the conclusion is clear: the adjective must go! This, in thoughts of one syllable, seems to be the line of reasoning taken by the statistical analysts of literary style.

It is true that adjectives can be overworked; often the precise choice of a noun or descriptive verb can eliminate the need for modifiers. But does the adjective really have a "subordinate" function? Let us begin innocently enough by asking someone, "Which house is Bob Fawcett's?" The answer is, "It's the house painted white with green shutters, the house just beyond the bank." The sentence is easy to analyze: subject, *it*; verb, *is*; complement, *house, house*. But try saying, "It is house, house." The words do not tell us the information we require. That information, the heart of the answer to our question, inheres in the adjective elements: "painted white with green shutters, just beyond the bank." Indeed, if our informant were in a great hurry, he might gasp out those adjective phrases as his full reply, and we should understand him readily. In literature, the carefully aimed adjective can be highly effective, as in the following description from Joseph Heller's *Catch-22*: "General Dreedle, the wing commander, was a blunt, chunky, barrel-chested man in his early fifties. His nose was squat and red, and he had lumpy white, bunched-up eyelids circling his small gray eyes like haloes of bacon fat." [2]

Take almost any literary passage at random and rewrite it, omitting the modifiers and see what you have left. Try, for instance, taking the adjectives out of Friar Laurence's lines in *Romeo and Juliet*, Act II, scene 3:

> The grey-eyed morn smiles on the frowning night,
> Chequering the eastern clouds with streaks of light;
> And flecked darkness like a drunkard reels
> From forth day's path and Titan's fiery wheels.

You will find that the essence of the lines resides precisely in the arresting adjectives. Or take this stanza from Coleridge's "The Rime of the Ancient Mariner":

> The fair breeze blew, the white foam flew,
> The furrow followed free;
> We were the first that ever burst
> Into that silent sea.

If this were reduced to "The breeze blew, the foam flew, the furrow followed; we were the first that ever burst into the sea," the spell is gone. Keats's "magic casements" cease to be magic when they are just plain casements.

Who would agree to read another two lines—from *Macbeth* this

142

time—as, "Out, out candle; life's but a shadow, a player . . ." Without the adjectives *brief, walking,* and *poor,* not only all poetry but almost all intelligibility vanishes.

It may reasonably be held that the adjective is normally as important a speech element as its governing noun, in that it is the function of the adjective to define or give point and sharpness to what would otherwise be a vague, general term. We may say *books* without any vivid image, but *old books, rare books,* are phrases to conjure with. By itself the word *school* does not convey very much; we want to know if it is a *grade school, art school, music school, graduate school, high school.*

But imprecise speakers and writers often use adjectives that are so vague as to be useless. A great many "utility words"—so-called because they can be used without much critical thought—are weak, anemic adjectives like *neat, swell, great, terrific, interesting,* and *nice.* Imagine the following dialogue between a housewife packing to go overseas and the moving man:

> MOVING MAN: How large is the bed?
> HOUSEWIFE: Oh, it's pretty big, but not too big.
> MOVING MAN: What does the refrigerator weigh?
> HOUSEWIFE: Well, it's kinda heavy.
> MOVING MAN: How many appliances do you have?
> HOUSEWIFE: Several.

When the actual packing is done, the moving man may conclude: "I hate to tell you, lady, but your sea freight is overweight."

Once there was a substitute park naturalist who knew very little about flora and fauna. When asked, "What kind of tree is that?" he would answer, "That's a big tree." To the question "What is that flower?" he would reply, "That's a pretty purple flower." Such descriptions are not very informative. On the other hand, you should be careful not to strain too hard for effect, as in "The fanged white cuspidors of dawn." (In this last example, the modifiers are also metaphors.) A number of readers claim to have taken up arms against James Joyce's "the snot-green sea."

Though the adjective does not deserve an automatic blue-penciling, it is advisable not to pile up too many modifiers, lest your prose develop a paunch: "Be a Much-in-Demand Highly-Paid Invisible Reweaver at Home . . . in Your Spare Time!" There is too much weight in front in "The handsome young frog's rich booming vibrato bass voice charmed the princess." Henry James's description of Harriet Beecher Stowe is more dizzying than dazzling when he wrote of "her extraordinary little, vaguely observant, slightly wool-gathering, letting her eyes wander all over the place, kind of little way." Piling up too many adjectives is a favorite device of journalists, who intend to make their prose compact but actually make it far too ponderous, smothering the noun and blocking the movement of the verb; e.g., "Former President of the Home for Aged Oxcart Drivers' Association Elmo Fink was arrested for drunken driving." Journalists are much too fond of putting a string of titles before a name: "Among the victims was Acting Punxatawny Wildlife Museum Director Homer Hartebeest." The titles are better put as a modifying phrase after the name of the titleholder: "The victims included Homer Hartebeest, Acting Director of the Punxatawny Wildlife Museum." Excessive use of compound adjectives reverses the movement of the sentence and brings the reader up against a blank wall, so that he has to go back and figure out what he has just read, as in, "The catalogue called for a 1:00 P.M. Wednesday afternoon November 27 Thanksgiving holiday commencement." This reads better as, "The catalogue states that the Thanksgiving holiday begins at 1:00 P.M. on Wednesday, November 27." Piling up adjectives separates the object from its verb or the object of a preposition from its preposition or the subject from its verb, as in "Difficulties in study-room scheduling at Erickson Hall exist." This reads better as, "There is difficulty in scheduling the study rooms at Erickson Hall." The massed modifiers are ambiguous in "Fire destroyed the 617 South Succotash Street home of Abraham Enloe early this morning." This implies that Enloe has other homes elsewhere; it should be changed to read ". . . the home of Abraham Enloe at 617 South Succotash Street."

Some modifiers are simply dead wood and should be removed. But sometimes piled-up adjectives can have an impressive cumulative effect. Hamlet denounces his uncle: "Bloody, bawdy villain!/ Remorseless, treacherous, lecherous, kindless villain!" The metaphors are memorable in Shakespeare's "mad mustachio, purple-hued malt worm." What reaction do you have to the New York *Herald Tribune*'s description of *Catch-22* as "A wild, moving, shocking, hilarious, raging, exhilarating, giant roller-coaster of a book?" Is this effective, or is it too much like Hollywood's technique of stacking up superlatives?

Sometimes the correct choice between alternative adjectives is controversial. One is the fast-disappearing distinction between *few*

144

and *little, fewer* and *less.* The precise grammarian uses *little* and *less* with a single unit or substance; *few* and *fewer,* with several units: "They had few rifles and little powder," "Waldo has less hair but fewer cavities than his brother." But one of the more ubiquitous ads promotes toothpaste that results in 37 percent "less cavities." This usage is growing but it is not yet accepted by careful stylists.

Adjectives ending in the suffix *-ish* often have a derogatory sense (*doltish, sluggish, foolish*); they should not be used inappropriately. *Manly* and *womanly* are complimentary in tone whereas *mannish* and *womanish* refer respectively to overly masculine women and effeminate men. *Large* is more positive than *largish,* which has the qualified meaning of "rather large."

A major mistake, already referred to in the discussion of pronouns, is the substitution of the objective third-person pronoun *them* for the demonstrative adjectives *these* and *those.* In cultivated circles this is a particularly strong shibboleth that connotes a lack of education, whether the person who speaks in this way (and many fine people do) is really uneducated or not. So avoid statements like "Them big brown eyes get me" or "Bring them books over here," both of which call for *those.*

Another frequent error is the omission of the terminal *-d* or *-ed* from past participles used as adjectives (*prejudiced, supposed*) or adjectives in similar form (*pigeon-livered*). This is more noticeable in writing than in speech and is in fact due to the slurring of the suffix in imprecise enunciation. Thus people mistakenly write of "a bias person," "a prejudice viewpoint," "an unaccustom procedure," "one-arm driving." All of these require a *-d* or *-ed* ending, as does *size* in, "One stroke of Mennen Speed Stick is so man-size, it protects almost 3 times the area of a narrow roll-on track."

Finally, an irritation to many clergymen is the use of the title *reverend* as a solitary noun: "Reverend, will you speak next Wednesday to the Thursday Club?" Even worse is, "Hey, Rev., how's everything?" The proper forms of address are "The Reverend Mr. Morgan," "The Reverend Jack Morgan," "Father Morgan," or "Mr. Morgan," but not "Reverend Morgan."

When several adjectives in a series all modify the same noun, there should be a comma between them but not between the last adjective and the noun: "There was a tall, thin, stoop-shouldered man at the door." But when the last adjective forms a unit with the noun or the first adjective modifies the second one, then there

145

should be no comma: "the big bad wolf," "a fuzzy purple worm," "the deep blue sea." "Greasy, kid stuff" is wrong; *greasy* doesn't modify *kid,* but *kid stuff*.

If by now you think English adjectives far from easy, Latin and German ones are even more difficult. We are fortunate that the modern English adjective is totally uninflected. By contrast, adjectives in Latin, German, and Old English are required to agree with their nouns in case, number, and gender. Latin adjectives have three different declensions and are inflected in both the singular and plural for five cases and three genders. Here is the breakdown for *bonus* ("good").

Singular

	MASCULINE	FEMININE	NEUTER
NOM.	bonus	bona	bonum
GEN.	bonī	bonae	bonī
DAT.	bonō	bonae	bonō
ACC.	bonum	bonam	bonum
ABL.	bonō	bonā	bonō

Plural

	MASCULINE	FEMININE	NEUTER
NOM.	bonī	bonae	bona
GEN.	bonorum	bonārum	bonorum
DAT.	bonīs	bonīs	bonīs
ACC.	bonōs	bonās	bona
ABL.	bonīs	bonīs	bonīs

Latin comparative and superlative adjectives also have full declensions. German adjectives have a strong and weak declension with three genders and four cases in the singular; all genders have the same four case-endings in the plural. Thus there are thirty-two possibilities, though some of the endings coincide. French adjectives are much simpler, but even they have two genders and a plural form. You can immediately forget all this and be thankful for the admirable simplicity of the uninflected English adjective. This simplicity includes the articles, which are a form of limiting adjective.

In modern English the simplest parts of speech are the definite article (*the*) and the indefinite articles (*a, an*). This was not true of

146

Old English, where articles were fully inflected, taking endings for case, number, and gender to match the noun they modify.

Modern English, praises be, is not bothered with these problems; as Gertrude Stein might have put it: "*The is a the is a the is a the.*" Still, there are some questions of usage connected with the article, and one is the distinction between *a* and *an*. Most people never have to think about this—at least, not in speaking—for it is generally used correctly as a matter of habit; but occasionally, in writing, the wrong article is used. *A* is used before words beginning with a voiced consonant ("*a kangaroo*") or with *eu* or *u* when pronounced *y* ("*a* European education," "*a* euphemism," "*a* university," "*a* unicorn," "*a* unique proposal"). A double consonant would cause a stuttering sound ("an nitwit"), but to have something to get our teeth into and to avoid grunting over two vowels (*a aardvark*), we use *an* before words beginning with a vowel ("an apricot," "an orang-utang") or with a silent *h* ("an heir," "an honor," "an hour"). It is acceptable but archaic to use *an* before *historical, habitual, university,* perhaps because these suggest a Cockney accent ("an 'istorical hepisode"). *An* rather than *a* should be used before initials and figures that begin with a vowel sound ("an RKO movie," "an RCA record," "an $18,000 house").

Repetition of the definite or the indefinite article before each noun in a pair or series places a rhythmic stress on the individual words ("*The Power and the Glory*," "A Stone, a Leaf, a Door"). If you don't want this stress, one article will do for all ("The Army and Navy forever. . .").

A frequent nuisance in student writing is the omission of the initial article from a title; thus one encounters "Frank Norris' the *Octopus*," "Norris' *Octopus*," "In *Grapes of Wrath,* Steinbeck . . . ," "Tennessee Williams' *Streetcar Named Desire.*" On the other hand, there is no article before *Adventures of Huckleberry Finn,* although some publishers mistakenly insert one. If titles of different works overlap, an omitted or inserted article might lead to confusion, as when a student wrote of Faulkner's *Hamlet* (*The Hamlet*). Another student, confused by *The,* thought *The Fountainhead* was a character (like the Batman) as well as the title of Ayn Rand's novel, and wrote: "In *The Fountainhead,* the Fountainhead was an architect who would not compromise his principles. The Fountainhead said . . ." This way lies madness. When the title of a publication is used as a modifier, the article is sometimes dropped; "a *New Yorker* story" or "a *Saturday Evening Post* cartoon" is used to avoid the double article in "a *The New Yorker* story" or "a *The Saturday Evening Post* cartoon."

Claiming that articles have no meaning and so are expendable, newspapers often omit them in order to achieve a telegraphic conciseness ("Senate Investigating Committee expresses belief that main agency of narcotics smuggling is Mafia"). But omitting articles does not really speed reading; it is likelier to make the reader pause and fill in the gaps. If articles were really useless, we doubtless would have gotten rid of them long ago, but *the* particularizes its noun, while *a* and *an* indicate one of a class. When some historical novelists attempt to give an archaic flavor to their prose by leaving out articles, they succeed only in writing stilted sentences like, "Bellegarde clapped hand to hilt, drew sword from scabbard, and pinked opponent in shoulder." Though the omission of articles can be awkward, their excessive or careless use can cause confusion. "Hector Heathcliff, the professor of English at Harvard University" implies that Harvard has only one professor of English. "Rousseau the French primitive painter" is proper because he is well enough known and because the modifier distinguishes him from Rousseau the philosopher. But sometimes *the* bestows a distinction that is unjustified. "Mañana Iguana the painter" may frustrate the reader with the feeling that he should recognize the name, whereas in this case the painter has a well-deserved obscurity.

There are a few special uses for the definite article. The proper form of address for ministers is "The Reverend Mr. Jones" rather than "Reverend Jones." Heads of Scottish and Irish families sometimes take *the* as in Robert the Bruce. And the official name of certain institutions, such as The John Hopkins University (vs. Duke University), requires the use of *the* in the title, sometimes even retaining it when the form is shortened (The Hopkins).

A and *an* are dead wood in such constructions as "kind of a dog," "sort of an impression." Though these forms are used fairly often by competent writers, it is better to use *kind of* and *sort of* without the article, on the principle that unless necessary in dialogue, any useless word is better omitted.

¶ ADVERBS

Whereas the adjective tells *which or what kind of* and describes single words (nouns, pronouns, and adjectives), the adverb modifies verbs, adjectives, other adverbs, and it may accompany both single

148

words and entire phrases and clauses. It answers such questions as *how, when, where, why,* and *in what direction*; but the term *adverb* is misleading, for adverbs are used not only with verbs.

Here are some examples of adverbs. *Carefully* tells how the nitroglycerine is to be carried in "Carry the nitroglycerine carefully." *Very* describes how *carefully* it is to be carried in "Carry the nitroglycerine very carefully." *Finally* answers the question of when Mr. Hyde turned and became Dr. Jekyll in "Mr. Hyde finally turned into Dr. Jekyll." *East* tells in what direction to turn in "Turn east." The adverbs are italicized in the following: "Do *not* make mistakes," "*Always* be careful," "Raccoons live *here now,*" "*Never* mind," "Practice *often,*" "Come *in,*" "Be *off,*" "Sit *down,*" and "We sail *tomorrow.*" And, of course, *how, when, where,* and *why* are themselves adverbs.

Sometimes a phrase or clause functions adverbially. In "At last Mighty Mouse arrived," *at last* answers *when.* So does *when he tried* in "When he tried, he succeeded in becoming a teen-age Frankenstein." In "Take off hell-for-leather," *hell-for-leather* explains *how.* *Because he forgot to watch the fire* explains why in "Because he forgot to watch the fire, Alfred burned the cakes."

Whereas the adjective generally precedes its governing word, the adverb may come almost anywhere in the sentence. Take for example "The monster began to revive" and see where the adverb *slowly* will fit. It may occur in any of four positions: "*Slowly* the monster began to revive," "The monster began to revive *slowly,*" "The monster *slowly* began to revive," and "The monster began *slowly* to revive."

Sometimes a noun functions as an adverb, for example, the italicized words in the following examples: "We went shopping *yesterday,*" "She died last *Wednesday,*" (tells when) "Jennie walked *miles,*" (tells how far) "Hawthorne and Melville talked *hours,*" (tells how long), "The idol weighed *tons*" (tells how much). Compare "The idol weighed tons" with "The explorers weighed the idol." In the first, *tons* is an adverb giving the answer to how much; in the second, *idol* is a direct object telling what was weighed. When a noun serves as an adverb, it can still have an adjective modifier like *twenty* in "Wakefield returned twenty years later," or *last* in "She disappeared last Wednesday." In Southern Appalachian speech, adverbs occasionally double as nouns: "A man has a rather about what he'll drink."

One of the most frequent specimens of nonstandard grammar is

149

the use of an adjective where an adverb is required. Yet it is often difficult to distinguish between the two. Often the same word is an adverb in one sentence and not in another. For instance, *very* is an adverb in "Fight very fiercely" but an adjective in "That's the very ingredient he needs." Conventionally *good* is an adjective and *well* an adverb: "Betsy is a good cook who cooks well." But *well* is also an adjective meaning *healthy*. "Smithers didn't feel *good,* but the doctors insisted that he was *well.*" Naturally this situation results in confusion, with the wrong word being used for an adjective, as in the ad: "A big delicious glass of orange juice (with ice in it) goes good with almost anything, or all by itself." Often, but by no means always, adverbs end in *-ly: surely, repeatedly, softly, hurriedly, commonly, gladly.* But adjectives may also end in *-ly;* we speak of "a timely book," "a kingly bearing," "a manly act," "a fatherly kiss," "a princely present." Some words ending in *-ly* are both adjective and adverb, like *early* and *leisurely.* We can take a *leisurely* drive and view the mountains *leisurely.* To confuse matters further, we have pairs of words, one with and one without *-ly,* in which both are adjectives: a *dead* king, a *deadly* poison; a *kind* queen, a *kindly* dwarf; a *low* branch, a *lowly* peasant; a *live* wire, a *lively* dance; a *sick* basset, a *sickly* invalid; *world* affairs and *worldly* possessions.

Usually when the same base appears with and without *-ly,* the plainer form is the adjective, and the *-ly* one the adverb; *light* vs. *lightly, bright* vs. *brightly, safe* vs. *safely, near* vs. *nearly.* But this is not always the case. *Hard* is an adjective, but the adverbial form is also *hard; hardly* has another meaning. You say, "The trunk closes hard; please slam it," not "The trunk closes hardly." Likewise, *lately,* though an adverb, is not the adverbial equivalent of *late* but instead means *recently.* Scott wrote "The gallant came late," not "The gallant came lately." Similarly, the meaning is different in "Travel light" and "Travel lightly" or "I like to drive cool" and "I like to drive coolly." In informal usage, some adverbs drop an *-ly* that might appear in more formal prose: both *loud* and *loudly, slow* and *slowly, quick* and *quickly, quiet* and *quietly* appear as adverbs, though formal usage prefers the latter of each pair. By overcompensation, some people add an *-ly* where there should be none and so create illegitimate words like *thusly, muchly,* and *firstly;* the only acceptable forms are *thus, much,* and *first.*

Sometimes it is impossible to distinguish adjectives from adverbs. Take, for example, the sentences, "True seeing is seeing charitably" and "Charitable seeing is seeing truly," where the same word *seeing*

150

takes adjective and adverb indiscriminately. Is *seeing* a noun or a verb? Functionally, of course, it is a noun; yet as a gerund, it is the present participle of a verb and takes an adjective. Yet how can a noun be associated with an adverb? Then there is *precisely* in "Precisely what I wanted lay there." Now *precisely* is the adverb form, by contrast to the adjective *precise*; yet *precisely* modifies the clause "what I wanted," which functions as the noun subject of the verb *lay.* Here again, then, we have what seems to be an adverb modifying a noun, in the teeth of every rule of grammar.

Observe the first word in "Comparatively few came." In form it is an adverb; in function, an adjective. Take "They are all equally complete, all equally sentences." Try this on your grammarian. First give him the sentence with the three last words omitted, and ask him what *equally* is, and what it modifies. He will reply that *equally* is an adverb modifying the adjective *complete.* Now spring the second *equally* on him and ask him what it is if not an adverb and what it modifies if not the noun *sentences.*

Nowadays the adverb seems to be losing its tail; *-ly* forms are dropped and the adjective form doubles with an adverbial function in much current usage. Telephone companies advertise, "Dial direct with us." (Contrast *dial directly* with *direct dialing.*) Stretchweave diapers "pin on easier, smoother, snugger." An ad for want ads quotes a student as saying, "I am very happy that I sold the banjo so quick." Aeroxon Fly Ribbons advertise "Catch flies safe & sanitary," making it appear that *safe & sanitary* are adjectives modifying *flies,* though of course they are used adverbially to modify *catch.* (The traditional adverbial forms are *safely* and *sanitarily,* or you could say "in a safe & sanitary way.") If you use Sea & Ski lotion, "You sure will tan, sure won't burn." Elvis Presley's first movie was *Love Me Tender,* and the title song goes on to urge that the lover "love me true." Sidney Bechet wrote an autobiography called *Treat It Gentle.* You are urged to "Shop early . . . shop easy for your personalized Hallmark Christmas cards." If you buy Christmas presents, get a mechanical dog: "Gaylord looks kind of crazy, moves kind of lazy." And the *Vogue Pattern Book* explains, "Frogs are made easiest if you work on a flat surface and pin loops." [3] In these examples, conservative usage would employ the adverbial forms: *directly, more easily, more smoothly, more snugly, quickly, safely, sanitarily, surely, tenderly, truly, gently, easily, lazily,* and *most easily.*

Thus many people say "awful slow," "Homer is hurt bad," "real good" when an adverb (*awfully, badly, very*) is required. At the same time, they use adverbs when adjectives are needed; one questionnaire found that three fifths of the students interviewed said "I feel well" rather than "I feel good," and two fifths said "I feel badly." This brings us back again to the question of predicate adjectives. Besides *to be* there are other linking verbs (*feel, become, act, seem, taste, grow, look, sound, turn, fall,* and others) that, in addition to having regular meanings of their own, can connect a modifier to its subject. In such cases, the modifiers are predicate adjectives: "He fell *silent*," "The beanstalk grew *tall*," "Prufrock became *old*," "She died *young*," "Natasha acted *odd*," "Boris seemed *uneasy*," "The slumgullion tastes *good*," "Fosdick looked *sick*," "The cider turned *sour*." Many people mistakenly use an adverb instead of the predicate adjective. But there is a difference between "Natasha acted odd" and "Elvis acted oddly." In the first, *odd* describes Natasha; in the second, *oddly* describes Elvis's acting. Thus it is nonstandard to say "Aunt Bossy is feeling poorly" (which seems to describe her ability to feel rather than the state of her health), "I hope your folks are all gaily," or "He acts toughly."

Sometimes it is a borderline case whether a word should be an adverb or a predicate adjective. In "Take it easy," does *easy* serve as an adverb modifying *take* (the usual adverb form is *easily*), or is it an adjective modifying *you* understood? In "Sin rises strong," does *strong* modify *rises* (should it therefore be *strongly*) or *sin?* In "He dresses *shabby*," should *shabby* be *shabbily* to modify *dresses*, or does it modify *he*? When a Southern restaurant advertised "Eat segregated in comfort," *segregated* does not modify *eat* but *you all* understood.

A great many advertisements use this sort of borderline adjective. We are urged to "Live modern—smoke an L&M," to "Shop smart," to buy Smirnoff Vodka and "Think tall." Here *modern, smart,* and *tall* could conceivably modify *you* understood, rather than the respective verbs. But what do you make of the grammar in "Go *Rambler*," "They eat *cute* in California," "Think *big*, raise elephants," "Think *pink*," "Think *crisp* with round Kix," "Go *jet-smooth* in a '63 Chevrolet," or "Think *young*"? Clearly the italicized words are adverbs, rather than objects of verbs, yet they are very oblique adverbs. Yet "Go Ramblerly," "Think pinkly," "Think crisply," "Go jet-smoothly" would never do. Perhaps we have here a new elliptical dimension.

Other ads combine the adjective used adverbially with a confusion between transitive and intransitive verbs. Thus we get the curious dimension of "Nestlé's Quik tastes best and fixes easiest," "The flavor [of Calvert Extra] is rich and full—yet it swallows easy," "Plastic rolling pin rolls light and easy . . . wipes clean," "Shampoo pours rich," "White Owl cigars taste so good, smoke so mild," and "The instruments looked strange, but they listened good." Here we approach a sort of dehumanization in which things fix, swallow, wipe, pour, smoke, and listen to themselves while devouring the adverb in the process.

If adverbial forms are widely neglected today, the language may not be degenerating so much as regressing to an earlier phase. In the sixteenth and seventeenth centuries, Englishmen often preferred the adjective form for adverbial function. This practice is a hallmark of the dialogue in Virgil Scott's historical novel *I, John Mordaunt*. Hamlet speaks of theatrical performances "come tardy off" and describes himself as "indifferent honest." In *Richard III*, Lord Hastings speaks of "the crown so foul misplaced." We would say *tardily, indifferently,* and *foully* but Shakespeare often dropped the *-ly*, "and sure he is an honorable man," as Anthony said of Brutus. *Sure* was used regularly instead of *surely* in Elizabethan English. In the early seventeenth century, *scarce* was common instead of *scarcely* as an adverb; William Bradford wrote that in Plymouth, "of 100 and odd persons, scarce 50 remained. An English folksong over four hundred years old has a farmer blow his horn "both loud and shrill." And throughout English and American literature, we find adjective forms used adverbially. In the following examples, the italics are mine.

> Through care of my parents I was taught to read *near* as soon as I was capable of it. . . .
> —JOHN WOOLMAN

> He that drinks fast, pays *slow*.
> —BENJAMIN FRANKLIN

> If one can think at all, in serious difficulties, one thinks *quick*.
> —WILKIE COLLINS, *The Woman in White*

> It is not necessary that a man should earn his living by the sweat of his brow, unless he sweats *easier* than I do.
> —HENRY DAVID THOREAU, *Walden*

> Every atom belonging to me as *good* belongs to you.
> —WALT WHITMAN

> . . . the Day/Turned and departed *silent*.
> —RALPH WALDO EMERSON

A bird with an angelic gift
Was singing in it *sweet* and *swift*.—ROBERT FROST

Do not go *gentle* into that good night.—DYLAN THOMAS

In conversation with Lillian Ross, Hemingway usually employed adjective forms adverbially: he shoots good, eats good, writes wonderful, moves pure, hits solid. On the other hand, he said, ". . . in war they talk profane, although I always try to talk gently." [4] Norman Mailer wrote that "James Jones can write as good as anyone who writes a book review." [5] Another reviewer claimed that David Stacton "writes quick and dry and funny. . . ." [6] And "A good way to end a story is, 'The prince and the princess lived happy ever after and the mice lived happy ever after too.' " [7]

Certainly it is too fastidious to insist that *quickly* rather than *fast* or *quick* must always be the adverb. "Get rich quick" has become a cliché. Many adverbs can appear either with or without -*ly*. *Loud, slow, quick* are all right after verbs but not before them. We can say "Drive slow," "Think quick," "He plays rough," "Talk louder," but not "Loud she sings in church," "Slow he eats dinner," or "Quick he slammed the door." We can say "He talks slow," but we must say "He talks slowly when he is thinking carefully." Sometimes sound requires that -*ly* not be added, especially if it will make a word end in -*lily*. In *Julius Caesar,* Brutus says, "How ill that taper burns." The line becomes ludicrous as "How illy that taper burns." So does "View the mountains leisurelily," "Juliet dances lovelily," "Step livelily," and so forth.

Despite Madison Avenue and other sources, it is not yet advisable to use adjectives indiscriminately as adverbs. There is still a difference between "Some kids can't speak English plainly" and "Some kids can't speak plain English." Two misused utility words are the adjectives *powerful* and *plenty* employed as adverbs in such constructions as "powerful lazy and powerful slow," "If you're hungry for flavor, Tareyton's got plenty—and it's plenty good," and "Marlboro cigarettes are plenty rich, yet plenty mild." Here the modifiers filter out the linguistic flavor. Likewise, you must be careful not to use adverbs indiscriminately: certainly the choice is askew in "Bulldozers *rapinely* crush tiny glades."

The adverb can be overworked until it becomes a mannerism. Henry James employed them somewhat noticeably in his late prose. For example, in "The Jolly Corner" we find, "But, quite beautifully, she had too much tact to dot so monstrous an *i,* and it

154

was precisely an illustration of the way she didn't rattle"; and " 'You came to yourself,' she beautifully smiled." As James himself put it of one of his characters, "He importantly qualified." In James, the adverbs are usually not too obtrusive, but they become markedly so in the Tom Swift books popular at the turn of the century. Whenever Tom uttered some dramatic (or even dull) statement, the author modified it adverbially. In 1963, this inspired a book and a game, "Tom Swifties," in which the idea is to make the adverb a pun on the main idea. For example, " 'I'm not so sure about the recipe for the spice cake,' she said gingerly," or " 'I barely avoided a collision,' said Tom recklessly." Joseph Heller's *Catch-22* is full of Tom Swift-type adverbs that contribute to the book's sardonic humor:

> "Did the dead man in my tent have a share?" Yossarian demanded caustically.
> "Of course he did," Milo assured him lavishly.[8]
>
> "I did try," admitted Milo gloomily. . . .
> "It's the end," Milo agreed despondently. . . .
> "Why don't you sell your cotton to the government?" Yossarian suggested casually. . . .
> Milo vetoed the idea brusquely. "It's a matter of principle," he explained firmly.[9]

Here the adverbs are part of the satire, but ordinarily it is advisable to use them with restraint.

In an essay, "Theory and Practice of Editing *New Yorker* Articles," Wolcott Gibbs wrote: "Writers always use too damn many adverbs. On one page recently I found eleven modifying the verb 'said.' 'He said morosely, violently, eloquently, so on.' Editorial theory should probably be that a writer who can't make his context indicate the way his character is talking ought to be in another line of work." [10]

¶ COMPARATIVES AND SUPERLATIVES

In their ordinary form, adjectives and adverbs are in the positive degree. The comparative degree indicates a contrast between two elements: the superlative degree, among three or more elements. To form these degrees, words of one or two syllables usually inflect by adding the suffixes *-er* for the comparative and *-est* for the superlative. Longer words usually keep the positive form, preceded by *more* for the comparative and *most* for the superlative. If the comparison is a diminished one, the positive form is used preceded by *less* for the comparative and *least* for the superlative. The use of the positive preceded by the modifiers (or function words) is sometimes called periphrastic comparison. A few words change their stem for the comparative and superlative degree: *good, better, best*; *bad, worse, worst*; *many, more, most*; and *little, less, least*.

Throughout the history of the language, people have used the superlative to give increased emphasis when the comparison is limited to two members; even such a careful stylist as Dr. Johnson did so. But conservative contemporary usage disapproves and calls for a careful discrimination. Thus you would write, "Who was stronger, King Kong or Godzilla?" and "Who is the stupidest of the Three Stooges?" Venus is *closer* to the sun than the earth is, but Mercury is the *closest* planet of all.

	POSITIVE	COMPARATIVE	SUPERLATIVE
ADJECTIVE	ugly	uglier	ugliest
	green	greener	greenest
	lovely	lovelier	loveliest
	lonely	lonelier	loneliest
	squeamish	more squeamish	most squeamish
	comfortable	more comfortable	most comfortable
ADVERB	late	later	latest
	hard	harder	hardest

If both the adjective and adverb end in *-ly,* the comparative and superlative can be formed by adding a suffix (*early, earlier, earliest*); but if the adverb already ends in *-ly,* it cannot add another suffix and so must be preceded by *more, most, less,* or *least*. No one ever uses *quicklier, wildliest, hopefulliest*. In other cases, the question of whether the alteration is made by adding a suffix or an auxiliary modifier does not depend absolutely on the number of syllables, but is partly a matter of idiom. Theoretically, a two-syllable word could use either method, but you'd never use *squeamisher* or *squalidest*. Most three-syllable words use periphrastic comparison; but there are exceptions; you'd never use *glamorouser* or *beautifulest,* but you could use *slipperiest*. Both *most unlikely* and *unlikeliest* are acceptable. The inflected form gives slightly more stress to the root and the quality it indicates (dear′ est), and the periphrastic *more* or *most* gives more emphasis to the degree. Thus, while one-syllable words usually inflect, we use *most* in speaking of "everything we hold most dear." Hamlet says, "This is most brave," " 'tis most sweet," and speaks of his father's "most dear life," where ordinarily the form would be *bravest, sweetest,* and *dearest.*

Often the comparative form is used without the second term of the comparison ever appearing; we hope for *better things,* speak of *lesser evils* and *baser metal,* support *higher education.* The periphastic superlative also is often used emphatically, with *most* being used for intensity without any specific comparison being indicated: "You are *most generous,*" "Orson is *most intelligent,*" "Caesar was *most ambitious*"; Hamlet frequently uses "most vile" in this way.

Theoretically, words that represent an absolute cannot be compared. Such words as *perfect, round, alive, dead, final, straight, pure, excellent, impossible, unique, black, white, complete* logically have no further degree of meaning. Yet we often modify them ("By gad, it's absolutely perfect"), and in practice they are often compared. There are, in fact, degrees of black and white; if these were absolutes, we wouldn't need such metaphorical clichés as "jet black," "black as pitch," "black as the ace of spades," "white as snow." Thus Shakespeare has Othello say of Desdemona that he "would not mar that whiter skin of hers than snow/And smooth as monumental alabaster." Shakespeare also used "most excellent." Though *pure* should be 100 percent, Thomas Gray wrote, "Full many a gem of purest ray serene,/The dark unfathomed caves of ocean bear. . . ." And our own Constitution begins with the intent "to form a more perfect Union." Often we admit a degree of comparison without actually using the comparative or superlative form of an absolute word itself; we speak of something as "more nearly perfect," "most nearly impossible," and so on. When used metaphorically, absolutes are often less than absolute and can be compared: "You look even deader than I do." *Unique* is often used informally to mean *rare* or *unusual,* rather than *one and only,* yet a critic for *Newsweek* called Arthur Miller's description of Marilyn Monroe as "most unique" a "barbarous locution." But there is, nevertheless, plenty of precedent, and Miller is certainly more a master of language than members of the *Newsweek* staff.

Modern grammatical convention forbids the use of both modifier and suffix to make a double comparative or superlative; e.g. "*The Attack of the 50-Foot Woman* is the most funniest movie I've ever seen." Shakespeare, on the other hand, often used a double

157

comparative or superlative: Mark Anthony calls the wound Brutus gave Caesar "the most unkindest cut of all"; in *Richard II,* John of Gaunt speaks of "the envy of less happier lands"; in *Othello,* Cassio says, "The worser that you give me the addition"; and Othello says, "she comes more nearer earth than she was wont . . ." These are clear and emphatic, and there is no reason why the double degree could not make a comeback, but at present such usage is considered nonstandard. For a century, people have been amused by the grammar in Nathan Bedford Forrest's statement of getting there "firstest with the mostest men."

¶ PSYCHOSEMANTICS

Sometimes vague, inappropriate, and misleading modifiers appear in sentences where they confuse or even reverse accurate meaning. *Semantics* is the study of the meaning of words; and some words are used in ways that are muddled, befuddled, psychotic, or downright sinister. Beginning with a harmless example, we encounter, "It was a literal picture-postcard of a day, and we lived every minute of it." *Literal* and *literally* are often used when the speaker really means *figurative* or *metaphorically*; but the careless speaker strives so hard for emphasis that he reverses the meaning and sometimes becomes ludicrous, as in "I literally blew my top." Then there is "Could we have about four folders, please?" Why *about*? Does the speaker really want three or five folders? If he wants exactly four, he should say so with no *abouts*; and if he is really trying to finagle half a dozen, he should ask for six. It is advisable to minimize and, whenever possible, eliminate timid qualifiers like *rather, somewhat, a bit,* and *little*. "Rather tasty," "somewhat attractive" are too uncommitted. The teacher who is grading a poor theme may pull his punches by noting, "This is a bit vague," or "This is rather routine." Likewise, intensive adverbs intended to serve as strengtheners,—such as *so, such,* and *very*—often weaken the force of sentences in which they appear. Consider, for example, "Sara sank into the nearest chair; she had had such a hard day, and she was so tired"; omit *such* and *so,* and you will find a distinct improvement. Schoolgirl style is sprinkled with such gushy emphasis that it only makes the prose soggy. In "Beneath her snow-white veil, the bride looked almost virginal," the intended effect of awe is ironically undercut by the qualifying adverb. And in "Scott said the Russian and probably American intelligence agencies undoubtedly knew

158

where the Red Chinese would produce nuclear weapons," the adverbs (*probably* and *undoubtedly*) contradict and cancel each other.

Then there are modifiers that mislead by not being what they seem. Merchandisers advertise, "Send 25 cents and a box top for your *free* thingamabob." Radio stations announce, "After this commercial we resume our program of *uninterrupted music.*" Many motion-picture theaters advertising "art" films do not show genuine art films by such directors as Ingmar Bergman, Federico Fellini, Sergei Eisenstein, Satyajit Ray, Akira Kurosawa, Stanley Kubrick, and Tony Richardson, but specialize in cheap striptease and nudist pictures. When a motion picture or television program lists someone as "guest" star, the matter is not one of hospitality but of calculated business transaction, whereby someone else gets top billing but the "guest" retains status by being a guest instead of a supporting or bit player. As for TV "immortals," they are lucky to last three seasons. How accurate is the word *average* in the sentence, "The average American sees 10,000 TV commercials a year?" To avoid making loose and faulty generalizations, you should omit words like *average, typical, all, every, always, most, never,* and *none* unless you possess reliable statistics, for all too often the sweeping *always* or *never* turn out to have a good many exceptions.

Voluntary is of questionable accuracy when you read in the newspaper, "Local action group wants to require voluntary school prayer" or "Stalin sent agents to capture a scientist and bring him back in a voluntary-compulsory manner." *Democratic* is certainly inaccurate when the Communist powers call themselves "democratic." In fact, practically all political adjectives—e.g., *liberal, conservative, realistic, austere, forward-looking, constructive, economical*—should be scrutinized, in the context in which they appear, for accuracy. Even *patriotic* becomes debatable in meaning when extremist groups calling themselves "patriotic" or "superpatriotic" accuse the Chief Justice and President of the United States of treason and indulge in abusive and seditious methods to brand as unpatriotic anyone who favors fluoridation, civil rights, academic freedom, the United Nations, public school integration, or social security. Should such slander be dignified by the word *patriotic*?

Often we use negative adjectives and adverbs in a favorable sense. "She's a mean cook" and "She slings the nastiest ankle in the dance hall" are meant to be admiring. People speak of being "dreadfully happy," "terribly fond of someone," and use words like *terribly, insanely, frightfully, horribly* as adverbs with *beautiful, desirable,* and

159

being in love. James Thurber found such semantics sinister in the modern age of anxiety and stated, "I think we must learn to brighten the human idiom, as well as make it communicable."

Both adjectives and adverbs can contribute to jargon. Pseudo-sophisticated ads recommend items that are *verve-y, un-huge, un-skintight,* or *loose-ish.* Observe in the "Negatives" chapter how the Newspeak of George Orwell's *1984* totalitarian society eliminates contrasting adjectives and different shades among near-synonyms by using, for example, *ungood, plusgood,* and *doubleplusgood* to replace *bad, better, excellent, splendid,* and other words that require exact critical judgment. To make adjectives in Newspeak, one adds the suffix *-ful* to nouns or verbs; and to make adverbs, one adds *-wise.* Thus *angry* would be *angerful,* and *angrily* would be *anger-wise.* Without any governmental pressure, we already seem to be moving somewhat in that direction. In some modern jargon, *proud* becomes *prideful, healthy* becomes *healthful,* and *fierce* adds a dead-wood suffix to become *fierceful.* The suffix *-wise* is far more prominent and has even become a joke on some occasions. Certainly the speaker who says, "Beethovenwise, you'll hear the Emperor Concerto," has a gray-flannel-suit mind. Shakespeare's "a muddy knave" would sound like a denizen of Madison Avenue if he were described as "a knave mudwise." What would happen to the poetry if the wise guys were to turn Macbeth's meditation into:

> Tomorrow creeps tomorrowwise and tomorrowwise
>   pettypacewise from day to day
> To the last syllable recorded timewise;
> And all our yesterdays have lighted fools
> Dustydeathwise. Out, out brief candle;
> Life's but a shadow walkingwise; a poor player
> That struts and frets hourwise, stagewise,
> And then is heard no more; it is a tale told
> Idiotwise, soundwise, furywise,
> Nonsignifyingwise.

'Tis devoutly not to be wished, consummationwise.

Exercise 12: In the following passages, underline the adjectives with a single line and the adverbs with a double line.

1. A brownish colored Java python, with a row of large, irregularly shaped black blotches down the back, is approximately ten feet long and measures up to five inches in diameter.

160

2. "The snow-white Northern Gannets, *Morus bassanus,* are strong, goose-sized sea birds with heavy, streamlined bodies."

—Back cover of *Zoonooz,* May, 1964.

3. "On the first day of Christmas my true love sent to me
A partridge in a pear tree."

4. "Inebriate of air am I
And debauchee of dew,
Reeling through endless summer days
From inns of molten blue."

5. The barred owl has a more emphatic hoot than that of the great horned owl, but his eight accented hoots are less deep.

6. "The morn in russet mantle clad
Walks o'er the dew of yon high eastward hill."

7. The ear tufts of the horned owl are larger and more spread apart than those of the long-eared owl.

8. Clad in pajamas, the deformed monster lumbered clumsily out of the smashed laboratory, carrying the doctor's daughter.

9. "The ram was fat behind, sir,
The ram was fat before.
He measured ten yards round, sir,
I think it was no more."

10. Some woodpeckers have white bars on their back or white rumps, but the hairy woodpecker is white backed.

11. "Last night you slept on a goose-feather bed,
With the sheet turned down so bravely O!
Tonight you'll sleep in a cold, open field,
Along with the wraggle-taggle Gypsies O!"

12. The olive-sided flycatcher appears to have a dark jacket unbuttoned down the front.

13. If you will come along with me
Under yonder flowering tree
I might catch you a small bird or two.

14. "Oh bring on your rubber-tired hearses,
Bring on your rubber-tired hacks.
They're taking Johnny to the buryin' ground
And they won't bring a bit of him back."

15. Blank verse is unrhymed iambic pentameter.

Exercise 13: Correct any faulty adjectives or adverbs in the following:

1. All us cats is high-strung, but I'm high-strungder than most.
2. Hegel was far-yonderer than Kant on some points.
3. A milch goat gives more richer milk than a mountain cow.
4. The Cherokees used seven different kind of woods to make ceremonial fires.

161

5. The Kuikuru are not offended if you refuse their food as long as you do it tactful.
6. General Forrest came instanter than General McClellan.
7. If the bear den is not uninhabited, we must run quick.
8. The one advantage of a pitch pipe over a piano is that it fits into your guitar case easier.
9. In southern Ohio, "You lackum wrapper" and "You like them riper" sound similarly.
10. The horse is afeard to jump across the chasm.
11. If the wind gets any worser, this cabin will blow off the mountain.
12. You'll be sorrow if you miss Dogpatch.
13. The hurrier I go, the behinder I get.
14. Bib-overalls are great for leisure living.
15. The pioneers had little rations left when they were finally rescued.
16. I hate them mice to pieces.
17. We were suppose to pick up our tickets before 8:00 P.M.
18. Henry VIII was a very mannish monarch.
19. We had 57 percent less mosquito bites after spraying with "Phew!"
20. The harpsichord was made from a eighty-five-year-old cherry tree.
21. Will you please put them pots in the sink?
22. The campers were unaccustom to dealing with an elephant in a state of must.
23. Clancy is the goodest left fielder since Casey was at the bat.
24. Rainy days are no time to have a active child around the house.
25. Bruno Bumpergarde, the physics professor at M.I.T., was mugged on an holiday to New York.

Exercise 14: Replace any adjectives with conventional adverb forms when the adverb is required in the following:

1. Cowboys weren't near as glamorous on the job as many people think.
2. The bears live peaceable if not provoked.
3. W. C. Fields was a juggler previous.
4. Zack can use a whip so accurate that he can pick flies off a mule's back.
5. The crocodile came out of the water prompt and hurried towards the cook beating the dinner gong.
6. I hate to see you give up so easy when you are almost finished.
7. The door shut very soft and quietly.
8. The huckleberries aren't doing so good this year.
9. The potato salad was made different tonight.
10. You can live cheaper in a warmer climate except for insect repellent.
11. The Hollywood system does not allow artists enough freedom in which to direct uninhibited.
12. I'm saving Confederate money in case the war's refought and comes out different.

162

13. Iced tea goes good with pizzas.
14. The bear looked suspicious at the artichoke.
15. Snakes have to be handled very careful.
16. If you tune your guitar too high, you may break a string.
17. You didn't divide up the gooseberry fool fair.
18. Play the snaredrums gentle or you'll wake up the poodles.
19. He's handy as a three-legged stool.
20. A sheik walks different from ordinary people.
21. The retreat was quick becoming a rout.
22. The old Moulmein pagoda looks lazy at the sea.
23. You have to quick shut the door to keep out the bugs.
24. Cades Cove eroded very gradual whereas some Western canyons show more spectacular erosion.
25. Auda ate slow without his false teeth.

Exercise 15: Underline the proper form of the comparative and super-lative modifiers.

1. Going down the Colorado River by boat was the (excitingest, most exciting) vacation I've ever had.
2. Which Invisible Man was the (invisiblest, invisibler, most invisible, more invisible) —Claude Rains, Vincent Price, or Jon Hall?
3. Which version of *The Prisoner of Zenda* did you like (better, best) — the Ronald Colman or the Stewart Granger one?
4. Clark Gable's *Mogambo* was a remake of *Red Dust* but was (most successful, more successful, successfuller).
5. The Clark Gable-Charles Laughton version of *Mutiny on the Bounty* was (more, most) dramatically effective, but the Marlon Brando version was the (more, most) colorful.
6. Which was the (funnier, funniest, more funny, most funny) Marx Brothers movie—*Duck Soup, Animal Crackers,* or *A Night at the Opera?*
7. My uncle preferred Hardy to Laurel, but my father thinks Laurel is (more, most) talented.
8. Of the actors who portrayed Napoleon in the movies, Charles Boyer was the (more, most) sympathetic, Marlon Brando was the (more, most) dynamic, and Herbert Lom was the (sinisterer, sinisterest, more sinister, most sinister).
9. In *Duel in the Sun,* Gregory Peck was supposed to gun down Charles Bickford; but Bickford had acted in so many Westerns that he was (quicker, quickest) and kept beating Peck to the draw.
10. This is the (fast-risingest, fastest rising) dough I've ever seen.

11 √ Ambiguous Modifiers

E. M. Forster, discussing motion pictures, wrote in *Abinger Harvest*, "American women shoot the hippopotamus with eyebrows made of platinum." Reading the book, James Thurber was brought up short at that point. "I have given that remarkable sentence a great deal of study," he commented, "but I still do not know whether Mr. Forster means that American women have platinum eyebrows or that the hippopotamus has platinum eyebrows or that American women shoot platinum eyebrows into the hippopotamus." [1]

Probably the most amusing grammatical errors—many downright ridiculous—occur because of ambiguous modifiers. There are two main causes for such ambiguity: dangling modifiers and misplaced ones. In "That bust looks like Beethoven with my glasses off," the modifier is dangling; "with my glasses off" should be describing the speaker, but seems instead to be describing Beethoven. Modifiers dangle when there is no word in the sentence for them to modify; when this occurs some part of the sentence must be rewritten to supply the missing noun or pronoun. Nothing needs to be added for most misplaced modifiers; they simply have to be moved next to whatever they modify. Occasionally a modifier can be both dangling and misplaced. "Did you ever eat chicken with false teeth?" Tasty, wasn't it? But "Did you ever, with false teeth, eat chicken?" is clumsy; the modifier has malocclusion. The solution seems to be, "Did you ever eat chicken when you were wearing false teeth?"

There are several ways for modifiers to dangle. In "He returned from the war with one leg, which he had lost," the modifier not only dangles but goes with the amputated leg, not the one that came home. A more common sort of error is, "Now ninety-two years old, his marriage has remained a happy one." This, obviously, is not the golden-wedding anniversary but a petrified one. Obviously it is the husband and not the marriage that is ninety-two

164

years old. In the sentence, "The first Bourbon king of France, his mistresses were many," how can the feminine plural *mistresses* be modifying the Bourbon king of France? "In his underwear, the tent was suddenly cold." Any self-respecting tent should be not only cold but downright embarrassed to be seen wearing only his underwear. "As a career wife, occasionally the apartment isn't immaculate." Maybe the apartment should get a divorce and marry the tent in the preceding sentence. "Before coming to Hollywood, Hector Troy's real name was Woffington Van Pelt III." But it was Troy, not his name, that came to Hollywood. In these examples, the modifier is an opening phrase followed by a shift of attention from what should have been the subject to the object, with the result that the original subject is omitted altogether and the object becomes the new subject. The solution is to make the thing modified the subject of the main clause.

> Now ninety-two years old, he has continued to have a happy marriage.
>
> The first Bourbon king of France had many mistresses.
>
> In his underwear, he found the tent suddenly cold.
>
> As a career wife, Phyllis occasionally fails to keep the apartment immaculate.
>
> Before coming to Hollywood, Hector Troy was known only by his real name of Woffington Van Pelt III.

On the other hand, the attention shifts from object to subject when Huckleberry Hound says, "As my prisoner, I have to see that you're comfortable." This is saner if it is changed to read, "Since you are my prisoner, I have to see that you're comfortable."

Many dangling modifiers are participial phrases that cause confusion by seeming to modify the subject of the clause that follows. "Dead in the moment of victory, few would not mourn for Wolfe." But it was Wolfe, not *few,* who was dead. In an even grimmer example, we find Anthony Nutting writing, "Being of only a very light weight, the boy's death-struggles were unusually prolonged." [2] But it was the boy himself, not his death struggles, that was light of weight. Mark Raskovitch wrote, "Being the embassy of Her Britannic Majesty, Queen Elizabeth II, there was no fear that proceedings would become boisterous." [3] Here we have an entire embassy dangling. "In turning the wheel, the truck went out of control and crashed into the fence." So did this sentence, for trucks are

165

unable to turn their own wheels. Neither do police arrest themselves, though the campus police saw fit to report, "When apprehended in their apartment, we found that the drapes had been cut with a razor blade so that they would fit the windows." As before, the remedy in each of these instances is to turn the phrase into a subordinate clause: "Because he was only a very light weight . . . ," "Since it was the embassy . . . ," "When he was turning the wheel . . . ," "When we apprehended them . . . ." The first example is trickier because of the word order. It can be clarified as "Few would not mourn for Wolfe dead in the moment of victory," but the drama is lost. A better solution would be, "Dead in the moment of victory, Wolfe would be mourned by many."

Many modifiers dangle because the verb is put in the passive voice, and the original subject, which would have been modified is therefore omitted. "With a family of five children, floor lamps are constantly being knocked over." A pity; Mama and Papa lamps should be treated with more respect. A manual for a foreign car advises, "When refilling the cooling system, the heating system should be bled by adopting the following procedure." Both present participles dangle here; certainly the heating system does not refill the cooling system. "While speaking of the sheriff, the deputy must not be overlooked." The remedy is to put the sentences in the active voice, restoring the original subject:

Since the Gooches have a family of five children, they are constantly knocking over floor lamps.

When refilling the cooling system, you should bleed the heating system by adopting the following procedure.

While speaking of the sheriff, you must not overlook the deputy.

Yet even professionals sometimes stumble into the pitfall of the passive. Irving Stone wrote, "After passing six years in the district school his first pair of long trousers was given to him . . . ." [4] Did Darrow's pants spend six years in school before they were given to him? Stewart Holbrook wrote, "Acting through Donald Smith, one of the Bay Company's big men, and George Steven, head of the Bank of Montreal, six million dollars was raised." [5] But no amount of money, not even in millions, can act through anybody. Norman Mailer wrote, "This way, failing to conquer Cuba, the road was left open for Khrushchev to commit a blunder as large as Kennedy's . . . ." [6] According to one newspaper, "The minister said his friendship with a Negro was 'treated as a subversive plot to

166

integrate the college' by members of the administration." Certainly we can't have administrators integrated with faculty. Again, the active voice clarifies the grammar, even if it doesn't enlighten the administration:

After passing six years in the district school, Darrow received . . .

Acting through . . . Bank of Montreal, they raised six million dollars.

This way, failing to conquer Cuba, we left the road open . . .

The minister said members of the administration treated his friendship with a Negro as a subversive plot to integrate the college.

In signs and advertisements, ellipsis often makes modifiers dangle, as in "Stop ahead when flashing" or "Not responsible if left over 60 days." "Amazing new easy way puts on pounds and inches of firm, solid flesh without overeating." It's gratifying that it is the way, rather than yourself, that puts on the flesh; apparently it also avoids overeating, whereas you might work up an appetite by watching it.

Sometimes, there are dangling infinitives, as in the following examples: "Life goes too fast to waste it," "To inspect the battery cells, a naked flame should never be used," "The pioneer is dressed in buckskins because civilization is too far away to get other clothing." Usually you can easily correct these by inserting a subject (in the objective case) for the infinitive: "too fast for us to waste it," "too far away for him to get other clothing." If there is a verb in the passive voice, make it active: "To inspect the battery cells, you should never use a naked flame."

Finally, a modifier may not dangle as much as be badly aimed: "As a result of the preceding paragraph, the hunter missed the duck." Experienced hunters should know better than to have paragraphs cluttering their line of fire.

"Did you ever drive a car with tired blood?" "Look at that fellow holding a submarine sandwich with a green sweater." The church bulletin announces, "Sermon: The Importance of Babies delivered by the Rev. Waldo Ralph Dimmesdale." These sentences are ridiculous because of misplaced modifiers. Modifiers naturally tend to modify the possibility nearest to them. Ordinarily correction is simple; merely move the modifier next to the word or phrase it modifies: "that fellow with a green sweater," "Sermon delivered by the Rev. Waldo Ralph Dimmesdale: The Importance of Babies." "Did you ever, with tired blood, drive a car?" is clumsy and requires rewriting: "Did you ever drive a car when you had tired blood?" If you did, you should see your doctor and learn what is wrong, since "tired blood" is not medically accurate. If your car doesn't have tired blood, did you ever hit a jack-rabbit doing eighty? If the rabbit was doing eighty, how fast were you driving? Here again a subordinate clause is needed: "when you were doing eighty."

Some misplaced modifiers, like "A man in a brown suit named Jones came into the room," are merely amusing. Others, less obvious, may twist the meaning, sometimes reversing what the writer intended to say. Thus a letter to the editors of the *Lansing State Journal* complained, "Already the government is in the electric power business with both feet, competing with investor-owned electric utilities with unlimited government money." If investor-owned utilities have unlimited government money, we'd better have an investigation. According to *Life,* "Project water is expected to increase greatly the alfalfa crop of Colorado, which already has about a million acres of alfalfa in the soil bank that no one is allowed to cut." [7] What can't be cut—the acres, the alfalfa, or the soil bank? Returning to the *Lansing State Journal,* we find an editorial stating, "The present harmonious tune of 'We're All for Lyndon' may strike some discordant notes, with the peaceful and illogical union under his banner of Northern big-city liberals and Southern conservatives falling apart at the seams." [8] The modifier was meant to go with *union,* but some Southern conservatives may indeed be falling apart at the seams. There is a patent contradiction in "Deists conceived of God as being good and not an angry God who had created things for delight." A journalism student wrote, "The death of Elijah P. Lovejoy at 35 by a mob, November 7, 1837, in defense of his fourth printing press presents today's newspapermen with a challenge to remain free." But the antiabolitionist mob did not murder Lovejoy in order to defend his press. After the defeat of the Confederacy, Thaddeus Stevens said vengefully, "We have conquered them, and as a conquered enemy we can give them laws . . ." The prose makes "as a conquered enemy" seem to modify "we," though nobody encountering Stevens in person would make such a mistake. Defending the amiable and harmless bloodhound, James Thurber ridiculed the misplaced modifier by quoting a sentence from an unscholarly article reviling the animal: "Terrible to look at and terrible to encounter, man has raised him [the bloodhound] up to hunt down his fellowman." Thurber was delighted that careless grammatical construction made man terrible to look at and terrible to encounter.

Other misplaced modifiers create marvelous implausibilities. The *Lansing State Journal* announced, "Bruce Gorsline, 14, views the totem pole of Sakau'Wan he carved shortly after it was raised Tuesday at Carl G. Fenner Arboretum." It's easier to carve totem poles before they are raised, but maybe this craftsman preferred to do things the hard way. When you read, "He had deep blue eyes and a beautiful plaid necktie that quivered with anticipation," you may conclude that he has a nervous Adam's apple. Though Emily Dickinson never married and spent all of her life in Amherst, Massachusetts, she seems to be going West to enter a *menage à trois* when a student writes, "The most serious of Emily Dickinson's loves, the Rev. Charles Wadsworth, was married when she met him and moved not long after to the Pacific Coast." According to the New Testament, Herod Antipas lusted after Salome, but according to the student who wrote the following sentence, he seems to have been a Sodomite: "He is referring to the niece of the king who tried to seduce John the Baptist." Moving the modifier will not cure this sentence: "He is referring to the niece who tried to seduce John the Baptist of the king." The remedy is to turn the partitive genitive (of the king) into an ordinary possessive: "the king's niece who tried to seduce John the Baptist."

Some misplaced modifiers cause a double take. According to one student paper on *The Octopus,* "Annixter had to fight against the exhaustion produced by a losing battle to save his home and a nervous stomach!" He did, in fact, eat prunes to cure a nervous stomach, but the student meant to write of "exhaustion produced by a nervous stomach and a losing battle." In *Catch-22,* Joseph Heller writes, "She would have been perfect for Yossarian, a debauched, coarse, vulgar, amoral, appetizing slattern whom he had longed for and idolized for months." [9] Because of their position, the modifiers seem to describe Yossarian, but of course they belong to *she.* "Though nineteenth century in origin, she's fond of a tall mahogany cubby-hole desk which she dates around 1820." Unless she is a great-grandmother, she is probably twentieth century in origin; the opening phrase needs to be turned into a subordinate clause: "Though it is nineteenth century . . ." Then there is the provocative statement, "I've got to buy some thread for my dress that I'm running out of." Evolution seems to be called into question in, "The wind blew down a branch that hit a man that had something to do with horses on the head." ". . . hit a man on the head that had something to do with horses" is still ambiguous;

169

". . . a branch that hit on the head a man who had something to do with horses" is awkward, but, at least, clear.

Sometimes the position of just one word is essential. "Yogi Bear is cordial to even strangers" should be corrected to read, ". . . even to strangers." A common but nonstandard colloquialism is the use of *anymore* at the beginning of a sentence, as in "Anymore the Cherokee don't play stickball as rough as they used to." The best solution here is to omit *anymore* altogether. Doubly nonstandard is the use of *anymore* for *nowadays*, as in "Anymore I mop the floor at night because the children are in the way" or "It's hard to tell boys from girls these days. Anymore they all have short hair and long pants." In these latter examples it is the meaning rather than the placement of "anymore" that is objectionable. To be logically precise, you should generally put "only" immediately after, and not before, the word it modifies; thus "Only apply to smooth, flat surfaces" would become "Apply only to smooth, flat surfaces." "I only like to go out on Saturday night" could be misleading, because the speaker doubtless likes to do other things as well, but he likes to go out only on Saturday night—never on Sunday. In practice, such concern about the placement of *only* is hairsplitting. Distinguished authors from Dryden to T. S. Eliot have placed *only* earlier in the sentence than the word it modifies. Cyrus Day of the University of Delaware cites examples from Joseph Addison, John Henry Newman, Thomas H. Huxley, Matthew Arnold, A. E. Housman, Havelock Ellis, George Moore, Somerset Maugham, Edna St. Vincent Millay, Robert Frost, Eugene O'Neill, Bertrand Russell, and Harry Levin, among others. Today it is almost a standard idiom, for *only* to come before the verb rather than later. As *Vogue* described the MG sports car, "It'll only carry two people, but it carries them in utter glory."

The placement of *not* is more important, "All are not" seems to be replacing "not all are" in common usage. In casual conversation the issue is not very important, but carefully written prose should avoid the illogic of such a statement as, "All anthologies are not books." Some of them are books. "All the busy executives aren't in offices." Where are they then? The adjective, rather than the verb, should carry the negation: "Not all the busy executives are in offices." Occasionally "all are not" leads to amusing oddities, such as "Being in show business, Barnum was regularly exposed to the charms of other women, and all of them were not freaks."[10]

170

Occasionally one encounters a combination of misplaced and dangling modifier. In Robert Lewis Taylor's *A Journey to Matecumbe,* a character says, "They were my father's squirrel rifles, that got killed in the war." It was, of course, the father and not the rifles that was killed. One of the best former oboe players in the nation announced, "This is Mitch Miller inviting you to help us open our Christmas mail, next in color, on NBC." Mitch's mail may come in color, but most people get theirs in white envelopes. "Next in color, on NBC" could modify Mitch, but it actually refers to the program.

Sometimes a preposition can make a modifier ambiguous: "The princess and the frog got into the coach with eight horses" sounds a bit crowded; "A coach pulled by eight horses" is clearer. Discussing the Salem witch trials, a student wrote, "The girls were dancing nude in the woods with a boiling pot containing a frog nearby." Were they dancing with a boiling pot, and did the pot contain a frog that was nearby it? "The girls were dancing nude in the woods, and a boiling pot containing a frog was nearby" is less intriguing but also less ambiguous. The Pennsylvania Dutch say, "Throw the horse over the fence some hay." Do you throw the horse over the fence? Does "over the fence" modify "throw" or "hay?" Probably the clearest version is, "Throw some hay over the fence to the horse." According to Peter Bart, "Miller was able also to win a significant tax saving . . . for one client who had purchased an expensive house only to have its pipes freeze soon after moving in." [11] Here the adverb modifying the infinitive suggests that the client's only purpose in buying the house was to have its pipes freeze. And sometimes punctuation is necessary to make a modifier unambiguous. "Give us Barrabas, live, on the Hallmark Hall of Fame" is a demand that seems to require some conjury. "*Give Us Barrabas,* live, on the Hallmark Hall of Fame" returns us to sanity, though the ratings may be lower. Finally, a double meaning can make a modifying phrase ambiguous even when it does not dangle, as in "Easter Matinee. Every child laying an egg in the usher's hand will be admitted free."

Sometimes a modifier may be amusingly incongruous. In a paper on *The Octopus,* a student wrote, "Suddenly, from the depths of an indignant rage against the railroad, Annixter notices Hilma Tree's white arms." You wonder how they stay white when you read, "Mingled among all the bloodshed, graft, starvation, and exploitation of the story is found Hilma Tree." Here she sounds more

171

mangled than mingled. Finally some modifiers are not so much ambiguous as downright nonsensical:

> At the end of "The Outcasts of Poker Flat," the bodies are very much purified, serene, and unable to tell which one had sinned the moast [sic] throughout her life.

> After she dies, Miss Watson does reconsider Jim's case and grant him his freedom.

R.I.P.

Exercise 16: Put the proper modifier in the blank.

1. Jane appears in (less, fewer) than half the Tarzan books. . . . .
2. I don't know why you are still (bias, biased) against oatmeal. . . . .
3. Can I have another of (those, them) travel folders on East Africa? . . . .
4. Pork skins are (wonderful, wonderfully) crisp. . . . .
5. "The Frog Galliard" is one of the (greatest, most great) pieces of music ever written, even though it is (comparative, comparatively) obscure. . . . .
6. West Branch, Iowa, was the (less, least) exciting of the historical landmarks we visited last summer. . . . .
7. This box of crayons has (much, many) different colors. . . . .
8. Have you become (accustomed, accustom) to the noise? . . . .
9. Joe Blfstk (?) is the (most unique, uniquest, most nearly unique) character I know of. . . . .
10. Boccherini's "Quintet in E for Guitar and Strings" is a (more masterful, masterfuller) composition than Tschaikovsky's symphonies. . . . .
11. How (much, many) more exercises do you have to do? . . . .
12. Pink is my (best, bestest) color. . . . .
13. *Thuvia, Maid of Mars* has a picture of Thuvia and a banth on (its, it's) cover. . . . .
14. The sky was (redder, more red) at dawn today than at sunset. . . . .
15. Stewart had (much more, many more) gray hairs after returning from the Amazon. . . . .
16. It is no longer respectable to be (prejudiced, prejudice) against minority groups. . . . .
17. Was Elmo Lincoln, Johnny Weismuller, Bruce Bennett, Gordon Scott, or Jock Mahoney (better, best) at giving Tarzan's cry of the bull ape? . . . .
18. Because of sprawling suburbia, there are (less and less, fewer and fewer) places where one can be alone in the woods. . . . .

172

19. The riders saddled (their, they're, there) mounts. . . . .
20. I have (less, fewer) wrinkles after using Murphy's Mud. . . . .

Exercise 17: Replace any incorrect modifiers with the proper form.

1. One-arm driving is dangerous.
2. You are suppose to report at 8:15.
3. He looks differently after the party.
4. Jaggars is a muchly disturbed lawyer.
5. Don't feel too badly about the philodendron.
6. They don't dare attack Mike direct, so they attack his friends.
7. There is a much ancient monastery at Mt. Sinai.
8. Herman is bad off after the hunting accident.
9. We were alarmed by his criminalistic behavior.
10. It was near impossible to prove his guilt.
11. Butch acts toughly, but he's really quite gentle.
12. Many fanatics are real sincere, but they'll kill you all the same.
13. The girl hippopotamus dances beautiful to "The Dance of the Hours."
14. *Ulysses* is muchly more difficult than *The Winning of Barbara Worth*.
15. It evident doesn't matter which route you take to Cudjo's Cave.
16. Firstly, we must have your credentials.
17. Edgar sudden heard a knocking at the lattice.
18. Dawn came quite earlily, before the cock crowed.
19. Natural, we need candles for a birthday cake.
20. Waldo became a full fledge eagle scout.
21. Albert felt quite sadly when his candidate lost the election.
22. Pepe reads English as good as he reads French.
23. Pogo once ran off to be a orphan like the girl in the funny papers.
24. You will probable feel better after a good night's sleep.
25. If it rains, let's have the picnic anyways.

Exercise 18: Correct any dangling and misplaced modifiers.

1. George Gundersdorf erected the statute in the museum which he carved.
2. Weighing 500 pounds and over 100 years old, Chadwick was impressed with the Galapagos tortoise.
3. Did you ever walk a dog in a plaid bathrobe?
4. Having been born in captivity, the zookeeper provides special care for animals neglected by their mothers.
5. When tending the desk, a volume of James Bond was read.
6. The Galapagos tortoises were taken to the San Diego Zoo, facing the threat of extinction.
7. Sleeping in the rain, a case of rheumatism was developed.
8. With horns 36 inches long, hunters prize the bongo of the African forest.

173

9. Growling hungrily, the keeper gave the Bengal tigers their noon meal.
10. The largest of all white rhinos, the hunter captured them in Rhodesia.
11. With her floppy ears cocked, the dowager frowned at the spaniel.
12. Sleeping in foxholes, trench foot sometimes breaks out.
13. Long thought to be extinct in their native habitat, the New Yorkers admired Przewalski's wild horses at the game farm.
14. Losing interest in mating, the zoo director explained that captive cheetahs become slack and indolent.
15. Grandmother used the fish in making the chowder we caught yesterday.
16. While walking by a stone fence, a snake struck at me and ignited the matches in my pocket.
17. The patrolman brought the wallet to the desk that he had found in the parking lot.
18. After spending a night at Camp Muir, a side trip is made to the Cowlitz Glacier in the morning.
19. A rarity in zoological collections, Dilsingham admired the marbled cat's white-patched ears and bicolored whiskers.
20. By providing the mother polar bear with privacy, she can have her cubs undisturbed.

Exercise 19: Correct any dangling and misplaced modifiers.

1. Breakfasting on acacia leaves at sunrise, Howard photographed the typical feeding posture of the gerenuk.
2. Formerly thought to run from 70 to 90 miles an hour, zoologists now find that few cheetahs can do more than 56 miles per hour.
3. An adult pair of Sclater's Crowned Pigeons, hatched in the rain forest of New Guinea, are shown with their month-old chick.
4. Having disappeared in Asia, maharajahs now import cheetahs to hunt from Africa.
5. Exploring the cave, a large deposit of bat guano was discovered.
6. We hardly saw any of the park bears.
7. The developer bought the property from a farmer that he later sold for an immense profit.
8. Walking along the beach, a strange footprint was encountered.
9. While going down to the cellar, a loose board made me stumble.
10. The landlord gave the old clothes to a Salvation Army worker that had been stored in the attic.
11. While climbing over a barbed-wire fence, the farmer's dog bit me.
12. Being only a sophomore, my advisor would not let me take graduate courses.
13. "The Greenland Fisheries" should be sung with a strong rhythm, paying careful attention to the dramatic details of the story.
14. Driving over Bear Mountain Bridge, the New York skyline can be seen.

15. Hiking the Appalachian Trail, shelter cabins are found every seven or ten miles.
16. Stacy brought the snake to the museum, which he later put on display.
17. Looking out of the bus window, a mother moose and young were seen grazing in the park meadow.
18. Exercising every day, thirty pounds were lost.
19. A bright orange specimen, Lothar carefully photographed the flame azalea.
20. Looking into the aquarium, a bottle-nosed dolphin was seen.

12 √ Confused Conjunctions and Prepositional Puzzles

Both conjunctions and prepositions are connectives, used in joining a word, phrase, or clause to the rest of the sentence. But whereas prepositions always form part of a phrase, conjunctions stand before or between grammatical units (clauses, phrases, words), which they connect or contrast. Conjunctions are essential to the balance, rhythm, and structure of sentences; the wrong choice can shift the weight, alter the tempo, splatter the punctuation, fragment the meaning, joggle the transition, and sink the sentence or give it a seasick lurch. The careful stylist must select conjunctions to give the exact shade he wants of coordination, subordination, pause, contrast, or other relationship. He must make certain his conjunctions carry appropriate weight—not too much or too little. Effective use of conjunctions is one of the more discriminating tests of style. The nonstylist uses them like buckshot, but the professional takes careful aim. Even use of the simple word *and* can become a matter of literary art. Ernest Hemingway told Lillian Ross, "In the first paragraphs of 'Farewell' [*A Farewell to Arms*] I used the word *and* over and over the way Mr. Johann Sebastian Bach used a note in music when he was emitting counterpoint." [1]

We shall consider conjunctions more thoroughly later in the chapter on sentence structure. Meanwhile, some classification may be helpful. Most people know of nouns, verbs, and adjectives (though one student, when asked to give an example of a verb said "sweater," and when asked what its past tense would be, replied "sweaters"), but cannot distinguish relative pronouns and the various kinds of conjunctions. Except in a classroom, if you should ask someone whether he can describe a subordinating conjunction, the chances are he'll decide you're a suspicious character—a lawyer or a spy. These classifications are not matters of common knowledge.

176

Teachers cannot count on their students' being familiar with them, as the students would be with a championship bout or the latest automobiles. Yet the distinction is not mere pedantry but is essential in constructing effective sentences.

¶ COORDINATING CONJUNCTIONS

Coordinating conjunctions (*and, but, or, nor, yet*) connect words or groups of words that are equal in grammatical form or rank. They can join two or more main clauses in a compound sentence. When they do so, they are preceded by a comma ("Johann Strauss wrote *Die Fledermaus,* and Richard Strauss wrote *Der Rosenkavalier*") but not when they connect two words ("Mutt and Jeff") or phrases ("Little John hit Robin Hood with a quarterstaff and knocked him into the stream"). When a coordinating conjunction is omitted between main clauses, it should be replaced with a semicolon, not a comma.

Some teachers have a taboo against beginning sentences with a coordinating conjunction. Competent professional writers have no such scruples and do not hesitate to start sentences with *and, but,* or other conjunctions. Dr. Herman Struck of Michigan State University found that such diverse writers as E. B. White and Loren Eiseley begin one tenth of their sentences with coordinate conjunctions and this is also true of one fifth of the sentences in F. L. Lucas's *Style,* whereas the timid style of doctoral dissertations shun opening coordinates as a breach of decorum. But obviously any decision about usage should be based, not on propriety, but on style and sense. If an initial coordinating conjunction coordinates effectively, use it; if it creates a false transition, use something else.

Some uses of *and* are too colloquial for expository prose. "Be sure and go there" should be changed to "Be sure to go there." *Good and* is emphatic ("good and hot," "good and mad") in casual conversation, but inappropriate for more formal style. *Took and* is even more so: "He took and fixed the huge machine."

¶ SUBORDINATING CONJUNCTIONS

Subordinating conjunctions are more difficult because there are more of them and because the function of connecting a subordinate, or dependent, clause is more subtle than coupling equal elements. As we have seen, the relative pronouns (*who, whose, whom, which, what, that*) have two grammatical functions, one of these being to double as subordinating conjunctions. Other subordinating conjunctions are:

after	before	so (so that)	where (wherever)
although	how	unless	whether
as (as if)	if	until	while
because	since	when (whenever)	why

Besides serving as connectives, conjunctions are often used to indicate contrast, comparison, result, or condition; some subordinating ones also have adverbial functions and may indicate time, direction, causal relationship, and interrogation. The subordinate clause that such conjunctions introduce may appear before, after, or within the main clauses, depending upon the relationship and rhythm:

Clark Kent ran to the phone booth *when* he heard the cry for Superman.

Li'l Abner refused to get married *until* his idol, Fearless Fosdick, supposedly married Prudence Pimpleton.

Unless the turnip termites are driven away, Dogpatch will perish.

I don't know *why* the Lone Ranger insists on wearing a mask *when* he has no alter ego to conceal.

Whenever Richard Cory went down town,
We people on the pavement looked at him: . . .

The legislators want to know *who* is responsible for the beer parties.

There are several specific problems with subordinating conjunctions. *While* should usually be used only in its sense of "at the same time"; if it is used for *although, and,* or *but,* it may cause confusion, as in "Boris Karloff played the monster in *Frankenstein* (1932), while Bela Lugosi played it in *Frankenstein Meets the Wolf Man* (1943)"; or in "I was born in Hackensack, while my father was born in Punxatawny."

After the verb *to be* it is best to avoid using a clause introduced by *when*: otherwise, you will find yourself stating that some noun is "when." All too often students produce such a sentence: "An eclipse is when the moon is between the sun and the earth," or "An example is when the Puritans persecuted the Quakers." "The reason is because . . ." is similarly awkward.

That is often omitted when necessary and inserted when unnec-

178

essary. It can be omitted in constructions like "She said that her hands were cold" or "He said that he would destroy the world." But sometimes common sense requires *that,* as in "The soothsayer said on March fifteenth Caesar would be murdered." He didn't say it on March fifteenth: " . . . said that on March fifteenth . . ." is the correct form for such statements. Again the missing *that* creates ambiguity in "He added the bill could be charged to the expense account." He did not add the bill; rather, he was talking and added that the bill could be charged. If you have two subordinate clauses, you may need two *thats* to keep the second clause from seeming coordinate, e.g., "The zookeeper said that the hippopotamus is expecting, and attendance is going up." Without a second *that,* you can't tell if the last clause is the writer's comment or part of the zookeeper's statement.

But that is awkwardly formal and should be avoided. In "I do not doubt but that students could read more than they do," *but* can be cut. To use *but what* with *doubt* is nonstandard, as in "We don't doubt but what the water level has risen." The use of *being as* for *because* or *since* is also nonstandard: "Being as Tarzan couldn't remember his parents, he thought his mother was an ape."

Than and *as* are used as conjunctions with comparisons in which something is smaller or greater than something else:

Henry V's army was much smaller than that of the French.

Despite popular legends to the contrary, Richard the Lion-Hearted was probably a worse ruler than his brother John.

As in these examples, *than* or *as* is usually followed by an elliptical clause in which the verb has been dropped. This can cause difficulty in using the proper case when a pronoun is the subject of a verb understood:

Dr. Horstwessel is madder than he (not *him*).
Herman is not as musical as she (not *her*).

¶ CONJUNCTIVE ADVERBS

Conjunctive adverbs (sometimes called transitional conjunctions) are used to connect two sentences or two main clauses requiring a heavier transition in meaning than coordinating conjunctions provide. As adverbs, they modify their entire clause. The main ones are:

accordingly	besides	indeed	still
also	consequently	likewise	that is
again	furthermore	moreover	that is to say
anyhow	hence	nevertheless	therefore
at the same time	however	on the contrary	thus

When used as conjunctions, they are preceded by a semicolon, and the more weighty ones are often followed by a comma. Sometimes a conjunctive adverb appears in the middle of a clause, rather than at the beginning: "Despite the death of Banquo, Macbeth felt uneasy upon the throne; he went, *therefore,* to consult the witches once more."

CONJUNCTIVE ADVERB: The giraffe's kick is strong enough to damage an automobile; consequently, the giraffe has the right-of-way on all highways.

ADVERB: Any physical exercise, however slight, is too much for Butch.

It is best to minimize the use of the heavier conjunctive adverbs. Too many weighty *howevers, neverthelesses,* and *moreovers* can sandbag your style. The prose is as heavy-footed as a hippo in "When Friday evening arrived, I was pooped; moreover, I had a headache; furthermore, my stomach was unsettled; nevertheless, I had to go bowling; however, I recovered sufficiently; indeed, I found that I had won the trophy; consequently, I was glad I had not gone straight to bed."

As an adverb, *too* can be synonymous for *also,* but it should not be used as a conjunctive adverb. At the beginning of clauses, *too* is an annoying affectation: "Too, she was wearing a mink stole." Most professionals find this as mannered as false eyelashes or *forsooth.*

¶ CORRELATIVE CONJUNCTIONS

These are sometimes called preconnectives because they signal that a connective is approaching and mark off the limits of the first connecting part. They include *as . . . as, both . . . and, either . . . or, neither . . . nor, not so . . . as, not only . . . but also,* and *whether . . . or.* Some grammarians find it illogical to use *both . . . and, either . . . or,* and *neither . . . nor* for more than two things. This would brand as incorrect the sentence, "He liked neither grammar, French, nor algebra." They also tell us not to

180

use *nor* as a correlative with anything but *neither*; not to say, for example, "He never shirked nor complained." Yet competent writers often disregard these warnings, both of which are broken in "Learning to spell is not a matter of intelligence, industry, nor logic so much as of memory." More useful is the advice to place correlatives in strictly parallel form. "It is neither the result of luck nor of wisdom" should be corrected so that neither is placed after *result*. Faulty parallelism sometimes results in ambiguity, as in "The authors both wrote sincerely and eloquently."

As . . . as can be awkward, with an *as* too many or two few. "T. S. Eliot is as influential as a critic as as a poet" stutters hopelessly. Yet in this sentence the third *as* completes the comparison, and the fourth is needed as a preposition with *poet* to balance the *as* with *critic*. The only solution is to rephrase the sentence: "as influential as a critic as he is as a poet" or "as influential in criticism as in poetry." Conversely, "Uncle Fudge says *Son of the Blob* is as good or better than *The Alligator People*" should be changed to "as good as or better than."

Sometimes *hardly . . . than* and *scarcely . . . than* turn up as correlatives. Wilson Follett calls these "intolerable"; whether they are so to you depends upon your degree of tolerance. Formal usage replaces *than* with *when* or prefers *no sooner . . . than*.

We shall return to coordination and subordination when we consider sentence structure. Meanwhile, we can proceed to another kind of connective.

¶ PREPOSITIONS

Then comes the thing that can of all things be most mistaken and they are prepositions. . . . I like prepositions the best of all. . . .

—GERTRUDE STEIN

For the person learning English as a second language, prepositions pose one of the greatest difficulties. Even native speakers find them a frequent headache. Formally, prepositions are quite simple; except for unusual constructions, such as "The week before's laundry came back this week," prepositions are never involved with inflectional endings. The difficulties come in the choice and function of prepositions and in the fact that many of these are idiomatic and illogical.

English uses prepositions to introduce a prepositional phrase and relate it to another part of the sentence. A highly inflected lan-

181

guage like Latin minimizes prepositions, using instead the inflected case endings of the genitive, dative, and ablative case. English is simpler, using prepositions for this function with uninflected nouns. Prepositions always have an object and show direction or relation between the object and the word or words it modifies:

He went home *for* lunch. (noun to noun)

Waldo was hungry *for* learning. (noun to adjective)

Irving dropped the watermelon *on* his foot. (noun to both noun and verb)

If we start with a boy standing at the door of his house, he may go *down* the walk, *up* the drive, *across* the street, *to* the school, *around* the block, *over* the bridge, *away* from home, *through* the door, *toward* a policeman. In all these phrases, the italicized word shows the direction of his going. Or imagine two people talking. They may talk *of* the weather, *in* low tones, *about* their friends, *for* an hour, *with* much enjoyment. Here the italicized prepositions do not show direction but indicate the relationship between the talking and *weather, tones, friends, hour,* and *enjoyment.*

The term *preposition* is misleading, for it suggests something placed *before,* whereas a preposition may, and often does, follow its object. Like a conjunction, it connects two or more parts of an expression. But unlike the weak conjunction, it not only joins but shows the nature of the relationship, and holds more individual meaning. In "go to the bank" and "go away from the bank," the words *to* and *from* are alike in showing the connection between going and the bank but they indicate opposite directions. Grammatically the object in a prepositional phrase takes the objective case. This is no problem with nouns, but occasionally causes difficulty with pronouns. The distinction is clearly indicated in Hamlet's question, "What's Hecuba to him or he to Hecuba?" A common and irritating error, probably caused by overanxiety about standards of grammar, is "between you and I," or "Give it to Carolyn and I." In conversation, the objective case is more and more disappearing in instances like "Who did you give it to?", the grammatically approved form being, "To whom did you give it?" *Whom* is unlikely to vanish altogether, being preserved in literature—*For Whom the Bell Tolls* is probably the best known example.

Many words that function as prepositions can also serve in other capacities. Some double as adverbs, as conjunctions, or as both. A few can even be nouns ("an *in* with the boss," "an *out* in case of in-

182

vestigation"). *Aboard* is a preposition in "Aboard the ship, mutiny was brewing," but it is an adverb in "Queeg went aboard."

PREPOSITION: Quick Draw McGraw went *after* the rustlers.
ADVERB: Jill came tumbling *after*.
CONJUNCTION: *After* the hurricane was over, the islanders began to rebuild.
PREPOSITION: The boat was tied *alongside* the pier.
ADVERB: The car pulled *alongside*.

Likewise, prepositional phrases can be adjectival modifiers ("the man *at the wheel*," "dinner *at eight*"), adverbial modifiers ("go *to school*," "jump *in the lake*"), or complements ("Arnold thought *of going to the movies*"). The last example has two prepositional phrases in a row. Usually prepositional phrases follow the nouns they modify: the lady *in the lake*," "ships *at sea*," "a time *to weep*." For some reason authors seem to favor using prepositional phrases for titles: *Of Time and the River, Of Human Bondage, Of Mice and Men, In Dubious Battle, In the Cage, To the Lighthouse, On the Road, By Love Possessed*. Many other titles contain prepositional phrases: *Life on the Mississippi, Portrait of a Lady, The Wings of the Dove, Intruder in the Dust, The Grapes of Wrath, This Side of Paradise*.

Prepositions can themselves be phrases (usually containing another prepositional phrase), as well as single words: "Jason sailed *in search of* the golden fleece." Stylistically it is best to minimize the use of long prepositions (*in accordance with, in relation to, by means of, in connection with, on the part of, in order to, in regard to*); they can usually be replaced with shorter ones. Some prepositions are composed of two words; *because of, instead of, next to, across from, down below*.

The idiomatic use of prepositions in English presents one of the great stumbling blocks to those who are not native born to the tongue, because this usage is neither rational nor predictable. We say not only *full of* but also *filled with, a victim of circumstances* but also *a victim to greed, by this means* but also *in this way* and *after this fashion*. One is guilty *of* a crime, and one also pleads guilty *to* it. If you beat somebody *up*, you may knock him *down*. The British say a building is *in* the street, when we say it is *on* the street. (Actually it is next to the street.) A house can *burn up* or *burn down*. You can drink something *up* or drink it *down*, but when you drink it *down*, it is all drunk *up*. But it always clouds *up*,

183

never *down*. And if you *live it up* too much, you may not be able to *live it down*.

Some prepositions are logical; *knock down and drag out* makes sense. But some combinations of verb and preposition have several quite different meanings. *Carry out* does not mean the same thing in "carry out the garbage" as it does in "carry out orders." When you get up in the morning, you put on some clothes and then put on some coffee. There may be no turn involved when something unexpected turns up. You look up to see an airplane, but you also look up someone in the phone book or look him up when you are in his neighborhood. And if things are looking up, they are improving. The warning "Look out!" is different from looking out the window. When you look over somebody's work, you look at it and through it but not over it. When you look after someone, you take care of him and do not stare after him. When you go through with a project, you may not go anywhere or with anyone. *Go about* can mean "to be occupied with"; *go along,* "to agree with"; *go by,* "to be known as"; *go in for,* "to have a liking for"; *go off,* "to happen"; *go out,* "to be extinguished, to become outdated, to sympathize, and to go on strike"; *go through,* "to suffer, to get approval, to spend"; and the number of similar idioms is legion. As the instructions advise on washroom paper towels, "Pull down and pull up to pull out."

Prepositions can also be combined with verbs to make nouns (*sellout, turnout, blowout, showdown, tossup, holdover, outlook, withdrawal, holdup, handout, sit-in, cookout, layout, layaway, layoff, hideout, hideaway*), with nouns to make nouns (*sundown, sunup, insight, inmate, outlaw, outboard, overhead*), with nouns or verbs to make adjectives (*overdue, outgrown, overland, outspread, underdone*), or with nouns and verbs to make new verbs (*outlaw, overlook, outrun, update*). When a preposition is tacked onto the end of a verb, the verb rather than the preposition is inflected, though one child recovering from the flu said, "Hey, I'm not throw-upping anymore."

Since prepositions occur on the average of one to a sentence, the possibilities for error are formidable. In one set of twenty-three high school papers, twenty-four errors in the use of prepositions appeared, including "It is to [in] my opinion correct," "Take the train till [to] Times Square," "Doesn't he resemble with his father?", "The contrast of [between] Portia and Calpurnia," and "Strike three times to [at] him."

184

Prepositions in English are the more difficult because the language itself sometimes shifts. *Averse,* coming from two Latin words meaning *from* and *turn,* should not logically have *to* following it, yet we say "He is not averse to studying," instead of the older "He is not averse from studying." *Oblivious* is just as remote from *to*; in Latin and less current English it was followed by *of,* yet we say "He was oblivious to his surroundings." *Of* used to function in the sense of *by,* as in "He was despised and rejected of men." People still die *of,* not *from,* something: "She died of a fever/With no one to save her,/And that was the end of sweet Mollie Malone."

The choice of prepositions is particularly controversial in several situations. *Different than* is forbidden by pedants, who demand *different from.* This is a hair-splitting distinction that is often justifiedly ignored. Margaret Nicholson has pointed out that Thomas Fuller in the seventeenth century; Addison, Steele, Defoe, Richardson, Goldsmith, and Fanny Burney in the eighteenth; and Coleridge, Southey, De Quincey, Carlyle, Thackeray, Newman, and others in the nineteenth used *different than* on occasion, and so do many competent writers today. Unquestionably *from* is the more grammatically precise preposition; but the conjunction *than* could be considered as introducing a subordinate clause with the verb understood: "different from me" or "different than I [am]." Of course, what you find is "different than me." The overfastidious therefore have a point in their denunciation of *different than me,* and if you want to be discriminating, you should stick with *different from.*

Another distinction is made in the use of *between* and *among.* Conventionally, *between* is used with two items ("between you and me," "between heaven and hell") and *among* with three or more ("life among the Polynesians"). There is no challenge when *among* is used in the sense of "in the midst of," but it is being threatened by *between* when a choice or comparison is involved. Thus Alexander Bumstead says, "The malt shop has 25 flavors, and it is difficult to choose between them," and *Vogue* describes a party that "will swirl between three different hotels." The careful grammarian would choose *among* in these situations.

There is frequent confusion in the use of *in, into,* and *in to,* for these are not interchangeable. You live *in* a house but go *into* it. If you go out, you might drive *in to* the city and go *into* a restaurant. If "Snideley Whiplash turned himself into the nearest Mountie station," he performed a remarkable magic trick; the preposition

185

should be *in to*. But sometimes there is unavoidable ambiguity, as in "The truck turned into the nearest garage." Usually, context and common sense make the meaning clear. *In* is stationary ("Fish live in the water"), *into* indicates movement from the outside to the inside ("Tarzan dived into the water"), and *in to* has a separate stress on each preposition. Logically, each of these prepositions is correct in "Put it [in, into] the box," but *in* is preferable because the inert enclosure, rather than the movement inward, is stressed.

As of is jargon and it is not an acceptable substitute for *at* or *on*. *On* is better in "As of Wednesday the store was still closed," and *at* is preferable in "As of six o'clock supper was not ready." *As of now* means simply *now*. *As per* is another bit of jargon in "Your assistance in proctoring the Natural Science Final Examination, as per [according to] the above schedule, will be appreciated."

With causes some awkward constructions as an adverbial preposition. "Horpington was the most popular member of his class with Fosdick in second place" calls for a double take. To keep from suggesting that he was popular with Fosdick, change *with* to *and*: "and Fosdick was in second place." "The second car crashed into the first one with the third going into a ditch" is ambiguous; "and the third went into a ditch" is clearer. How would you remove the confusion in the following?

> Schmertz fed the wombat with the koala bear waiting for his turn.
>
> She bit him on the ear with her cigarette burning his lapel.

Like the omnivorous *-ness* suffix, *on* seems to be gradually eliminating all other prepositions. The appropriate choices are in brackets in the following examples:

The administration questioned Horpington on [about] his drinking.

The public can be satisfied on [as to] my candidate's honesty.

The cast was disappointed on [at] the poor attendance.

The city council is waiting on [for] medical testimony about fluoridation.

Some success has been made on [in] cancer research.

Security controls have been lifted on [from] the new aircraft.

We are educating underdeveloped nations on [in] better methods of agriculture.

Whenever you are in doubt as to the proper choice of a preposition, it is advisable not to guess but to consult your dictionary.

Another point of contention is *due to* versus *because of*. In

186

conservative grammar, *due* is an adjective followed by the preposition *to*; thus *due* can modify only nouns and pronouns, not verbs. Yet *due to* as an adverbial preposition has become so widespread that it must be recognized (if not accepted) as standard. Porter G. Perrin's *Writer's Guide and Index to English* cites Professor John S. Kenyon who in 1930 conceded, albeit reluctantly, that much as he personally disliked the prepositional *due to,* it was established in the work of reputable writers. Perrin also cites Margaret M. Bryant's report, based on a survey of thousands of books and periodicals, that *due to* appeared as a preposition in 56 percent of the cases, *because of* in 25 percent, and *owing to* in 19 percent. Even so, the more conservative grammarians condemn the prepositional *due to*. It is illogical to be indignant against it, but if you want to avoid their criticism, you should use *because of* in constructions similar to "We arrived late due to an error in the program announcement." The following examples illustrate the contrast in traditional practice:

The demonstrations were *due to* disagreement over the census count. (Adj.)
The game was called *because of* darkness. (Prep.)
The ship ran aground *because* the captain was drunk. (Prep. Not "due to the captain's drunkenness.")
Professor Crabshaw's reputation was *due to* his study of Richard III. (Adj.)
Because of bad weather, the picnic is postponed. (Prepositional adv.)
The postponement is *due to* bad weather. (Adj.)

¶ AS YOU LIKE IT

One of the hottest conflicts between prescriptive and descriptive grammarians is over the use of *like, as,* or *as if* in a metaphor or comparison. The prescriptive position is that *as* and *as if* are subordinate conjunctions used between clauses, whereas *like* is a preposition that can be used only to introduce a prepositional phrase and never to introduce a clause. The issue is complicated because *as* is also used as a preposition in some comparisons: "black as pitch," "hot as blazes," "cool as a cucumber." By and large, *as* causes no trouble; the cries of alarm and anguish come when *like* usurps the role of conjunction. Purists protested bitterly, particularly denouncing the cigarette slogan "Winstons taste good like a cigarette should" as a symbol of linguistic decay. The Winston people respond by having the Flintstones sing the jingle, thus giving it unquestioned antiquity.

187

Actually if we look back, we find the Elizabethans combining all the rivals in *like as if, like as, like to,* and *like unto.* Thus Shakespeare's Richard III complains of looking "like to a chaos or an unlicked bearwhelp." One of Edmund Spenser's sonnets begins "Like as a ship that through the ocean wide," and another, "Like as a huntsman after weary chase . . ." The King James Bible is thoroughly inconsistent. In The Song of Solomon we read, "Thy neck is as a tower of ivory; thine eyes like the fishpools in Heshbon, by the gate of Bath-rabbim: thy nose is as the tower of Lebanon which looketh toward Damascus," and again, "His head is as the most fine gold . . . His cheeks are as a bed of spices, as sweet flowers: his lips like lilies, dropping sweet smelling myrrh." And "This thy stature is like to a palm tree . . ." Today we would use *like* in all of these comparisons, and the Revised Standard Version does so. In St. Matthew we read, "The kingdom of heaven is like to a grain of mustard seed. . . . like unto treasure hid in a field. . . . like unto a merchantman" but also "The kingdom of heaven is as a man traveling into a far country." Again, the Revised Standard Version replaces all of these with *like.*

Today we seldom see *as* misused for *like* ("She looks as her mother," he looks as King Kong"). Most complaints come when *like* is used for *as* and *as if.* Yet authors from Shakespeare to Keats to John F. Kennedy have used *like* in this way, and they are hardly vulgarians. As long ago as 1923, James Thurber observed that Joseph Conrad and Henry James used *like* for *as,* but that he didn't care because he admired their style and content. Certainly the use of *like* as a conjunction antedates the Winston ad. "Let's All Sing Like the Birdies Sing" and "If You Knew Susie Like I Know Susie" are earlier.

Tyrone Guthrie was careful to make the traditional distinction when he wrote of an actor: "He can coo like a dove, roar like a lion, shriek like a banshee, rattle like a machine gun, sing like an angel and curse like—well, as only Australians can." [2] So was the translator in ". . . he behaved like a king, and as if the young sovereign were merely his heir." [3]

On the other hand, Lawrence Durrell violated the prescriptive rule when he wrote, "He had, in fact, been nailed to this tree by bullets for all the world like the body of a jay is nailed to a barn door, as a warning." [4] John Dos Passos also did so several times in *Midcentury.* Sir Laurence Olivier said that Othello must "stand like a strong man stands, with that sort of ease, probably straight-

188

backed, straight-necked." Princeton historian Eric Goldman wrote in *The New York Times* of "a novel which sounds like it should be light reading." And President Kennedy said of Khrushchev, "I would suspect he has his good months and his bad months like we all do."

Clearly it is not proof that you are vulgar or illiterate if you use *like* in place of *as*. A descriptive grammarian would say that conservative usage opposes the use of *like* as a conjunction; that if you want to play it safe, you should follow conservative practice; but that many educated people do use *like* for *as* and that this is no sign of degeneracy or cause for alarm. Perhaps the choice is one more of diction than of grammar. Certainly *like* is inappropriate when at the climax of the movie *Phaedra,* Anthony Perkins (in a role analogous to that of Hippolytus in the ancient Greek drama) says, "She loved me like they did in the good old days." Here the flat, modern colloquial style fails to sustain the mood of high tragedy the film was trying to achieve. The weakness is not alone in the grammar of *like* but equally in the diction of "they did in the good old days."

Webster III outraged purists by presenting *like* as if it were a synonym for *as*. It did not make this reversible, with *as* a synonym for *like*. In fact the two are not interchangeable. "Like an Indian, I made my way through the forest" is quite different from "As an Indian, I made my way through the forest." In the first, the narrator is walking like an Indian; in the second, he is impersonating an Indian. Notice the difference that occurs if the title of John Howard Griffin's *Black Like Me* is changed to *Black As Me*. Sometimes a wrong use of *like* or *as* can cause ambiguity and confusion. "Code 10 disappears into the blotter like it disappears into your hair" may use *like* as a conjunction, but it is at least clear, whereas "Code 10 disappears into the blotter as it disappears into your hair" suggests that it disappears into the blotter at the same time that it disappears into your hair. "I'm going to throw that typewriter out the window just like General What's-his-name" suggests that the general is going to be tossed out the window; the sentence is clearer as "I'm going to throw that typewriter out the window just as General What's-his-name did." The meaning is also ambiguous in "The State Library serves students just like any Michigan citizen." This might be interpreted as meaning that any citizen serves students the way the library does, whereas the real meaning is that the services of the library are the same for students and citizens alike. Again, *like* makes the modifier ambiguous in "Joy'll treat your hands just like a bubble bath." In the ad for "Beatnik Wigs . . . look like they just got off the boat," the confusion is caused not by *like* but by the picture of the wigs walking through customs. In his attack on *Webster III,* Wilson Follett denounces "that darling of the advanced libertarians, *like* as a conjunction, first in the meaning of *as,* secondly (and more horribly) in that of *as if.*" These uses he calls "no more than a regional colloquialism." [5] But regional colloquialisms are not nonstandard, though they may be highly inappropriate outside their own setting; and the use of *like* as a conjunction is certainly not confined to nor characteristic of any particular region. Besides, what is so horrible about the practice, even if it is a borderline case? *Like* can be a conjunction if usage so determines; and in fact Mr. Follett admits that it was used this way in the Middle Ages, but claims that this usage, once dropped, is not entitled to make a comeback. Why not? Stylistically, *as if* may be awkward and *like* more effective: "It looks like we're late" vs. "It looks as if we're late."

Looks like, though unacceptable to purists, is rapidly becoming idiomatic. Certainly in casual speech, it has a smoother sound than *looks as if,* which shifts gears an extra time: "She looked like she'd wink" comes naturally; "She looked as if she'd wink" seems grammatically self-conscious. On the back cover of *Mad* (January, 1964) we read, "Next week my company starts using a new-type can, and I'll be able to stuff those eight great tomatoes in that little bitty can without ending up looking like [more effective than as if] I've been attacked with a meat cleaver." And "It looks like the octopus got him" is far more likely to be heard than "It looks as if the octopus got him."

But to conform with formal and conservative practice, replace the use of *like* as a conjunction with *as* in the following:

"I thought I'd boil off the whale blubber, like the Eskimos do," said the museum director.

Eat the sucker when you're through
Or save it like the squirrels do.   —*Holiday Inn menu*

Like I always say, if at first you don't succeed, do something sneaky.
                                        —HOKEY WOLF

I wish he'd bury his bones like other dogs do.

I brought in Snideley Whiplash like I said I would.   —DUDLEY DO-RIGHT

190

Conservative usage and traditional grammar prescribe the use of *such as* in "a pan like you cook brownies in," and *as if* or (preferably) *as though* in "Seems like the whole country's gone Dial happy," or "Your hair looks like you bleached it twice." But for all practical purposes, *like* has become a conjunction, and you should not be outraged that such is the case. Depending on the situation, you may so use it yourself. If you are indignant at the Winston ad, you can switch to tea, for "Lipton's satisfies as no other tea can." The important question about Winstons is whether they really taste good.

¶ ENDING SENTENCES WITH A PREPOSITION

What would we really know the meaning of? —RALPH WALDO EMERSON

. . . this only is reading, in a high sense, not that which lulls us as a luxury and suffers the nobler faculties to sleep the while, but what we have to stand on tip-toe to read and devote our most alert and wakeful hours to.
—HENRY DAVID THOREAU

That the Bastille was attacked with an enthusiasm of heroism, such as only the highest animation of Liberty could inspire, and carried in the space of a few hours, is an event which the world is fully possessed of.
—THOMAS PAINE

The prison to which the new ministry were dooming the National Assembly, in addition to its being the high altar and castle of despotism, became the proper object to begin with. —THOMAS PAINE

Clearly the Ipswich minister was a fighting as well as a praying parson, whom Cromwell should have delighted in. —VERNON L. PARRINGTON

Stewards in church and state, he would have none of.
—VERNON L. PARRINGTON

For whom would a poem on Spring be by? —ROBERT FROST

Had Lincoln been born in a sweatshop he would never have been heard of.
—EUGENE DEBS

> The undiscover'd country from whose bourn
> No traveller returns, puzzles the will
> And makes us rather bear those ills we have
> Than fly to others that we know not of.
> —WILLIAM SHAKESPEARE

I am as lonesome and as happy as I can be in that town we lived in and worked and learned and grew up in, and then fought our way back into.
—ERNEST HEMINGWAY, *quoted by Lillian Ross*[6]

191

In Shakespeare I always try to reassure the audience initially that they are not going to see some grotesque, outsized dimension of something which they can't understand or sympathize with.   —SIR LAURENCE OLIVIER

It's the kind of music we love to sink our collective teeth into.

—THE BROTHERS FOUR

THOU SHALT NOT END A SENTENCE WITH A PREPOSITION!!!

This is one of the few widely known "rules" of grammar and a totally false one. If it is such an absolute command, why do so many superior writers ignore it? Because, as we discussed earlier, it was never based on actual usage. It was John Dryden, sitting in his study one day in the late seventeenth century, who decreed that English sentences must never end with a preposition, and prescriptive grammarians have preached the dogma ever since, although as a matter of actual fact, some sentences can end no other way. For example, how is it possible to end Hamlet's declaration, "My head should be struck off," without using a preposition? In *The Prince and the Pauper,* when Tom Canty is asked what he used the Great Seal of England for (not for what he used it), he answers, "To crack nuts with!" Should he have said, "With which to crack nuts?" Consider the awkward alternatives to placing the preposition at the end in the following:

On what did I step?	What did I step on?
At what are you laughing?	What are you laughing at?
I'm going up to live it.	I'm going to live it up.
For what is this?	What is this for?
We must prevent war out from breaking.	We must prevent war from breaking out.
Of what are you scared?	What are you scared of?
Ten cents is a fraction of for what it sells.	Ten cents is a fraction of what it sells for.
His sister is very particular about with whom she out goes.	His sister is very particular about whom she goes out with.
On what the hell am I sitting?	What the hell am I sitting on?

There is a well-known story that when a secretary revised one of Winston Churchill's sentences so that it would not end with a preposition, Churchill wrote a note, "This is the sort of impertinence up with which I will not put." When a writer goes out of his way to avoid ending a sentence with a preposition, his prose usually has an overstuffed Victorian sound, as in the following passages from Edgar Rice Burroughs' *Tarzan and the Lost Empire*:

192

The first few steps that von Harben took onto the grassy meadow land revealed the fact that it was a dangerous swamp from which only with the greatest difficulty were they able to extricate themselves.

They had been paddling for hours, and the heat and the monotony had become almost unbearable, when a turn in the water-lane revealed a small body of open water, across the opposite side of which stretched what appeared to be low land surmounted by an earthen rampart, along the top of which was a strong stockade.

Thus when such a careful stylist as Edmund Wilson writes, "Neither the Soviet Russians nor we were very much beloved by the peoples in upon whom they had moved," the sentence seems curiously contrived.[7]

The preposition "rule" is one that not even the most adamant purist can always follow. In *Pygmalion* (and *My Fair Lady*) Professor Higgins finally loses his temper and tells Eliza, "Marry some sentimental hog or other with lots of money, and a thick pair of lips to kiss you with and a thick pair of boots to kick you with." [8] This piles up terminal prepositions almost as much as Ehrich von Kanehl's statement that Pop art "gives the observer something he is familiar with and emotionally with to look at and identify with."

The reason that a preposition is so often placed at the end of a sentence, in spite of prescriptive grammarians' thunderings, is that we do not think of the preposition as taking an object but as being linked to the verb that immediately precedes it and forming with it a verbal unit. A preposition following a verb usually has an adverbial function as well, so that it is normal and natural to keep them together. The prepositional-adverbial relationship is disturbed in a contruction like "To whom did you talk?" Breaking the normal speech pattern, it seems too strained and contrived for easy, relaxed conversation.

Conservative grammarians also object that ending a sentence with a preposition often causes people to put what is actually the preposition's object in the subjective case: "I don't know *who* these earmuffs belong to," "*Who* did you give them to?" Usually this occurs in direct or indirect questions where, as we discussed earlier, the use of *whom* as an interrogative pronoun is already vanishing anyway.

Clearly it is nonsense to ban the use of a final preposition when leading writers from Shakespeare to Shaw have used it. Even that fastidious stylist Henry James often ended sentences with a preposition. Despite the critics of *Webster III* and other pedants, we are not being corrupted by "Music to pour Sugar Smacks by" or Quick Draw McGraw's explaining, "These packages are not to draw on; they're to eat out of." The real problem about Quick Draw is, "Where docs El Kabong hang his rope from?" When Tussy "In-a-wish" mascara advertises, "Now you can have the kind of lashes you would sell your soul for," you should worry more about the theological implications than the grammar. Again, the logic rather than the language is demented in this quotation from Joseph Heller's *Catch-22*: "The case against Clevinger was open and shut. The only thing missing was something to charge him with." [9] In the same book, General Dreedle asks, "You mean I can't shoot anyone I want to?" [10] This statement calls for a psychiatrist, not a grammarian.

Sometimes the too self-conscious person, trying to avoid ending with a preposition, fumbles and inserts an extra one from habit: "He is the man to whom I was talking to." A student wrote that sharecroppers "had not owned the farms upon which they were living and working on." In Norman Mailer's *The Naked and the Dead,* a nervous officer says, " 'You said you had been to a place to which . . . *in which* you hadn't even been within a mile of.' In the midst of his anger, [General] Cummings felt a mild contempt at the way Binner had mangled the sentence." [11]

Sometimes sentences end with two prepositions: "Something should be done away with." But it is far better not to pile up prepositions, especially at the end of a sentence, lest you stumble into some such trap as "What is that box for the birds to be fed out of inside for?" or "He would have nothing to compare the creed he is looking into with."

Though it is permissible to end sentences with a preposition, it is not always advisable to do so. "Thoreau says the individual has the right to oppose any law which he does not agree with" has a weak climax; *with* should have been placed before *which*. Likewise, the climax is destroyed in "Steinbeck reveals the unethical policies of the merchants whom the migrants are forced to deal with." By placing *with* before *whom,* you end with the proper stress on *deal*. If you have a *whom,* it is best to put *with* before it and avoid the stumblefootedness of "In the movie there is a scene in which the sailor whom Billy Budd had the fight with dies while on duty." "This turtle may be symbolic of the Joad family, who Steinbeck centers his story around" is doubly weak, both because it trails off with an unemphatic preposition and because the relative pronoun is in the wrong case; *around whom* solves both problems. On the other hand, because *lived with* seems to form a verbal unit, "Flameless electric home heating is the most comfortable heat we've ever lived with" is better than ". . . with which we've ever lived." So the only standard should be clarity and grace.

For careful grammarians, one of the most objectionable signs of linguistic vulgarity is ending a sentence with *at* after the verb *to be*: "I don't know where the theatre is at." Actually, this construction is undesirable not because of the preposition at the end of the sentence but because *at* is redundant. Plenty of likeable people ask "Where is it at?" and there is no good reason for scorning them personally, but the stigma is still there, so you are warned. In fact a final stressed *at* is an ugly, grating sound. In the middle of sentences, *at* is usually slurred as a rapid *ut,* but at the end it is usually drawn out to sound like *aayht.* In "That was what I was laughing so hilariously at," *at* is not dead wood, but the sentence is more logically constructed and has more euphony if it is changed to "That was what I was laughing at so hilariously." "What are you looking at?" is perfectly acceptable; there *at* is not dead wood and is not overstressed. But dead wood is doubly objectionable, and the *at* should be cut from such a sentence as, "Where's the vacuum cleaner at?" Why not ask, Where is it *on, under, in,* or *behind*? The trouble is that people think of *is at* as a unit, as in "He is at the chicken-pluckers' convention" and so use *at* habitually and indiscriminately after the verb *to be*. Some day we may even hear "I think, therefore I am at."

¶ DOUBLED IN DEAD WOOD

There are a great many prepositions besides *at* that can be used meaninglessly. The final word should be cut from "What have you been doing of?" "Where will it all end up?" and "Where's the opener to puncture this can with?" Dead wood can occur anywhere in a sentence, but it is not always easy to get a coroner's certificate. Clearly the second word should be pruned from the following pairs: *inside of, parallels with, despite of, near to, revert back, off of.* It is sufficient to cancel; you need not cancel *out.* Following orders is enough; you need not follow them *out.* *Up* is useless in "up until three years ago." You don't need *about* in "studying about chemistry." You don't crave *for* something; you simply crave it. A criminal confesses his guilt instead of confessing *to* it. It is enough to

195

meet and to marry; you are overdoing it to *meet up with* or *marry up with* someone. If something is *over* (finished), why make it *over with*? *Up and* is pointless in "He up and died," especially if he died in bed. Some prepositions can be shortened: *because* is better than *on account of* and *behind* than *in back of*. The interrogative *why* is better than *what for* in "What did you do it for?"

Yet many redundant prepositions are borderline cases. *Over* may seem dead wood in "He lives over in Deadwood"; you wouldn't say, "The President lives over in Washington." Yet *over* may be legitimate if it suggests some geographical barrier—"over [the mountains, the river, the hills and far away] in [name of place]." Shakespeare's Coriolanus speaks of "what we have compounded on," though *on* is not needed. We are particularly prone to add *up* to verbs where the preposition is not strictly necessary: *hurry up, lock up, fatten up, chain up, clean up, fill up, open up, eat up, check up on, divide up, fix up, foul up,* and *end up*. It is enough to hurry, lock the gate, fatten the pigs, chain the bear, clean the stables, fill the tank, open the door, eat the steak, divide the loot, fix the machinery, foul the works, and end without doing all these things *up*. Yet *up* adds intensity and underscores the idea of completion or thoroughness, as in the difference between doing something and really doing it up. "Drink it up" is more emphatic than "Drink it." If you eat something, you may not finish it; but if you eat it up, there's none left. You rarely if ever hear someone tell a gas station attendant, "Fill her," instead of "Fill her up." There is a genuine difference between cutting something and cutting it up. *Follow* means to go after or pursue, whereas *follow up* means to follow closely and persistently or to continue with even more of the same; *follow out* means to carry out fully; and *follow through* means to continue and complete.

When you have unequivocal dead wood, remove it. *From* is wrong in "A crowd of from fifty to sixty thousand was expected," "Receipts of from two to three hundred dollars were received." Meteorologists seem addicted to needless prepositions: "Logan, Utah, received [from] four to six inches of rain last night," "High winds [of] between forty and seventy miles an hour are predicted." *At about* should be simply *at* in "I'll call for you at about eight." *Rather* is wrong in "Deism seems to be more of a philosophy rather than a religion." *Of* is unnecessary in "good of an idea" or "that small of a child." Yet even great authors are not immune to this sort of failing; Hemingway wrote Lillian Ross, "Time is the least

196

thing we have of." [12] Imagine Robert Penn Warren's novel retitled *All of the King's Men.*

On the other hand, unstressed prepositions are sometimes dropped in casual speech, whereas a well-formed style requires them:

> A couple [of] hamburgers.
> What type [of] music do you like?
> Play the record [at] its right speed.
> What size [of] shoe do you wear?
> There is plenty [of] homework for tomorrow.

It is all right to omit the preposition in constructions such as "Write [to] me," "Give me," "Show me," but less acceptable to do so in "Give it [to] me" and "Show it [to] me."

You need not repeat a preposition when two verbs or nouns both use it ("Give it to Min and Bill"); but when a sentence has two words that require different prepositions, both are necessary:

> The life of Prufrock's drawing-room and teacup society
> far *removed* [*from* not needed] and *sheltered from*
> the vital questions of existence.
>
> Abner is *interested in* and *addicted to* movies.
>
> Naturalists are *concerned for* and *fascinated by* wildlife.

The accurate use of prepositions contributes considerably to effective style and is sometimes crucial for clarity. But quarrels over *like, as,* and *as if; different from* and *different than; between* and *among; due to* and *because of;* and the issue of ending a sentence with a preposition are too often mere quibbles. It is advisable to be as precise as possible, but sniping at *different than* is not going to save the English language because *different than* is not the real danger. The genuine threat to clarity and style is jargon, dead wood, bumblery, circumlocutions, verbosity, vague and slovenly diction, and other impediments to logical thought and clear communication. Critics should not waste their ammunition on trivia but go after the main target.

Exercise 20: Identify and underline the subordinating conjunctions in the following sentences:

1. When you study speech, the subject you begin with is phonetics or sounds.

197

2. It is the column of air that enters or leaves the lungs that forms the basis for sounds.

3. Proving this air current escapes unobstructed, it forms the sound which we write as *h*.

4. What obstructs the air current is some one of the speech organs.

5. The lips, teeth, tongue, nose, palate, and vocal cords are called speech organs because they help produce sound.

6. After the air leaves the lungs, it passes through the larynx, where the vocal cords are located.

7. If these vibrate, the sound which results is called a voiced sound; *h*, on the other hand, is a breath sound.

8. The simplest voiced sound is *ah,* as it is made with open unobstructed throat.

9. That is why doctors tell you to say *ah* when they want to see your throat.

10. If you want to know how voiced and breath sounds differ, compare *p* and *b*.

11. Whenever the bell was rung, Pavlov's dogs salivated.

12. If you want to know whether mushrooms are edible or poisonous, eat some and see how you feel the next day.

13. The lancers found that the telegraph wires had been cut.

14. I don't understand how people who love animals can also enjoy hunting.

15. I did but see her passing by, yet will I love her till I die.

16. There is a message from Count Alucard, who wants to know when we can deliver the coffins to the old abbey.

17. The reinforcements never saw the bugler again after he climbed the walls of Fort Zinderneuf.

18. Mark Twain said that he would rather be damned to John Bunyan's heaven than have to read a novel by Jane Austen.

19. Henry James criticized *War and Peace* because he thought it was too sprawling and formless.

20. The wolf man becomes Laurence Talbot until the next full moon transforms him again.

Exercise 21: Eliminate unnecessary prepositions from the following:

1. The austerity program should cut expenses by from 50 to 100 thousand dollars.

2. Hercules had to clean up the Augean stables.

3. Have you finished all of the kickapoo joy juice?

4. The freeway should shorten driving time by from two to three hours.

5. Quasimodo was chosen as king of the Carnival of Fools.

6. The smugglers' hideout was near to the cliffs.

7. Ever since Sputnik, Americans have been aware of the need for trained scientists.
8. The Barebones Parliament was named for a Puritan member named of Praise-God Barebones.
9. Movies were silent up until 1927.
10. Placing of the area under quarantine was necessary.
11. Fearless Fosdick knocked the robot off of the bridge.
12. Nobody saw King Kong enter into the cave, carrying Fay Wray.
13. It is evident that, if everything goes along as planned, that the project will be a huge success.
14. The grass doesn't need mowing for a couple of more days.
15. Look out of the window; a bear has knocked over the garbage can.
16. Where is the grapefruit native to?
17. There is a cow up on the ridge over across the valley.
18. Tyrone Power sliced through the candle in *The Mark of Zorro* without knocking it off of the candlestick.
19. Basil Rathbone, who did the candle bit with Tyrone Power, repeated it over in a burlesque scene with Danny Kaye in *The Court Jester*.
20. There were approximately about ten percent more visitors this year.

Exercise 22: Replace any inappropriate prepositions or conjunctions in the following sentences.

1. He won't come in without you ask him.
2. Will you join me in a slice of watermelon?
3. In *The Son of Frankenstein,* Lionel Atwill stuck darts into his wooden arm while waiting on his turn to throw.
4. We bought some fruit jar whiskey of a moonshiner.
5. Emma Bovary died from arsenic poisoning.
6. What is Admiral Bilgewater protesting for?
7. Africans and Europeans had different ideas of what slavery consisted in.
8. When you're in the Great Smokies, be sure and visit Cades Cove.
9. This rifle belonged of my great uncle Thad.
10. You can't have pearls without you find oysters.
11. Ramon Navarro played Ben Hur in the 1925 movie while Charlton Heston played him in the 1959 remake.
12. Being as we shall be out late tonight, you must take a nap.
13. We don't know but what the murderer is in this room.
14. Beowulf tore off Grendel's arm. Too, he pursued Grendel's mother and killed her.
15. Neither poor eyesight or faulty memory seems to faze Mr. McGoo.
16. We had scarcely begun the picnic than a bear turned over our ice chest.
17. Follow the Appalachian Trail til the turn off to Mt. LeConte.
18. The contrast of the white rhinoceros and the black rhinoceros is provocative.

199

19. Concentrating on his work, Handel was oblivious of his household.
20. The apostles divided the loaves and fishes between the five hundred.

Exercise 23: Put the appropriate traditional preposition or conjunction in the blank.

1. The Indian elephant's ears are different (than, from) the African elephant's.   . . . .
2. Crispy Critters already have sugar (like, as) Froot Loops do. . . . . .
3. There were so many new records that Jethro couldn't choose (between, among) them.   . . . .
4. The Brysons divide their vacation (between, among) the mountains and the beach.   . . . .
5. (As of, On) Labor Day, most seasonal park rangers go home. . . . . .
6. Inspector Bucket was discouraged (on, by) the lack of evidence.   . . . .
7. The Round Bottom caravan was canceled (due to, because of) high water at Straight Fork.
8. Pogo tried to disguise himself (like, as) Little Orphan Annie. . . . .
9. (Owing to, Because of) storm and shipwreck, many ships of the Armada never reached Spain.   . . . .
10. Neither Simpatico del Sarto's (or, nor) Mañana Iguana's style approach the simple symmetry of Pasquatanx's.   . . . .
11. The victory at Crecy was (due to, because of) the English archers.   . . . .
12. As the mad monk in *Rasputin and the Empress,* Lionel Barrymore looked (like, as if) he had crawled out of the woodwork.   . . . .
13. (Being as, Since) they hardly ever make them anymore, Jethro wrote his latest lyrics in Spenserian stanzas.   . . . .
14. Francis X. Bushman played Messala (while, and) Charlton Heston played Ben Hur.   . . . .
15. I wish we could have an air-conditioned lawn mower (like, as, such as) all the other kids have.   . . . .
16. I don't know (but what, whether) "The Three Ravens" is prettier than "Whoops, Do Me No Harm, Good Man."   . . . .
17. John Keats died (from, of) tuberculosis and not (of, due to) harsh literary criticism.   . . . .
18. In the Renaissance, most painters had to look (at, to) wealthy patrons for support.   . . . .
19. Grace thought the giraffe was (as good, as good as) or better than the twelve-string guitar.   . . . . .
20. Luther wrote that man is justified (on, by) faith alone.   . . . . .

200

13 √ Negative Negatives

One of the most frequent and obvious signs of nonstandard English is the double or multiple negative. When H. L. Mencken translated the opening of the Declaration of Independence into burlesque vulgar usage, he multiplied every possible negative: "without asking no permission from nobody . . . not trying to put nothing over on nobody . . . nobody ain't got no right to take away none of our rights . . . nobody else ought to have no say in the matter." Actually, Mencken overdid it; even speakers of nonstandard English don't go that far. But the use of the double negative serves as a powerful shibboleth; statements like "I don't want no supper," brand a person as a clod or a clown, and it is certainly better to avoid them.

The songwriters of "You Ain't Nothing but a Hound Dog" and "I Don't Want No Ricochet Romance" self-consciously use the double negative for contrived folksiness. A less obviously planned double negative often occurs with the words *hardly* and *scarcely,* for these adverbs being indirectly negative require a positive verb. Thus "I couldn't scarcely eat a thing," "There wasn't hardly any furniture in the house," and "She can't scarcely see ten feet" should be corrected to read "could scarcely," "was hardly," and "can scarcely."

But prescriptive grammarians often give illogical reasons for commanding, "Thou shalt not use the double negative." Certainly there is no sensible reason for an absolute injunction against it. The French have always doubled the negative with *ne . . . pas, ne . . . jamis,* and *ne . . . rien.* Old and Middle English regularly used a multiple negative, and Shakespeare employed it on occasion: "I never writ, nor no man ever loved." Today custom frowns on it, but it could make a comeback if usage so determined. The only commonsense argument against double negatives is that they are superfluous—a sort of dead wood. On the other hand, it can be argued that multiple negatives, though nonstandard, increase a statement's emphasis and intensity, as in these examples from the Great Smokies: "I hain't got nary none," "That boy never done nothin' nohow," "I can't get no rest nohow," and "It holped a man not to be beholden to nobody." The Appalachian "Hit don't make no nevermind" has the wrong verb form as well, but is certainly more vivid than "It doesn't matter."

The argument that two negatives make a positive is a faulty analogy from mathematics. Meaning is not mathematics; and when a person says, "He doesn't read no books," he does not mean he does read *some* books, no matter what purists may argue.

Standard English does sometimes use a double negative but for an evasive rather than an emphatic effect, as in "There is no one who does not sometimes make mistakes." It is clearer and more direct to write, "Everyone sometimes makes mistakes." But jargon often prefers evasion and likes to weaken statements by the non-commital negative, particularly the *not un-* formation, where two negatives do not quite make a positive but rather a diminished affirmative. "I'm not certain that it is honest" is less forceful than "I think that is dishonest." *Not infrequent* is less forthright than *frequent*; *was not faithful* is less blunt than *betrayed*; *not very worthwhile* is less emphatic than *practically worthless*; and *not very attractive* is less damning than *ugly*.

Apparently many people today hesitate to commit themselves. In "Politics and the English Language," George Orwell cites as a horrible example the following sentence from Professor Harold Laski's *Freedom of Expression*: "I am not, indeed, sure whether it is not true to say that the Milton who once seemed not unlike a seventeenth-century Shelley had not become, out of an experience ever more bitter in each year, more alien [*sic*] to the founder of that Jesuit sect which nothing could induce him to tolerate." This is a poor example of unfettered literary expression, for Laski gets so tangled in negatives that he conveys the wrong meaning, using the negative *alien* when he means *akin*. This sort of style erects a series of barriers, like the false turns in a labyrinth, and a reader may never find the exit. The *not un-* is a hesitant construction and may thus, as Orwell suggests, give banal statements an appearance of profundity. A reader should not be taken in by it and should avoid it in his own work. As a cure, Orwell recommended memorizing, "A not unblack dog was chasing a not unsmall rabbit across a not ungreen field."

Besides the tangle of jargon, negative implications are difficult to remove; sometimes they raise needless doubts that then have to be removed. The Department of Agriculture urges its writers to think positively and not to drag in negative suggestions that must later be canceled. Thus, "We cannot fail to be impressed" should be changed to "We are greatly impressed."

Negative affixes are sometimes a problem. Sometimes they do not actually negate. The undead are not exactly alive; vampires and zombis are hardly living dolls. (When in the film *White Zombi,* some tourists in Haiti see zombis slaving in a grist mill—zombis usually seem to slave in grist mills—and ask their coachman about these strange people, he replies, "Them's not people; them's dead *bah-*ties [bodies].") A nonbook is still a book; and currently, e.g., in such terms as *nonperson, nonmusic, nonbook, nonsentence,* the prefix *non* means "illegitimate" or "debased" or "deficient," rather than "not." Neither does the negative with an adjective necessarily indicate the opposite. *Not right* doesn't have to mean "absolutely wrong"; *not my friend* doesn't mean "my enemy"; *not full* doesn't have to mean "empty." There are degrees of shading and contrast for subtleties of distinction.

Since subtleties require thought, the totalitarian thought controllers of George Orwell's *1984* manipulate language and enormously reduce vocabulary to purge the diction of critical thinking and make unorthodoxy impossible. One way is to eliminate positive opposites (and hence choice) by replacing them with the prefix *un-.* "Given, for instance, the word *good,* there was no need for such a word as *bad,* since the required meaning was equally well— indeed better—expressed by *ungood.* All that was necessary, in any case where two words formed a natural pair of opposites, was to decide which of them to suppress. *Dark,* for example, could be replaced by *unlight,* or *light* by *undark,* according to preference." [1] By this method and others, language is impoverished until only the rigid jargon of Newspeak remains, in which dehumanized people express the dogmas of the Party.

Both prefixes and suffixes can be used to negate a word, but you should not use both on the same root. *Irregardless* is undesirable not mainly because it is considered vulgar but because the suffix is sufficient; *regardless* is proper; the prefix, worthless and irritating. There are many negative prefixes: *a-, anti-, contra-, contre-, counter-, de-, di-, dis-, dys-, ig-, il-, im-, in-, ir-, mal-, mis-, non-,* and *un-.* These cannot be used interchangeably, but custom is the only rule governing their use, so you have to learn each word individually.

Thus we have *achromatic, antithesis, disarrange, ignoble, illiterate, immature, incomplete, irreverent, misbehave, nonrestrictive, unscientific.* Some words with a negative prefix have no positive counterpart; there is no *mune, effable, cessant, delible, ane, nominy, ert,* or *dignant,* for *immune, ineffable, incessant, indelible, inane, ignominy, inert,* and *indignant.* Some negative prefixes have other meanings as well, and occasional confusion results. *Inflammable* means that the substance can catch fire, but some people seeing the sign on trucks thought that the prefix meant *not,* so *inflammable* has been replaced by *flammable,* which means the same thing.

Many contractions are negatives with an auxiliary verb: *can't, couldn't, won't, wouldn't, doesn't, don't, didn't,* the practically obsolete *shan't, shouldn't,* and the notorious *ain't.* A frequent error here is the omission or misplacement of the apostrophe, which should be between the *n* and *t* to replace the *o* in *not.* Often careless writers misplace the apostrophe, and even the novelist John W. De Forest wrote, "It wo'nt burn!" Not all contractions duplicate in shortened form the original word; *won't* is not literally a combination of *will* and *not* but strictly speaking, a new word used to express the idea. The actual contraction, which one four-year-old girl coined by analogy, is *willn't.* Sometimes small children confuse the negative contraction with the infinitive and precede it with the positive verb. The aforementioned four-year-old asked questions like, "Why could he couldn't play?", "Why did she didn't go to nursery school?", "Why did they didn't say hello?", "Why would they wouldn't fall off the mountain?", and once stated, "I'm going on the back porch where the hornets are aren't."

Though the bête noire of purists, *ain't* is quite as logical as *won't;* it simply isn't sanctioned. *Ain't* replaces *am not* ("I ain't"), *is not* or *isn't* ("he ain't"), and *are not* ("they ain't"). *Isn't* is a slithery word, and *ain't* may be more euphonious. In question, *ain't* is used for *are not* (*ain't I* vs. *aren't I*). *Aren't I* is technically ungrammatical though approved; the logical but unpronounceable form is *amn't I,* and formal English would use *am I not.* *Ain't got no* and *ain't got none* are triply unsanctioned. Besides the double negative, *ain't* here is a contraction of *has not* or *have not.* Hence the contraction is illogical, with no audible relation to the actual verb. Perhaps the soundest argument against *ain't* is that it could easily become an indiscriminate catch-all contraction.

Possibly more common than *ain't* in nonstandard English is the erroneous use of *don't* for *doesn't* in the third person singular ("he

204

don't"). Another fallacy with contractions is the use of *didn't ought* or *hadn't ought*. Since *did* and *had* are meaningless here, the proper form is *ought not,* which you sometimes hear (but seldom see written) in the contracted form of *oughtn't.*

Do with a negative often loses all meaning and becomes purely functional, with the infinitive carrying the full sense, as in "I do not think so," "I don't know," "He doesn't want any." Older English might omit *do* and instead use the form, "I think not so," "I know not," "He wants none," with the negative following the verb.

Sometimes those asking negative questions expect affirmative answers, as in, "Don't you want to take a nap?" or "Why don't you wash your hands before supper?" The danger here is that children are apt to reply, "No, I don't," or "Because I don't want to." In such situations grammar fails, and other persuasions must take over.

Exercise 24: Correct any multiple or unacceptable negatives in the following:

1. It doesn't cost only thirty cents.
2. Fish aren't biting nohow in this rain.
3. Father's not working none; he's just trafficking around.
4. With a not inconsiderable number of supporters, Ringo Starr made a not unmemorable campaign for President.
5. Lon Chaney looked horrifying as the Phantom of the Opera, but Claude Rains wasn't hardly scary even without his mask.
6. In the coldest weather some New Englanders don't wear no coat.
7. Errol Flynn was a not insensitive actor when he had a script that was not unworthy of his intelligence.
8. In the mountains you won't find nary a person that says a good word for the revenuers.
9. James Thurber couldn't hardly picture Henry James confronting Brigitte Bardot.
10. Allen insists on going without no reservations.
11. Not even the chains couldn't hold King Kong when the flashbulbs went off.
12. It didn't take scarcely a moment for Quasimodo to swing down from the scaffold and whisk Esmeralda to safety.
13. It is a not unreasonable claim that *The Carpetbaggers* is a not unlikely candidate for the worst novel ever written.
14. There wasn't no black bean soup in stock at Shaheen's supermarket.
15. A not unsooty raven was making a not uncacaphonous caw in a not un-apple tree in the not unmowed field at Oconaluftee.

16. There is not, according to literary scholars, no reliable evidence to show that Shakespeare did not write his own plays.
17. To say that Bacon wrote Shakespeare is not scarcely different from claiming that Darwin wrote *Vanity Fair*.
18. Ben Gunn was disappointed that Jim Hawkins did not have no cheese in his pocket.
19. After the disastrous opening night of *Guy Domville,* Henry James did not want no more active connection with the theater.
20. After losing money on foolish speculations, Mark Twain became cautious and did not buy no stock in the new Bell Telephone Company.

14 √ Sentence Structure

Knowing how to use the parts of speech is not very helpful if you cannot use them to construct effective sentences. It is quite possible to use correct grammar and have a totally undistinguished style. H. L. Mencken wrote that President Warren G. Harding's prose reminded him "of a string of wet sponges." Harding enjoyed making speeches ("I like to go out into the country and bloviate," he said), but few people enjoyed listening to them. Instead of "bloviating," you need to organize your thoughts logically and then express them in a clear and orderly fashion. If your paragraphs and pages are to be persuasive, you must not rely on sheer bulk of argument or narrative, but must construct each sentence carefully. For a few writers, the sentence rather than larger units, holds the essence of their art. Emerson and Thoreau often ramble in their wording, seeming to neglect logical development and transition, but their individual sentences are polished like gems. *Walden* is largely a mosaic of brilliant sentences, which Thoreau had written years before he placed them in a larger organization.

Unfortunately, many people are unsure when they have written a sentence. It is as necessary for the writer to know the structure of a sentence as for a mechanic to know that of his machines. First we must differentiate between phrases and clauses. A phrase is a group of words combined as a unit without a subject and a verb. It may form all or part of the subject or all or part of the predicate, but both are needed for a clause. In the following examples, the phrases indicated by the italicized words function in each sentence in a different way grammatically:

> *The magic word "Shazaam"* turned Billy Batson into Captain Marvel.
>   (Phrase is subject.)
> Snoopy is *Charlie Brown's dog.* (Phrase is complement of the verb.)
> Superman emerged *from the phone booth.* (Phrase modifies verb.)

207

Without his mask, the Lone Ranger might have better eyesight. (Phrase modifies subject.)

L'il Abner's hair is parted on whatever side *faces the reader.* (Phrase is a predicate.)

Alice the Goon *has not appeared* lately in the "Popeye" comic strip. (Phrase is a verb.)

Each of these sentences has several other phrases beside the ones italicized. Sometimes there are phrases within phrases. In "Mighty Mouse rescued Pearl Pureheart *from the clutches of Oilcan Harry,*" the over-all phrase modifies the verb *rescued,* and *of Oilcan Harry* modifies *clutches.*

¶ MAIN CLAUSES AND SIMPLE SENTENCES

There are two types of clauses: main (or independent) and subordinate (or dependent). Both must have a subject and a verb. But a main clause is self-contained and does not function as a subject, modifier, or complement. It can be an independent simple sentence, consisting of just a subject and a verb: "She sells." To this we can add an object ("She sells seashells") and assorted modifiers ("She sells overpriced seashells by the seashore"). A main clause can have two subjects ("Jack and Jill went up the hill") or two verbs ("Jack fell down and broke his crown") or two subjects for the same two verbs ("Frankie and Johnnie went to the bar and had a few drinks"). Two or more main clauses can be combined to make compound sentences:

Art is long. (One main clause as a simple sentence.)

Art is long, but *time is fleeting.* (Two main clauses joined as a compound sentence.)

Mark Twain was a realist and *so was Henry James,* but *they didn't like each other's work.* (Three main clauses joined as a compound sentence.)

A main clause can have a number of qualifying phrases and still the whole will be an independent simple sentence: "Our hearts, though stout and brave, still, like muffled drums, are beating funeral marches to the grave." This has only one subject (*hearts*) and one verb (*are beating*). In a compound sentence, the main clauses must be connected either by a coordinating conjunction (*and, but, for, or, nor, yet*) preceded by a comma or by a semicolon with no conjunction. Use of a comma alone constitutes a comma splice, a serious flaw in punctuation. If the clauses are simply run together with no conjunction or punctuation, then there is a run-on sentence; this is rightly considered an even more serious flaw.

¶ SUBORDINATE CLAUSES

A subordinate (or dependent) clause has its own subject and verb, but it cannot stand alone. Usually introduced by a relative pronoun or a subordinating conjunction, it depends upon the main clause and functions as subject, modifier, or complement:

John Wayne is the only actor *who killed two giant squids.* (Clause modifies *actor.*)

As soon as the fire alarm rang, Smokey Stover was on the job. (Clause modifies *was.*)

I don't understand *why Prudence Pimpleton puts up with Fearless Fosdick.* (Clause is complement of verb *understand.*)

Why Beetle Bailey isn't promoted or discharged is a mystery. (Clause is subject of *is.*)

Orphan Annie is the girl *whose eyes are blunked out.* (Clause modifies *girl.*)

Occasionally, the connective is omitted ("Lois Lane is the girl *Clark Kent loves*"). A sentence may contain several subordinate clauses: "*When Ming was ruler of Mongo,* he ordered *that all men must be bald.*" Sometimes the subordinate clause is elliptical, with the verb understood: in the sentence, "Blackstone gave away more rabbits *than any other magician,*" the verb *did* is understood.

Subordinate clauses introduced by conjunctions can have various positions in a sentence, whereas those introduced by an interrogative or relative pronoun usually cannot. "I don't understand *how Popeye eats spinach through his pipe*" has fixed word order, as does "Jack Jawbreaker is the man *who robbed the bank.*" "Only the Shadow knows *what evil lurks* in the heart of man," is the normal word order, though this could conceivably be phrased, "*What evil lurks in the heart of man,* only the Shadow knows." "When I go to a ball game, I don't like to sit in the rain" could just as well be "I don't like to sit in the rain when I go to a ball game." Notice that a subordinate clause is followed by a comma when it precedes the main clause, unless it is the subject of that clause, but is not set off by a comma if it comes after the main clause.

Sentences with one subordinate clause and one main clause are

209

called complex sentences. Those with two main clauses and one or more subordinate clauses are compound-complex sentences, like Thoreau's "One value even of the smallest well is, that when you look into it, you see that earth is not continent but insular."

Though subordinate clauses can serve as a verb's subject, object, or complement, they are not always used this way effectively. According to *Time*, ". . . President Kennedy told his press conference that just because some merchant has Polish ham in his shop does not brand him as unpatriotic." [1] In this complex sentence, "just because some merchant has Polish ham in his shop" is not grammatically adequate as the subject of the verb, *does*. Similarly, "Just because Babbitt rebels" is not an adequate subject in "Just because Babbitt rebels does not mean that he becomes genuinely liberal." As complement, a subordinate clause can be equally clumsy, as in "A baby is so you could be the boss" and "Marriage is so your brothers and sisters should grow up and get married and then you could be the only child," [2] though not always with such comic effect. The clumsiness of "One thing no good about a big brother is when you hit him he hits you right back" [3] can be cured by additional subordination—the insertion of *that* between *is* and *when*. But then the sentence isn't as much fun.

¶ VARIETY IN SENTENCE STRUCTURE

Books for beginning readers are usually written in a sequence of simple sentences, and elementary writers often follow suit: "Once upon a time there was a hippopotamus. His name was Harry. Harry ate too much one night. He ate 275 cabbages. He ate 312 bananas. He ate 25 bags of potato chips." Or they connect a series of short main clauses by *and* with monotonous regularity: "Harry ate 46 hamburgers, and he ate 79 pounds of peanuts, and he ate 13 cantaloupes, and he drank 32 bottles of root beer, and he ate 115 pizzas, and for dessert he had seven gallons of fudgi-wudgi ice cream. Then Harry felt sick, and he went to the wise old owl, and the wise old owl told him to go to the magic spring and drink some water from it. Harry asked where the spring was. The wise old owl told him it was three mountain ranges away. Harry felt too sick to go there, so the wise old owl told him to get some help." This is not quite as deadly as "See Spot run. Run, run, run. Run, Spot, run," but it has little variety. Grammatically such prose is correct, but stylistically it is flat unless it is done by Hemingway, who

210

achieved considerable subtlety with deceptively simple grammatical repetition. Possibly the best example of terse statement packed with what now seems comic implication is the climax of the pot-boiler novel *The Sheik*: " 'I haven't!' 'You aren't!' She was." Some students go to the other extreme and get lost in a tangle of involved verbosity. Clarity is essential, but so is a degree of variety—though a writer should never strain to achieve it. Paragraphs in which most sentences have the same length and structure plod along with the monotony of an ambling nag:

Thoreau's *Walden* is partly an autobiographical narrative. It tells about the two years and two months and two days that Thoreau spent in the woods. He went to the woods to simplify his life. He also wanted to prove that men could live adequately without a lot of money. He borrowed the land from Emerson and bought a railroad shanty. He worked little so that he could read and study nature. Thoreau did not urge everybody to do as he did. He wanted each man to find his own solution. According to Thoreau, most men lead lives of quiet desperation.

If Thoreau had written no better than that, no one would read him today. On the other hand, too much variety may seem like tutti frutti: "Those who could fled, until at last there were no more to pay the penalty for a deed, which, while not beyond them, they were, nevertheless, not guilty of." [4] This involved, stumbling construction seems punctuated with panting pauses so that writer and reader can catch their breath. If Burroughs' sentences were so clumsily complicated consistently, his readers would have soon lost patience. Though their sensibilities were worlds apart, the mandarin prose of Henry James's late period sometimes resembles this specimen from Burroughs. In "The Altar of the Dead," James wrote, "He had found little change indeed, he had brought the little change back; it was the little change that stood there and that, do what he would he couldn't, while he showed those high front teeth of his, look other than a conscious ass about." In his later writing, James inserted a great many hesitant parenthetical qualifications that sometimes made his style so involuted that it became asthmatic.

Sometimes subordination and combination can help give variety and improve transition:

It was the beginning of February, 1821. Two ships of imperial Russia, the *Vostok* and the *Mirnyi,* rounded Cape Horn. They cruised South into the ice-choked Weddell Sea. They were searching for uncharted land. The Russians hoped this might prove the existence of the legendary Antarctic

211

continent. Captain Thaddeus von Bellingshausen commanded this small squadron. Twelve months before it had explored the islands east of the Cape. Now it was a year and a half out of Kronstadt. It was completing a circumnavigation of the world in the south polar latitudes.

Here is the beginning of an interesting story botched by a bumpy style. Notice the improvement in the following:

At the beginning of February, 1821, two ships of imperial Russia, the *Vostok* and the *Mirnyi,* rounded Cape Horn and cruised south into the ice-choked Weddell Sea searching for uncharted land that might prove the existence of the legendary Antarctic continent. This small squadron, under command of Captain Thaddeus von Bellingshausen, had twelve months before explored the islands east of the Cape and was now, a year and a half out of Kronstadt, completing a circumnavigation of the world in the south polar latitudes.

Here the first sentence of version one is turned into a phrase; the subject in sentence two picks up the verb in sentence three and cuts the repeated subject; sentence four becomes a participial modifying phrase; and sentence five becomes a subordinate clause. What changes are made to combine the remaining sentences?

Sometimes making a clause subordinate is undesirable. "There's a whole lost city that nobody knows where it is" is grammatically off the track. The sentence should be coordinated to "There's a whole lost city, and nobody knows where it is." Subordinate clauses, especially those beginning with *which,* can be dangerous in that they tend to proliferate out of control: "He took his daughter to see the penguins in the Vancouver Zoo, which was located across the isthmus which bridged Stanley Park, which had been set aside by the city and which included twelve miles which have both beaches and almost virgin forests which are penetrated only by a few paths which are always well tended." *Which* clauses not only sprawl but often pile up passive voice constructions: "It was an obsolete car, for the repair of which a diligent search for spare parts was required and for which a mechanic occasionally had to make a new part." James Thurber writes that "Trying to cross a paragraph by leaping from 'which' to 'which' is like Eliza crossing the ice. The danger is in missing a 'which' and falling in." [5] In "Rufus went to the zoo, which was in the park, which had his favorite rhinoceros which he liked to feed and calmed his nerves," the twittering "whicher" dropped the last *which* before *calmed.* Sup-

212

pose you write, "It is a program which we must adopt or go bankrupt." Something is wrong here, so you plunge in and try, "It is a program which we must adopt or which will go bankrupt." You run your fingers through your hair and try, "It is a program which we must adopt or by which we will go bankrupt." Foiled again, you shake your head grimly and write, "It is a program which we must adopt or which, if we do not adopt, will bankrupt us," and so on. By the time you get the sentence straightened out ("We must adopt this program or go bankrupt"), you may have gone bankrupt yourself.

¶ PERIODIC SENTENCES

When an introductory subordinate clause, a long introductory phrase, or a group of modifiers comes before the main clause, we have a periodic sentence. Depending on their content, periodic sentences can be simple, compound, complex, or compound-complex. Such sentences are often effective in opening with an emphasis and building to a climax: "From the time Tarzan left the tribe of great anthropoids in which he had been raised, it was torn by continual strife and discord. . . . As Terkoz reached the group, five huge, hairy beasts sprang upon him." [6] One of the most spectacular examples of a periodic sentence occurs in Whitman's "Song of Myself," where we find one sentence eighty lines long, with the subject and verb in the last line preceded by a series of modifiers modified by other modifiers. By all rules this should not work, but it succeeds as one of Whitman's finest pieces of poetry:

By the city's quadrangular houses—in log huts, camping with lumbermen,
Along the ruts of the turnpike, along the dry gulch and rivulet bed,
Weeding my onion patch or hoeing rows of carrots and parsnips, crossing savannas, trailing in forests,
Prospecting, gold-digging, girdling the trees of a new purchase,
Scorch'd ankle-deep by the hot sand, hauling my boat down the shallow river,
Where the panther walks to and fro on a limb overhead, where the buck turns furiously at the hunter,
Where the rattlesnake suns his flabby length on a rock, where the otter is feeding on fish,
Where the alligator in his tough pimples sleeps by the bayou,
Where the black bear is searching for roots or honey, where the beaver pats the mud with his paddle-shaped tail;

213

Over the growing sugar, over the yellow-flower'd cotton plant, over the rice in its low moist field,

Over the sharp-peak'd farm house, with its scallop'd scum and slender shoots from the gutters,

Over the west persimmon, over the long-leav'd corn, over the delicate blue-flower flax,

Over the white and brown buckwheat, a hummer and buzzer there with the rest,

Over the dusky green of the rye as it ripples and shades in the breeze;

Scaling mountains, pulling myself cautiously up, holding on by low scragged limbs,

Walking the path worn in the grass and beat through the leaves of the brush,

Where the quail is whistling betwixt the woods and the wheat-lot,

Where the bat flies in the Seventh-month eve, where the great gold-bug drops through the dark,

Where the brook puts out of the roots of the old trees and flows to the meadow,

Where cattle stand and shake away flies with the tremulous shuddering of their hides,

Where the cheese-cloth hangs in the kitchen, where andirons straddle the hearth-slab, where cobwebs fall in festoons from the rafters;

Where trip-hammers crash, where the press is whirling its cylinders,

Wherever the human heart beats with terrible throes under its ribs,

Where the pear-shaped balloon is floating aloft, (floating in it myself and looking composedly down,)

Where the life-car is drawn on the slip-noose, where the heat hatches pale-green eggs in the dented sand,

Where the she-whale swims with her calf and never forsakes it,

Where the steam-ship trails hind-ways its long pennant of smoke,

Where the fin of the shark cuts like a black chip out of the water,

Where the half-burn'd brig is riding on unknown currents,

Where shells grow to her slimy deck, where the dead are corrupting below;

Where the dense-starr'd flag is borne at the head of the regiments,

Approaching Manhattan up by the long-stretched island,

Under Niagara, the cataract falling like a veil over my countenance,

Upon a door-step, upon the horse-block of hard wood outside,

Upon the race-course, or enjoying picnics or jugs or a good game of base-ball,

At he-festivals, with blackguard gibs, ironical license, bull-dances, drinking, laughter,

At the cider-mill tasting the sweets of the brown mash, sucking the juice through a straw,

At apple-peelings wanting kisses for all the red fruit I find,
At musters, beach-parties, friendly bees, huskings, house-raisings;
Where the mocking-bird sounds his delicious gurgles, cackles, screams, weeps,
Where the hay-rick stands in the barn yard, where the dry-stalks are scatter'd, where the brood-cow waits in the hovel,
Where the bull advances to do his masculine work, where the stud to the mare, where the cock is treading the hen,
Where the heifers browse, where geese nip their food with short jerks,
Where the sun-down shadows lengthen over the limitless and lonesome prairie,
Where herds of buffalo make a crawling spread of the square miles far and near,
Where the humming-bird shimmers, where the neck of the long-lived swan is curving and winding,
Where the laughing-gull scoots by the shore, where she laughs her near-human laugh,
Where the bee-hives range on a gray bench in the garden half hid by the high weeds,
Where band-neck'd partridges roost in a ring on the ground with their heads out,
Where burial coaches enter the arch'd gates of a cemetery,
Where winter wolves bark amid wastes of snow and icicled trees,
Where the yellow-crown'd heron comes to the edge of the marsh at night and feeds upon small crabs,
Where the splash of swimmers and divers cools the warm noon,
Where the katy-did works her chromatic reed on the walnut-tree over the well,
Through patches of citrons and cucumbers with silver-wired leaves,
Through the salt-lick or orange glade, or under conical firs,
Through the gymnasium, through the curtain'd saloon, through the office or public hall;
Pleas'd with the native and pleas'd with the foreign, pleas'd with the new and old,
Pleas'd with the homely woman as well as the handsome,
Pleas'd with the quakeress as she puts off her bonnet and talks melodiously,
Pleas'd with the tune of the choir of the whitewash'd church,
Pleas'd with the earnest words of the sweating Methodist preacher, impress'd seriously at the camp-meeting;
Looking in at the shop-windows of Broadway the whole forenoon, flatting the flesh of my nose on the thick plate glass,
Wandering the same afternoon with my face turn'd up to the clouds, or down a lane or along the beach,

My right and left arms round the sides of two friends, and I in the middle;
Coming home with the silent and dark-cheek'd bush-boy, (behind me he
   rides at the drape of the day,)
Far from the settlements studying the print of animals' feet, or the moccasin
   print,
By the cot in the hospital reaching lemonade to a feverish patient,
Nigh the coffin'd corpse when all is still, examining with a candle;
Voyaging to every port to dicker and adventure,
Hurrying with the modern crowd as eager and fickle as any,
Hot toward one I hate, ready in my madness to knife him,
Solitary at midnight in my back yard, my thoughts gone from me a long
   while,
Walking the old hills of Judaea with the beautiful gentle God by my side,
Speeding through space, speeding through heaven and the stars,
Speeding amid the seven satellites and the broad ring, and the diameter of
   eighty thousand miles,
Speeding with tail'd meteors, throwing fire-balls like the rest,
Carrying the crescent child that carries its own full mother in its belly,
Storming, enjoying, planning, loving, cautioning,
Backing and filling, appearing and disappearing,
I tread day and night such roads.

Not until the last line are the subject *I* and the predicate apparent. All of the preceding lines tell where and how Whitman treads—by the houses, in huts, camping, along the ruts, weeding, prospecting, scorch'd, hauling; then comes a series of subordinate clauses modifying *hauling*: where the panther, the buck, the rattlesnake, the otter, the alligator, and the bear live; then follow another series of modifiers of *I*—over this and that, scaling, walking (followed by dozens of lines modifying where he walks)—followed by another series telling how he walks, pleased with this and that, looking, wandering, coming home, etc., and so on down to the nine present participles in the second and third lines from the end.

The periodic sentence is sometimes necessary for climax. "We won the game after having ten penalties and fumbling the ball twelve times" leaves the impression of penalties and fumbles rather than victory. "After having ten penalties and fumbling the ball twelve times, we won the game," gives the necessary chronological explanation, contrast, and culmination. Again, the subordinate clause is an ambiguously placed modifier in "Adam and Eve did not have to go out into the cruel world and work until they had sinned." Sinning was not the result of too much work, so the word order should be, "Until they had sinned, Adam and Eve did not have to

216

go out into the cruel world and work." Periodic sentences are often stately and sometimes static. Since they weigh down the structure so heavily before reaching the sentence's subject and predicate, they may impede the forward movement of narrative action. And after too much of a build-up, the action may seem too trivial. How effective is the following? "Unversed in jungle craft, overwhelmed by the enormity of the catastrophe that had engulfed him, his reasoning faculties numbed by terror, Wilbur Stimbol slunk through the jungle, the fleeing quarry of every terror that imagination could conjure." [7] Perhaps the verb *slunk* is insufficient to carry so much weight. At any rate, be careful not to make your sentences top-heavy.

¶ INVERSION AND WORD ORDER

Since emphasis and stress normally fall at the beginning and end of the English sentence, a skillful writer often inverts normal word order to place what he wishes to have emphasized at the sentence's beginning or end. This is particularly common in poetry. "Divine am I inside and out," wrote Whitman, more dramatically than if he had written, "I am divine inside and out." "Exploitation there was . . ." wrote C. Vann Woodward about the Jim Crow laws. Emerson's "In self-trust all the virtues are comprehended" is more emphatic than, "All the virtues are comprehended in self-trust." By omitting an auxiliary verb, inversion can make a line of poetry more dramatic and concise: Macbeth's "Saw you the weird sisters? Came they not by you?" has more urgency than "Did you see the weird sisters?" "Infected be the air whereon they ride," he curses. On the other hand, sometimes inversion is used to delay the climactic word until the end, as in Richard III's "Than my Lord Hastings no man might be bolder."

Milton was particularly prone to use inversions in both his poetry and his prose. As a result, his work is sometimes more stately than vigorous. Critics have observed that Homer has the *Iliad* well under way but Milton is still invoking his inverted muse after a dozen lines. Sometimes, poetic inversion forces the reader to straighten out the lines in order to clarify the meaning. The Puritan poet Edward Taylor wrote:

> This thing
> Souls are but petty things it to admire.
> Ye angels, help! This fill would to the brim
> Heaven's whelmed-down crystal meal bowl . . .

217

Prose would say, "Souls are but petty things to admire this thing. . . . This would fill Heaven's whelmed-down meal bowl to the brim." How would you straighten out the following lines from Chaucer?

> Of his complexioun he was sangwyn. . . .
> An housholdere, and that a greet [great], was he;
> Seint Julian he was in his contree [country]. . . .
> With-out bake mete [meat pie] was never his hous,
> Of fish and flesh, and that so plenteous
> It snewed [snowed] in his hous of mete and drink.

Word order is one of the subtlest and most important problems of style. There are no rules or reliable guidelines; the best way to learn how best to order a sentence is to read widely among skilled writers and educate your ear to possible rhythms. Sometimes word order involves logic, as with misplaced modifiers. "Lowell's essay on Thoreau suffers from lack of argument and wandering purpose" is clearer as "Lowell's essay on Thoreau suffers from wandering purpose and lack of argument." Otherwise, lack of wandering purpose may seem to be what the essay suffers from. But usually the issue is more one of style than sense. "Life, Liberty and the pursuit of Happiness" has exactly the right order. The meaning is as clear, but something is lost in "Life, the pursuit of Happiness, and Liberty," "Liberty, Life, and the pursuit of Happiness," or "The pursuit of Happiness, Life, and Liberty." ". . . we mutually pledge to each other our Lives, our Fortunes and our sacred Honor" again has the inevitability of the right word order. Had Jefferson written, "our Lives, our sacred Honor, and our Fortunes," the proper culmination would be missing. Again, contrast "Man does not live by bread alone" with "Man doesn't live only on bread." Not only the style but even the connotative meaning is subtly altered. Effective word order is as much a matter of intuition as rationale. Why is Shakespeare's "Something wicked this way comes" better than "Something wicked comes this way?" Perhaps a slight shift in the normal word order creates dramatic tension. Ordinarily a modifier should be placed next to the word it modifies, but notice how delaying the key word until the end gives it an explosive power when James Baldwin writes, "Yes, it does indeed mean something—something unspeakable—to be born, in a white country, an Anglo-Teutonic, anti-sexual country, black." [8]

Some problems of word order are dealt with in other chapters in this book, particularly in the sections on jargon, circumlocution, and dead wood. Sometimes people talking too rapidly, carelessly, or fumblingly toss off sentences with staggering structure or use redundancies, such as "All I did was, I did . . ." or "So what I decided to do, I decided . . ." Or they start a subordinate clause with *that,* fail to follow up the subject with a verb, and get sidetracked into some other clause: "He was playing the kind of pool that you knew he was a professional." Holden Caulfield often uses such constructions in *The Catcher in the Rye,* but they are appropriate only when creating ficitional dialogue. In "All we did, we just went to see the walrus," the first clause should be eliminated, as it should in "What I did was, I pulled his hat over his ears."

Some grammarians warn against piling up adjectives or nouns, but at times these can be effective. The nouns are weirdly formidable in the ad for Chrysler's marsh screw amphibian: "For water, mud, marsh, sludge, slosh, slough, bog, fen, morass, quagmire, snow, slush, sand, silt, muck and mire." This is not a complete sentence, but doubtless the author was unable to slog along any farther. More artistically, John Donne piled up nouns like a series of hammer blows in:

> Thou'rt slave to Fate, chance, kings, and desperate men,
> And dost with poison, war, and sickness dwell . . .

Ultimately the arrangement of words is an artistic rather than a strictly grammatical matter. Styles vary from the stark sentences of early Hemingway to the full diapason of Faulkner, whose open-stopped sentences sometimes go on for as long as six pages, full of subordination upon subordination, participle upon participle, and parentheses within parentheses. Most writers settle somewhere between these two extremes.

¶ PARALLELISM

Parallel constructions contain two or a series of units identical in form grammatically, balancing ideas of equal weight. When these parallel elements are not in similar grammatical form, the balance is upset and the syntactical logic weakened. Thus, "The polar bear likes eating, sleeping, and to swim" as the combined object of *like* two present participles and an infinitive. This faulty parallelism can be corrected by using either three participles ("eating, sleeping, and swimming") or three infinitives ("to eat, to sleep, and to swim"). The parallel structure may be clearer if printed:

| African wildlife is endangered by | the growth of agriculture and industry, the activity of poachers, the callousness of trophy hunters, | and the resultant destruction of the balance of nature. |

Here the verb *is endangered* has four nouns as objects: *growth, activity, callousness,* and *destruction*. If any of them were changed to another part of speech, the balance would be destroyed, e.g., "endangered by the growth of agriculture and industry, the activity of poachers, to satisfy trophy hunters, and the resultant destruction of the balance of nature."

"To err is human, to forgive divine." In this line by Alexander Pope, we have a parallel contraction of two infinitives, followed by *is* (the second understood) and a predicate adjective. If the line were altered to read, "To err is human, to forgive being divine," the sense remains unchanged, but the style is sabotaged. Rhythmical measure and balance in both poetry and prose is often the direct result of effectively using parallel structure. Emerson wrote, "There is a time in every man's education when he arrives at the conviction that envy is ignorance; that imitation is suicide; that he must take himself for better for worse as his portion; that though the wide universe is full of good, no kernel of nourishing corn can come to him but through his toil bestowed on that plot of ground which is given to him to till." Here the succession of parallel subordinate clauses beginning with *that* holds the sentence together in stately procession. "There is a time in every man's education when he arrives at the conviction that envy is ignorance and it is suicide to be imitative because he must take himself for better or even worse as his portion . . ." destroys the parallelism and makes Emerson's muse a crippled pedestrian. Again, Emerson wrote, "What we are, that only can we see. All that Adam had, all that Caesar could, you have and can do." How much less effective this is as, "We are only what we can see. You can have all that Adam had and can do what Caesar could do." The paraphrase is still in parallel structure, but the ordered, cumulative rhythm of the original is ruined.

Lacking Emerson's style, a student wrote, "Thoreau says to live free and uncommitted and that a farm can imprison a man." Here *says* has two complements joined by *and*—an infinitive and a subordinate clause. For proper parallelism they must be in the same grammatical form: "Thoreau says that a man should live free and uncommitted and that a farm can imprison him." This is still not a brilliant sentence, but it holds together. According to another student, "Reading Thoreau and of *Walden,* we become aware of another world around us." Here the opening participle has a direct object parallel to a prepositional phrase. There are various remedies: "Reading Thoreau, we become aware . . . ," "Reading *Walden,* we become aware . . . ," "Reading Thoreau's *Walden,* we become aware . . . ," or "Reading of Thoreau's life at Walden, we become aware . . ."

Even worse are lumpy series without parallelism, such as "Three things prevail. These are man's inhumanity to man, worth of things is not determined by dollars and cents, and the migrants' condition was uncontrollable by them." This combines a noun (*inhumanity*) and two coordinate independent clauses in a senseless hodgepodge. One girl described her boy friend: "Jerry is six feet tall, brown eyes, black unruly hair, and weighs about one hundred and sixty pounds." Lest it seem that Jerry is eyes and hair, this series needs an inserted *has* before *brown eyes,* so that there will be three verbs (*is, has, weighs*) in parallel construction. "Everyone in *Babbitt* has the same type of homes, dress very similar, must give the same type of parties, ect.," is triply botched. The singular subject needs singular verbs, but the sentence shifts from *has* to the plural *dress* to *must.* Perhaps the student was thinking backward from *must give* to *must dress* but skipped the first *must.* Finally, *ect.* is both misspelled and unnecessary. Too often *et cetera* or *etc.* is used when the writer can think of no further examples and wishes the reader to think for him. "The tenant farmers' futile attempts at shooting bulldozers, etc., were ineffective" is ineffective; certainly it takes more than one example to make a series.

Infinitives, present participles, and subordinate clauses often get tangled in faulty parallel constructions. "Casy wasn't satisfied telling them that sometime they would have a better life and just to suffer until then" links the subordinate "that . . . they would have" with the infinitive "to suffer." The sentence needs two subordinate clauses, instead. "Franklin made many contributions in the field of science and by forming such things as a postal system, a library, and a college" joins a noun (*contributions*) to a participle (*forming*). Actually, this sentence should not be parallel; the cure is simply to cut *and.* "Franklin believed virtue was something to be

221

developed through conscientious effort and which in the end would be rewarding" combines a passive infinitive (*to be developed*) with a relative subordinate clause (*which . . . would be*). The remedy is to turn the first into a subordinate clause ("something which could be developed").

Finally, the omission of a necessary past participle often mars parallel constructions: "Americans have [fallen] and will continue to fall short of this idealism" and "The perfect naturalistic novel has not [been] and never will be written."

When the reader encounters a parallel construction, he expects the writer to continue it. If incongruous elements intrude, both the sound and the sense are jarred. So if you begin using nouns, adjectives, infinitives, present participles, or relative clauses in a grammatical series, continue with nouns, adjectives, infinitives, participles, or relative clauses until you reach the end. When you use a coordinating conjunction (*and, but, for, or, nor, yet*), make sure the elements it joins are coordinate. In conversation it is sometimes difficult to keep track of parallel units, but you should be able to do so in your writing, by revising it if necessary.

¶ FRAGMENTARY SENTENCES

To be grammatically complete, a sentence must contain a main clause capable of standing independently. It is too vague to say that a sentence must contain a complete thought. Actually, sentences may contain several complete thoughts, and a fragmentary sentence may have a complete thought and yet be grammatically incomplete. "As the giant sloths were about to attack him, Mandrake gestured hypnotically." Here, "Mandrake gestured hypnotically" is a main clause that could be a separate sentence, whereas "As the giant sloths were about to attack him" is subordinate to or dependent upon the main clause and cannot stand alone. Occasionally one encounters what seems to be a main clause that cannot stand alone; e.g., "One value even of the smallest well is" in "One value even of the smallest well is, that when you look into it, you see that earth is not continent but insular." Here the problem is that the three clauses making up the rest of the sentence are really complements of *is* and thus are part of the main clause. Such a pattern of concentric clauses is the exception.

There are many situations in which fragmentary sentences are perfectly acceptable. Some are simply interjections or exclamations:

222

"Great gobs of goose grease!" "Donner and Blitzen!" "Great Caesar's ghost!" Some are questions or answers to questions: "One lump or two?" "Two, please." "About ten o'clock." Others are balanced expressions like "Better late than never," "First come, first served," or Robert Frost's "No surprise for the writer, no surprise for the reader." Conversation and informal writing often use fragmentary sentences with perfect legitimacy. So does advertising, which often consists of a series of phrases like "*Secret Fighting Arts of the World by John F. Gilby. Suppressed for generations!* Twenty of the world's most secretly guarded fighting techniques vividly described in one volume: the Oriental delayed death touch; the destruction wrought by the fingertips of an obscure Mexican; the shout of doom; the lightning-like destruction inflicted by a Peoria bookworm—and many more vicious fighting tricks."

Certainly there should be no absolute injunction against fragmentary sentences, or minor sentences as they are sometimes called. Most modern authors use them at times, and they are often necessary in dialogue. But they are acceptable only when they work stylistically. The professional writer, when he uses fragments, does so intentionally to achieve a desired effect. Most unacceptable fragments occur when the writer simply fails to understand what constitutes a sentence. Usually he severs a subordinate clause, verbal, phrase, or participial phrase from the rest of the sentence to which it belongs. In the following examples, the italicized passages are faulty fragments.

SENTENCE FRAGMENT	INTERPRETATION	CORRECTION
I was raised with a gun in hand and am a fairly good shot. *My best score being 91 out of a possible 100.*	Italicized passage is a participial phrase modifying the main clause.	I was raised with a gun in hand and am a fairly good shot, my best score being 91 out of a possible 100.
In the early hours of the morning, the city is like a graveyard. *The buildings resembling huge tombstones and monuments and the barren streets paths between the graves.*	Again, we have a participial phrase modifying the main clause.	In the early hours of the morning, the city is like a graveyard, the buildings resembling huge tombstones and monuments and the barren streets paths between the graves.

SENTENCE FRAGMENTS	INTERPRETATION	CORRECTION
Fearless Fosdick dived into the garbage can. *When the machine guns opened fire.*	Italicized passage is a subordinate clause modifying *dived*.	Fearless Fosdick dived into the garbage can when the machine guns opened fire.
The Human Torch never burns up. *Although he often throws part of himself as fireballs against criminals.*	The italicized clause is subordinate and cannot stand alone.	The Human Torch never burns up, although he often throws part of himself as fireballs against criminals.

In all of these examples, the writer used a period when he should have used a comma. These period faults are easy to correct. But some fragments require a bit of rewriting. For instance, "Popeye could not decide. Rescuing Olive Oyl or salvaging his spinach," needs to be changed to "Popeye could not decide whether to rescue Olive Oyl or to salvage his spinach." "It was a dreadful ordeal for the climbers. Surviving a blizzard, suffering frostbite, and driving off the abominable snowman." Here the fragment consists of a series of gerunds that should be turned into verbs or used as modifiers: "In a dreadful ordeal, the climbers survived a blizzard, suffered frostbite, and drove off the abominable snowman" or "The climbers had a dreadful ordeal, surviving a blizzard, suffering frostbite, and driving off the abominable snowman." "What she wants to know is. Will a silver bullet kill a teen-age werewolf?" This should be an indirect question: "She wants to know whether a silver bullet will kill a teen-age werewolf."

Sentence structure brings us to the matter of structural linguistics, which are alternately praised and denounced in current grammatical controversies. There is a difference between descriptive grammarians and structural linguists. The latter are descriptive rather than prescriptive, but they often go a step further and discard traditional grammatical terms and methods. Structural linguistics is related to anthropology and was developed from the study of Oriental, African, and American Indian languages, which are structurally quite different from Indo-European ones. Some of these exotic tongues use no verbs, and many depend upon tone and pitch for word meanings. Applying to English the scientific method used in examining these diverse and often unwritten languages, structural linguists stress form more than function and generally reduce ques-

224

tions of meaning to "same" or "different." According to W. Nelson Francis, "Meaning is such a subjective quality that it is usually omitted entirely from scientific description." Structural linguists like to use jabberwocky sentences to illustrate form independent of meaning; e.g., "Blindfolded garages burp violently." This is nonsense, yet the formal relation of the words is clear. Of course there must be some meaning, or there can be no structural pattern, even though the meaning may be absurd. In "Blagenbogen grizzafapple bynapoz veeblefetzer," there is no grammar. Structural linguists separate words into "form-classes" that can fit function slots. Thus the slot in "The . . . is brilliant" can be filled with such forms (formerly labeled nouns) as *painting, ballet, drama, novel,* and *sunlight* but not with *erroneous, tangential, consequently,* or *yawned.*

Lincoln Barnett claims that structural linguists are incapacitating school children and making them incapable of clear writing. Many students are indeed incapable of clear writing, but structural linguistics is not to blame, for the simple reason that it is not being taught in elementary and secondary schools, except in a few avant-garde situations. The overwhelming majority of English teachers have studied and continue to teach traditional grammar. Probably the real villain is not the sort of grammar but the fact that over-worked teachers with overcrowded classes sometimes lack sufficient training in language and almost always lack time to teach writing adequately. The sheer burden of grading weekly themes for hundreds of students is murderous. And to be really effective, the English teacher must give his students a good deal of individual attention, having them revise, correct, revise again, and examine every sentence and paragraph for the best diction, rhythm, organization, and lucidity—in short, he must teach not merely grammar but logic and style. In most teaching arrangements today, this is impossible. Ultimately the effective writer teaches himself.

Exercise 25: Identify the italicized elements as (1) phrase, (2) main clause, or (3) subordinate clause.

1. Wonder Woman deflected the bullets *with her bracelets.* . . . .
2. Some Asians think *that the rhino's horn is magic.* . . . .
3. Sergeant McChesney *arrested Sergeant Archibald Cutter for* insubordination. . . . .
4. With a rifle butt, *Auda smashed his Turkish false teeth.* . . . .

5. "I was armed to the teeth with a pitiful little Smith & Wesson's seven shooter, *which carried a ball like a homeopathic pill,* and it took the whole seven to make a dose for an adult."
—Mark Twain . . . .
6. Turhan Bey fed the mummy boiling tana leaves *in order to keep it alive.* . . . .
7. *Sergeants McChesney and Cutter put elephant elixir in the punch* in order to remove Higginbotham from the expedition.
8. When the first World War broke out, Lawrence was in the Near East *working with an archaeological team.* . . . .
9. When Marco Polo returned to Venice, *he told of cheetahs at the court of Kublai Khan.* . . . .
10. *Winslow Homer made some of the best drawings* of the Civil War. . . . .

Exercise 26:   Underline the subordinate clauses in the following:

1. They knew that Mighty Mouse would save the day.
2. When Dick Tracy was a prisoner of Mrs. Pruneface, she fed him two forkfuls of water a day.
3. Though the Mullins family have entered the affluent society, Kayo still sleeps in a bureau drawer.
4. I'm glad to hear that the Green Hornet is back on the radio.
5. Only the Shadow knows what evil lurks in the heart of man.
6. Why did it have to rain when the Human Torch was about to throw his forearm at the criminals?
7. Ranger Smith said that if Yogi Bear once more broke regulations, he would be sent to the St. Louis Zoo.
8. The train ride from Asheville to New York is still essentially as Thomas Wolfe described it.
9. Before McChesney could stop him, the guru jumped into the cobra pit.
10. At first Annie collapsed after she took the elephant elixir.

Exercise 27:   Correct any comma splices and run-on sentences in the following:

1. Paul Gauguin deserted his family to become a painter eventually he left France for the South Seas where he died.
2. Melville and his friend Toby deserted the whaling ship *Acushnet* at Nukuheva, then they were captured by the Typees.
3. For revolutionary activities Dostoevsky was condemned to death, a mock execution was held before the victims were told their sentences were commuted to Siberian imprisonment.

226

4. Vincent Van Gogh was a fine writer as well as a painter, his letters to his brother Theo are literary masterpieces.

5. Stephen Crane's style has been called prose impressionism because he used bold color effects like, "The red sun was pasted against the sky like a wafer."

6. Henry James never managed to write a successful play ironically his novels and stories adapted for the stage, movies, and television have been very well received.

7. Copernicus worked many years on his magnum opus, *The Book of the Revolutions of the Heavenly Spheres*, not published until after his death, it was one of the worst-sellers of all times.

8. Some hunters make sound shots they can't see anything but they shoot at any sound and sometimes kill their companion.

9. My wife is a great admirer of the poems of Matthew Arnold she likes best "The Forsaken Merman," "Thyrsis," and "Rugby Chapel."

10. Ernest Dowson fell off a bar stool and died he was courting a twelve-year-old girl named Adelaide at the time.

11. Akaba is fast becoming the Acapulco of the Near East it doesn't seem so long since Lawrence of Arabia captured it.

12. Jonathan Edwards was driven from his pulpit at Northampton, where he had been the minister for a quarter of a century.

13. Boccherini spent some years at the Spanish court he later wrote for the guitar.

14. Ralph Vaughan Williams' skill as an essayist is not as well known as his music but it is quite impressive.

15. Sinclair Lewis turned down the Pulitzer Prize for *Arrowsmith* in 1925, he should have received it for *Babbitt* but the judges were overruled.

16. When Nathaniel Hawthorne was dismissed from his job at the Salem Customs House, his wife gave him the money she had saved from house-keeping and said now he could write his novel.

Exercise 28: Rewrite any fragmentary sentences to make them grammatically complete.

1. The American Pronghorn being the only animal that is as fast as or faster than the cheetah.

2. Baby clouded leopards not to be confused with the marbled cat.

3. We must insist that our customers list the articles in their bundle. Otherwise our count will be taken as correct.

4. The Detroit zoo the most successful at raising polar bear cubs.

5. A pursuit that also leads to finer products, new ways to serve you better.

6. Zookeepers failed to realize. That rhinos may be mating when they batter each other.

227

7. We found the Volkswagen was right at home in the Alps. And would recommend a similar trip to anyone.
8. Her father having a large record collection of frog calls.
9. Fitsi fitsi a kind of bush spirit.
10. The revenuers used to ride their horses up the streams, and when the horses would no longer drink, because the stream contained fermented slops from a still.
11. Never having heard a transistor radio before. The Eskimo thought it was an instrument of torture.
12. Tree kangaroos and birds of paradise dwelling in the San Diego zoo.
13. Deposits of bat guano fifty feet deep located in Carlsbad Caverns.
14. Death rates are being lowered. Because of improved medical care and sanitation.
15. Zoos establishing special survival centers for animals in danger of extinction.
16. Did you see the pygmy hippo? Resting in its bathing pool?
17. Some mountain people used Victorian euphemisms well into the twentieth century. It was startling to hear one hunter say. That his rifle wouldn't stay roostered.
18. Most people these days. Seem to think that privacy is very bad form.
19. White rhinos requiring undisturbed privacy in mating season.
20. The cars were backed up half a mile. At the point where the bear was holding up traffic.

Exercise 29: Revise the following sentences to correct any errors in parallelism.

1. Aunt Minnie likes shops full of things and to putter.
2. There is an instrument for each member of the family and to accompany Mother on the piano.
3. The idea of the hero as good looking and smooth dialect prevails in TV Westerns.
4. Hilma Tree's appearance, attitudes, and personality are all perfect, daughter on the farm, earthy characteristics.
5. At the low wages that were being paid, a man could not get enough money to feed his family, much less putting it to work to earn more money for himself.
6. We are taught to believe in truth as an absolute and that things are either always true or not true at all.
7. Americans have and will use pragmatism many times without realizing it.
8. His opponents said that such things as a lack of occupation, a vagrant to civil duty, or never attending church were characteristic of Thoreau.
9. Guilt by association is unfair, dangerous, and threatens civil liberties.

228

10. The chairman said that we would discuss the supplementary readings at the next staff meeting and to study the list carefully before then.
11. Eugene said that movies are often stupid and ridiculous and he was addicted to them.
12. It is absolutely untrue that bloodhounds are vicious, terrifying, and attack people fiercely.
13. King Kong showed his ability to wrestle dinosaurs, strangle pterodactyls, rescue Fay Wray, and how to climb the Empire State Building.
14. For the sake of your health, your nerves, and in the interests of your sanity, don't translate *Finnegan's Wake* into Arabic.
15. Poe gives no moral such as occurs in many of Hawthorne's stories, but rather how art can be its own justification.
16. Hippopotamuses are awkward on land but often leaping gracefully over underwater barriers.
17. Mrs. Warren told the laundryman she wanted either two new sheets or her own sheets being returned.
18. Reading widely has contributed to my becoming a more liberal person and to help me think more logically.
19. *Moby Dick* gives a documentary account of whaling and how a mad captain destroys his crew for the sake of egotistical monomania.
20. Henry James admired Hawthorne's fiction and how he made use of moral allegory.

15 √ The Pitfalls and Pratfalls of Punctuation

Everybody agrees that a sentence must end with a period, question mark, or exclamation point. That is almost the only form of punctuation about which there is unanimity. Various instruction manuals dictate rules for punctuation, but practice differs widely, from manual to manual and office to office. What is standard operating procedure in business correspondence may be heresy in military reports. Some organizations require a rigid conformity to their particular punctuation policy; if you work for such an outfit, you had better learn its rules and follow them. In creative writing, individualism is rampant; authors, editors, and publishers differ widely on details of punctuation. Though many composition teachers used to uphold an inflexible set of punctuation rules (doubtless some still do), it should be self-evident that there can be no absolutism here. Nor is punctuation in any way connected with effective use of spoken language. And language is essentially spoken; writing is merely a symbolic representation of our thoughts or speech. Punctuation is visual, a set of printer's artificial marks to indicate the pauses and vocal stresses of our speech. In written English, we need signs to break up the otherwise uninterrupted flow of words. Even the space between words is a sort of punctuation. Anglo-Saxon manuscripts have no punctuation, sometimes not even a clear break between words; the translator therefore has to decipher before he can translate. Chaucerian punctuation is minimal, and Elizabethan is extremely haphazard, so editors sometimes substitute modern punctuation for clarity. In fiction, if a character's mind is unclear and his subconscious thoughts run together by free association, the author may eliminate punctuation for paragraphs or even pages, as in

230

the Quentin Compson section of Faulkner's *The Sound and the Fury*. In an attempt at greater realism, Faulkner makes the reader follow the erratic flow and abrupt shifts of Quentin's stream of consciousness. This makes difficult reading, but its very confusion brings ultimately a greater understanding.

E. E. Cummings, who was a painter as well as a poet, novelist, and essayist, used the visual quality of punctuation and typography to illustrate his verbal imagery. For the word *look,* why not give it eyes bracketed by cupped hands?: *l (oo) k*! Cummings developed this technique in elaborate and witty forms. Of course, the visual quality is lost when the poems are read aloud, and some have their words so rearranged that they can only be appreciated when seen, not heard.

Punctuation, therefore, is flexible, but only to a degree. Some consistency is needed for clear communication and common sense. Effective punctuation enables the reader to read faster and with better comprehension, whereas missing or misplaced punctuation slows him up, makes him retrace his ground to be sure he has the sense of the passage. Thus punctuation may be compared to the center line and the speed, curve, hill, and warning signs on a highway that help the driver to proceed with greater assurance and accuracy.

When speaking, we indicate our meaning by vocal inflection as well as by diction and grammar. In written English, the meaning can be ambiguous without punctuation. When the playwright Richard Brinsley Sheridan was serving in Parliament, he was once required to apologize to a fellow member of Commons. Sheridan rose and replied, "Mr. Speaker I said the honorable member was a liar it is true and I am sorry for it," adding that the honorable member could place the punctuation marks where he pleased. If the fellow member had a grain of wit, he would have realized that the insult had been repeated. Once a college class was given the following sentence to punctuate: "Woman without her man is a savage." There was a revealing difference between the interpretation by boys and girls. Most of the former wrote, "Woman, without her man, is a savage," while the girls wrote, "Woman! Without her, man is a savage."

Certainly, punctuation must be precise in love letters. In the old sixteenth-century play *Roister Doister,* the oafish hero bungles his wooing of Dame Custance by sending her the following love letter. (I have modernized the spelling.)

231

Sweet mistress whereas I love you nothing at all
Regarding your substance and riches chief of all,
For your personage, beauty, demeanor and wit,
I commend me unto you never a whit.
Sorry to hear report of your good welfare.
For (as I hear say) such your conditions are,
That ye be worthy favor of no living man,
To be abhorred of every honest man.
To be taken for a woman inclined to vice.
Nothing at all to Virtue giving her due price.
Wherefore concerning marriage, ye are thought
Such a fine paragon, as ne'er honest man bought.
And now by these presents I do you advertise
That I am minded to marry you in no wise.
For your goods and substance, I could be content
To take you as ye are. If ye mind to be my wife,
Ye shall be assured for the time of my life,
I will keep ye right well, from good raiment and fare,
Ye shall not be kept but in sorrow and care.
Ye shall in no wise live at your own liberty,
Do and say what ye lust [desire], ye shall never please me,
But when ye are merry, I will be all sad,
When ye are sorry, I will be very glad.
When ye seek your heart's ease, I will be unkind,
At no time, in me shall ye much gentleness find.
But all things contrary to your will and mind,
Shall be done: otherwise I will not be behind
To speak. And as for all them that would do you wrong
I will so help and maintain, ye shall not live long.
Nor any foolish dolt shall cumber you but I.
I, who ere say nay, will stick by you till I die.
Thus good mistress Custance, the lord you save and keep,
From me Roister Doister, whether I wake or sleep.

When Dame Custance charges him with writing her an arrogant, nasty, and insulting note, poor Roister Doister denies he wrote the letter. He had, in fact, paid a scrivener to write it for him; and the scrivener points out that Roister Doister must have copied it wrong, fouling up the phrasing and punctuation. The letter should have read:

Sweet mistress, whereas I love you, nothing at all
Regarding your riches and substance: chief of all
For your personage, beauty, demeanor and wit
I commend me unto you: Never a whit

Sorry to hear report of your good welfare.
For (as I hear say) such your conditions are,
That ye be worthy favor: Of no living man
To be abhorred: of every honest man
To be taken for a woman inclined to vice
Nothing at all: to virtue giving her due price.
Wherefore concerning marriage, ye are thought
Such a fine paragon, as ne'er honest man bought.
And now by these presents I do you advertise,
That I am minded to marry you: In no wise
For your goods and substance: I can be content
To take you as your are: if ye will be my wife,
Ye shall be assured for the time of my life,
I will keep you right well: from good raiment and fare,
Ye shall not be kept: but in sorrow and care
Ye shall in no wise live: at your own liberty,
Do and say what ye lust: ye shall never please me
But when ye are merry: I will be all sad
When ye are sorry: I will be very glad
When ye seek your heart's ease: I will be unkind
At no time: in me shall ye much gentleness find.
But all things contrary to your will and mind
Shall be done otherwise: I will not be behind
To speak: And as for all they that would do you wrong,
(I will so help and maintain ye) shall not live long.
Nor any foolish dolt shall cumber you; but I,
I who ere say nay, will stick by you till I die.
Thus good mistress Custance, the lord you save and keep.
From me Roister Doister, whether I wake or sleep.

Thus punctuation can be a lover's undoing. Even the simple "Will you marry me?" can be altered to the imperative "Will, you marry me!" We use punctuation marks both to separate ideas and to group together the related words that express an idea. We also use them to indicate pause and emphasis. Thus punctuation is like a measure of music, with symbols to indicate cleft, key, tempo, tune, time, staccato, legato, volume. Because punctuation is an aid to interpretation, it is closely allied to grammar. Before you can end a sentence with a period, you have to know when you have written a sentence. If you cannot recognize sentences, clauses, appositives, serial and parallel constructions, restrictive and nonrestrictive modifiers, parenthetical insertions, or distinguish direct from indirect questions and quotations, you cannot punctuate properly. Even to use the apostrophe correctly, you need to know the detailed workings of nouns and verbs. However, even effective grammarians and stylists are sometimes unreliable in punctuation, especially if they write rapidly. The hurried writer may know when he needs punctuation, but he will not take time to consider the kind of punctuation, and he is apt to use commas and dashes indiscriminately or to omit punctuation altogether except to stab in a period at the end of a sentence.

¶ THE PERIOD

1. The main use of the period is to mark the end of a declarative sentence. If you fail to use a period, your sentences will be what is known as fused or run-on. If you use a period before the sentence is completed, you have written a sentence fragment. ("When I bit down on the roll. I lost my filling.") Both errors are annoying and indicate that the writer's thoughts are not clearly organized. Many amateur writers love to use exclamation points for mildly emphatic statements, but a simple period is usually preferable, just as a plain suit carries more authority than a screaming sport shirt. Sometimes students confuse declarative with interrogatory sentences and fail to distinguish between the use of a period and a question mark. An indirect question takes a period:

> I asked her if she liked Beethoven.

> WRONG: I asked her if she liked Beethoven?

> CONFUSED: When Huck Finn considered that Jim was a runaway slave, he wondered why was Tom Sawyer helping Jim escape?

The last example is a mixture of a declarative and interrogative sentence, and it is better not to mix the two. The solution is to make the question indirect and end the whole with a period:

> When Huck Finn considered that Jim was a runaway slave, he wondered why Tom Sawyer was helping Jim escape.

2. A period is used with certain abbreviations. Practice varies here; the military does not use a period (Ft Knox), and some abbreviations (CIO) do not customarily have periods. It is best to check your dictionary or the policy of your employers. Conventionally a period is used after abbreviated titles (*Dr., Rev., Mr., Mrs., Capt.*), names (*Edward G. Robinson, George C. Scott, Francis X. Bushman, E. B. White*), months (*Jan., Sept., Dec.*), states (*Cal., S. Dak.*). A title used alone without a proper name, should not be

234

abbreviated; students are wrong who write that the *Dr.* performed the operation. In such cases the word should be spelled out and put in lower case.

3. A period is used between dollars and cents ($2.99) and before a decimal (".07 of his income," "a .30 caliber machine gun").

4. Three spaced periods (. . .) called ellipses are used to indicate the omission of words in a quotation. If the omission comes at the end of a sentence, a fourth point—the period for the sentence—is added. Some students indiscriminately use ellipsis points instead of dashes and semicolons, and/or use dashes, hyphens, or half a dozen (instead of three) ellipsis periods to indicate omission. You should avoid this sort of splatter punctuation. Ellipsis points can also be used to indicate a pause ("Does she . . . or doesn't she?"). Schoolgirl style favors a peppering of gushy ellipses, but the careful stylist shudders at saccharine paragraphs like: "When all the little children are abed . . . scrubbed nestling cherubs clutching teddy bears and rabbits . . . when quiet house and warm hearth fire make a haven . . . when, sitting peacefully in a rocking chair, mending little garments, you muse over the small happenings of the day . . . then you know that no career . . . no glamorous job . . . could ever be as satisfying . . . as . . . MOTHERHOOD."

5. Most experienced writers in this country place a period at the end of a quotation inside the quotation marks whether it is part of the quotation or not:

Mad printed a burlesque of Melville, called "Morbid Dick."

¶ EXCLAMATION AND QUESTION MARKS

1. The exclamation mark (!) is used after strongly emphatic words or sentences and after particularly emphatic imperative commands:

> "Tiger! Tiger! burning bright"
>
> "Poets to come! orators, singers, musicians to come!"
>
> " 'Courage!' he said, and pointed toward the land"

Amateur writers tend to overuse the exclamation point to the extent that it loses its emphasis, like the boy who cried wolf. The real emphasis must be conveyed by the wording itself; if the language is inadequate, punctuation will not help. Ads like "Remove unwanted body hair!" fail to create a sense of urgency. Poetry and fiction use exclamation points more freely than does expository prose, where they are rarely called for. And even great poets overwork the exclamation point. It is needless after a line like Browning's "Notice Neptune, though,/Taming a sea-horse, thought a rarity,/ Which Claus of Innsbruck cast in bronze for me!" A university student used(¡), reversing the exclamation point, to show that he couldn't care less.

2. (a) The question, or interrogation, mark (?) is used at the end of every direct question:

Didst thou not fall out with a tailor for wearing his new doublet before Easter?

Tybalt, you ratcatcher, will you walk?

(b) When a request is put in the form of a question, it may be followed by a question mark in a formal statement, but the question mark is not necessary generally:

FORMAL: Will you please present your credentials to the secretary?
GENERAL: Will you please be seated.

(c) The question mark is not used after an indirect question.

RIGHT: Sir Palamedes asked the churl if he had seen the Questing Beast.
WRONG: Hamlet asked Polonius if he had a daughter?

(d) It is awkward to combine a declarative statement and a question in a single sentence, although this practice is becoming more and more common.

Emerson is an inspirational writer, but how long does the inspiration last?

Tom Tryon, a cowboy type without the light of thought, spirituality or emotion in his square-jawed pan, is a hero that must make everyone in the theatre feel if he can make it, why not me?   —DWIGHT MACDONALD

(e) The question mark in parentheses is used after questionable statements and uncertain dates: Ben Jonson 1573 (?)–1637. It is sometimes used in this manner as an ironic commentary but is a feeble form of sarcasm:

Your courtesy (?) is greatly appreciated.
We enjoy the soup (?) very much.

(f) The question mark is placed inside the quotation marks when it is part of a quotation but is placed outside if it is not part of the quotation:

Juliet asked, "Art thou not Romeo, and a Montague?"

Have you read "The Snows of Kilimanjaro"?

Only one question mark should be used after a double question:

Did Alfred E. Neuman really ask, "What, me worry?"

¶ THE SEMICOLON

The semicolon (;) is not interchangeable with the colon or the comma. It has several special uses of its own. If you learn these, you are reasonably safe in using the comma for those other situations where you might be tempted to use the semicolon.

1. The main use of the semicolon is to separate two main or independent clauses that are not joined by a coordinating conjunction (*and, but, for, or, nor, yet*).

Nobody but teen-agers could see the monsters from outer space; the adults refused to believe they existed.

The monsters from outer space were all eyeball; nothing could destroy them but the headlights from teen-agers' hot rods.

The drive-in theatre is getting another science-fiction film next week; it's a new one called *Teen-agers from Outer Space*.

A comma is not strong enough to mark the break between two independent clauses; a semicolon or period is needed to indicate break, so that the reader does not run one clause over into the other. If there were no punctuation at all, we would have run-on sentences. When there is only a comma, we have a comma splice. In very short sentences comma splices are all right ("Take your umbrella, it's raining"), and some established authors (e.g., Alan Moorehead in *The Blue Nile*) use them fairly regularly, but as a general rule, they are better avoided.

2. A semicolon is used before a conjunctive adverb bridging two main clauses. These connectives are too weak to take only a comma. The most common of them are *accordingly, also, anyhow, besides, consequently, furthermore, hence, however, in addition, indeed, likewise, moreover, nevertheless, still, then,* and *therefore*. The heavier of them take a comma after them:

Huck Finn had been taught that slavery was proper; consequently, he tried to turn Jim in.

Henry James revised some of his early works in his later style; however, not all critics think this is an improvement.

Theodore Dreiser's brother Paul was a popular song writer; indeed, for a time Paul was the better known of the two.

Ben Jonson killed an actor in a duel; hence he was branded on the thumb.

When these conjunctive adverbs are used parenthetically, they are enclosed by commas and not preceded by a semicolon:

Jonson, however, escaped hanging because he could read like a clerk.

3. A semicolon may be used before a coordinating conjunction joining two main clauses if (a) there is internal punctuation between the clauses or (b) the sentence is unusually long. Otherwise, a comma is used before a coordinating conjunction.

4. A semicolon should be used to separate the items in a series that contains internal punctuation:

Mark Twain traveled to St. Joseph, Missouri; Salt Lake City, Utah; Carson City, Nevada; Virginia City, Nevada; and finally to San Francisco.

The runaway camel knocked over Mr. Koontz, the milkman; Dr. Ijams, the dentist; P. E. Funk, deliveryman for the Capital Laundry; and Alfred E. Neuman, representative from Ballantine Books.

If commas were used instead of semicolons, it might seem that Mark Twain went to St. Joseph *and* to Missouri *and* to Salt Lake City *and* to Utah, and so forth, or that the camel knocked over Mr. Koontz *and* the milkman *and* Dr. Ijams *and* the dentist and so on.

If none of these four situations exist, do not use a semicolon. It should not be used after an introductory subordinate phrase or clause, between a main clause and a following subordinate phrase or clause, or to replace the colon before a formal quotation or a long list or series. Gertrude Stein claimed that semicolons "really have within them deeply within them fundamentally within them the comma nature"; but if so, it is better to go against nature.

¶ COMMAS

The comma is the most common and the most frustrating of all punctuation marks. Its omission where it is necessary is an obstacle to clear, rapid reading, and so is its inclusion where it is not necessary or where some other mark of punctuation is required. Too many students punctuate with the comma intuitively, instead of

238

rationally. When asked why they used a comma in some particular case, they answer, "I don't know; I just felt I should put something there." This guesswork approach is like splatter painting; successful results are largely accidental. You should avoid this method and know when and why to use the comma. When there is no reason for it, don't use one. According to Gertrude Stein, "Commas are servile and they have no life of their own. . . ." This is true in spoken language, where we use vocal inflections and pauses instead; but in writing, there are specific uses for the comma together with some optional ones.

1. The comma is used before a coordinating conjunction (*and, but, or, nor, yet*) connecting two main clauses. Some writers omit a comma here, and it is better dropped in very short sentences, but its omission is usually a nuisance and can sometimes cause confusion:

Bartleby at first does an immense amount of copying, but he soon refuses to do small jobs around the office and then announces that he has given up copying altogether.

Notice that there is a comma before *but* but not before *and*; a comma is not needed between two verbs with the same subject:

WRONG: I think I shall lie down, and take a nap.

In "A sniper's bullet killed a Negro woman and three men were wounded by gunfire Monday night in Jacksonville," a comma before *and* is needed for clarity, as well as for separating the clauses; otherwise it seems at first glance that the bullet killed a woman and three men. A similar confusion occurs in "Scabs were fighting strikers and little children were throwing bottles at trucks." A comma is needed to show that scabs were not fighting little children. A reader can make out the meaning of these sentences without a comma, but he has to read them twice to do so.

Many people mistakenly put a comma both before and after a coordinating conjunction (*,but,*); but there should never be one after such a conjunction unless some parenthetical insertion requires it. Also there should be no comma after a coordinating conjunction that connects words or phrases, rather than main clauses:

WRONG: Jack, and the beanstalk.

2. A comma is used after an introductory subordinate clause or a long phrase preceding the main clause:

239

When Mark Twain's brother went to Nevada, he took a six-pound un-abridged dictionary with him.

If you get there first, save me a place in line.

Having eaten 425 cabbages, Harry the Hippopotamus felt sick.

After several generations of neglect, Melville's work was rediscovered by modern literary critics.

A comma is not necessary if the introductory matter is quite short and/or closely related to the main verb:

UNNECCESSARY: For supper, we are having grits and grunts.

3. In a compound-complex sentence where there is a main clause followed by a subordinate clause that encloses another subordinate clause, a comma is used at the end of the enclosed subordinate clause. Obviously you have to be able to recognize clauses to punc-tuate effectively.

Mark Twain observed that when Brigham Young was given a whistle for one of his children, he had to buy a hundred and ten whistles to make his other children happy.

Brigham Young told Mark Twain, "And if ever another man gives a whistle to a child of mine and I get my hands on him, I will hang him higher than Haman!" (Here the *if* subordinates both the *man gives* and *I get* clauses.)

4. When a subordinate clause or phrase follows a main clause, a comma may precede it if the clauses are not smoothly related or es-sential to the sentence's principal meaning.

Melville deserted on his first whaling voyage, jumping ship in the Mar-quesas.

Melville could not support his family by literature, though his first books had been popular.

Finally Melville settled into obscure security when he got a job as customs inspector. (No comma needed.)

Don't tell me you were late because you missed the bus. (No comma needed.)

5. Commas are used to enclose nonrestrictive clauses but not to enclose restrictive clauses. A restrictive clause is one that is essen-tial to specify or identify the word it modifies. In the sentence "Henry V was the king *who won the battle of Agincourt*," the itali-cized modifying clause is restrictive because it is needed to indi-cate a specific fact that identifies the king. If there is only one king

240

and no question as to his identity, then we would have a nonrestrictive modifier: "Take this pie to the king, who is sitting in his countinghouse." The modifier is clearly restrictive in "It is necessary for a democratic government to have laws [no comma] that will give men justice."

RESTRICTIVE	NONRESTRICTIVE
Michigan is one of many states that have abolished the death penalty.	There are a great many lakes in Michigan, which calls itself the "Water Wonderland."
Utah is the only state that has executions by firing squad.	The Mormons were the first settlers in Utah, which they called Deseret.
People who are afraid of heights should not try parachute jumping.	Parachutists, who have careful training, have a low accident rate. (This might be considered restrictive, depending upon the weight given the modifier.)

Usually a nonrestrictive modifier can be left out of a sentence without making it meaningless, whereas the omission of a restrictive modifier mangles the sense. There is a crucial difference between "Soldiers who give information to the enemy are traitors" and "Soldiers . . . are traitors" or between "Everybody who goes to Africa must have yellow fever shots" and "Everybody . . . must have yellow fever shots."

Unless it occurs at the end of a sentence, a nonrestrictive modifier must be set off by two commas, one before and one after it. If the second comma is missing, the results may be confusing, as in "A path meanders from the house across Wapsinonoc Creek, where Hoover paddled as a boy to the new Herbert Hoover Library, repository for many of the former President's official papers." Without a comma after *boy*, it seems that Hoover paddled to the new library when he was a boy.

6. Commas are used to enclose parenthetical or appositive constructions not sufficiently pronounced to require parentheses or dashes:

The lettuce, you will no doubt admit, is not improved by boiling.

The mother bear, understandably enough, was annoyed at the tourists.

Next weekend, with luck, we shall finish tunneling through the walls.

The elephant, she says, is eating cabbages.

If the commas are omitted, there can be a confusion in meaning:

Hemingway did not like Ambrose Bierce disappear over the border.

Unless there are commas around *like Ambrose Bierce,* it seems at first glance that Hemingway did not like Ambrose Bierce. Such an error occurred in a Michigan newspaper, which printed, "Bartlett says Hatch demonstrates a lack of understanding," reversing the actual statement, "Bartlett, says Hatch, demonstrates a lack of understanding."

Conjunctive adverbs are often set off by commas when they are parenthetical or introduce a sentence:

The pirates, however, were pursued by giant land crabs.

Furthermore, the pirates forgot where they had buried the treasure.

7. Commas are used to enclose appositives. Appositives are identifying phrases equivalent to the noun or pronoun they explain:

William James, *brother of Henry James,* was a distinguished pragmatist.

Some students confused William James with Will James, *author of cowboy novels.*

Julia A. Moore, *the Sweet Singer of Michigan,* was a model for Mark Twain's Emmaline Grangerford.

Similarly, commas set off a title following someone's name: Sir Walter Scott, Bart.; Geoffrey Crayon, Gent.; H. M. Pulham, Esq.; Felix Flutz, Ph.D.; Sam Spade, Private Eye.

Do not confuse appositive phrases with restrictive or nonrestrictive modifiers, which are usually relative clauses. When an appositive is obvious and unstressed, it should not be set off by commas. No comma is needed in *my uncle Jules* or *his brother James.* Commas are needed for the first appositive but not the second in "Tarzan, lord of the jungle, made friends with Tantor the elephant."

8. Commas are used to set off names and other nouns directly addressed, whether they occur at the beginning, middle, or end of a sentence:

I had a dream, dear.

Go down, Moses, way down in Egypt's land.

242

Madam, I protest that you misunderstood me.

That is not, sir, an adequate explanation.

All right, you clods, stop yodeling in the halls.

I think, Dr. Frankenstein, that you have gone too far.

Apparently direct address is implied in the title *Rabbit, Run*. A misplaced comma can change the meaning radically. Notice the difference between *Call Me Madam* and *Call Me, Madam*; between *I Remember Mama* and *I Remember, Mama*; and between "That's North Carolina honey" and "That's North Carolina, honey."

9. Commas are used to separate items in a series:

The recipe for Kickapoo Joy Juice calls for formaldehyde, alarm clocks, skunk oil, white lightning, and anything else you care to throw in.

The survivors were a Peruvian policeman, an unemployed zoo-keeper, an Eskimo craftsman, two juvenile delinquents, a missionary to the Tuckapoo Indians, and an ex-bullfighter who would eat only frijoles.

Philip Guedalla divided the works of Henry James into three periods—James I, James II, and the Old Pretender.

If a comma is omitted, there may be ambiguity, as in the difference between *James Joyce and Proust* and *James, Joyce, and Proust*. Again, a program for *The Duchess of Malfi* listed among the cast; "Attendants, servants, madmen executioners." There are no *madmen executioners*, but there are madmen *and* executioners, so a comma is needed between the last two items. When there is an *and* before the last item in a series, a comma before it is optional; *Farrar, Straus and Cudahy*; *Holt, Rinehart and Winston*; or *bacon, beans, and beer*. If there are conjunctions between each of the items in the series, commas should not be used: "Ham and eggs and onions make a tasty omelet." If the items contain internal commas, semicolons should be used to seperate the units.

10. When adjectives are used in a series, a comma should be inserted between them:

There was a drooling, fanged, hunchbacked monster at the window.

You niddering, dunderheaded, thimble-brained, invertebrate imbecile!

In the first example, each adjective modifies *window*; in the second, each modifies *imbecile*.

Missing punctuation creates confusion; for example, in "Dinosaurs became extinct and smaller, less massive creatures took their place," it might at first glance seem that dinosaurs became extinct and smaller, and that less massive creatures then took over. This is illogical; the proper punctuation should be, "Dinosaurs became extinct, and smaller, less massive creatures took their place."

11. A comma is placed before a negative appositive element:

Mañana Iguana is a painter, not a sculptor.

Evidence reveals that it was a werewolf, not a wolf.

Call the Southern highlanders "mountain people," not "hillbillies."

A comma is not used for a *not this but that* construction: "Mañana Iguana is not a painter but an imposter."

12. Commas are inserted between the various elements in place names, addresses, dates, and numbers:

Mozart lived in Salzburg, Austria. (Comma between city and nation or state)

Los Angeles, California, may soon be the largest city in the world. (Comma between city and state and after state)

Sherlock Holmes lived at 21B Baker Street, London. (Comma between street and city)

Both Shakespeare and Cervantes died on April 2, 1616. (Comma between day and year)

How much money does Daddy Warbucks have—$1,345,798, $999,999,001, or $2.00 Confederate? (Comma between each three figures)

13. A comma is used after an introductory *yes, no, oh,* or exclamation:

Yes, I was in Macao in January, 1932.

Oh, no, the soldier ants are coming!

Curses, it's that muscle-bound mouse.

What, me worry?

14. Commas are used to set off direct quotations from the rest of a sentence:

Emerson wrote, "A foolish consistency is the hobgloblin of little minds."

"And now," said Snagglepuss, "I shall exit stage left."

"Nuts and berries—yeech," grumbled Yogi Bear.

Neither commas nor quotation marks are used with indirect quotations.

Hemingway said that *Huckleberry Finn* is the best American novel.

244

See the discussion of quotation marks for a fuller treatment of punctuation with quotations.

15. A comma may be used wherever necessary for clarity. Missing punctuation has caused confusion in several songs. Many people think the Christmas carol goes "God rest you, merry, gentlemen," whereas it should be phrased "God rest you merry gentlemen" with *merry* modifying *rest*. And there is no *Alice Ben Bolt*; the song asks, "Oh! don't you remember sweet Alice, Ben Bolt?" Probably Ben Bolt has forgotten her. In the sentences, "Through this spiritual Negro laborers expressed their oppression," there should be a comma after *spiritual,* lest it seem that *spiritual* modifies *Negro laborers*. Occasionally a comma is needed to keep separate elements from running together. In "It is necessary to recognize clauses. Students who do not often write fragmentary sentences," a comma is necessary after *not* to make clear that *not* modifies *do* rather than *often*.

The above cases involve a modifier that could belong to two different words. Other parts of speech might have two possible functions. A noun subject might be mistaken for the object of a preceding verb: "When the burglar left, the house was stripped of all valuables." (Not "When the burglar left the house. . . .") "After the storm struck, the water rose rapidly." (Not "After the storm struck the water. . . .") Conjunctions and prepositions too can cause confusion: "She cried out, for an elephant was standing on her foot." (Not "She cried out for an elephant. . . .") And finally a comma is customarily used between a word that occurs twice together: "What the boss's wife does, does not interest Betty." Then there are idiosyncratic errors. A book list alphabetized by authors listed:

Macaulay, *History of England*

Mill, *On Liberty*

Mill, *On the Floss.*

16. The comma should not be misused. Perhaps the most common misuse is the already discussed comma splice. Some students carelessly place a useless comma between subject and verb:

At present, some government agencies, retain patent rights on research and development discoveries.

Another reason to criticize the validity of the trials, stems from the handling of evidence.

There is no point to the commas inserted after *agencies* and *trials*. Again, there is no need for a comma between the indirect and direct object in "Bruce Catton gives the Southern troops and their leader, the credit due them." In "Still, the scientific observer, Hale tries to find evidence either way," the comma after *still* interrupts what should be a unit modifying *Hale*. There should be no comma in "William Faulkner's novel, *The Sound and the Fury*," because Faulkner wrote many novels; and *The Sound and the Fury* is a restrictive appositive. The commas are even more ridiculous in "Steinbeck's, *The Grapes of Wrath*, is filled with religious symbolism." Here the title is the subject, and *Steinbeck's* modifies it.

The tendency today is to minimize punctuation and to omit it if there is an option. Victorian writers often punctuated to excess, just as they favored ornamental excess in architecture and interior decoration. Though modern students are more apt to omit even necessary punctuation, some punctuate with flamboyant garishness. James Thurber complained of *The New Yorker's* overuse of commas. A professor of English once asked Thurber why there was a comma in "After dinner, the men went into the living room." Thurber answered that it "was Ross's way of giving the men time to push back their chairs and stand up." [1] As an example of excess, try this added punctuation for Shakespeare's lines:

> If, it were done, when, 'tis done, then, 'twere well
> It were done, quickly. . . .

¶ THE COLON

The colon (:) is not interchangeable with the semicolon, but has several specific uses of its own.

1. The colon is used after the salutation in a formal letter, whereas a comma is generally used in an informal one:

Dear Sir: Dear Dr. Karloff: Gentlemen: Dear Madame: Dear Mrs. Schultz: (as opposed to the casual *Dear Pete, Dear Herbie,* and *Hiya, Honeybun*).

2. The colon is used before a relatively long list of appositives or a formal series:

Here is the reading list for the oral examination: *The Odyssey, Oedipus Rex, Troilus and Criseyde, King Lear, The Duchess of Malfi, Paradise Lost, An Essay on Man, Tom Jones, Don Juan, Bleak House, Walden,*

246

Leaves of Grass, Moby Dick, Huckleberry Finn, The Return of the Native, The Waste Land, and *A Farewell to Arms.*

Do not use a colon before a brief, casual series. Wrong: "The sports I like best are: skiing, fencing, and girl watching." Here there should be no punctuation after *are.*

3. The colon can be used before a long or formal quotation:

Thoreau explained his purpose in going to Walden: "I went to the woods because I wished to live deliberately, to front only the essential facts of life, and see if I could not learn what it had to teach, and not, when I came to die, discover that I had not lived."

4. A colon can be used before a clause that is a restatement, illustration, or explanation of a preceding one:

Fitzgerald once quarreled with Hemingway: the latter had made a disparaging reference to him in "The Snows of Kilimanjaro."

Thurber tried to be demoted at *The New Yorker*: he had been hired as an editor but wanted to be a writer.

Naturalistic writers denied that man has a soul or free will: they claimed that the same laws govern the stones of the roadway and the mind of man.

In summary, the colon is used to set off material that explains or sums up something anticipated in the preceding expression. It creates a telegraphic brevity and conciseness (for which reason some news magazines favor it); but when it is used excessively, it becomes a mannerism.

¶ THE DASH

Some casual students use the dash indiscriminately whenever they wish to indicate a pause, clause, or stop. But this is merely slapdash. Both Queen Victoria and Jack Kerouac used dashes instead of commas and periods; this is all they had in common, and Kerouac's editors changed his punctuation. Unlike the tight colon, with which it is often confused, the dash creates a loose prose that too easily becomes limp. The dash has several specific purposes and is otherwise best kept under restraint.

1. A pair of dashes are used to set off interpolations that are both logically and grammatically interruptions:

Abner Bieberman—he once played Young Toad Face in *Gunga Din*—now directs some programs for *The Twilight Zone.*

247

What could D'Arnot do against Sabor—or if Bolgani, the gorilla should come upon him—or Numa, the lion, or cruel Sheeta?[2]

—EDGAR RICE BURROUGHS

Being an American, it was impossible you should remain what you were born, and being born poor—do I understand it?—it was therefore inevitable that you should become rich.[3] —HENRY JAMES

Such constructions sometimes take parentheses instead of dashes, but parentheses make the interruption even more pronounced. When the interpolation comes at the end of a sentence, only one dash is needed.

It is not money, it is not even brains—though no doubt yours are excellent.[4] —HENRY JAMES

2. A dash is used to set off a final explanatory or summarizing word or statement:

What's it made of—hammered gold?

To abolish slavery, John Brown committed another crime—murder.

Valentin de Bellegarde lived in the basement of an old house in the Rue d'Anjou St. Honoré, and his small apartment lay between the court of the house and an old garden which spread itself behind it—one of those large, sunless, humid gardens into which you look unexpectedly in Paris from back windows, wondering how among the grudging habitations they find their space.[5]

3. A dash is used to indicate an unfinished or interrupted statement:

"I'm sorry," she said, "but the lettuce—"
"The lettuce seems to have been washed in detergent," he remarked dryly.
"Yes, er—yes—that is—" and she rushed from the table.
"Why, I wanted the *adventure* of it; and I'd a waded neck deep in blood to—goodness alive, AUNT POLLY!"

Sometimes a double dash is used to indicate an interruption at the end of a speech. Ellipsis points can also be used for this sort of construction.

4. After a quotation, a dash can be used to set off the source.

I loafe and invite my soul,
I lean and loafe at my ease observing a spear of summer grass.

—WALT WHITMAN

Sagebrush is free. Stuff some in your trunk.
—FEARLESS FERRIS

Commas cannot substitute for dashes in an appositive interruption.

I have lived in various states, [should be dash] Ohio, Indiana, and Florida, [should be dash] and I have spent vacations on the east coast; but never have I encountered the demoralizing, disagreeable weather offered by the state of Michigan.

In typing, two hyphens (--) make a dash.

¶ PARENTHESES

Parentheses ( ) are used in pairs to enclose interruptions, asides, explanations, illustrations, and cross references:

South-eastward from the Cape, off the distant Crozetts, a good cruising ground for Right Whalemen, a sail loomed ahead, the Goney (Albatross) by name. —HERMAN MELVILLE, *Moby Dick*

Look at his hump, which would be as fine eating as the buffalo's (which is esteemed a rare dish), were it not such a solid pyramid of fat. —*Ibid.*

Only one of Henry VIII's wives (Katharine Parr) outlived him.

(*Cf.* p. 897)   (See Appendix B)   (Consult *The Dictionary of American Slang*)

Amalgamated Chicken Wire sells for seventy-five dollars ($75.00) a share.

When a parenthetical insertion occurs at the point where a comma is needed, the comma goes after the second parenthesis:

When the first man brought the first dog to his cave (no doubt over and above his wife's protests), there began an association by which Man has enormously profited.[6] —JAMES THURBER

Either dashes or parentheses can be used to set off a distinct interruption, but usually that with dashes is sharper. Sometimes both occur in the same sentence. As Thurber wrote about a mother dog with her pups,

For six weeks—but only six weeks—she looks after them religiously, feeds them (they come clothed), washes their ears, fights off cats. . . .[7]

Brackets are used for parentheses within parentheses, but parentheses are used for insertions in a passage set off by dashes.

249

My mother had never liked the congressman—she said the signs of his horoscope showed he couldn't be trusted (he was Saturn with the moon in Virgo) —but she sent him a box of candy that Christmas.[8]

It is possible to overwork parentheses. William Faulkner has parenthetical passages that run for several pages, with parentheses within parentheses within parentheses. Faulkner is a master of narrative by indirection, but even he sometimes stumbles, and the ordinary writer should keep parentheses within reasonable limits.

¶ BRACKETS

Brackets [ ] are used mainly to enclose writer's or editor's inserted commentary or explanation within a quotation. Sometimes when a quotation is taken out of context, an explanatory word or phrase is necessary.

An early exponent of pragmatism was [William] James.

To Bobby [Kennedy] the world is black and white.—Gore Vidal

When Henry James published his first novel, *The American* [actually, it was his second], he was already a master of the form.

When a reproduced text has unclear, incomplete, or omitted words or punctuation, the editors may add material within brackets to give an explanation or fill in the omission.

In his Majesty['s] service—in this ship indeed—there are Englishmen forced to fight for the King against their will.   —HERMAN MELVILLE, *Billy Budd*

If a quoted passage contains an error, you can place *sic* in brackets immediately after the word to indicate that the error is not yours but is in the original: "Cooper's *The Bathfinder* [*sic*] is the fourth novel he wrote in the Leatherstocking Series."

Brackets are also used to indicate parentheses within parentheses.

Most typewriters do not have bracket keys, but you can make brackets by using the diagonal with an underscore above and below, thus: /̅ ̲/

¶ THE DIAGONAL

The diagonal is used to indicate alternative or fusion in situations like either/or, both/and, and/or. "A program for a modern-dress version of *The Duchess of Malfi* indicated the time as 1504/con-

250

temporary." The diagonal is also used to separate lines of poetry when they are run together in a text: "The patent of a lord/And the bangle of a bandit/Make argument/Which God solves/Only after lighting more candles."—Stephen Crane.

¶ THE HYPHEN

Like the hydra, the hyphen is many-headed and full of deviltry. It has so many and such varied uses that one can go mad trying to catalogue them all. Mostly it is copy editors who go mad, since the hyphen is more their problem than the writer's. For writers who do their own copy editing, an explanation of the more common uses may help. Basically, the hyphen is used to join two or more words into a compound and to divide an overlong word at the end of a line. In printing, hyphenation is sometimes unavoidable to make the right margin even, but in manuscript or typescript, you should try to avoid line-end hyphenations; it is better to crowd the margin or carry the entire word to the next line. If you must break a word, do so between syllables. Never hyphenate a one-syllable word nor a short two-syllable one. Students sometimes make errors similar to the following:

ta-	lo-	ea-	lo-	lau-	gas-	re-
ke	ve	t	oked	gh	p	ad

These are even worse when the first half is at the extreme right margin and the second at the extreme left. If you must hyphenate, try whenever possible to do so between prefix and root or root and suffix.

manu-	dis-	bio-	phil-	marriage-
script	locate	chemistry	harmonic	able

Avoid separating merely the first letter from the rest of a word.

	WRONG: A-	u-	F-
	merican	niqueness	rench

Never separate a suffix of less than three letters from the rest of the word. It is all right to separate -*ing*, but not -*ed, -al, -le, -ly*.

CORRECT: construct- WRONG: perpetu- construct- complain- usual- princip-
    ing   al   ed   ed   ly   le

If you hyphenate compound words, keep each part of the compound intact.

motor- boat	sun- shine	moon- light	lawn- mower	bath- room

When you are uncertain where to divide a word, consult your dictionary.

The greatest difficulty with hyphens is the problem of compound words. There are three ways of writing compounds: as two separate words (*freight train*), as one word (*playboy*), or hyphenated (*teenager*). Sometimes the same word can be written any of the three ways. There is an increasing tendency to write compounds as one word, especially if each half has one syllable (*mailman*), but there is sufficient variety so that the only reliable guide is a current dictionary. A few generalizations may be helpful.

1. A hyphen is sometimes used in fractions and always in compound numbers beginning with *twenty-one*: *one hundred forty-four, five-eighths, seven-tenths, one sixty-fourth.*

2. A hyphen is used when a prefix is joined to a proper noun or adjective: *anti-McCarthy, pro-Churchill, un-American, pre-Roosevelt, pre-Shakespearean.*

3. A hyphen is used between *ex-* ("former") and a noun: *ex-governor, ex-husband, ex-convict.*

4. A hyphen is used with *in-law* family relationships: *mother-in-law, sister-in-law.*

5. Most compounds beginning with *self* are hyphenated: *self-love, self-esteem, self-serving, self-control, self-sufficient,* but not *selfless, selfsame,* or *selfhood.*

6. Sometimes a hyphen must be inserted to avoid confusion with a similar word: *re-signed* vs. *resigned, re-claim* vs. *reclaim, re-act* vs. *react, re-cover* vs. *recover.*

7. A hyphen may be used in joining a prefix ending in a vowel to a word beginning with the same vowel: *re-enlist, re-elect, re-enter, re-enact, pre-empt, co-ordinate.*

8. The most common use of the hyphen is in compound modifiers before a noun. These include compound numbers.

a bug-eyed monster	a ninety-seven pound	a high-pitched scream
English-speaking peoples	weakling	
a run-on sentence	a seven-room house	a muscle-bound brute
a poverty-stricken family	a worn-out shirt	a burnt-out case
	a feeble-minded clod	a beat-up bum

252

Sometimes you may wonder whether you need a comma between two or more adjectives preceding a noun, or a hyphen with a compound modifier. The answer depends on your meaning. Note the difference between *dark-rimmed glasses* and *dark, rimmed glasses*; the rims are dark in the first and the lenses in the second. The focus is off in *a high, pitched scream,* which makes the modifier separate adjectives rather than a unified compound. Occasionally a hyphen is needed for clarity in otherwise ambiguous modifiers. A *new home-owner* is new at owning a home; a *new-home* owner may have owned many old homes before buying a modern one. In *a deep blue pool, deep* modifies *pool*; whereas it modifies the color in *a deep-blue pool,* which might be shallow.

When a compound modifier follows a noun, it usually is not hyphenated.

She wore a seventeenth-century costume.
The costume is seventeenth century.
There was a horrible-looking fiend.
The fiend was horrible looking.

Longer compounds are usually hyphenated, no matter where they occur: *up-to-date, face-to-face, tête-à-tête, never-to-be-forgotten, twenty-one-year-old, pay-as-you-go.*

9. Arabic numerals before modifiers and letters before nouns are hyphenated: *L-shaped room, 8-hour day, 40-hour week, A-bomb, U-boat, 5-string banjo.*

10. A hyphen is not interchangeable with a dash. Students often make this error in typing because there is no actual dash on the typewriter. To type a dash, you need two hyphens--otherwise you lack a sufficient break.

Except to clarify ambiguity, the hyphen is a purely mechanical device that has no relation to the writing of effective English. It is far more essential in mathematics. A hyphen omitted from an equation could cause the destruction of an $18,000,000 rocket designed to probe Venus. Fortunately editors are free from this sort of red ink.

¶ QUOTATION MARKS

There are two sorts of quotation marks: double (" ") and single (' '). Double quotation marks are more common in the United

States; single ones, in Great Britain. Both are equally valid; and single quotes, which are neater, are gradually gaining acceptance in the United States.

1. (*a*) Quotation marks are used to indicate the actual words of a speaker or writer:

According to Emerson, "For nonconformity the world whips you with its displeasure."

What novel opens with the line, "Call me Ishmael"?

The Queen of Hearts shouted, "Off with her head!"

"So," he sneered, "you thought to betray us."

Quotation marks are also used to enclose words attributed to a speaker, though he did not say them.

Since Patrick Henry's speech to the Virginia delegates is a reconstruction by William Wirt, Henry probably did not say, "Give me liberty, or give me death."

If a quotation is interrupted by *he said, they exclaimed,* etc., two sets of quotation marks are necessary. Some modern fiction writers do not use quotation marks for dialogue. This is sometimes an annoying obstacle to the reader.

When you are quoting a real statement, rather than writing fiction, you must be careful to quote verbatim, including the original punctuation and spelling. An approximate quotation will not do when the authentic one is available. If all you have is an approximation, you should indicate this. Inaccurate quotation is unscholarly. In politics it can be dangerous. Unscrupulous demagogues make a practice of distorting quotations, wrenching them unfairly out of context, or even inventing fictitious quotations and attributing them to their enemies. The fact that the late Senator Joseph McCarthy did all these things was one reason he was censured by the Senate for conduct bringing disgrace on that body.

Likewise, if you use the words of another author, you must enclose them in quotation marks and acknowledge your source. Otherwise you are guilty of plagiarism. Some students—either through ignorance or through unwillingness to do their own work—take paragraphs from other writers, change a few words here and there, and consider that they have made an acceptable paraphrase. But something like "Fourscore and seven years ago our ancestors [fathers] brought forth on this continent a new country [nation],

254

conceived in freedom [liberty], and dedicated to the concept [proposition] that all men are born [created] equal" is still in every essential, despite the replacement of some words by synonyms, the work of Abraham Lincoln. This is a blatant example, but such inadequate paraphrasing often occurs with less obvious material. If you quote three or more consecutive words from another's writing, you should enclose them in quotation marks. If you paraphrase, do so completely.

(*b*) Quotation marks are never used in a paraphrase or for indirect discourse and quotation:

DIRECT QUOTATION: Huck Finn said, "All right, then, I'll go to hell."
INDIRECT QUOTATION: Huck Finn said that he would go to hell.
WRONG: He said "that he would be late for the game."

(*c*) If a quotation continues for several paragraphs, opening quotation marks should be placed at the beginning of each paragraph (to indicate that the quote is continuing, but closing quote marks are used only at the end of the last paragraph, where the quotation itself ends. Usually in dialogue a separate paragraph is devoted to each speaker. On the other hand, an appropriate quotation may be placed in the body of a sentence without any form of break.

(*d*) You may indicate a lengthy quotation from a piece of writing by indenting it, centering it on the page, and single-spacing it. In print, such quotations are generally put in smaller type. When you single-space and center a quotation, you do not need to use quotation marks. For example:

Why should we be in such desperate haste to succeed and in such desperate enterprises? If a man does not keep pace with his companions, perhaps it is because he hears a different drummer. Let him step to the music which he hears, however measured or far away. —HENRY DAVID THOREAU, *Walden*

2. To indicate a quotation within a quotation, use the alternate form of double or single quotation marks than those in the outer quotation. In other words, if your outer quotation marks are double, use single quotes in marking the inner quotation, and vice versa.

3. Quotation marks are often used to show that a word is being considered as a word, to be defined, or explained:

"Animism" is the word given to primitive man's belief in ghosts and spirits in natural objects.

What does "potrezebie" mean in *Mad*?

The English dog, after centuries of pure breeding, does not have a powerful constitution and is subject to certain virus infections and a destructive stomach ailment called "bloat." [9]   —JAMES THURBER, *Thurber's Dogs*

Bloodhounds are frequently handicapped by what is technically known as the "fouling" of a trail by sightseers and other careless humans.[10]—*Ibid*

Notice the difference between "There is scholarship in the dictionary" and "There is 'scholarship' in the dictionary." In print, instead of quotation marks italics can be used to designate words specified as words.

4. When a word is called into question or is particularly ironic, it may be enclosed in quotation marks:

Immigrants were given "free" transportation to America, but their fare was deducted from their wages, so that they were immediately plunged into debt.

Sometimes slang words and phrases or familiar figures of speech are put in quotation marks. This is an annoying mannerism. If the words are inappropriate, do not use them. If they are appropriate, use them straight. Some students protest that their teachers told them to put all mild colloquialisms in quotation marks. The result is that they enclose every third word in quotes and produce pages resembling a swarm of gnats. Movie ads are becoming addicted to putting the names of characters in quotes: Tony Curtis as "Antoninus," Peter O'Toole as "Lawrence." This is a feckless device, even when the character is fictitious. Certainly Lawrence of Arabia did not sign his name T. E. "Lawrence." In the old days, Charles Laughton simply played Henry VIII, not "Henry VIII." One of the fussy mannerisms of Henry James's later prose is the setting apart of ordinary words by quotation marks "He had come —putting the thing pompously—to look at his 'property'. . . . He was the owner of another, not quite so 'good'. . . . He could live in 'Europe' as he had been in the habit of living. . . ."—"The Jolly Corner"

5. Quotation marks are used to enclose the titles of articles, short stories, chapters, short poems, and songs. Titles of books and periodicals are underlined or italicized. Never mark a title by both quotation marks and italics, or underlining.

WRONG: Arthur Miller's "*The Crucible*."

RIGHT: "Baker's Blue-Jay Yarn" first appeared in Mark Twain's *A Tramp Abroad*.

"The Rime of the Ancient Mariner" was in the 1798 *Lyrical Ballads*.

"Old Man River" is a Jerome Kern song from *Showboat*.

In footnotes and bibliographies, the titles of chapters and of the sections or divisions in a published book or periodical are put in quotation marks. The first example following is for a footnote; the second, for a bibliography:

James Thurber, "The Secret Life of Walter Mitty," *My World—and Welcome to It* (Harcourt, Brace and Company, New York, 1942), p. 73.

Fujimura, Thomas Y., "The Appeal of Dryden's Heroic Plays," *PMLA*, Vol. 75, March 1960, pp. 37-45.

6. You should avoid loose, indiscriminate use of quotation marks. An Iowa City mortuary displayed an ad urging "Mark every grave." The sign was not quoting anyone but the signmaker, so there was no point to the punctuation. "Mark every grave."— George Washington. This might lend some authority but could lead to charges of inaccuracy. "Mark—every grave" has a dramatic pause, and "Mark every grave!" might arouse some urgency, but perhaps the most appropriate punctuation is "Mark every . . . grave?"

¶ QUOTATION MARKS WITH OTHER PUNCTUATION

Practice varies somewhat on the position of other punctuation marks in conjunction with quotes. The following advice is safe.

1. Put the period or comma at the end of a quotation inside the closing quotation marks, whether or not it is part of the quotation. Other punctuation marks go inside the closing quotes only when they are part of the quotation:

"It appears," said the Rajah, "that you have forgotten about the cobras."

Maury Maverick coined the word "gobbledygook."

Note that there are not two periods at the end.

2. When the quotation is a direct question, the question mark is placed inside the closing quotes; in other cases, it is placed outside:

"Am I a coward?" asked Hamlet.

What play contains the line, "My kingdom for a horse!"?

Have you read Faulkner's "Dry September"?

On bended knee, Horpington tenderly asked Patricia, "What's for lunch?"

(There is no need for a period after the question mark.)

Hardly a man takes a half-hour's nap after dinner, but when he wakes he holds up his head and asks, "What's the news?" as if the rest of mankind had stood his sentinels. —HENRY DAVID THOREAU, *Walden*

3. The same practice holds for exclamation marks as for question marks:

Hamlet cried, "O, horrible! O, horrible! most horrible!"

"O, I am fortune's fool!" said Romeo.

Don't call me a "fink"!

4. Semicolons and colons always go after end quotes.

"That is right," he said; "I do come from the Carpathian Alps."

Ronald Colman said, "It is a far, far better thing I do than I have ever done"; then the camera moved up past the guillotine.

Note that in the first example, the semicolon between the two main clauses is placed after *he said* rather than inside the first end quote.

5. Ellipsis points at the beginning or end of a quotation are placed inside the quotation marks:

Thoreau wrote, ". . . I would have each one be very careful to find out and pursue *his own* way, and not his father's or his mother's or his neighbor's instead."

If a fourth point is added to indicate the end of the sentence after an ellipsis, it is also placed inside the quotation marks.

Thoreau explained, "My purpose in going to Walden Pond was not to live cheaply nor to live dearly there, but to transact some private business with the fewest obstacles. . . ."

6. When a quotation is broken off by a dash, the dash is placed inside the quotation marks, and it is not followed by a period even if it ends the sentence.

"It's perfectly clear, my good man, but—Good heavens—"

258

¶ UNDERLINING AND ITALICS

In handwritten and typed copy, underline words that would be *italicized* in print.

1. Underline complete titles of books, periodicals, plays, motion pictures, and the names of ships, planes, and trains. Titles of songs and short poems are put generally in quotation marks, rather than italicized. Titles of chapters, articles, and short stories are also put in quotation marks:

Fitzgerald's "Babylon Revisited" was published in Taps at Reveille.
Melville's "Bartleby" is one of the Piazza Tales.
Many of Faulkner's stories first appeared in The Saturday Evening Post.
"Passage to India" is one of the major poems in Whitman's Leaves of Grass.
A Passage to India is a novel by E. M. Forster.
Many novels of intrigue take place on the Orient Express.
The mutiny aboard H. M. S. Bounty occurred in 1789.
Will Rogers was killed in the crash of the Winnie Mae.

If the title of an article includes the title of a book, underline the book and enclose the whole title in quotation marks: "A Study of James's The Ambassadors." Be careful to underline all the words in a title and no words that are not in the title.

WRONG: The Autobiography of Mark Twain or The Autobiography of Mark Twain
RIGHT: The Autobiography of Mark Twain
WRONG: The Maritime History of Massachusetts
RIGHT: The Maritime History of Massachusetts

Students frequently fail to underline the article in a title and so commit such errors as "Cooper's the Deerslayer," "Norris's The Octopus," "Hemingway's a Farewell to Arms." Again, students sometimes take the heading used in an anthology for the book's actual title, writing such absurdities as, "In Thoreau's From Walden . . . ," "In Paine's From Common Sense . . . ," or "Billy Budd and the Critics is Melville's final novel."

2. Underlining or italics may be used to emphasize a word or phrase.

"$12.95—for a magazine?"
"Well, what did you say, then?"
". . . ef you en Huck fetches a rattlesnake in heah for me to tame, I's gwyne to leave, dat's shore."

259

Mark Twain used this device effectively, but it can easily be over-worked by less skillful writers.

3. Words and phrases still considered foreign (consult your dictionary) are underlined or italicized: Gemütlichkeit, coup de grâce, Zeitgeist, memento mori.

4. Words and phrases considered specifically as words can be underlined or italicized. They may, alternatively, be put in quotation marks, a practice more common in writing or typing than in printing:

Curfew comes from the French couvre feu ("cover the fire").
To coöperate in the highest as well as the lowest sense, means to get our living together. —THOREAU, Walden

¶ CAPITALIZATION

There are many words that require a capital, or upper-case, letter. Editorial practice varies, but most uses follow well-established conventions. If you are writing for an organization with special rules of style, you should consult its manual (e.g., the *Government Printing Office Style Manual*); otherwise, the following instructions are generally held acceptable.

1. The first word of a sentence is capitalized. When a complete sentence is enclosed in parentheses, the first word is capitalized if the sentence in parentheses stands outside the preceding sentence; but if the parenthetical matter is inserted to stand within a sentence, the first word starts with a small letter.

Mt. Rainier is not the highest mountain in the continental United States (it is 14,410 feet high), but it has the most spectacular rise from sea level.

The first word of a quoted sentence is capitalized, but if the sentence is broken into during the course of the sentence, the continuation does not begin with a capital letter until another complete sentence.

Thoreau wrote, "The mass of men lead lives of quiet desperation."

"I think," he said casually, "that all hell is about to break loose."

"Come, Goodman Brown," cried his fellow-traveller, "this is a dull place for the beginning of a journey."

"You jest," he exclaimed, recoiling a few paces. "But let us proceed to the Amontillado."

260

When a phrase, not of dialogue, is quoted, it does not usually begin with a capital letter.

Christopher Cranch drew a cartoon of Emerson as "a transparent eyeball."

If the beginning of a quotation is omitted (sometimes it is replaced by ellipses), the quotation is not capitalized unless it begins with a proper noun.

According to Thoreau, ". . . a man is rich in proportion to the number of things which he can afford to let alone."

2. Proper names are capitalized. These include the names of people (Alfred E. Neuman); races, nationalities, and tribes (Mexican, Indian, Cherokee, Eskimo); places (New Zealand); languages (German, Yoruba); months; days of the week; holidays (Groundhog Day, the Fourth of July, St. Agnes' Eve); historical events and periods (the Boxer Rebellion, the Battle of the Bulge, the Reformation, the Enlightenment, Reconstruction, the New Deal); documents (the Ten Commandments, the New Testament, the Bill of Rights, the Monroe Doctrine); names of ships (*The Golden Hind*); religious denominations ("Methodists, beware Mormon crickets"); organizations and institutions (Loyal Order of Moose, Prudential Insurance, State University of Iowa).

Adjectives from proper nouns are capitalized unless they have become too common: *Elizabethan, Shakespearean, Darwinian, Platonic, Thomistic, Restoration drama, Petrarchan sonnets, German philology, Jacobean drama.* Some proper nouns and their adjectives have become common nouns and are no longer capitalized: *boycott, bologna, bourbon whiskey, brussels sprouts, chinaware, cordovan leather, french dressing, lynch, maverick, mercurial, portland cement, sandwich,* and many others.

German simplifies matters by capitalizing all nouns, but in English, only common nouns are generally written with a small letter. Sometimes the distinction is difficult. Seasons of the year are not capitalized, though the months are. Compass directions are not capitalized unless they designate a region of the country (and this distinction is weakening).

To find the Moose Hall, turn north two blocks, and then go east a mile.

There was sectional antagonism between the industrial North and the agrarian South.

Many words are uncapitalized common nouns unless they are used in a title; common among them are *school, college, university, church, hospital, hotel, street, park, fort, city, mountain, river,* and *island*:

Lyndon Johnson once taught school.

Thomas H. Johnson teaches at the Lawrence School.

Most colleges and universities are expanding.

Michigan State University has 27,000 students.

After the battle at the fort, the casualties were taken across the river into the city; there they were lodged in hospitals, churches, hotels, and some in the streets and parks.

The inspectors visited Fort McHenry, Patterson Park, Charles Street, the Johns Hopkins Hospital, the Patapsco River, Old St. Paul's Church, and the Lord Baltimore Hotel. Then they flew to Salt Lake City.

Sometimes, capitalizing a noun will change its meaning or make it more specific. Uncapitalized, *depression* is a common noun; capitalized, it refers to the decade following the crash of 1929. Similarly, *red* is a color, whereas *Red* is a political designation. There have been lots of armadas, but the *Armada* is the one that sailed from Spain in 1588. Many things have been restored; the *Restoration* denotes the return of the Stuart monarchy to England in 1660. Notice the difference between *friend* and *Friend, genesis* and *Genesis, virgin* and *Virgin, advent* and *Advent, catholic* and *Catholic. Army, navy, marines, air force* are not capitalized unless they refer to a specific organization:

Tarzan saw an army winding its way over the mountains.

Most navies had abolished flogging by 1850.

Senator Joe McCarthy was revealed as a demagogue in his attack on the Army.

3. Professional and official titles are capitalized when followed by a proper name or when used to stand for a specific person. When used as a general term, they are left in lower case. *Sir, Lady, Mr., Mrs., Miss, Master,* and *Mistress* are capitalized before a proper name:

Is there a doctor in the house?
There's a phone call for Dr. Sawbones.
Some professors have to publish or perish.
The dean told Professor Crabshaw to publish or perish.

A colonel and several generals were drunk.
Aunt Agatha sent a billet-doux to Admiral Bilgewater.
"As I live and breathe, it's the Major," said Snagglepuss.
Nell Gwynn was Charles II's mistress.
Falstaff liked to sponge off Mistress Quickly.

When referring to the United States government leaders, *President* and *Vice-President* are always capitalized:

When Franklin Pierce was President, he made Hawthorne consul to Liverpool.
The First Lady entertained the delegation from Opar.

4. Names of relatives are not capitalized unless they are followed by the relative's name or clearly stand for a specific individual. *Mother, father, mom, pop, uncle, aunt, brother, sister*, etc., without the name are not capitalized if preceded by a modifier (usually a possessive noun or pronoun) but are capitalized when used alone as proper names. Sometimes an author departs from this practice. *We Escape from Madrid* contains the sentence, "Stewed cat cost mother and me a dollar a plate in Madrid."

The princess's twelve brothers were turned into ravens.
Sir Joseph Porter had sisters, aunts, and cousins by the dozens.
Tom Sawyer often bamboozled Aunt Polly.
Mrs. Day was shocked at Father's language.
Thomas Wolfe's letters to his mother have been published.
"Just before the battle, Mother . . ."
Most fathers aren't excited by the P.T.A.
"Come up from the fields, Father."
Oscar Homolka played Uncle Chris in *I Remember Mama*.

When used as slang, *brother* and *sister* are not capitalized:

Listen, brother, you better pay protection money, or else.
Just remember, sister, don't get smart with Rocco, see.

5. Titles of books, stories, articles, songs, and organizations customarily have the first and last words capitalized, and generally all others except articles, conjunctions, and short prepositions.

The Sound and the Fury	*The Ides of Mad*
Much Ado about Nothing	The Fraternal Order of Eagles
The Last of the Mohicans	*A View from the Bridge*
The Portrait of a Lady	*Once upon a Mattress*
"Smoke Gets in Your Eyes"	*The Middle-Aged Man on the Flying Trapeze*

In business correspondence each letter in a title may be capitalized, so that the typist won't have to stop to underline: HOW TO IMPROVE YOUR VERBAL SKILLS. Sometimes an author, like e. e. cummings, does not want any of his title's words capitalized; and, of course, titles and all other words in books written by a cockroach who can't hit the shift key of his typewriter must be in small letters.

Titles of school courses are capitalized (History 204), but except for languages, school subjects in general are not; "Lumpington was studying history, math, physics, French, Russian, and psychology; he was carrying too many hours."

6. The pronoun *I* is capitalized; otherwise, it might easily be lost among the words with more letters (e.g., "They wondered why i insisted upon skiing"). The French *je* has an additional letter for support and so is not capitalized. Likewise the English vocative *O* is capitalized, though *oh* usually is not.

7. Nouns standing for the name of the Deity are capitalized; usage is divided on pronouns. This practice has no necessary connection with a writer's religious beliefs, though a militant nonbeliever might make a point of using a small letter. When used in a general sense, *god* should not be capitalized: "The ancient world believed in many gods." Otherwise, *God, Christ, Jehovah, Allah,* and the like are treated as proper nouns. So are words like *Saviour, Redeemer, Messiah,* the *Lamb,* the *Trinity, Father, Son,* and *Holy Ghost* that refer to the Christian Trinity. Unitarians probably would not capitalize pronouns referring to Jesus; Trinitarians often do, though the Gospels do not. Deists used to capitalize *Reason,* and some humanists capitalize *Man* and *Mankind.* Pantheists might capitalize nature; Frank Lloyd Wright said, "I put a capital *N* on nature and go there." But pronouns referring to *Reason, Man,* and *Nature* or to mythical deities are left uncapitalized.

The Almighty will protect us by His Providence.
Christ told His Apostles that He would be with them always.
The Lord does not always reveal His will.
I know that my Redeemer liveth.
Saturn devoured his children.
Athena carries the head of the Gorgon on her shield.

8. Abstract nouns are often capitalized if they are personifications or if they denote institutions or ideals.

Where then shall Hope and Fear their objects find?
Must dull Suspense corrupt the stagnant mind?
—SAMUEL JOHNSON, "The Vanity of Human Wishes"

With close-lipped Patience for our only friend,
Sad Patience, too near neighbor to Despair:
—MATTHEW ARNOLD, "The Scholar Gipsy"

Can Honor's voice provoke the silent dust,
Or Flattery soothe the dull cold ear of Death?
—THOMAS GRAY, "Elegy Written in a Country Churchyard"

The Constitution requires the separation of Church and State.

By the same token, nouns standing for a nation's flag are capitalized: *Old Glory, the Stars and Stripes, the Stars and Bars, the Tricolor, the Oriflamme, the Union Jack.*

9. Customarily the first letter in each line of verse is capitalized, though poets are free to follow any practice that they wish. Sometimes the entire first word is capitalized:

MUCH madness is divinest sense
To a discerning eye;
Much sense the starkest madness.
'Tis the majority
In this, as all, prevails.
Assent, and you are sane;
Demur,—you're straightway dangerous,
And handled with a chain.—EMILY DICKINSON

10. Solitary letters followed by a hyphen to form a compound are capitalized: *A-bomb, H-bomb, L-shaped, T-square, X-ray, U-boat.* So are Roman numerals except for prefatory page numbers, which are printed in small numerals.

11. Authors can, at their discretion, capitalize words for emphasis or stylistic effect:

If all these companies have their way, and it looks as if they will, our country will have the sweetest-smelling people in the world, If they don't turn green first.

¶ A FINAL WORD

This chapter does not attempt to cover all the possibilities in punctuation. Many situations are too specialized and may require you to consult a manual of professional or business style or to use your

265

own initiative. This chapter has been rather prescriptive in setting forth rules. In practice, not all of them are hard and fast. Some offices and some editors may be rigid, but practice varies among them. In creative writing you should feel free to experiment and suit punctuation to your style and subject. Clarity is ultimately the only test.

A few final words of advice may be in order. You should never begin a new line of typing, or writing, with any punctuation except quotation marks. Some confused students begin a new line with a comma or semicolon that belongs with the words on the previous line. One, unable to finish his paragraph at the end of a line, wrote as his last line:

. . . ."

Neither should you end a line with the quotation marks belonging to the words on the next line:

WRONG: Hemingway said, "
            Morals are what you feel good after."

Exercise 30:   Correct any errors in capitalization.

1. Last hallowe'en, uncle Hermie took mom and pop to a Witches' sabbath.
2. Last year Horpington studied Geology, History, American Literature, and Chicken Plucking.
3. Cardinal Newman's brother translated *Hiawatha* into Latin and Arabic.
4. In parts of the American west there are still fewer than ten people per square mile.
5. In High School, Lumpington excelled at cafeteria attendance.
6. In *The Plumed Serpent,* D. H. Lawrence's characters try to revive the aztec Religion.
7. All presidents of the United States except Jackson and Franklin Roosevelt have been Baptized after death in the mormon church.
8. Don't write "According to Webster." Webster has been dead for over a century, so indicate what Dictionary you are using: e.g., Webster's new collegiate dictionary.
9. Don Marquis is the author of *the lives and times of archy and mehitabel.*
10. Grandmother does not know Brigitte Bardot is french.
11. Rölvaag wrote *Giants In the Earth* in norwegian.
12. In some Schools, Freshmen still wear beanies.

266

13. The United States has thirty-one National Parks.
14. Rita Hayworth, as Salome, tried to save John the baptist and ended listening to the sermon on the mount.
15. The Johns Hopkins University band used to wear ROTC uniforms dyed black and blue and sam browne belts.
16. Bernard winterset, Art Critic, leaned back in his chair and surveyed with distaste the Bearded creature before him.
17. Thangbrand O'connel saw the siamese cat stalking him and said tentatively, "Here, Kitty, Kitty."
18. His name is wu the Inscrutable; don't call him "kitty"—he doesn't know he's a cat.
19. Edgar Rice Burroughs wrote twenty-two Tarzan Novels, ten Mars books, and three books about Pellucidar, the Land that Time forgot.
20. Henry the eighth had six wives, but Charles the second had innumerable Mistresses and tried hard to be the Father of his Country.

16 √ The Antic *'s*

The one advantage German has over English is the lack of apostrophes. There was no apostrophe in Old or Middle English. It appeared during the Renaissance along with printing, and it has plagued us ever since. Basically, the apostrophe is a printer's mark rather than part of the language proper. It is never used in speech except by Victor Borge, yet no one ever has any trouble distinguishing meaning without it. In written English it is more of a nuisance than a help. Its rules are inconsistent and full of exceptions; and students, advertisers, and journalists often use it incorrectly, omitting it when required and inserting it when it is not called for. It would be better to have no apostrophe at all than to have it so misused, and George Bernard Shaw did try to get rid of it. You might welcome its early demise; but as long as it is still required, you should know how to use it properly.

1. The apostrophe is used to indicate the possessive case in nouns. A singular or plural noun not ending in *s* adds an apostrophe and *s* to form the possessive ("man's hat," "women's hats"). A singular or plural noun already ending in *s* or an *s* sound adds the apostrophe only (Essex' execution, Leibnitz' philosophy, Jesus' parables, Apostles' Creed), though it is also acceptable to add an apostrophe and *s* to singular nouns even when they already end in *s* (either "Charles' head" or "Charles's head").

This seems simple enough, yet it is often confused by people who don't look carefully at the original noun. If it already ends in *s*, the careless reader is apt to put the apostrophe before the *s* and so make a bungled back formation. Thus students mistakenly write of "Henry James's fiction," "Yeat's poems," "Robert Grave's criticism," and "Jonathan Edward's theology." One student even wrote of "John Dos Passo's *U.S.A.*" Some usage is relative, but these errors are always and absolutely wrong, and display sheer carelessness or an inability to read clearly. Of course, there is no Jame, Yeat, Grave, Edward, or Dos Passo; the proper possessive is *James', Yeats', Graves', Edwards',* and *Dos Passos'* (or alternatively, *James's, Yeats's, Graves's, Edwards's, and Dos Passos's*). Again, people write the wrong form by adding a nonexistent *s* to a singular noun and then using the apostrophe. Thus Theodore Dreiser is transformed to Dreisers when a student writes of "Dreisers' *Sister Carrie.*" Students are not the only ones at fault; several learned correspondents, including a Harvard professor and Pulitzer Prize winner, wrote to *The New York Times Book Review* to comment on a history by Will and Ariel Durant, which they indicated as *the Durants's* book. But the singular is *Durant;* the plural, *Durants;* and the possessive plural, *Durants'.*

Elizabethan English sometimes avoided the apostrophe by pronoun constructions, such as "the king his army." This may serve as a clue to modern usage; in "the cat his pajamas," the word *cat* has no *s* and so needs both it and an apostrophe when written in our possessive form, whereas in *the cats their pajamas, cats* already has the *s* and needs only the apostrophe.

2. In compound nouns, the *'s* is added to the element nearest the object it modifies ("mother-in-law's house," "attorney general's action," "Jason Robards, Jr.'s performance").

3. Joint possession or possession in a series usually takes the possessive case only in the last item ("Simon and Schuster's office"; "Harcourt, Brace & World's new dictionary"; "Montgomery Ward's catalogue"), but for individual or alternate possession, each item should be in the possessive case:

Do you prefer Cecil B. deMille's or Ingmar Bergman's movies?
The wombat's and the koala's feeding habits are significantly different.
St. Bartholomew's Men's Club is having Ladies' Night.
Have you read Hemingway's and Faulkner's fiction?

4. For titles, geographic names, and names of organizations, follow the official form, whatever it may be. Often these are contradictory. Thus we find *St. John's College* but *St. Elizabeths Hospital, King's College* and *Queens College,* the *Teamsters Union* but the *International Ladies' Garment Workers' Union.* Sometimes there is no apostrophe even though possession is implied, as in *Peoples Church, Painters Supplies, Investors Mutual.* There are no apostrophes in *Rutgers* or in *Johns Hopkins University,* since *Johns*

269

was Hopkins' first name and *Hopkins* modifies *University* just as [John] *Harvard* does. Thus *John's, Hopkin's,* and *Hopkins'* are all wrong. Increasingly the apostrophe is being dropped from official names, where it is simply a bother. The U.S. Geographic Board has ruled it out of places with a possessive proper name: e.g., *Harpers Ferry, Devils Courthouse, Pikes Peak, Hells Canyon, Huggins Hell, Silers Bald,* and *Charlies Bunion.* As yet there is no evidence that anyone has lost their way because of the missing punctuation.

5. As a general rule, no apostrophe is used in words more descriptive than possessive that end in *s*:

Massachusetts law (vs. Gresham's law)
teachers college
Actors Studio
Home Owners Policy

United Nations Assembly
United Auto Workers Local
White Citizens Councils
Hotels-Restaurant Employees & Bartenders International Union

An exception is *Veterans' Administration,* because the apostrophe is in the enabling statute. There are some other exceptions, including *rogues' gallery* (which is plural as opposed to *rogue's march*). If the modifier is a personal name ending in *s,* people sometimes confuse it with a possessive; thus the *Michigan State News* turned *Olds Hall* into *Old's Hall.* There should be no possessive in *United States Constitution,* but it is sometimes written as *United States' Constitution,* or worse, *United State's Constitution.*

6. Possessive personal pronouns (*ours, yours, hers, its, theirs*) never take an apostrophe, but impersonal ones require it.

anybody's game
anyone's guess
each other's families

everybody's choice
everyone's dismay
one's self I sing

nobody's business
someone's child
but someone else's mistake

7. The apostrophe is used in such general phrases as:

author's royalties
baker's dozen
confectioner's sugar

lamb's wool
pitcher's elbow
printer's devil

sailor's hornpipe
shepherd's pie
traveler's checks

8. An apostrophe is used to indicate the omission of letters or figures and the plural of letters, numbers, and symbols.

270

a '59 Thunderbird	p's and q's	wouldn't
a '22 Stutz Bearcat	6's and 7's	you're
the spirit of '76	MP's	won't
the 49'ers	VIP's	it's (it is)
'em (them)	¶'s	ne'er

The apostrophe is not used in spelled-out words or numbers (*twos and threes, ifs and buts*) unless it is needed for clarity (*do's and don'ts*). In some abbreviations and contractions the apostrophe is now omitted: *til, Frisco, Halloween.* Many people no longer realize that the latter, spelled alternatively *Hallowe'en,* is a contraction, for All Hallow Even meaning the evening before All Hallow (All Saints') Day; and the apostrophe has vanished along with the religious connotation. As for contractions, when we are talking, we no longer think of them as a combination of two words, but use them habitually as independent words (even the pronunciation of *don't* is different from *do not*), so there is no reason except custom for retaining the apostrophe. As it is, some people confuse any final *nt* with a contraction and so create absurdities like *mean't* and *len't.*

9. The apostrophe is never, never, never, never used to form the subjective and objective plural of nouns or the third person present singular of verbs. Yet many people, indiscriminately associating a terminal *s* with the possessive, mangle plurals and verbs grotesquely. Inadequately sophisticated suburbanites label their houses as "The Morrison's," "The Glub's," or send invitations for a party at "the Jone's." The errors here are doubly dyed, being wrong in number as well as case; there is no *Jone,* and no one uses *the* with the singular in referring to a family's name. Morrison, Glub, and Jones want the subjective or objective plural, which is *Morrisons, Glubs,* and *Joneses.* This confusion of the plural with the possessive is increasingly common in slipshod advertising and journalism, as well as in student writing. Thus one reads of "Roy Acuff Exhibit's" in Gatlinburg, and sees ads for "Bagel's Toasted and Buttered," "Poncho's for Sale," "Hat's on Sale Reduced," or "Save $100 or more on piano's." Students write "The early Puritan's considered the Indian's to be servants of Satan," and "The Joad's could not afford adequate food and clothing." *Redbook* advertises "Christmas with the Kennedy's and Queen Elizabeth," and journalists write that "Reporters covering receptions may only watch the guests arrive and ask the Kennedy's to pose for pictures." Though ex-

271

tremely common, these faulty plurals remain illogical and unacceptable. Often they are combined with fuzzy thinking, as in two statements from the reactionary Cinema Educational Guild, Inc.: "In 1918, Woodrow Wilson, the first of their [i.e., "Communist traitors" like J. P. Morgan, John D. Rockefeller, and Bernard Baruch] Benedict *Arnold's* was elected President," and "[President Kennedy and] the INVISIBLE COMMUNIST GOVERNMENT OF OUR COUNTRY forbid the Cuban *refugee's* to organize an invasion Army to try to regain their country." (Italics mine.)

Sometimes the error is compounded when the plural is spelled differently from the singular. *Negro, hero, banjo* and similar words add an *es* to form the plural. So when one advertises "banjoe's weighing up to fifty pounds" or writes, "During Reconstruction, most Negroe's endured great hardship," he has a misspelled singular possessive instead of the desired subjective plural.

When a noun ending in *s* is to be used in the possessive plural, many students are totally dumbfounded, since they don't even know how to form the noun's plural. Thus, for *the Phelpses' farm* in *Huckleberry Finn,* students wrote *Phelp's farm, Phelps' farm, Phelps farm, Phelpes' farm, Phelpeses' farm,* and *Phelpeses farm.* But the case is simple enough: singular—*Phelps,* plural—*Phelpses,* possessive plural—*Phelpses'.*

Similar to the confusion over the plural is the mistaken use of the apostrophe and *s* to form the third person present singular of verbs. The proper procedure is simply to add an *s* to the infinitive (*eat—he eats*) unless the verb ends in *y,* in which case you turn the *y* into an *i* and add *es* (*carry—he carries*). But again, some people cannot resist using an apostrophe with any final *s,* and so they write "he try's," "she sing's," "it rumble's." (In a Roadrunner cartoon, Wile E. Coyote ordered a weapon labeled "Acme boomerang return's to owner.") Another difficulty is that some simple verbs are confused with contractions. Since *let us* is contracted to *let's,* one student wrote by faulty analogy, "The landlord let's us cook in our room." Later this same student omitted a necessary apostrophe from a contraction, writing "Lets go to the circus."

The apostrophe is so extremely idiosyncratic in practice that one sign even transformed *cafe* into *caf'e.* This way lies schizophrenia, and we would do well to follow German and get rid of the apostrophe altogether. Where we write "brother's hat," the Germans write "Bruders hut." In spoken English we don't need the apostrophe; and in writing as well, context would make the meaning clear so that one could tell *my brothers term paper* from *a Marx Brothers* script and both from *The Brothers Karamazov.*

Exercise 31: In the following sentences some words lack a necessary apostrophe and others have apostrophes incorrectly used. If there is an error, enter the proper form in the blanks.

1. When Huck first arrived at the Grangerford's, he found them hospitable. . . . .
2. Horpington is studying Henry Adam's *Mont-Saint-Michel and Chartres'.* . . . .
3. Dwight Macdonald claimed that the last good Hollywood movie was Orson Welles's *The Magnificent Amberson's.* . . . .
4. The Indian's sold enormous tracts of land for trinkets. . . .
5. E. E. Cumming's *The Enormous Room* is one of the best World War I novels. . . . .
6. My wife made me watch *The Mummy's Curse* on the Late Late Show. . . . .
7. You're one of the lucky one's. . . . .
8. Spencer Tracy won his first Academy Award for *Captains' Courageous.* . . . .
9. Many critics think *Howards End* is E. M. Forster's finest novel. . . . .
10. *Thurbers Dog's* is now out in paperback. . . . .
11. Theres no use arguing; I won't lend you my copy of *Mad.* . . . .
12. You cant borrow *The Brothers Mad,* either. . . . .
13. Spencer Tracy won his second Academy Award the next year for *Boy's Town.* . . . .
14. This pfeffernuss is made with Mrs. Evan's cookie recipe. . . . .
15. Horpington couldn't understand the vocabulary in James Gould Cozzen's *By Love Possessed.* . . . .
16. James Baldwin is an eloquent spokesman for Negroe's rights. . . . .
17. Don't confuse Dos Passos' *Three Soldiers* with Kipling's *Soldier's Three.* . . . .
18. Can you sing "St. Jame's Infirmary"? . . . .
19. I refuse to watch *My Brothers Talk's to Horses* on the Late Late Show. . . . .
20. Nobody knows how many member's there are in the Mafia. . . . .
21. Critics admired Douglas Fairbanks's, Jr., performance in *The Prisoner of Zenda.* . . . .
22. "Help," cried Una O'Connor; "the monsters coming! Look at it's horrible face." . . . .
23. Spencer Tracy played Robert Rogers in the movie of Kenneth Roberts' *Northwest Passage.* . . . .

273

24. Theres no use arguing; you can't keep an aardvark in the cellar. . . . .

25. "Fill er up," Horpington told the attendant, as he parked his 33' Duesenberg. . . . .

26. Several students collapsed with writers' cramp.

27. Funk's and Wagnall's company is well known for its dictionaries and encyclopedias. . . . .

28. The syllabus seemed confused; the course required *The Doctors Dilemma, Roget's International Thesaurus, All the King's Men, Pigeon Feather's, Lysistrata,* Holme's "The Chambered Nautilus," and Howells *A Modern Instance.* . . . .

29. Spencer Tracy murder's Ingrid Bergman in *Dr. Jekyll and Mr. Hyde.* . . . .

30. The flame azaleas in the Great Smokies are at their best on Gregorys Bald. . . . .

Exercise 32: In the following sentences, correct any grammatically inaccurate words or constructions.

1. Them cattle is speckled, spotted, and ringstraked.
2. You hadn't ought to tell a good dream until it has come true.
3. Is you finished washing of your hands?
4. I thought I had losted my plastic bottles.
5. Groundhogs is the same as them woodchucks whom some people call whistle pigs.
6. You got to be having a visa to enter Egypt.
7. Mother Hubbard's dog was eaten her outen house and home.
8. Why come is the buzzards waiting here?
9. I resembles my brother William—Bill, us calls him.
10. They is a lot of work to do before supper.
11. I isn't made up my mind which way to vote.
12. Them sudden stops can make a fellow seasick.
13. Carter is got some very peculiar tastes.
14. I already seen *The Three Stooges Meet Hercules.*
15. Them's not moth holes; them's bullet holes.
16. The Cherokees, which was the most civilized Indians, wouldn't hardly write no sentences as this one.
17. They was seventeen cattle friz solid in a stack.
18. Skinks is different than skunks.
19. Is the campground got any vacancies?
20. You should not of lost your temper that way.
21. I don't believe the bloodhound is ran away.
22. Give me back my glasses so's I can see you.
23. I never knowed you were so fond of liver mush.

274

24. Us has got the same color hair but different color eyeballs.
25. Claude talks like he must of run for Congress.

Exercise 33: Add any necessary punctuation and remove any unnecessary punctuation from the following:

1. Since it is the desire of every woman in Africa to get children if she doesn't get a husband it will make her unhappy.
2. In vain did all the rain doctors of the locality, engage in the formidable task of controlling the weather.
3. The first son of the late chief, brought the cow, immediately afterwards.
4. Then the oldest woman, advised the seven wives of the late chief, to give account of themselves, since they lost their husband by death, a couple of years ago.
5. The first wife, walked to the cenotaph and said "You know that I have carried out all the necessary formalities according to custom. If I did not may today, be, my last day on earth.
6. In this solemn and thought provoking way, the remaining six women, gave account of themselves.
7. Everybody was in great suspense, as to what would be the outcome, of this historic ceremony.
8. As the animals were trying to escape the people pursued them and killed them, with hatchets.
9. The villagers argue that if the juju fails to operate the result will be bloodshed.
10. Courage he said and pointed toward the land
   This mounting wave will roll us shoreward soon.
11. Anybody, with any experience in the ways of the West, would have known better than to stop in the Sierras with a storm brewing.
12. I did not like the strange behavior of the begonia trees said the matriarch.
13. Do you want to go to the Birunga, gorilla sanctuary
14. But it amused us to hear a Kuikuru at some unexpected moment muttering under his breath chick chick quack quack oink oink.
15. Bob Hawk will pay you as he hollers Yes you're a Lemac now.
16. I do not like your aunt want to look at all the shops in Fleagle street.
17. Dejah Thoris was captured by Matai Shang the Holy Hekkador of the Sacred Therns.
18. I have just come from the doctors mother and he says my baby is due in six weeks.
19. Susy Clemens said mama loves morals and papa loves cats.
20. Orphan Annie says Gee Willikens Sandy and Little Annie Rooney says Gloriosky Zero.

21. William Walton one of Englands leading contemporary composers wrote the musical scores for Laurence Oliviers films of Henry V, Hamlet, and Richard III.

22. Do you remember the scene in The *invisible Man* when Claude Rains ran down the street in his underwear singing Here we go gathering nuts in may.

23. Samuel Johnson liked pussycats, but disliked Whigs and Scots.

24. The boys, who sprayed paint on the Blue Ridge Parkway bridges, were fined and ordered to remove the damage.

25. Errol flynn ran basil rathbone through in captain Blood and the Adventures of robin hood tyrone power ran rathbone through in The mark of zorro a french peasant stabbed him in a tale of two cities richmond's troops killed him in *The Tower of london* gary cooper threw him into a tiger pit in the adventures of marco polo and joan fontaine crushed him with a suit of armor in frenchman's creek but he escaped the frankenstein monster and killed the hound of the baskervilles.

17 √ Grammar Is Not Enough: A Digression on Diction

Language is the source of all misunderstanding.
ANTOINE DE ST. EXUPERY

Having finally polished her grammar, Eliza Doolittle is ready to make her appearance in society. Picture, then, a group of supremely nonchalant, elegantly dressed spectators at the Ascot races. With the aristocrat's disdain for vulgar emotion, they languidly observe the horses coming in for the finish. Then, from among the superbly stylish ladies, Eliza cries out, "Come on, Dover!!! Move your bloomin' arse!!!" [1] The grammar is perfectly acceptable, but the diction is hilariously inappropriate to the setting.

Diction as well as grammar reveals a good deal about one's background—geographically, occupationally, educationally, and socially. Though we share a common language, there are hundreds of differences in British and American speech and vocabulary. For a long time, the British looked down upon Americanisms, while Americans tended to consider the British affected. But there is no real linguistic advantage gained whether you use the British *lorry, petrol, spanner, bonnet,* and *windscreen* or the American *truck, gasoline, wrench, hood,* and *windshield.* You can play the same record on a *gramophone* or a *phonograph* and see the same picture at the *cinema* or the *movies.* There are many regionalisms within both Britain and the United States, and considerable differences in diction between Australia and South Africa. Various occupations have their own terminology and jargon, and a habitual use of substandard slang or of precise diction can place you on the social scale. There is no magic value in words themselves, though many primitive peoples believe there is and use them for charms,

277

curses, and incantations. The only moral or social value in a word is the way in which we have been conditioned to respond.

But there are different levels of diction, and they should be used appropriately. Kenneth Roberts complained of a British novelist who had a wealthy Detroit manufacturer on a safari say, "Wa-al, I reckon I guess we ain't fur from the lion-huntin'!" The author claimed that he was using regional dialect for local color, though such fake folksiness is more like Dogpatch than Detroit. Roberts retaliated by writing a scene wherein a British lord and his son discuss an American professor:

> The earl bit savagely at the end of a moist, black cigar. "Coo!" he said bitterly. " 'Ere's a ruddy nuisance! 'Oo's goin' to look after this blighter if 'e comes bargin' abaht?"
> The Hon. Vivyan smiled affectionately at his father. " 'Old your 'osses, guv'nor!" he said. "Don't get your blinkin' wind up over this Yank! 'E's nuffin to worry abaht, not 'alf!"

This is certainly not the speech of English aristocrats. Again, Roberts imagined a Cotswold shepherd and his wife complaining of the imminent sale of their cottage.

> "Blimey!" he says in his rough, shepherd's voice, "blimey, but it's cruel 'ard to be chucked out of one's digs wivout a blarsted word! Eighty-two years come Michaelmas Oi'm lived in these 'ere digs, by Cripes, an' now 'ere Oi be, throwed out like a bloomin' old straw 'at!"[2]

This burlesque Cockney speech is ludicrous in the mouth of an ancient Cotswold peasant. It would be equally ridiculous to have a London clergyman talk in the dialect of "Waltzing Matilda" or a Boston professor of 1964 sound like a Nevada miner in the days of the Comstock Lode.

Thus style and diction are as important as grammar—perhaps ultimately more so. Correcting grammar is a mechanical process, whereas style and diction require a degree of literary art. Great writers may violate grammatical conventions, while many a hack has ground out reams of grammatically proper but totally undistinguished prose. Often students write sentences that are grammatically correct but hopelessly awkward. Many themes are wordy and witless, with fumbling language betraying fuzzy thoughts. The careless writer chokes his prose with mumbled meanderings and uses any approximate word, rather than find one most suitable for sound and sense. The prolific British novelist John Creasey says

278

that the most devastating criticism he has ever encountered was Dorothy Sayers' evaluation of his mystery novels: that if the author "cannot think of the right word, anything vaguely approximating it in sound will serve." [3] The literary artist does not rely upon hackneyed diction nor employ the first word that comes to hand, but makes a conscious, deliberate choice, for as Dr. Johnson stated, "What is written without effort is in general read without pleasure."

¶ LEVELS OF DICTION

Standard English has several levels of diction. *Popular words* are those that we all know and use regularly without having to think twice about them. In fact several linguists claim that nine words comprise 25 percent of our speech, though they disagree as to which are the nine. G. H. McKnight votes for *and, be, have, it, of, the, to, will, you*; Godfrey Dewey claims *a, and, in, is, it, of, that, the, to*; and the Bell Telephone Company tabulates *a, I, is, it, on, that, the, to, you*. McKnight claims that thirty-four more words (including the competitors for his nine) make up another 25 percent, so that forty-three words make up 50 percent of our speech. Most people have a vocabulary of from ten to twenty thousand words but actively use only a small fraction of these, the others being recognition or recall vocabulary. If all words were popular, there would be little need for dictionaries except for foreigners, but other words are less commonly known, though well-educated people use many of them in conversation. Others, largely literary, are used mostly in writing, while others are so specialized that they send even scholars to the dictionary. The last three groups are learned words having increasing degrees of unfamiliarity. The length of a word is no measure of its learnedness (*ventilation* is popular, whereas *laud* is learned), but many learned words are coined or borrowed from Greek or Latin:

POPULAR	LEARNED	POPULAR	LEARNED
fire	conflagration	letter	epistle
imprison	incarcerate	show	evince
chew	masticate	sixty-fourth note	hemidemisemiquaver
house	domicile	wordy	verbose
will	volition	very long words	sesquipedalia
neglect	dereliction	brave	intrepid
lash	scourge	agree	acquiesce

279

POPULAR	LEARNED	POPULAR	LEARNED
surrender	capitulate	rashness	temerity
think	cogitate	boast	gasconade
stolen	purloined	improve	ameliorate
elephant	pachyderm	self-denial	abnegation
childish	puerile	hard to understand	abstruse, recondite

If you use learned words to unlearned people, you are apt to be resented as a snob. A stock comic figure is the hobo professor, patent medicine peddler, or seedy Thespian who likes to display his elaborately extensive vocabulary. Some of William Faulkner's Southern aristocrats use a grandiose vocabulary with recurrent immolations, commiserations, relinquishments, abrogations, suzerainty, intransigency, recalcitrance, effluviums, sentience, apotheoses, avatars, and things circumambient; but even Faulkner's full-blown style consists mainly of popular words; the grand manner is more in the rhythm than the diction. Also in the South, some characters in *Pogo* use a mad mixture of grandiloquent rhetoric and swampy slang.

Words or phrases that are used mainly in casual conversation are termed colloquialisms. These are perfectly acceptable in standard English. There is nothing vulgar about them, though some may be inappropriate for more formal levels of usage. Some are clipped words (*prof* for *professor, exam* for *examination, home ec* for *home economics, psych* for *psychology*); others have the breezy character of:

okay	swell	tough (difficult)
pal	sure enough	jam (difficulty)
buddy	you bet	nifty
buy	nope	hold on (wait)
scram	corny	hot dog (food and enthusiasm)
beat it (leave)	uh, uh	awfully (very)
done with (finished)	yep	kids (children)
doggone it	nix	kidding (joking)
flunk	lousy	pooch

Some colloquialisms are actually slang; others have more status.

¶ SLANG

Slang has long been controversial and is sometimes considered the sign of linguistic disreputability. As defined by Ambrose Bierce,

"Slang is the speech of him who robs the literary garbage-carts on their way to the dumps." Walt Whitman, trying to break the barriers of Victorian gentility, was sometimes deliberately and aggressively slangy in the poetry that he called his "barbaric yawp." In very unslangy language, he described slang as "the wholesome fermentation or eructation of those processes eternally active in language, by which the froth and specks are thrown up, mostly to pass away, though occasionally to settle and permanently crystallize." But Whitman was attacked by the same prudes who condemned the language of *Huckleberry Finn*. *The London Critic* (1856) wrote, "Walt Whitman gives us slang in the place of melody, and rowdyism in the place of regularity. . . . Walt Whitman libels the highest type of humanity, and calls his free speech the true utterance of a man; we, who may have been misdirected by civilization, call it the expression of a beast." Such criticism was directed partly at Whitman's ideas but also at his language. Even in *The Oxford English Dictionary* slang is defined in part as "the special vocabulary used by any set of persons of low or disreputable character."

This is a sweeping generalization and only partially accurate. According to Sir William S. Craigie, co-editor of the *OED,* "The nation's best textbook of slang is the Congressional Record . . . ." [4] In fact everyone uses slang, and a good deal of it is perfectly respectable, though perhaps not appropriate for formal occasions. Stuart Flexner, one of the lexicographers of the *Dictionary of American Slang,* estimates that the vocabulary of the average American includes about two thousand slang words, or approximately 10 percent. When the term *slang* originated in the eighteenth century, (slang, without a label, is as old as civilization), it referred to the special cant of criminals, rogues, and beggars—a sort of code known only to the initiate. Today various subgroups have their special vocabulary and idioms, partly for shoptalk but partly as passwords for a clique, separating the initiated from the outsiders. Prominent among these subgroups, Stuart Flexner lists hobos, immigrants, the army, navy, and merchant marine, the underworld, narcotic addicts, jazz musicians and fans, financial-district employees, college students, high school students and teen-agers, railroad workers, baseball players and fans, show business people. Slang is the more widely used speech of these subgroups. Obviously some of them are more legitimate than others. Many slang phrases include obscenities; some are grammatically nonstandard; but many are perfectly proper in a casual context. In fact, as we saw above,

281

it is not always possible to distinguish between slang terms and colloquialisms. Some slang terms become standard; others continue for centuries without social recognition. But most slang is ephemeral and is lucky to last a decade. Nothing dates dialogue in fiction more clearly than its slang, much of which has gone the way of twenty-three skiddoo."

The drawbacks of slang are two. First, it is a communication barrier to the uninitiate. The British edition of *Babbitt* had to have a special glossary explaining Sinclair Lewis's slang terms. "Waltzing Matilda" has to be decoded for non-Australians. When an American GI asked an Austrian tavern owner if there was a one-armed bandit (slot machine) in the joint, she said indignantly that she ran a reputable establishment with no thieves on the premises. See how comprehensible is W. E. Henley's rendition of François Villon's ballade of medieval Parisian criminal cant into the slang of the London underworld:

VILLON'S STRAIGHT TIP TO ALL CROSS COVES

Suppose you screeve? or go cheap-jack?
  Or fake the broads? or fig a nag?
Or thimble-rig? or knap a yack?
  Or pitch a snide? or smash a rag?
  Suppose you duff? or nose and lag?
Or get the straight, and land your pot?
  How do you melt the multy swag?
Booze and the blowens cop the lot.

Fiddle, or fence, or mace, or mack,
  Or moskeneer, or flash the drag?
Dead-lurk a crib, or do a crack,
  Pad with a slang, or chuck a fag;
  Bonnett, or tout, or mump and gag;
Rattle the tats, or mark the spot;
  You cannot bag a single stag—
Booze and the blowens cop the lot.

Suppose you try a different tack,
  And on the square you flash your flag?
At penny-a-lining make your whack,
  Or with the mummers mump and gag?
  For nix, for nix the dibs you bag!
At any graft, no matter what,
  Your merry goblins soon stravag—
Booze and the blowens cop the lot.

It's up the spout and Charley Wag
With wipes and tickers and what not;
Until the squeezer nips your scrag,
Booze and the blowens cop the lot.

Unlike learned jargon, which signifies an in-group all its own, most slang is short and sassy. It favors one-syllable words rather than elaborate gobbledygook, preferring to voom than to locomote itself. But like jargon, slang becomes a collection of clichés—handy phrases to fill a linguistic gap without bothering to find more precise words. This is drawback number two, for too much reliance on slang dilutes clear thinking. Some slang is deliberately vague, avoiding the need for precise logic or evaluation. Things are *cool, hep, crazy, skizzy, dullsville, square,* or *weird,* with no reasons given. A *kook* or a *weirdie* can be anything from a mongoloid idiot to a nuclear physicist; what makes him weird is some sort of nonconformity, the fact that he differs from whatever group is deriding him. And by rejecting others with automatic thoughtlessness, the slang-slinger affirms his intuitive rapport with his group of cool cats. Thus a great many teen-age slang words are vague terms of praise and condemnation.

Mr. Flexner observes that "Slang . . . always tends toward degradation rather than elevation" and that with reverse morality, "much of our slang purposely expresses amorality, cynicism, and 'toughness.' " [5] Perhaps for this reason or because much slang is occupational rather than domestic, more men than women make and use slang.

On the credit side, many slang terms are attempts at colorful and unconventional speech. Some are humorous hyperboles and comic metaphors; e.g., moonshine whiskey is rattlesnake juice, white mule, corpse reviver, white lightning, and a person who has too much liquor can be jug-bitten, pie-eyed, loaded, half-seas over, listing to starboard, three sheets in the wind, tanked up, or high as a kite. These too easily become trite, though the French *"Mes yeux ne sont pas en face des trous"* ("My eyes aren't opposite the holes") has not yet gone stale.

The issue is not if you should use slang but if you can use it effectively. Dwight Macdonald observes that *jalopy* is more concise and vivid than *dilapidated automobile,* but often slang is more feeble than fresh. Of course, *bug, crazy, cool, drag, drip, neat, heap,*

283

pad, tiger, rumble, octopus, and others are old words that become slang only in an idiomatic context, whereas *jalopy* was a new word. Anyhow, if you want to be ginchy instead of a goopus, get with it, dad; be an abominable snowman and all that jazz, but play it cool and know when to knock it off, so you'll be in orbit and not out to lunch.

Learned words, popular words, colloquialisms, and some slang are all valid in the speech and writing of educated people, but they may not be equally valid at all times and in all situations. Just as there are several levels of style for clothing, so are there for language. Some occasions require formality; others are more casual. Formal style is more often literary than spoken, though it is used at certain ceremonial events. Highly rhetorical, it is characterized by long, stately sentences (often in an inverted word order), introductory participial phrases and subordinate clauses, conservative grammar, learned words, and the avoidance of colloquialisms and contractions. It is the language of the Declaration of Independence, the Gettysburg Address, and other dignified documents. Its danger is that it may become pompous and ponderous. John Milton, Samuel Johnson, Edward Gibbon, and many classic prosodists regularly used a highly formal style. In such masterful hands, it functions like a Rolls-Royce; but for most writers, it is unmaneuverable, poor on mileage, and subject to frequent breakdowns.

Colloquial style has a casual manner, favoring the use of popular words, relaxed grammar, contractions, a liberal helping of colloquialisms and slang, and frequent incomplete sentences. It is used in writing for light humor, friendly correspondence, appropriate dialogue, and palsy-walsy advertising, such as:

And for the Morning After—Executive Eye-Opener. When you've had a little too much of some things, or a lot too little of others, let pure USP Oxygen take up the slack, make up the lack.

Or

Should you wear paisley underwear with a beret? Certainly. But never to the opera. For such an occasion we suggest Carter's knit boxers in Persian Squares: lively but not aggressive. . . . Best friend a well-dressed knit-picker ever had.

Or to be really colloquial,

Look, chum, why don't you skadoodle over to Moe's and really live it up with a mug of Mumblebrau—the brew that's true for you. Just ask Moe— he's a gasser.

284

In between these two extremes is informal—the style most commonly used. A highly formal style is disappearing, along with the top hat and tails; scientific and bureaucratic jargon is replacing it with the stylistic equivalent of the space suit; but if you don't wish to be a jargonaut, you will find that informal style is appropriate for most occasions. It is the prose of most novels, magazine articles, and untechnical essays that want to avoid the extremes of stately formality and chummy colloquialism.

The answer to which style is best depends upon the occasion. You do not wear blue jeans to a ball nor a tuxedo to a picnic, and a scuba and skin-diving suit is highly specialized. Even more incongruous is mixing levels of style. Imagine getting dressed with indiscriminate articles of apparel. You might combine Bermuda shorts with a tuxedo shirt, a cowboy bandana, ski socks, a frogman flipper on one foot and a sandal on the other, a motorcycle jacket, and a deep-sea diving helmet. You would be dressed but hardly ready to go anywhere except out of your mind. Yet the inattentive writer sometimes mixes levels of style almost as ludicrously. Once you decide what style suits your purpose, you should stick to it and avoid inconsistencies such as appear in the following:

When Napoleon invaded Russia in 1812, he was seemingly at the height of his power. He anticipated little resistance from the Russians, whom he considered a *bunch of freaps*. Personally leading the Grand Armée, he struck at Smolensk and then *booted* the Russians back to Moscow. Engaging the forces of General Kutuzov at Borodino, *Boney* expected to *clobber* his opponents with little difficulty. The battle was bloody but indecisive. The French held the field but lost so many men that they could not sustain their victory. With the threat of winter and increased Russian resistance, Napoleon decided to *take it on the lam*. In the light of burning Moscow, set aflame by incendiaries, the French began to *vavoom out of there*. The retreat became a disaster. Winter caught the ill-prepared *Frogs*, and Russian guerrillas harassed *Boney's boys*, turning the ordeal into a nightmare. The haggard survivors were a mere ghost of the invincible *dogfaces* that had set out so confidently.

This is admittedly an extreme example, but students write scrambled statements like "Jonathan Edwards was gung-ho on religion," "Walt Whitman was more gung-ho American than T. S. Eliot," or "Emerson and John Winthrop would have had quite a rhubarb had they lived during the same time." It is not appropriate to write chummily of Henry James, "In 'Madame de Mauves,' Henry tells of a rich young girl that is tricked into marriage to a slob." (Despite

285

our American folksiness, it is crude to address or write of celebrities or political dignitaries by their first name or a nickname—Ike, Winnie, Eleanor, Jackie, Lyndon, Liz, or even Nikita.) One student wrote, "Emerson was a real weirdy in some of his beliefs." According to another, "Whitman believed in pantheism and the oversoul and all that stuff," and yet another explained, "J. Alfred Prufrock can't cut the mustard."

Ministers sometimes mix Biblical quotes and archaic seventeenth-century phraseology with current colloquialisms. Mark Twain complained of James Fenimore Cooper's tendency to "divide each sentence into two equal parts: one part critically grammatical, refined, and choice of language, and the other part just such an attempt to talk like a hunter or a mountaineer, as a Broadway clerk might make after eating an edition of Emerson Bennett's works and studying frontier life at the Bowery Theatre a couple of weeks." According to Mark Twain, the rules of literary art "require that when a personage talks like an illustrated, gilt-edged, tree-clad, hand-tooled, seven-dollar Friendship's Offering in the beginning of a paragraph, he shall not talk like a negro minstrel in the end of it."

It is often essential to suit your style to the level of your audience. This does not mean adopting nonstandard grammar and diction for the sake of conformity. But it is obviously ineffective to talk over or under the heads of your audience. Instructions for the assembly or operation of equipment are worthless if they are not clear. It is hardly appropriate to lecture an elementary Sunday school class in the language of Paul Tillich or to teach primer lessons to seminarians. A highly formal style is too pretentious for friendly correspondence, and a slangy style too frivolous for scholarly publications. Style indicates something of one's attitude toward his subject. Contrast "Gimme a little kiss, willya, huh?" with this speech by Cyrano de Bergerac:

> And what is a kiss, when all is done?
> A promise given under seal—a vow
> Taken before the shrine of memory—
> A signature acknowledged—a rosy dot
> Over the i of Loving—a secret whispered
> To listening lips apart—

and so on. Cyrano is undoubtedly too florid for modern girls, but clearly his style makes both the kiss and the bestower of it more

286

important than does the slack-jawed, gum-chomping style of the first request.

Some statements seem to be acceptable in formal prose that would be objectionable on another stylistic level. There is a story ("That's a joke, son") about a boy who saw some bow-legged men and said to his mother, "Mama, mama, look at the bow-legged men." She smacked him on the hand and told him not to say such things, but the next week he saw them again and once more shouted, "Look at the bow-legged men." This time his mother made him study Shakespeare for a month to teach him more dignified language. The next time he saw the men, he remarked, "Lo, what manner of men are these/That walk with their legs in parentheses!"

¶ JARGON

The formal style of Dr. Johnson and other neoclassic men of letters may have been heavy but it was not clumsy. It was usually as graceful as an intricate dance pattern and could be eloquent or ironic. Though it was sometimes slow, it was always clear and often quotable.

Is not a Patron, My Lord, one who looks with unconcern on a Man struggling for Life in the water and when he has reached ground encumbers him with help? The notice which you have been pleased to take of my Labours, had it been early, had been kind; but it has been delayed till I am indifferent and cannot enjoy it, till I am solitary and cannot impart it, till I am known, and do not want it.

This excerpt from Johnson's letter to Lord Chesterfield slowly but powerfully gathers force until the total effect is devastating.

By contrast, much modern formal prose is frozen into jargon— ugly, unrhythmic, unmelodious chunks of verbiage that go together as gracefully as two freight cars coupling. A species of pretentious bumblery, it is long-winded, unnecessarily difficult, and sick with what James Thurber called carcinonomenclature. Thus *food* becomes *units of nutritional intake, baby sitters* become *custodial supervisors of juvenile activities and recreation,* and Donald Duck's Dubble Fudgi-Frost is identified on the wrapper as "a quiescent frozen product."

Some jargon is legitimate within limits: the technical terminology of various sciences, trades, and professions. Presumably such terminology is clear and necessary in its proper context. But too often people borrow or imitate it for prestige in other areas. In some schools, bureaus, and publications, it seems more important to know the orthodox jargon than to show any critical and original thought. In fact, once you learn the jargon, it almost does your thinking for you. Decide to use Freudian, Marxian, or any other esoteric terminology, and your criticism automatically falls into place. Moreover, you will be a member of that particular in-group and can feel superior to the uninitiated. In literary and artistic criticism, the jargon addict may show considerable ingenuity in finding verbal and symbolic devices to fit his subject into the pattern, but the pattern is standardized. Thus Richard Chase writes, "The psychoanalyst might say that Billy Budd has avoided the Oedipus struggle by forming an attachment to the mother at the prephallic level of 'oral eroticism' and has allayed his fears of castration by symbolically castrating himself (by being consciously submissive) and by repressing his rage and hostility against the father in order to placate him." [6] Sometimes such ritualized dialectic creates distortion; for example, in one criticism of Hemingway, Sam the cook in "The Killers" becomes "the wooing mother-surrogate," "the dark hermaphroditic mother-guide." On the other hand, some invent their own jargon that seems to have no pattern at all in such pretentious nonsense as: "The latest painting by Trudwick Zerch reveals the subliminal thrust of the tender tendrils of resurrection against a bleak background suggestive of a Bach toccata played by an Eskimo band before the northern lights as the Plutonian antipodal winter is about to engulf the Proserpine equinox."

Some literary critics subject their subject to excessive analysis— more weight than the traffic can bear. H. L. Mencken called Thorstein Veblen's prose "a cent's worth of information wrapped in a bale of polysyllables." Too many scholars turn prose and poetry into pedantry. Graduate students and even established scholars have claimed that they were required to rewrite material because their style was too clear and their arguments too lucid. Apparently it is felt that if the material is too accessible, the scholar loses status; the veil of the temple is rent and the sacred mysteries revealed. Thus the jargon of Academia is sometimes more incantation than communication. Many matters are indeed so complex that they cannot be reduced to the popular level; but obscurity or devious elaboration is not desirable for its own sake, and some writing is unjustifiably difficult.

And dull. There are different species of jargon, and a lot of it is not learned or profound but merely long-winded. It creates obscurity when there is nothing obscure. To conceal a lack of ideas, the experienced bumbler beats around the proverbial bush, turning verbs into phrases, snarling his syntax, preferring polysyllabic and learned words to short and direct ones and abstract words to concrete ones. Thus we find the following sorts of inflation, given to the right of their simpler equivalents:

if	in the eventuality that
this refers to	this is in reference to
useless	devoid of usefulness
imprecise	reveals a lack of preciseness
I think that	My trend of thought leads me to the conclusion that
I feel	I have a feeling that
I conclude	It is my conclusion that
many	a not inconsiderable number of (or a substantial number of)
repair	restore to operational condition
failed	did not succeed in achieving its objective
prefer	demonstrate a preference for
dislike	manifest an antipathy towards
supports	is supportive to

To the unsophisticated, such jargon may suggest scientific detachment, an attempt to avoid subjective interpretation and hasty conclusions. Actually it is a lot of blah, a species of circumlocution and dead wood, expansive and elaborately vacuous. If your mind is empty or your thoughts not clearly organized, it is helpful to have a handy collection of jargon, cliché terms and phrases; they are a falsely impressive and more elaborate way of saying "and . . . uh . . . er . . ."—of clearing your throat while groping for what next to say.

Such gobbledygook bloats the language with a verbal elephantiasis that destroys its grace and impairs its vigor. It can be dangerous, for as George Orwell wrote in "Politics and the English Language": "the slovenliness of our language makes it easier for us to have foolish thoughts. . . . The great enemy of clear language is insincerity." In politics, jargon can be a way of avoiding direct statements, or it can be a means of channeling thought. Its pseudo-scientific terminology tends to turn people into abstractions or statistics and reduce the individual to a member of the mass. As a sort of bureaucratic slang, it can have the same effect in avoiding

289

the need for precise logic or evaluation and in causing people or concepts to be accepted or rejected by a more elaborate name-calling. Whether that of the Communists or that of the ultraconservatives, political jargon offers a set of stock phrases that can evoke the desired response with a minimum of intellectual effort.

T. S. Hsia, a scholar at the University of California in Berkeley, says Communist China is using military jargon to condition its people for war. Thus workers are "fighters," work forces are "armies," production drives are "major battles," and facing obstacles is "declaring war against heaven." A woman who works well is called a "Mu-Kuei-ying," after a legendary medieval woman general. When the Shantung province organized eight million people to combat drought, it announced that it put eight million "Wu Sungs" to work. (Wu Sung was a legendary twelfth-century hero who killed a tiger with his bare hands.)

Some jargon employs euphemisms to make things more attractive than they are. Thus hydrogen bombs have been called "thermonuclear deterrents" as if they are a defense against hydrogen bombs. We also are working on "clean" bombs, which can kill millions of people with one explosion but leave no dirty fallout. Leonard R. N. Ashley calls these "the Ultimate Detergent." Even "the free world" is partially euphemistic jargon, since it includes South Africa, Franco's Spain, Duvalier's Haiti, Tito's Yugoslavia, and various right-wing dictatorships around the world. They are free only by token of not belonging to the Communist bloc. At home, various reactionary hate groups call themselves by various patriotic names, though by "patriotism," they mean censoring textbooks, impeaching the Chief Justice, denouncing the United Nations, condemning civil rights, opposing public education, and slandering as subversive anyone who favors fluoridation, mental health, social security, conservation, academic freedom, the Bill of Rights, or democracy.

This distortion of meaning is as new as *1984* and as old as history. In the fifth century B.C., Thucydides wrote that under demagogues, "The meaning of words had no longer the same relation to things but was changed by them as they thought proper. Reckless daring was held to be courage; prudent delay was the excuse of a coward; moderation was the disguise of unmanly weakness; to know everything was to do nothing. Frantic energy was the true quality of a man. . . . He who succeeded in a plot was deemed knowing, but a still greater master in craft was he who detected one."

A good deal of jargon is a by-product of bureaucracy, in both government and corporations. Secretary of Agriculture Orville Freeman told his staff, "The fright of verbs is one of the most dismaying, but most characteristic attributes of the language of big bureaucracies. Why? Maybe because the language is originated by people who feel far removed from decision and action, and therefore, who subconsciously shrink from such bold, plain, and clear expressions as 'We think' or 'We will tell you' and retreat behind some form of the static and listless verb 'to be' coupled with a prepositional phrase denoting a condition ('of the view that . . .') in place of owning up to the active decision which is the actual fact that should be communicated." Thus "We are of the view that . . ." should be "We think . . . ," and "Request is hereby made to establish . . ." should be "Please establish . . ." "You may be assured that careful consideration will be given to all the facts" should be changed from the passive to the active, "We will consider carefully all the facts."

One pitfall of jargon is the overused passive. The passive voice is by definition less active than the active voice, and too many passive constructions create a negative movement like the Army definition of marching in place: "You's going, but you ain't going no *where*." When the subject really is the passive recipient of action, when the actor is indefinite rather than specific, or when the verb indicates a general procedure, the passive voice is appropriate. (Cf. p. 112.) But too much scientific and sociological writing and bureaucratese deliberately prefers the passive even when an active verb is more effective. The rationale is that active verbs in the first person ("I did," "I think," "We propose") lack the required flavor of scientific objectivity and organizational impersonality. The jargonaut considers the passive more clinical even though it may be clumsy and obscure. Despite this self-effacing manner, things are not done by themselves; people do them, and in some instances it is hypocritical to hide behind the passive. The passive eliminates the actor and leaves only the act; there is nobody to get the credit or the blame. Scientific objectivity is commendable, but scientism (as in Aldous Huxley's *Brave New World*) can reduce the individual to a cipher; and in bureaucracies, where the office is more important than the official, the excessive passive voice is an additional harness on the organization man. Hannah Arendt, in her study of Adolph Eichmann, found him merely an extreme example of the bureaucrat who disclaims responsibility and seeks refuge in passivity: "I was ordered, I was instructed, I was required to obey." The passive is also a tool of the informer and inquisitor in a police state. "It is charged, it is reported, it is known . . ." You are accused, but there is no visible accuser. In such cases it may be necessary to distinguish between the active and passive. In *A Man for All Seasons,* Sir Thomas More, persecuted for refusing to approve Henry VIII's marriage and the Act of Supremacy, says to the King's prosecutor, "So I am brought here at last."

> CROMWELL: Brought? You brought yourself to where you stand now.
> MORE: Yes—Still, in another sense—I was brought.[7]

Some government agencies are finally recognizing the inefficiency of jargon and are trying, like Secretary Freeman, to eliminate it. The State Department is giving its officers courses in elementary composition so that they will be able to understand each other's communications. The Postmaster's office no longer approves calling post offices "major mail-handling facilities" or garages "postal lubritoriums" and criticizes such gobbledygook as, "Space will be available for balloons for accommodation distribution, and creepers will be installed to assist personnel in the cannibalization of bums."

Still, jargon continues like a creeping fungus. Pentagonese flourishes with words like *deprojectmanagerize.* When the Army bought portable showers for workers to wash off spilled rocket fuel, it called the showers "rocket propellant personnel neutralizers." Merchandising gets into the act with instructions (for Replicap Bottle Resealer) like: "The inner carbonation retention structure for this successful resealer is such that application should be from the back of the bottle mouth—forward—using the heel or palm of hand to ease cap into resealing position." Sociologists are said to call orgies "sexual educational group dynamics." (Washington University has begun a $135,000 a year project to turn sociological jargon into plain English.) Educationists—as distinct from teachers—are often addicted to a ponderous prose that James D. Koerner (in *The Miseducation of American Teachers*) calls "Educanto." In a search for pseudoscientific status, teachers become "instructional personnel"; the classroom is "the teaching situation"; bright students are "fortunate deviates"; collecting information becomes "assemblizing imponderables"; and the teacher (or rather "director of experience") gets ahead by using ritual words such as "insightfulness" and progressing to formidable phrases like "the progressive

292

familial subcultural mental retardation," "the normative generalization reference cue," or "the extrinsic dualistic organization of
coordinate administration." Mr. Koerner observes that such jargon
"masks a lack of thought, and in fact makes thought of any important kind extraordinarily difficult." [8] This is true of jargon in
general; it becomes a sort of mechanical litany like the brainwashed chanting of party slogans. Most jargon is more muddled
than sinister, but it is second-hand—and handy, so that when you
fumble for a thought, you can draw an automatic phrase from the
stockpile of jargon. Even if the terminology is technical rather than
bumbled, it can be constricting. Thus Norman Mailer writes, "Psy-
choanalysis. An artist must not explore into himself with language
given by another. A vocabulary of experts is a vocabulary greased
out and sweated in committee and so is inimical to a private eye." [9]

Even religion is not immune from jargon. For some ministers
and seminarians, *kerygma* and *didache* are more prestigious than
preaching and teaching. Koinonia is more imposing than *fellowship,*
though it sounds less inviting. German sounds more learned than
English, so *angst, Wissenschaft, Kirchliche Dogmatik,* and *Heils-
geschichte* replace *anxiety, knowledge, church dogma,* and *salvation
history.* Academia generally is fond of *Zeitgeist, Weltanschauung,
Weltschmertz,* and other German jawbreakers. Some terms, though
syllabically segmented as a centipede, are a shorthand; *redaktions-
geschichte* is briefer than "the historical study of how the written
gospels were edited from the oral teaching of the early church." [10]

To avoid jargon, cut all unnecessary words, eliminate *not-un*
constructions, minimize the passive voice, replace vague verbal and
prepositional phrases with active verbs, cut or replace colorless adjectives, do not pile up nouns, and whenever possible use short
English words instead of long, foreign, and pretentiously scientific
ones.

¶ PSEUDOLITERARY LANGUAGE

Some amateurs, trying too hard to be literary, come up with strained
metaphors and overly ornate diction. On the one hand they become
turgid, like the *Time* movie reviews cited by Dwight Macdonald:
"Like a giant caldron the screen boils with life, and Kurosawa's
telescopic lenses, spooning deep, lift the depths to the surface and
hurl the whole mess in the spectator's face"; or "The Bergman who
made this picture still had akvavit in his veins. Intellect, that glit-

tering and treacherous Snow Queen, had not yet struck her icy sliver into his heart." [11]

Or they lace their language with archaisms, affected allusions, learned insipidities, and feckless effusions. Certainly "It stinks" is more authentic than "A fragrance like to that of the celebrated Augean stables arises in our vicinity and, wafted by gentle zephyrs, permeates the dewy air and penetrates my proboscis, thus offending my olfactory senses." This is a deliberately grotesque example; but one sometimes encounters a simpering style "With many holiday and lady terms" (as Hotspur put it). In *Hamlet,* the foppish Osric speaks thus, and Hamlet parodies him: "Sir, his definement suffers no perdition in you; though, I know, to divide him inventorially would dozy th'arithmetic of memory, and yet but yaw neither in respect of his quick sail. But, in the verity of extolment, I take him to be a soul of great article, and his infusion of such dearth and rareness as, to make true diction of him, his semblable is his mirror, and who else would trace him, his umbrage, nothing more." Such phony elaboration is obviously pseudoliterary. While avoiding such blatant extremes, some writers create more sound than sense with strained pseudoliterary clichés, such as: "Chicago mothers all peoples, rich or poor, famous or unknown. In the shadows of towering, austere skyscrapers are huddled crowded masses of humanity. Yet this city of steel, din, and confusion envelopes her people with a stubborn and protecting love. Buffeted by the tormented Lake Michigan waters and swept by the Iowa prairie winds, Chicago stands firm and unyielding." Perhaps, but such trite and over-emphatic prose falls on its face.

There is no special language for literature, though it may draw upon a larger vocabulary than ordinary conversation. It is most effective when it uses contemporary idiom. Even a poetic drama like T. S. Eliot's *Murder in the Cathedral,* about the twelfth-century tragedy of Thomas à Becket, avoids conscious archaisms and uses modern diction. But eighteenth- and nineteenth-century writers did often employ a special literary language consisting largely of imitation Shakespearean and Biblical grammar and vocabulary. The Bible was a profound stylistic influence and was the only book many people ever read. Even Thomas Paine wrote of Deism in the cadences of the King James translators: "The Creation speaketh an universal language . . . ." Much eighteenth-century style has a commendable clarity and directness, but some authors wrote elaborately ponderous prose full of polysyllabic Latinate words; and

294

some became so addicted to false elegance that they favored such circumlocutions as calling fish "the finny folk" and birds "our little feathered friends." Wordsworth called for a new poetry written in the language of the people, though he did not always follow his own advice. The popularity of historical novels from Sir Walter Scott on gave new life to archaisms, and the genteel tradition encouraged them as a sign of elevated purity. The result was often ludicrous and provoked the ridicule of Mark Twain, Artemus Ward, and other satirists. When "middle-aged female No. 2" asked Artemus Ward's landlord, "Dost never go into the green fields to cull the beautiful flowers?" he replied, "I not only never dost, but I'll bet you five pound you can't bring a man as dares say I durst." In another episode, Ward describes encountering an evangelist for women's rights:

"I hope, marm," sez I, starting back, "that your intensions is honorable! I'm a lone man hear in a strange place. Besides, I've a wife to hum."

"Yes," cried the female, "& she's a slave! Doth she never dream of freedom—doth she never think of throwin off the yoke of tyrinny & thinkin & votin for herself?—Doth she never think of these here things?"

"Not bein a natral born fool," sed I, by this time a little riled, "I kin safely say that she dothunt."

In modern literature, realistic dialogue prevails, even while poets and novelists have found new and surprising resources in the language. If they sometimes wrench the language violently, they do so with originality, whereas a special literary diction and grammar is a sort of jargon. Deliberate archaisms still appear in historical fiction and are sometimes burlesqued; Snagglepuss as Robin Hood declaimed, "I robbeth from the richeth and giveth to the pooreth." Ersatz Biblical language also fossilizes some legal documents:

Memorandum of Agreement made this 31st day of February, 1972, between Herbert Homefreeze, party of the first part (hereinafter called the "Author"), and party of the second part (hereinafter called the "Publisher"), Witnesseth: that whereas the said Author desires that a work be published and put on the market by the said Publisher: Now, therefore, in consideration of the premises and of one dollar to each in hand paid by the other, the receipt whereof is hereby acknowledged, the parties hereto do covenant and agree as follows.

The language of Hollywood Biblical epics usually sounds as musty as Samson's jawbone of an ass. Yet priests and ministers still favor

Jacobean jargon. Perhaps they do so to be consistent with Biblical readings in the services. Still it sounds strange to have prayers for the President of the United States couched in the phraseology of the Tudor and Stuart monarchs. The Rev. Dr. Krister Stendahl, professor of Biblical studies at Harvard, urges Protestants to dispense with archaic *thees* and *thous* and verb endings (*Thou speakest, he goeth,* etc.). He observes that Jesus favored plain language and taught that God is a father rather than an inaccessible deity who can be addressed only in a special sacred language. As literature, the King James translation surpasses any modern ones, but for "language understanded of the people" there are several excellent versions in contemporary diction and style. Among some religious extremists these later translations have been denounced and even burned as infidel and subversive, though the original testaments were written in Hebrew and Greek, not in seventeenth-century English. On the other hand, a version of the gospels in modern teen-age slang fell completely flat and reduced to absurdity the majesty of the original. Still, a special ecclesiastical style can lead to exchanges like "Wilt thou take this woman to be thy lawful wedded wife?" "I wilt."

¶ DEAD WOOD

Not all dead wood is jargon; a lot of it is just clumsiness or the unwillingness to find more exact language. In J. D. Salinger's *The Catcher in the Rye,* Holden Caulfield lets his sentences dangle with "and all," "and everything," or "or something" when it's too much strain to be more precise. These loose phrases are quite legitimate for Salinger's realistic dialogue, but they serve no purpose aside from characterizing Holden. How informative are "measles and all," "Hallowe'en and all," "my Sunday school teacher and all," "Errol Flynn and all," "September and all," "bathtub ring and all," "an intellectual and all," "geology and all," "nervous and all," "science fiction and all," "a doctor or something," "homework and all that stuff," "Utah and everything," "asleep or something," "soup or something," "a porpoise or something," and "without a hat on or anything?" Sometimes such phrases are even more ludicrous, as when a student wrote about a literary character, "She was illegitimate or something like that." What is something like that?

Much dead wood is mere redundancy, like "this modern-day world of ours in which we live," which should be shortened to "this

296

modern world." "Visitors gaze in awe at the magnificent panorama before their eyes." Where else, if they gaze? So cut "before their eyes." Since celebrities are by definition famous, *famous* should be cut in "In the Via Veneto, famous celebrities are hounded by reporters." "To the present day" is obvious and hence unnecessary in "since the beginning of time to the present day." Again, the last phrase should be cut from "Our vocabularies have been broadened through the introduction of new words with which to communicate." What else do we do with words? In the following examples, consider why the dead wood (enclosed in brackets) is unnecessary:

National parks offer many recreational activities [for anyone interested in participating in them.]

Some students don't want to work as waiters [as far as a job is concerned].

Horpington has trouble writing [verbally].

Society is becoming more complex. As a result [of this situation], people are becoming frustrated.

The reason for this situation is [due to] the fact that neither side understands the other.

Despite advertising, people usually buy the brand [of product] they like [the] best.

Most people read for enjoyment or to gain knowledge [on a certain subject].

An example is [that of] automation.

Thoreau was opposed to living [life] in a hurry.

It has been said that a lot of litter is not literature. As a general rule, never use superfluous words. Whenever possible, replace rambling phrases with single words. "Healthy" is better than "in a state of health." "A socialistic form of government" can be reduced to "socialism." "Many desire" is preferable to "It is the desire of many." "Many years ago" is briefer than "many years prior to this day." "Except for a few exceptions" can be "with a few exceptions." "Defined" is better than "expressed a definition of." "Frost's writings in the form of poetry" means simply "Frost's poems." "The quote of Jefferson's relating that those who labor in the earth are the actual chosen people of God is a statement that needs consideration" should be condensed to "Jefferson's statement that those who labor in the earth are the actual chosen people of God needs consideration." Besides, Jefferson was not quoting anyone. Note how cutting dead wood (in brackets) can tighten the following:

297

"The quote [should be "Jefferson's statement"] 'The legitimate powers of government extend to such acts only as are injurious to others,' [by Thomas Jefferson] is somewhat [of a] misleading [statement] when taken out of context [from Jefferson's writings]."

The following example of student writing (about a poem of Edward Taylor's) is so wordy that the writer stumbles over his own dead wood.

The imagery of the second stanza is of a very effective nature. The stanza contains what is called a word paradox. It is of such a manner that the use of the paradox and metaphorical type imagery was an effective method describing the everlasting love of God conjoined in an embodiment of man to form Christ.

This can be greatly condensed and clarified:

The second stanza makes effective use of paradox and metaphor to describe the everlasting love of God conjoined and embodied for man in Christ.

"Bret Harte's characters are mining and gambling individuals" is better as "miners and gamblers." A particular nuisance is the bracketed dead wood in "Professor Crabshaw stated [this following quote] in his book, [quote], 'Richard III was unjustifiably maligned by Tudor historians.' [Unquote.]" Another is "In Martin's *Civilizing Ourselves,* he describes the modern barbarian," which is better as "In *Civilizing Ourselves,* Martin . . ." And sometimes there is simple repetition: "Overpopulation is one of the greatest problems in the world. It is a problem that is of great importance everywhere."

The dead-wood addict, whether jargonaut or simple bumbler, particularly likes to change verbs into nouns and then add weak and needless verbal phrases:

There was a difference in their criticisms.

There was is the grammatical subject, but it is meaningless; the significant word is *criticisms,* and the idea is both strengthened and shortened as "Their criticisms differed." *There is, there are,* and similar constructions can often be dropped:

There is something in your attitude that bothers me.
                              vs.
Something in your attitude bothers me.

298

There were several people who walked out of the meeting.

vs.

Several people walked out of the meeting.

There is a probability that the bill will be passed.

vs.

Probably the bill will be passed.

There was a dislike of Mark Twain for Henry James's novels.

vs.

Mark Twain disliked Henry James's novels.

Whenever possible, turn nouns back into verbs:

The discussion in the committee was about parking fees.

vs.

The committee discussed parking fees.

The statement of the faculty is that salaries should be increased.

vs.

The faculty state that salaries should be increased.

The proposal of the engineers is that they should dam the canyon.

vs.

The engineers propose to dam the canyon.

Besides the weak verb *to be,* the past participle of other weak verbs can turn the real verb into a noun. Such feeble constructions include:

accomplish	bring about	give	provide	show
achieve	cause	make	result	take place
affect	exist	occur	serve	transpire

These are so general that they are often interchangeable:

Elimination of inefficiency has been accomplished.
Elimination of inefficiency has been achieved.
Elimination of inefficiency has been brought about.
Elimination of inefficiency has occurred.
Elimination of inefficiency has taken place.

To really eliminate inefficiency, turn the noun back to a verb:

"Inefficiency has been eliminated."

A frequent type of dead wood is the use of *the . . . of . . . the* with gerund phrases. Perhaps influenced by *The Taming of the Shrew* or by the lines of the Christmas carol, "The rising of the sun/And the running of the deer,/The playing of the merry organ,/Sweet singing in the choir," people write clumsy constructions like "She is responsible for the washing of the dishes," or "The Constitution called for a setting up of a Supreme Court." Again, clauses or phrases can sometimes be condensed by an infinitive: "Al Capp proposed psychological tests for the screening of candidates for the Senate" rambles with its two awkward *fors*; "tests to screen candidates" is better. "Opportunity for the betterment of himself" is better as "to better himself."

But yet, but nevertheless, and etc., revert back, return back, and *where is it at* are redundant. So are many prepositions, which are all right in colloquial speech but should be pruned for a concise effective style: e.g., fix *up*, flatten *out*, parallels *with*, crushed *down*, follow *out* orders, hurry *up*, and so on. *I have got* can be shortened to *I have*, though *got* may be more emphatic (cf., "I've got rhythm" and "I have rhythm"). Since *impossibility* is an absolute, there is no need for the adjective in "a complete impossibility." Savages are by definition uncivilized, so "an uncivilized savage" is as redundant as "a vegetarian who doesn't eat meat." Finally we have dead wood in a circular argument: "Booster Club meetings in *Babbitt* show how childish grown men can really be because they carry on in a most childish manner." But occasionally dead wood is all right for inverted emphasis, as in Doggy Daddy's saying, "If there is one thing I can't stand, it's a lamp that says *Yowtch!*" Otherwise the best thing to do with dead wood is to cut it out.

¶ THE PRECISE WORD

The ability to think in abstractions is a sign of intellectual maturity, but abstractions must be based on and related to specific details if they are to have any vitality or validity. Too much academic prose consists almost entirely of abstract words, which create a lifeless style that seems to divorce the content from reality. John Dewey was an extremely influential figure in modern philosophy and education, yet even his admirers find his prose almost unreadable because of its abstract diction. The ideas may be provocative, but they are presented in a style largely impenetrable.

On a less scholarly level, students often water their writing with vague words like *nice, great, swell, interesting, different, unusual, strange* that offer only the feeblest concrete evaluation. "How was the play?" "Oh, it was terrific" (or *tremendous* or *great* or *not bad* or *fair* or *lousy*), which is not very enlightening. Such modifiers have been called *utility words,* because you can use them with no intellectual effort. Usually a general quality or action can be made more specific. Note how many related words *Roget's International Thesaurus* gives for each general one. The verb *walk* might variously be more accurate as *stride, shuffle, limp, amble, strut, pace, tread, stroll, march, saunter, shamble, flounce, swagger, scuttle* depending upon the occasion. *Sword* can be subdivided into *saber, rapier, broadsword, cutlass, smallsword, claymore, scimitar, falchion, hanger.* Of course these are not all interchangeable. In dialogue, *he said* and *she said* can be monotonous and might be varied by more descriptive verbs: *suggested, replied, snorted, snarled, chuckled,* etc. However, such diction can be overworked until it calls attention to itself and the reader again longs for a plain *he said.*

Words have degrees of specificity; *dog* is more specific than *animal* but less so than *dachshund.* From left to right the following examples become increasingly specific, like the guessing game "animal, vegetable, mineral" that requires players by an ever-narrowing of category to hit upon the exact object that one person has chosen:

structure	house	igloo
America	North America	Mexico
breakfast food	cereal	Froot Loops
TV program	cartoon show	Yogi Bear
plant	vegetable	spinach

The situation determines how precise a word you need. If someone invited you over to his fraternity house to see the new pet, you might like to know in advance whether you are to see a terrier or a tarantula. When you ask, "What's for supper?" you may find "food" an inadequate answer. It might turn out to be filet of fenny snake, eels in eel broth, or haggis.

To be effective, writing must often present precise detail in an exact vocabulary. The amateur sometimes hits well off target, failing to select the exact word among near synonyms or missing the right word altogether: *willfully* is not interchangeable with *willingly.* In "Ring Lardner accomplished in giving vivid realism to the characters of his story," the verb should be *succeeded. Perceptively* should be *perceptibly* in "The daily routine of the average American home slows perceptively after dinner." *Gradually* makes no sense in "If a person accused of witchcraft did not confess, he would gradually be hanged." *Notorious* should be *notable* in "John Dewey was affiliated with four notorious universities." Jack Frost

Confectionery Sugar XXXX intended to use *induced,* not *influenced,* in "The velvety smoothness of the frosting is influenced by sufficient beating." The emphatic *wallop* is absurdly weak in such journalism as "50-megaton bomb delivers wallop," and so is *punch* in "New missile has sufficient punch to destroy 50-mile area." And the adjective is altogether unsuitable in "Billy Budd went to his death with a boisterous prayer."

Some people distort words by mangling or inflating them, bloating *virtue* into *virtuousness, unconventional* into *unconventionalized, excess* into *excessiveness, mediocre* into *mediocratic, savage* into *savagerous, criminal* into *criminalistic, loyal* into *loyalistic, confidence* into *confidentiality, potential* into *potentiality, analysis* into *analyzation, orient* into *orientate, bias* into *biasness,* and *excess* into *excessiveness. Disobedience* gets warped into *disobeyance, chrysanthemum* into *chryseantheum,* and *defeatist* is blurred into *defeatus* ("a defeatus attitude"). Jargon gets into the act with such pseudo-sophisticated modifiers as *verve-y, un-huge, un-skin-tight, loose-ish,* and *Beethovenwise.*

Then there are ludicrously mixed metaphors: "a sweeping statement that will not hold water," "a deep-seated hatred of long standing," "floods sparked by the hurricane," "uranium rolling out of our ears," "scrubbing the floor with a fine tooth comb," or "industrialism suddenly snowballed." One student wrote, "To really over-balance the apple cart, Poe placed much emphasis on morbidity, and to add the topping to the pudding, he allowed a ship containing dead people to overtake the ship and pass it." Students are not alone in this. In a passage of *The Octopus,* Frank Norris describes the railroad as a galloping monster with iron hoofs, bellowing hoarsely, with a Cyclopean eye, "the leviathan with tentacles of steel," "the monster, the Colossus, the Octopus." Someone wrote that "Socrates died from an overdose of wedlock, but before he went he had the crowned heads shaking in their shoes." This combines mixed metaphor with malapropism, as does "We are living on the edge of an abbess that stands ready to crush us."

¶ MALAPROPISMS

A malapropism is a ridiculous confusion of words, usually an unintential pun, in which a word with a similar sound but entirely the wrong meaning is used instead of the precise word. The name comes from Mrs. Malaprop, a character in Sheridan's eighteenth-century comedy *The Rivals,* who blundered into such phrases as "an allegory [alligator] on the banks of the Nile." Such confusion is still with us today when writers have a tin ear, can't spell, or fail to proofread. Thus we are told that an octopus is a person who hopes for the best and that the big dogs that rescue people in the Alps are called Sarah Bernhardts. Students write that Arabs wear turbines on their heads and that the Christian custom that allows a man to have only one wife is called monotony. In a movie review, the *Michigan State News* (January 21, 1963) printed: "Melina Mercouri as Phaedra is superb, but she is surpassed by Raf Vallone who spays [plays] her husband, a wealthy Greek shipowner, sacrificed in Phaedra's fire." *The Lansing State Journal* wrote of Euripides' *Media* (*Medea*)—mass media, no doubt. The Greeks took another beating when a student wrote of the Four Horsemen of the Acropolis. Another thought that euthanasia (mercy killing) was Youth in Asia. As for religion, we read of gregarious chants in honor of the Lord's annotated. One student wrote of the Quakers, "The Quackers were called Quackers because they quacked when they received the Holy Spurt [Spirit]." (Another wrote of the San Francisco earthquack.) As for the Puritans, "They thought every event was significant since it was a massage from God." But some Puritan colonists became ill or starved and "parished in the wilderness." Other pioneers went west and eventually crossed the Appellations. Some Puritans believed that "the rich are virtuous and the poor are viscous. But as man can only attain true happiness through virtuosity, God wishes a virtuous human race." On the other hand, "Thomas Paine believed it was an absolute waist of time to go to church. Paine says if you want to know God, go out and imbrace a tree or bush, ect." What does *etc.* mean here, let alone *ect.*? Perhaps the student meant to write *eccch.*

Continuing with malaprop American history, we read of "ragged individualism" and learn that "John Marshall knew that if the Constitution of the United States was to last through the years it must be interrupted liberally." We find that "Poe was kicked out of West Point for gamboling." He wrote "tales of the supper natural" and at one point "had a romance with Mrs. Stanard that was purely plutonic." His contemporary Emerson wrote that "A foolish consistency is the hemoglobin [hobgoblin] of little minds." One student explained that Whitman was influenced by Emerson and wrote, "I was simpering, simpering [simmering] and Emerson brought me to a broil [boil]." According to another, "Whitman

303

used much illiteration and compacked verse. He often wrote long and rumbling [rambling] lines." And so we could continue to mangle American literature clear down to *The Christian Science Minotaur.*

In concussion we might attribute some of these faults to spelling, others to careless listening, and some simply to ignorance. Taking notes, one student wrote Karl Marx as Carl Marks. Dimmesdale becomes Doomsdale, Hurstwood becomes Hearsewood, and everything ends in a state of chassis (chaos). Some people slur their speech and so write *another words* for *in other words, next store* for *next door, apart* for *a part* and confuse *pastime* with *past time.* Sometimes a person responds to standard pronunciation with, "Oh, you mean flars [flowers]," "Oh, you mean a bray [beret]," or "Oh, you mean a pome [poem]," Chicago has a Goethe street, but if you ask a taxi driver for it, he's apt to say, "Huh? Oh, you mean Go-eethy Street [or Gertz or Gooth or Goath Street]." So in diction, you can't take pronunciation for granite.

Proofreading is important. The misstriking of one letter on the typewriter can turn *interior* to *inferior, internal* to *infernal, bigger* to *bitter, daughter* to *laughter, ping pong* into *king kong,* while reversing two letters can change *alter* into *later.*

¶ TRANSLATIONS

The problem of finding the right word or idiom is particularly evident in translation. The difficulty is increased because the translator must not only find the denotative equivalent of the original but must also find the right level of diction and avoid wrong connotations. Homonyms and near synonyms increase the translator's headache, and unintentional puns turn it into a nightmare. We often hear of a literary work that it loses in translation. This is particularly true of poetry or of fiction where dialect and slang are involved. *Huckleberry Finn* must seem strange in German. The French are particularly fond of William Faulkner's fiction, but his Mississippi dialect must be odd with a Gallic flavor. James Thurber owned a collection of Western dime novels in French, in which the Redskins were *les Peaux-Rouges,* several of whom taunted a captured scout with the comment, *"Vous vous promenez très tard ce soir, mon vieux!"* In Germany, all Hollywood movies have dubbed dialogue. It seems incongruous to hear Gary Cooper or Errol Flynn speaking fluent German, but it is even more startling

304

to see Randolph Scott gallop up to a Sioux chief, say "How!", and have the Sioux answer, "Wie gehts?" It is really enlightening to see *King Kong* in German as *König Kong, der Herr des Urwalds* and to hear exotic savages crying, "*Ach, hilfe! Kommt der Kong!*" Besides creating the wrong atmosphere, the dialogue is often inexact in dubbed translations. In French versions of Westerns, *redeye* is *vin rouge,* while in Japan, the *OK Corral* is the *Yes Corral.* There is nothing new about this; the late seventeenth-century play *Love's Last Shift* was translated into French as *La Dernière Chemise.*

Americans are equally guilty of inept translation. The French sometimes call De Gaulle "le grand Charles," which *Life* vulgarized into "Big Charlie." Again, someone translated Albert Einstein's "*Raffiniert ist der Herr Gott, aber boshaft ist er nicht*" as "God's tricky, but he ain't mean," which is an inappropriate level of both grammar and diction. One English version of the *Iliad* turns Achilles' manly breast into his shaggy bosom, transforms the ashes of Anchises into cinders, and says of Apollo that "his arrows jiggled as he jogged along." Often a literal translation will not do: the English equivalent of the French *haut peuple étranges* ("strange noblemen") is not *high strange people.*

Grammar as well as diction can be inept in translation, especially if the translator has not mastered the language into which he is translating. The German who translated the instruction book for a German automobile made many dangling modifiers and clumsy passive voices. Dutch translators came up with some amusing sentences when they rendered into English some Amsterdam and Rotterdam criticisms of a visiting American pianist: "In his phrasing he made light rubato's and a little reservation before each heavy chord gives to the melody a friendly heave, which makes the whole movable and also moved and a sensitivity that is originally musical. . . . It is only a few pianists given to play the Mephisto Wals the way the young American pianist . . . did. The temperament both of this work and it's interpretor covered each other entirely and the exorbitant technical difficulties were conquered by . . . overcourage and bravoure. . . . Throughout, he gave evidence of his tender toucher. It is seldom that an audience greets a performing artist with feettrample."

Probably a machine could do as well as this translator. In fact there are electronic translators now converting Russian into English at the rate of about 2,400 words a minute. Its operator needs no knowledge of Russian, and the machine can turn out in half a minute a page that it would take a person forty-five minutes to translate. Considering the vast bulk of scientific and political material that needs to be translated, such machines are invaluable. But they have no sense of style and no ability to distinguish subtleties of diction. One machine turned "The spirit is willing but the flesh is weak" into "The wine is available but the meat is poor." Jargon makes language itself too mechanical. In an essay on Boris Pasternak as a translator, George Reavey wrote: "The babel of modern civilization, the unprecedented and appalling eructation of ambiguous verbiage, and the apparent superfluity of means at man's disposal, have perhaps so inflated his [man's] disordered ego as to lead to some unreflecting contempt for a traditional labor of love."[12]

Samuel Johnson wrote that "No book was ever turned from one language into another, without imparting something of its native idiom," but it is more likely that the native idiom will be lost and replaced by mechanical substitutions or inappropriate connotations. Sometimes these can be unintentionally insulting or ludicrous. In the Nigerian novel *Things Fall Apart,* a missionary to the Ibos keeps mistranslating the word *myself* as *my buttocks,* to the derisive amusement of the Africans. There is no word for *virgin* in the Algonquian language, so the Puritan John Eliot who translated the Bible into Algonquian had to render the wise and foolish virgins as young men.

Some phrases cannot be meaningfully translated. James Baldwin observes in *Giovanni's Room* that "find yourself" is not in any other language and that the phrase reveals something crucial about the American way of life.

¶ CIRCUMLOCUTIONS

Circumlocution is related to jargon in that they are ways of evading a direct statement by talking around a subject. Some politicians are such masters of circumlocution that they can give an impression of integrity and profundity when they have actually said nothing but only emitted a blast of hot air. The technique is to discourse in pompous platitudes that are totally vague or else to bumble over a sequence of polysyllabic, pretentious, and preferably abstract words. The listener may not discover any sense in them, but he is apt to be stunned into awed admiration.

In *Roughing It,* Mark Twain had fun bringing together a slangy

306

Nevada miner with a circumlocutory minister fresh from an Eastern seminary. Scotty Briggs, delegated to find someone to bury Buck Fanshaw, asks the minister, "Are you the duck that runs the gospel-mill next door?" When the clergyman is perplexed, Scotty asks again if he is "the head clerk of the doxology-works next door?"

"I am the shepherd in charge of the flock whose fold is next door."

"The which?"

"The spiritual adviser of the little company of believers whose sanctuary adjoins these premises."

After Scotty has proceeded to explain that Buck Fanshaw has "passed in his checks" and that his friends need "to roust out somebody to jerk a little chin-music for us and waltz him through handsome," the minister, increasingly bewildered, pleads, "Would it not expedite matters if you restricted yourself to categorical statements of fact unencumbered with obstructing accumulations of metaphor and allegory?" Scotty replies with more slang from card-playing; he'll have to pass, because he "cant neither trump nor follow suit." Finally he explains that Buck Fanshaw has "gone up the flume," "throwed up the sponge," "kicked the bucket—"

"Ah—has departed to that mysterious country from whose bourne no traveler ever returns."

"Return! I reckon not. Why pard, he's *dead*!"

So getting to business, Scotty asks "if we can get you to help plant him—"

"Preach the funeral discourse? Assist at the obsequies?"

After more explanation, the minister asks, "Had deceased any religious convictions? That is to say, did he feel a dependence upon, or acknowledge allegiance to a higher power? . . . Well, to simplify it somewhat, was he, or rather had he ever been connected with any organization sequestered from secular concerns and devoted to self-sacrifice in the interests of morality?"

"All down but nine—set 'em up on the other alley, pard."

Despite the minister's display of learning, Scotty's language is more vital; and when he eventually becomes a Sunday school teacher and tells Biblical stories in slang to the Nevada small fry, he is immensely successful.

A stock-in-trade comic figure is the long-winded professor addicted to painfully learned and circumlocutory prose. In *Tarzan of the Apes* we find Jane's father, Professor Porter, and his companion Mr. Philander lost in the jungle. The latter breaks into Porter's conversation to inform him that they are being pursued by a lion, but the professor is more annoyed than alarmed:

> "And now I find you guilty of a most flagrant breach of courtesy in interrupting my learned discourse to call attention to a mere quadruped of the genus *Felis*. As I was saying, Mr.—"
>
> "Heavens, Professor, a lion?" cried Mr. Philander, straining his weak eyes toward the dim figure outlined against the dark tropical underbrush.
>
> "Yes, yes, Mr. Philander, if you insist upon employing slang in your discourse, a 'lion.' But as I was saying—"13

Obviously, *lion* is not slang, and the jungle is no place for the professor's jargon. Henry James, in his later fiction, tried to make his characters and prose so refined in subtlety that his paragraphs are often monuments of circumlocution. Edith Wharton recalled James's trying to ask an old man the directions to the King's Road at Windsor:

> "My good man, if you'll be good enough to come here, please; a little nearer—so," and as the old man came up: "My friend, to put it to you in two words, this lady and I have just arrived here from *Slough*; that is to say, to be more strictly accurate, we have recently *passed through* Slough on our way here, having actually motored to Windsor from Rye, which was our point of departure; and the darkness having overtaken us, we should be much obliged if you would tell us where we now are in relation, say, to the High Street, which, as you of course know, leads to the Castle after leaving on the left hand the turn down to the railroad station."

Receiving a dazed look, James went on:

> "In short, in short, my good man, what I want to put to you in a word is this: supposing we have already (as I have reason to think we have) driven past the turn down to the railway station (which in that case, by the way, would probably not have been on our left hand, but on our right), where are we now in relation to . . ."
>
> "Oh, please," I interrupted, feeling myself utterly unable to sit through another parenthesis, "do ask him where the King's Road is."
>
> "Ah—? The King's Road? Just so! Quite right! Can you, as a matter of fact, my good man, tell us where, in relation to our present position, the King's Road exactly *is*?"
>
> "Ye're in it," said the aged face at the window.14

This episode is harmlessly amusing, but some readers find Henry James's late prose frustrating and flawed by strained and needless circumlocution. James, however, revised much of his early work to make it conform to his late style, and the results are sometimes unfortunate. In the 1877 edition of *The American,* the hero "was clean-shaved"; in the 1907 revision, "he spoke, as to cheek and chin, of the joy of the matutinal steel." There is no gain in refinement, merely a loss of strength.

¶ EUPHEMISM

Related to circumlocution is euphemism—the avoidance of a direct word or phrase by the substitution of a more genteel, fastidious, prestigious, abstract, or indirect one. Usually a euphemism is intended to make something blunt, ugly, or unpleasant seem more attractive or less offensive. In Melville's *Billy Budd,* we find euphemism and circumlocution combined, when the villainous Claggart says, " '. . . the man in question, had entered His Majesty's service under another form than enlistment.' At this point Captain Vere with some impatience, interrupted him: 'Be direct, man; say impressed men.' "

In a science-fiction story where babies are illegal because of surplus population, a Congressman tells the Director of the Population Planning Agency he has heard that "a bounty has been offered for infants born after the grace period."

"That is false," the director said. "Absolutely incorrect. It is true that remuneration has been offered for information leading to the recovery of illegal infants, but this is in no sense a bounty."

"To many people," the chairman said, "it might appear to be a distinction without a difference."[15]

Some sinister political euphemisms have become so familiar that they have lost their innocent connotations. *Purge* and *liquidation* no longer have any associations other than the blood baths they actually are. Others do not attempt to fool anyone but are used as a matter of discretion, such as calling someone a *prevaricator* instead of a *liar.* John T. McNaughton, the Defense Department's counsel, told a colleague, "Never, under any circumstances whatsoever, use the word 'lie.' Don't use it negatively; don't use it positively. If you have to tell the committee you want to lie down, say 'recline.' " (*The Reader's Digest,* LXXXIII, August, 1963, p. 40.) Elizabethan duellists made a fine art of giving the lie; there were ingenious evasions, but if one wished to send a formal challenge, an expert advised, "In this writing it also behooveth to use all plainness of

309

words and phrases, leaving aside eloquence and ambiguity of speech."

Other euphemisms are not so deadly but can be hypocritical, like the military's speaking of *planned withdrawal* when a retreat takes place or like television's disguising censorship by the term *continuity acceptance* and calling its censors *editors*. Many jobs get euphemistic titles, to avoid unfavorable connotations and gain prestige. Whenever possible, the addition of *engineer, expert, technician,* or *scientist* is helpful. Thus *undertaking* becomes *mortuary science, embalming* is *restorative art, cemetary salesmen* are *memorial counselors, cemetary operators* are *cemetarians,* and the whole death business becomes *grief therapy.* (Of course, *death* and *corpses* are never mentioned on pain of . . . of being launched into eternity.) The Purina Pet Care Center discovered a stupefying variety of euphemistic titles for dog-catcher: *Dog Officer; Dog Constable; Supervisor of Dog Control; Dog Law Enforcement Officer; Stray-Dog Supervisor; Dog Pound Superintendent; Poundkeeper; Canine Controller; Pet Rehabilitation Officer; Chief Humane Officer; Mongrel Administrator; Supervisor, Missing Dog's Bureau; Chief, Dog-Depot Section;* and *Director of the Animal Regulation Division of the Department of Public Health. Garbage men* became *sanitary engineers, pawn brokers* became *loan experts,* and we may find *window washers* becoming *transparent wall engineers.* You might be tempted to say *bull* to all this, but in Puritan communities you'd better not. Victorian society was so outwardly prudish that it refused to mention directly anything physical, lest it seem vulgar or even suggest s-e-x. Obviously, then, *bull* must be a taboo word, and in some places it still is. In America, New Englanders called it a *critter, sire, toro,* or *top cow;* Midlanders referred to it as an *ox, sire,* or *mule cow;* and Southerners termed it a *steer, male cow, beast,* or *brute.* On the prairies, pioneers often built fires with bison manure, made more attractive by the term *buffalo chips.*

Motivational researchers in advertising are particularly practised at using euphemisms to avoid unpleasant financial or physical connotations and have a genius for making bad breath, body odor, gluttony, nausea, constipation, false teeth, pimples, obesity, general pathology and creeping debility seem glamorous or at least palatable. Certainly *halitosis, overindulgence, gastric distress, nature's tardiness, dentures, blemishes* sound more respectable. If you do not survive, at least the aforementioned grief therapists will see you off with extreme unction. No one will call you a stiff. But we do

310

find books in semi-stiff (e.g. paperback) bindings; and if the trend continues, we may find orators giving speeches not from soap boxes but detergent packaging. Euphemisms have become so much a way of thinking that they appear even when there is no point to them. Thus submarines no longer sink; they have *negative buoyancy*.

The opposite of euphemism is the more infrequent dysphemism: for example, naming a restaurant *Sloppy Joe's* or *The Greasy Spoon*, calling butter *axle grease*, drinking *bug juice*, driving a *tin Lizzie*, referring to one's father as *my old man* or to one's wife as *my old lady*.

¶ WORDS AND CENSORSHIP

Sometimes squeamishness leads to demands for censorship. The self-styled pure in heart (apparently not so secure in their purity) challenge the right of authors to use realistic dialogue and description. There are unscrupulous peddlers of pornography who should be prosecuted, but too many censors lack critical discrimination. Some, when questioned, have admitted that they rarely read, have seldom if ever seen a play, have no interest in the arts, but still insist that they are qualified to be arbiters of what should be available to the public. Often, on the basis of book lists or because of the cover or title, they condemn books that they have not read. If they have read the books, they usually select words, phrases, and scenes out of context and use them to show that the entire work is contaminated. But most significant literature, from the Bible to Shakespeare to the latest Nobel Prize winner, has words or passages that may be objectionable by themselves but in the context of the entire work are justified as part of a realistic portrayal of people and conditions. Any work intended to arouse moral indignation at some injustice or inhumanity will have to portray scenes that can create that indignation. Thus they may include the horrors of war, starvation, murder, sexual degradation, bigotry, slums, in order to make the reader fully aware of what is wrong with these things. The issue, therefore, is not whether a book contains certain words and scenes but what the purpose and the effect of these are upon the normal adult reader. Obviously many books are unsuitable for children, but this does not necessarily justify making them unavailable to responsible adults. If an adult has lewd or psychopathic reactions to reading Chaucer, Shakespeare, Hemingway, or Salinger, then he had better consult a psychiatrist rather than clamor for a censor.

Practically no one is so sheltered that he has escaped hearing profane or obscene words, and encountering them in a passage of literary realism is not going to make him profane or obscene unless he is so already.

Actually, no word is good or bad in itself. Words are simply sounds to which we have attached meanings. Thus a Yugoslavian immigrant just learning English asked a teacher which words were improper, for she wanted to avoid them but couldn't tell them just from listening or from the dictionary. Most of the taboo words are four-letter monosyllabic ones of Anglo-Saxon origin. The same excremental acts that they name are expressed by other terms that are perfectly acceptable, though they may not be appropriate for dinner-table conversation. It is therefore not the natural acts themselves but simply the mental associations we have evolved that make some words forbidden and their synonyms acceptable. Still, the mental associations are there, so it is advisable not to shock people by offensive language. But in literature such language may be necessary for realistic portrayal. This is not necessarily "strong language"; some people of limited vocabulary and impoverished imagination rely so heavily upon a few favorite four-letter words that their speech is insufferably stale.

Often the genteel tradition is ridiculous, as when the Victorians draped the legs (or rather "limbs") of their pianos lest they arouse lascivious thoughts. Such prudery is really dirty-minded, seeing dirt where a wholesome mind would find none. Certainly anyone who responded lecherously to piano legs was in a bad way. The absurd delicacy of nineteenth-century Puritanism appears in Edward Ellis's *The Hunter's Cabin*. In a perilous moment, Annie, the genteel heroine, is trapped with the heroic hunter Ferrington in a cabin besieged by Indians. Seeing some movement in the bush, Ferrington utters the uncouth statement:

"It is a devilish Indian contrivance—"

" 'Sh, George; do not speak thus," she interrupted, noticing the expression, in spite of the tumultuous feelings that reigned in her breast.

"I beg pardon. It is an Indian contrivance, and there are Shawnees hid behind that same bush."

When Whitman and Mark Twain broke some of the taboos, to use a more realistic language of the people, their works were denounced for using vile obscenities. *Huckleberry Finn* was banned in some communities for containing such impure words as *dern* and *sweat*.

312

In *Pygmalion,* George Bernard Shaw had fun with the proper Edwardians' squeamish shibboleth against *bloody.* Henry Higgins' housekeeper tells him:

. . . there is a certain word I must ask you not to use. The girl has just used it herself because the bath was too hot. It begins with the same letter as bath. She knows no better; she learnt it at her mother's knee. But she must not hear it from your lips.

Today, when the ban against *Tropic of Cancer* and *Lady Chatterly's Lover* has been lifted, it seems as if almost any language can be allowed, provided the author has a serious purpose and is not merely trying to give his readers a cheap excitement. Usually there is no need for an author to indulge in ubiquitous obscenities. Yet some censorship groups and even some teachers try to prohibit writing which contains even the mildest profanity. It is a truism that beauty and vileness are in the mind of the beholder. In John Steinbeck's *The Grapes of Wrath,* Casy says "Maybe you wonder about me using bad words. Well, they ain't bad to me no more. They're jus' words folks use, an' they don't mean nothing bad with 'em." [16] Certainly *hell* and *damn,* as used colloquially, have lost any theological meaning and are merely expletives and intensifiers, as when something is called "damned good," "damned fine," "important as hell," "colorful as hell," "sleepy as hell," or "a helluva great guy." When you read that "All hell broke loose," you are not likely to be converted to diabolism.

One of the books most often attacked by would-be censors is J. D. Salinger's *The Catcher in the Rye.* At the climax, the protagonist encounters the most notorious of all four-letter words scrawled on a school wall. He is revolted and tries to erase the word, which he sees symbolising the modern loss of innocence. In context, the word makes the empathic reader share Holden's and Salinger's moral indignation, whereas the would-be censors are mistakenly indignant at Salinger. The rest of the book is sprinkled with *hells* and *damns* used in a purely harmless fashion. These passages do not make Holden corrupt, nor will they corrupt any reader in his right mind. The lesson to be learned here is not that the book should be censored, but that Holden has, as he admits, a lousy vocabulary.

Hell and *damn* have become trite utility words that the careful stylist should avoid unless they are appropriate in dialogue. As for well-meant profanity, *The New Yorker's* editor Harold Ross once told John McNulty, "Well, God bless you, McNulty, goddam it," and James Thurber observed that Ross had two deities, one upper and one lower case.[17] Conversely, an Australian clergyman denied that bullocks cannot be driven without blasphemy. To prove his point, he cracked the whip and roared, "You rapturous archangels! You sublimated cherubim! You sanctified innocents! Get ye up and hence!" And they did.[18] Which shows that profanity is more in the mind and the manner than in the words themselves. As the Virginian says, "When you call me that, smile."

The controversy in California over the *Dictionary of American Slang* can best illustrate the inverted thinking of some censors. The dictionary, a scholarly reference work, includes among its more than 20,000 definitions about 200 that contain obscene words. Since these are part of American English, the compilers had no choice but to include them. A person consulting the dictionary might run across them, but they are not in a context that would give a normal person any erotic or antisocial ideas. Yet in the spring of 1963, a student using an assumed name checked out of the Sacramento library a copy of the dictionary and turned the stolen volume over to a state assemblyman. The California State Superintendent of Public Instruction denounced the book as "a practicing handbook of sexual perversion," and recommended that schools censor the dictionary on the grounds that it is unfit for children. Stuart Flexner, one of the authors, replied that many books are not written for children, e.g., *Advanced Geometry, Gone with the Wind, How to Prepare Your Income Tax*.[19] And American courts have ruled it unconstitutional to ban books for adults because they are not suitable for children. Most librarians protested the pressure for censorship, and the book's defenders pointed out that any dictionary contains the word *sin* and defines most of the individual sins without in any way tempting readers to commit them. Yet some of the would-be censors, when challenged, said that they could not control themselves when they encountered a suggestive word in print. Who then, has the dirty mind? Some would-be censors refused to look at the book, but others carefully excerpted all the taboo words and compiled lists of them. Various ultraconservative organizations and hate groups joined the fray, denouncing as immoral and probably subversive the politicians, teachers, and librarians who defended the book. Some self-appointed custodians of public morals wanted to discharge the entire state school board. No one ever tried to condemn the book under the state penal code against obscenity, because they knew they did not have a legitimate case; instead they tried to ban the book and its defenders without due process of law. Censorship groups urged others to reproduce their lists of "dirty words" and circulated them widely throughout the state, distributing them indiscriminately on street corners and in housing units, stores, and parking areas. Many fell into the hands of children, but one censor insisted, "I don't care if every teen-ager in California reads the filthy excerpts we're showing. What we're trying to do is protect unborn generations." [20] One distributor of the lists said he hoped to cover the state with 100,000 copies, to make sure that nobody missed reading the "dirty words." A mother wrote Mr. Flexner that she had never heard of any of the taboo words and that his dictionary defined them all wrong. Another correspondent "suggested the Constitution be rewritten on 'sound principles' to eliminate freedom of speech and guarantee 'each one a wholesome . . . life' instead." [21] Ultimately the furor died down; all it succeeded in doing was to provide an outlet for various social and political frustrations and to give the self-righteous would-be censors a chance to make certain that everybody learned the words that they wanted concealed from everybody. When a woman congratulated Dr. Johnson for omitting indecent words from his dictionary, he replied, "So you have been looking for them, Madam?"

Exercise 34: There are 320 words in the following passage from James Fenimore Cooper's *The Deerslayer*. By cutting all surplus diction and lifeless detail, Mark Twain reduced the passage to 220 words; and the omission of 100 words tightened the episode and made it more dramatic. Without changing any of Cooper's words, underline those that can be omitted, and see if you can do as well as Mark Twain.

In a minute he was once more fastened to the tree, a helpless object of any insult or wrong that might be offered. So eagerly did every one now act, that nothing was said. The fire was immediately lighted in the pile, and the end of all was anxiously expected.

It was not the intention of the Hurons absolutely to destroy the life of their victim by means of fire. They designed merely to put his physical fortitude to the severest proofs it could endure, short of that extremity. In the end, they fully intended to carry his scalp into their village, but it was their wish first to break down his resolution, and to reduce him to the level of a complaining sufferer. With this view, the pile of brush and branches had been placed at a proper distance, or one at which it was thought the heat would

315

soon become intolerable, though it might not be immediately dangerous. As often happened, however, on these occasions, this distance had been miscalculated, and the flames began to wave their forked tongues in a proximity to the face of the victim that would have proved fatal in another instant had not Hetty rushed through the crowd, armed with a stick, and scattered the blazing pile in a dozen directions. More than one hand was raised to strike the presumptious intruder to the earth; but the chiefs prevented the blows by reminding their irritated followers of the state of her mind. Hetty, herself, was insensible to the risk she ran; but, as soon as she had performed this bold act, she stood looking about her in frowning resentment, as if to rebuke the crowd of attentive savages for their cruelty.

"God bless you, dearest sister, for that brave and ready act," murmured Judith, herself unnerved so much as to be incapable of exertion; "Heaven itself has sent you on its holy errand."

Exercise 35: Condense or revise the following sentences to make them as concise as possible. For example, "The wealth of industry is market creating" can be reduced to "Industrial wealth creates markets."

1. The basis of the purpose of the novel *Babbitt* is to expose vulgarity and intolerance.
2. The test of the poet is to use simplicity and precision in his usage of words.
3. Conwell's first statement concerning the attainment of wealth states that a man can attain it at home.
4. George Stevens budgeted for the spending of $15 million for *The Greatest Story Ever Told*.
5. When a person entertains today, it seems imperative that he must have liquor on hand.
6. Today there are many countries that practice a democratic form of government.
7. Many years prior to this day, Richard III was killed at Bosworth.
8. The hope is in some of our minds that we can finish ahead of the schedule that we have.
9. If people try to express views other than what the group feels to be right, they are ostracized and a great dislike for these individuals arises.
10. This is symbolic of how God's love is of an evil crushing quality.
11. Without any pause for the sanitation of showering, he went directly to the pool.
12. Wolfert stood apart by himself alone, observing the scene with an indifferent eye.

316

13. The Batman descended down from the roof by means of a rope.
14. The chestnut blight killed the life of all the mature trees.
15. Ebenezer secretly thought to himself that the weather seemed ominous.
16. Margarine is cheaper than the seventy-cent spread, and it doesn't cost as much.
17. The hardened jargonaut never uses one word when he is able to make employment in addition of several other words besides.
18. It is advised and cautioned that endemic ursine creatures not be offered digestible sustenance within the confines of the park.
19. The electric coffee pot is something that I wonder how I got along without before I had it.
20. If one should chance to partake of an illicit beverage that is the product of domestic distillation, he may endanger his ocular faculties to the point of blindness or may even render himself a member of those who are not of the living, if the beverage under consideration was vaporized and condensed not in a copper cooking utensil and curvilinear tube but was produced in those containing the malleable metal symbolized as Pb, the chemical sign for lead.

Exercise 36: Underline the dead wood that should be cut from the following:

1. In my opinion I consider Billy Budd to be a tragic hero.
2. A Deistic belief was that of the concept of God as a prime mover.
3. Not everyone approved of the placing of the defeated territory under military rule.
4. In contrast to frontier life, life today seems to be of a more pessimistic nature.
5. A battered house greets the family the day as they move in.
6. One of the main characters in *The Octopus* is that of Buck Annixter.
7. Gatsby does nearly everything with the idea in his mind of winning Daisy again.
8. Huck is from a family quite dissimilar to that of Tom's.
9. There has been tyranny in nearly all the governments that man has created during his existence.
10. In *Walden* Thoreau wrote the results of the experience of the living in a state close to that of nature.
11. I came back to my room and was shocked by all the bags, clothes, and boxes that were piled high in my room.
12. Since the beginning of time to the present day, man has been afraid of crocodiles.
13. Godzilla felt the same towards King Kong also.
14. Freezing foods has become one of the most popular methods of food preservation.

317

15. Every time I walk past Bessey Hall, I imagine in my mind seeing about ten students in each room wearing striped uniforms, scraping tin cups across the windows.
16. Because of her very nature of foundation, society must fight individuality.
17. Another unjustifiable rule is the rule that prohibits freshmen from having cars on campus.
18. For the past couple of three weeks we have been studying about anatomy.
19. That's too good of an idea.
20. Sharecroppers did not own the farms upon which they were working and living on.
21. We met a fellow named of Gonzales Pilkington O'Toole the Fourth.
22. The accused did not reply back when the prosecutor asked him to confess to his guilt.
23. The doctors never saw that small of a child.
24. This type of thump keg is a good type of thump keg because it takes the impurities out of the whiskey.
25. That is the way in which Americans would like to be in the modern society of today.

Exercise 37: Replace the malapropisms on page 303 with the right words.

Exercise 38: Replace any faulty diction or typographical errors in the following sentences:

1. Lincoln waited until 1863 to issue his Emaciation Proclamation.
2. Scott Fitzgerald's stories are full of long, blonde women, beautiful and sofasticated.
3. In Faulkner's *The Bear,* Isaac McCaslin learns of his grandfather's miscegenation and discovers the tinted line of his ancestors.
4. Many of Hawthorne's stories are moral allergies.
5. Blanche DuBois became notarized in her town for her loose morals.
6. It was all many a pioneer could do to eek out an existence.
7. The Rev. Mr. Hale became dissolutioned with the Salem withcraft trials.
8. Professor Crabshaw felt that the murder of the princes could not be contributed to Richard III.
9. In *The Grapes of Rath,* the Joads were depraved of almost everything.
10. In Faulkner's "Dry September," Miss Minnie Cooper went down town wearing a shear dress that was a reveling garment.
11. Holden Caulfield was hesitant about excepting adult responsibilities.

318

12. The P. and S. W. Railroad charged exuberant freight rates.
13. Horpington felt that the lack of electives narrowly circumsized the curriculum.
14. The Arias disbelieved in the Christian trinity.
15. School droopouts contribute to juvenile deliquency.
16. After a long, hot day, the cook was in a state of nervous prostitution.
17. Poe's poetry intensifies the aurora of mystery.
18. The A & P was full of costumers the day before Thanksgiving.
19. Zachary went to business school to learn bookeeping.
20. The bubonic plaque devastated England in 1349.
21. The Puritans would not tolerate any religious hearsay.
22. The villian tried to destroy the newlyweds' martial bliss.
23. We now have freeways where formally there were farms.
24. The Jerrybuilders are creating a housing development next store to the high school.
25. A swarm of gnats inflitrated the campground.

Exercise 39: Underline the dead wood that should be cut from the following:

1. Social workers have been working for years in trying to find a remedy to this problem.
2. In Stephen Crane's "The Open Boat" the story is written in an impressionistic manner.
3. Smurdly is too kind of a man to take advantage of anyone.
4. Grendel took and swallowed the thane.
5. Babbitt and his friends urged for conservative politics.
6. I made matching muu-muus for the whole entire family, but Grandma she wouldn't even try hers on.
7. Has it ever occurred to you that chicken soup with rice it should be chicken with rice soup?
8. The Greenland whale was a-twitching of his tail.
9. Martin Eden realized that he did not have a big enough of a vocabulary.
10. "I wonder who it is at the door," she said, clutching the monkey's paw in her hand.
11. This here man is to have apartment B1B1.
12. Built in 1901, the Oconaluftee pioneer farmhouse is not so old of a building.
13. Here comes the Good Humor man coming up the road.
14. There wasn't nobody noticed the hidden secret passage through the fireplace.
15. You've eaten an entire whole package of Necco candies.

319

16. That there speck on Mt. Rushmore it is James Mason chasing Cary Grant up around on George Washington's nose.
17. In *The Lost Weekend,* Ray Milland hung whiskey bottles out of the window and hid them secretly up in the chandeliers.
18. What sort of a coffin contains sacred earth in it?
19. Hawkeye went and followed the trail of the treacherous Huron.
20. What is the unknown secret ingredient put in the salad?

18 √ The Grammar of Mars

What, it is often asked, is the language coming to? Are we making progress in communication and literacy, or were the critics right who saw in *Webster III* the opening blast of some linguistic Armageddon? Can we arrive at a universal language that can overcome the barriers of tribalism, provincialism, and nationalism and thus promote the cause of international understanding and cooperation? Will we become strangled in the red tape of jargon or be brainwashed by some totalitarian Newspeak? If we develop an international tongue, will local ones become dead and forgotten? Should we, and can we, streamline and simplify grammar and spelling by regulation rather than by linguistic evolution?

From the Middle Ages until almost modern times, Latin served as the international language of Western scholarship and diplomacy, but its knowledge was confined to scholars and diplomats. During the eighteenth century, on the continent, French largely replaced it as the language not only of diplomacy but of the cultured aristocracy. At the time of Napoleon's invasion of Russia, many Russian nobles, living in the artificial, sheltered world of court and privilege, spoke only French, then suddenly the language of the enemy. Nevertheless, obviously, national barriers had not been overcome.

So why not have a new language altogether? As early as 1887, Dr. L. L. Zamenhof invented Esperanto (hope), a synthetic language for international use, based on a streamlined combination of various Romance languages. Esperanto did not come into general use; and when the United Nations was founded and the need for communication acute, technology and simultaneous translation provided a solution to the problem. Michael Fraym in *The Manchester Guardian* parodied the Esperanto approach in his proposed anthem for the Common Market, which concludes:

321

Wir werken ensemble kos wir laik es dass Weh,
Nous sommes ein gemütlich and schnug Familie-Grupp—
Spaghetti pour Breakfaast und Schnitzel pour Tee—
So Gott geb lang vita au grand Kommun Krupp!

We are unlikely to have such a spoken smorgasbord, but there
have been linguistic simplifications. Turkish and Japanese introduced the Roman alphabet, and Russian and Arabic (in some
areas) were simplified. German has dropped the old Teutonic type
and is streamlining its script. The Communist Chinese government
decided in 1956 to simplify some of its complicated brush-stroke
characters, but the program backfired when people all over the
country started inventing their own abbreviated characters, creating illegible inconsistency. One newspaper complained of the resultant breakdown in the postal service and sighed, "Who would
have thought that the reliability, which was unshaken by civil
wars, would succumb to the vagaries of writing reform." The Chinese claim that they plan ultimately to replace their ideographic
characters with the Roman alphabet.

On the other hand, there have been twentieth-century movements to re-establish an older national tongue, such as Gaelic in
Ireland and Hebrew in Israel. (Because of Nazi nationalism, Hitler
closed the six hundred schools of Esperanto in the Third Reich.)
But these "reforms" seem to lack urgency for the ordinary people,
who do not give up their habitual vernacular and embrace some
unfamiliar tongue just because of government pressure and propaganda, any more than Americans could become fluent in Algonquian if politicians decided that its revival would promote national
pride.

Instead, the trend is to the more widely used languages, to the
extent that some local ones may be completely lost except to scholars; and in some cases, with no written form and no recordings,
may be entirely lost. Cherokee, the only American Indian language
with a written form devised by one of its own members, is a case in
point. Sequoyah's Cherokee syllabary, with a character for each
syllable (eighty-six) rather than each phoneme in the language,
may well be a more efficient system than our own alphabet. Now
the Cherokees are almost all English-speaking; and if another language is to be taught in their schools, they are interested in learning one of the major European ones to broaden their education.
Those who still speak Cherokee learn it only at home. In its writ-

ten form, it may be one of the few Indian tongues that will escape oblivion, but the spoken form is dying out.

A similar situation exists in India and parts of Africa, where English, from the days of the British Empire, has been taught in the schools and is the language of the civil service and of the governmental and diplomatic elite. It also serves as a means of communication between dialects and tribes. Except for Communist China, English is increasingly used in Asia to conduct business, banking, transportation, science, and politics. First the British and now the Americans have exerted tremendous political and economic pressure in the Orient, with the result that despite emergent nationalism, English has become a status symbol. In Hong Kong it is the official language as well as the elite tongue of the upper classes. Since World War II, the Japanese and the Koreans have made English compulsory in the public schools. Despite former Dutch colonization, the Indonesians use English in advanced university courses. In Malaysia, English rivals Malay as one of the two legal languages. Tagalog is the official language of the Philippines, but in practice, English breaches dialectal barriers and is the language of the law, newspapers, the schools, politics, and business. In India, it was the legal language, and the thirteen million who can use it are the dominant power. When in 1965, Hindi replaced English as the official language, a series of bloody riots ensued in which a railway station was burned and over seventy people were killed. The rioters were not inspired by a love of English but by a resentment that Hindi, the language of northern India, was superimposed over their regional tongues. English is no longer official in Pakistan, but it is required in the schools and is necessary for communication between Bengali in the East and Urdu in the West. In Africa, English is the official language of Nigeria (which has over 250 regional languages or dialects), Ghana, Sierra Leone, and Gambia, and is widely used from Capetown to Cairo. Even in Latin America, English is competing with Spanish as the language of commerce. And in Europe, many schoolchildren elect or are required to study English for some years, especially in Germany, Scandinavia, and Russia.

English may receive a profound impact by its use as a lingua franca in countries which are now ready to develop industrially and participate fully in international affairs. Perhaps it will be modified by the native tongues of those who use it around the

323

world. Pidgin English has been in use in Africa and in the Orient for some time. This is basically English words (altered by local pronunciation) grafted onto the local syntax, or sometimes used with no apparent syntax at all, with tense, number, case, and gender all jettisoned. It can be much more elaborate than "no tickee, no shirtee." A sailor might be "him fella allatime belong boat," and an often quoted specimen is the Chinese servant's explanation that his master's sow had produced a litter: "Him cow pig have kittens." In Edgar Rice Burroughs' *The Monster Men,* the Chinese servant warns the heroine, "No talkee so strong, walle have ear all same labbit." Since pidgin was used to conduct trade, the word is a slurring of *business* into *bidgin* into *pidgin.*

Pidgin is completely unacademic, but even when Orientals have studied English, they sometimes produce a strange amalgam. Here is an essay submitted by an Indian for a civil-service examination in 1961 and reprinted by Evelyn Wood in *Thought,* published in Delhi, January 20, 1962:

The cow is one wonderful animal, also he is quadruped and because he is female he gives milk, but he will do so only when he is got child. He is same like God sacred to Hindu and useful to man. But he has got four legs to-gather. Two are forward and two are afterwards.

His whole body can be utilized for use. More so the milk. What it can do? Various ghee, butter, cream, curds, whey, kova, and the condensed milk and so forth. Also he is useful to cobbler, watermans and mankind generally.

His motion is slow only. That is because he is of amplitudinous species and also his other motion is much useful to trees, plants as well as making flat cakes in hand and drying in sun.

He is the only animal that extricates his feeding after eating. Then afterwards he eats with his teeth whom are situated in the inside of his mouth. He is incessantly in the meadows on the grass.

His only attacking and defending weapons are his horns especially so when he has got a child. This is done by bowing his head whereby he causes the weapons to be parallel to the ground of the earth and instantly proceed with great velocity forwards.

He has got tail also, but not like other similar animals. It has hair on the other end of the other side. This is done to frighten away the flies which alight on his whole body and chastises him unceasingly whereupon he gives hit with it.

The palms of his feet are so soft unto the touch, so that the grasses he eats would not get crushed. At night time he reposes by going down on the ground and then he shuts his eyes like his relatives the horse which does not do so.

This is the Cow! [1]

This has a weird eloquence, unlike the examples of supposedly elegant English seriously offered in J. da Fonseca's and P. Carolino's *The New Guide of the Conversation, in Portuguese and English* that seems to have been inspired by a drunken nightmare in Hong Kong:

"It delay me to eat some wal nutskernels: take care not leave to pass the season."

"Be tranquil, i shall throw you any nuts during the shell is green yet."

"The artichoks grow its?"

"I have a particular care of its, because i know you like the bottoms."

Only Chinese rivals English in the number of people speaking it. It seems that many Westerners consider Chinese an incredibly difficult and inefficient language, but this is far from the case. In the twentieth century, there has been a profound linguistic revolution in China. Long before the Christian era the written language of China had become archaic. It had stood still while the spoken language was changing through the centuries; and gradually the rulers realized that governmental ordinances, philosophical writings, legal statutes, and classical literature were all unintelligible to the ordinary person. Said the Prime Minister Kung Sun Hung, about 120 B.C., "The imperial edicts and laws . . . are not generally understood by the poorly educated public officials, who are incapable of explaining them to the people." Here was a major administrative problem, yet conservatism smothered common sense. One emperor, Shih Huang Ti (200 B.C.) saw the need for modernization, but in trying to bring it about he ordered a complete holocaust of Chinese books and so outraged the scholars that they cordially detested him for the next two thousand years.

There evolved in China a civil service system in which the scholar was supreme. Fitness for administrative service was determined by the candidate's knowledge of the difficult, dead literary language and the philosophy written in it. Accordingly there grew up a scholastic class or hierarchy, which passed the precious learning from hand to hand, often from father to son. Ostensibly democratic, the system became very nearly hereditary. Imagine a country far more populous than the United States, where every candidate for public

325

office, whether judge, tax assessor, policeman, or dog catcher, had as the sole test of fitness to pass an examination on *Beowulf* in the original Anglo-Saxon ("Hwaet we gar-dena in geardagum. . . ."), using Anglo-Saxon himself in his examination paper. Imagine, moreover, not a fairly simple *Beowulf* in alphabetic symbols, but a rebus *Beowulf* expressed in pictures, each word having its individual picture, and each picture a complicated arrangement of lines having small observable relation to the idea expressed. Imagine further a *Beowulf* which is not a story but an exposition of the most abstruse philosophical ideas which the candidate is expected not only to remember but to understand.

There you have the system which ruled China, with some interruptions, for several millennia. Under it the mandarin class continued to rule until 1905, when the Manchu Empress agreed to abolish the examinations, together with the many abuses which had grown up around them.

Quite apart from this elaborate literary-political-philosophical system were the various vernaculars of the common man—of the Cantonese in the south and the northerner in Peking. No one bothered about this vulgar speech, yet little by little it developed a literature. It appeared first in the early centuries of the Christian era, in anonymous popular songs and ballads. In the ninth century, vernacular prose began to appear, to flower magnificently in the great anonymous novels of the sixteenth century. Yet at the beginning of the twentieth century, this living language and literature were ignored by classical scholars except for entertainment.

The breakdown of the traditional civil-service examinations was followed by the revolution of 1911, after which the vernacular came into its own. For the first time, the actual speech of the people was officially recognized. The new national language was the northern dialect, which was simpler and more mature than the southern and which was intelligible to nine out of ten Chinese. It was not the same as the tongue of the old novels and ballads, for the Chinese vernacular had changed just as Middle English developed into Modern English. According to Hu Shih, professor of philosophy at Peking before the Communists took over, the new idiom is "the most highly developed language in the world." If so, and because of its numerical rivalry to English, it deserves a comparison with English. In alphabet and orthography, English is infinitely superior to the Chinese pictographic characters. It is in grammar that Chinese may be better developed. It is an inflectionless language that uses form words instead of changed endings to express tense, number, case, and so on. Modern English is developing in the same direction, using the form words *has, have,* and *had* instead of inflections to indicate the perfect tenses of the verb. In certain constructions, *do, it, there,* and *to* have lost all definiteness of meaning to become merely formal units. Instead of the termination *-ess,* the feminine gender is often indicated by the formal use of *she, girl,* or *woman* (*a she-wolf, a girl bandit, a woman lawyer*), and other constructions are comparable (*a child prodigy, the child-buyer, a hound-dog man, the god-seeker*). Chinese is a monosyllabic language, with a sentence order much like English (usually subject-verb-object).

Perhaps the most significant likeness between Chinese and English is functional shift, by which a word can function as various parts of speech, being a modifier in one sentence, a noun in another, a verb in a third, and so on. Thus *round* may be a noun in "a round of golf," a verb in "to round the cape," an adjective in "a round ball," a preposition in "round the house," and an adverb in "to walk round." Functional shift is one of the distinctive features that gives modern English its flexibility. Chinese has gone even further in this direction; there are no distinctive parts of speech but just words whose function determines their classification. English has not yet attained this ideal state, but it is heading that way. In the cold war, the two languages are not apt to influence each other, and it is ironic that they have so much in common.

It is notable that the efficient simplicity of Chinese came about because it developed for twenty centuries unimpeded and uninterfered with by the literary class. As a result of this complete freedom, the language underwent a revision more logical and more thorough than any other in the world. This could not have happened so completely without scholarly neglect. Scholarly attention would have tried to arrest the process of growth, and the good fortune of Chinese was its complete freedom to change.

Today the Communists seem to be tampering with the language, developing political jargon and propagandistic juggling. Meanwhile, in English there is an increasing gap between the terminology of science and the language of literature and between the jargon of bureaucracy and everyday speech. The linguistic gap between the advanced scientist and the man in the street is almost as wide as it was when Latin was the language of scholarship. (In fact many scientific terms are borrowed or coined from Latin.) We have, in addition, a pseudo-scientific approach, perhaps comparable to the medieval astrologer or alchemist, used in various businesses and particularly in advertising. While the scientist and the sociologist are busy trying to strip words of connotations and arrive at "operational definitions," Madison Avenue makes words fairly reek with connotative meaning. And with the proliferation of new drugs, fabrics, and cosmetics (legend has it that all possible syllables are dumped into a computer which obediently grinds out all the possible combinations for names) and new products by more conventional coinages (from *rayon* and *nylon* we now have a suffix *-on* or *-lon,* as in *Ban-lon, Herculon, Corlon, Fabulon,* and even *Silk-a-lon*), scientific and advertising activity produces a linguistic fallout which is sifting into the vernacular.

Can we predict at all the future of the language? We have noted several patterns of development: the spoken language is written down, the writings become "scripture," the "scriptures" become the language of scholarship and a new vernacular develops, sometimes by peaceful evolution and sometimes by conquest. The pattern of language and the main linguistic problem is in the balance of freedom and authority. Arthur Miller writes, "I will listen to anything that leads toward lucidity, to nothing that only simplifies." [2] Can you, should you regulate a living language without fossilizing it? Language has a way of regulating itself, and it is unlikely that we shall ever have complete anarchy. If we have another separation of the "scriptures" from the vernacular, it will probably be specialized jargon—administrative, military, scholarly, sociological—from the main current of English. This is not necessarily sinister, but George Orwell in *1984* eloquently described the dangers of Newspeak.

And then there's Mars. Two favorite devices of science-fiction writers are: either the people in outer space are beings of superior intelligence who know all about us already or who learn English with phenomenal ease, or they use telepathy, or both. We in turn may have developed ESP, LSD, and subliminal advertising on Telestar to work out an Esperanto for outer space. Let us hope so if we do find intelligent life there. We have enough linguistic problems on our own planet.

Exercise 40: Here is your chance to play editor. In the following sentences, identify the errors and put the appropriate symbol in the blank: Frag = sentence fragment; Paral = faulty parallelism; Case = error in case; PA = error in pronoun-antecedent agreement; SV = error in subject-

328

verb agreement; REF = faulty pronoun reference; DM = dangling modifier MisM = misplaced modifier; RO = run-on sentences; CS = comma splice; Dead = dead wood; Verb = faulty form of the verb; OK = no error.

1. Each homestead was located near cool spring water which provided them refrigeration as well as drink. . . . .
2. There are crayon stomped into the kitchen floor. . . . .
3. A parent does not want to drug their children to keep them quiet. . . . .
4. Mrs. Garth wants more women in politics and to run things. . . . .
5. Blackstone was mastered by the time he was twenty-two. . . . .
6. The cat's in the cream jar painted blue. . . . .
7. Hounds has better noses than curs, but they won't tree a bear. . . . .
8. The men from North American weighed the cartons on our scales here before they took them away, and it came to about 270 pounds. . . . .
9. A cave on the far side of the peninsula in which were found two mummified bodies. . . . .
10. Iago counted upon Othello being gullible about Desdemona's alleged faithlessness. . . . .
11. The road-runner is a cuckoo called geococcyx californianus. . . . .
12. Whenever Wile E. Coyote orders Acme equipment to catch the roadrunner, they always misfunction. . . . .
13. You may, while frozen, brush the crab cakes thoroughly with butter and heat in the oven. . . . .
14. When the white rhino advances, their mouth works like a lawn mower. . . . .
15. The white rhino being an exceptionally harmless and docile animal. . . . .
16. T. E. Lawrence is the last person who one would have thought to be a military genius. . . . .
17. Most soils in Africa is poor in humus and leaches easily. . . . .
18. Being a large bear, the ranger approached it cautiously. . . . .
19. Mother said we'd have dinner and to save something for Uncle Gus. . . . .
20. The new part of the Blue Ridge Parkway is graded, it's going to go through the Biltmore forest.
21. Sleeping in church, the verger nudged Lothar with a candle snuffer. . — . .
22. African family and kinship groups are much more tightly bound than those in Western society in some ways the Africans have more security. . . . .

23. The three weird sisters are the extra cook whom we think will spoil the broth.   . . . .
24. It is impossible to tell what prehistoric man really looked like. Or what skin color he had.   . . . .
25. The management of the laundry is not responsible for fastness of colors, jewelry left in clothing, or in case of fire.   . . . .

Exercise 41: Using the symbols from the preceding exercise, identify the errors in the following sentences.

1. Undisturbed since 1636, vandals recently mutilated the tree.   . . . .
2. In Thomas Wolfe's *Look Homeward, Angel,* he wrote about his youth in Asheville, North Carolina.   . . . .
3. Lots of trees has been tossed and broken to kindling by the storm.   . . . .
4. "Everybody should keep their promises," said the frog to the princess.   . . . .
5. Being a large child, the teacher put Sam at the end of the row.   . . . .
6. The story was clear, dramatic, and variety.   . . . .
7. Dr. Bruse and me brought back a collection of African bronzes.   . . . .
8. The British in Africa has tried to establish courts and written law.   . . . .
9. Frederick Remington wrote about the West at some length. As well as his paintings.   . . . .
10. The horned lark breeds from the Arctic to Texas, and they sometimes frequent golf courses.   . . . .
11. How does Orphan Annie and Sandy see with blanked eyeballs?   . . . .
12. Riding a mule down the trail, three big-horned sheep were seen.   . . . .
13. Most people do not know about Timbuctu having an important university in the Middle Ages.   . . . .
14. Hurricane Ysolde came as a surprise, the weather men were not prepared for it.   . . . .
15. Was you ever in the Yukon when it was 65 degrees below zero?   . . . .
16. Who was the Baltimore lady who wrote detective stories with a man's name?   . . . .
17. Mrs. Browning dabbled in spiritualism, which caused some friction with her husband.   . . . .
18. A rattleless rattlesnake? Never heard of, you say, but found in Isla Santa Catalina.   . . . .

330

19. Baudelaire was an ardent admirer of Poe's stories and poems and even suggested that he was a reincarnation of him. . . . .
20. Passing along a corridor of the Louvre, the Mona Lisa suddenly was seen. . . . .
21. Is it true that bears is all left-handed? . . . .
22. The tropics do not have winter and summer instead they have a rainy and a dry season. . . . .
23. Being overweight, the doctor ordered me to diet and exercise . . . .
24. Did you ever ride a horse in striped pants? . . . .
25. Honey was obtained by keeping bees in a hollow black gum log. . . . .

Exercise 42: Identify the errors in the following sentences as Frag, Paral, Case, PA, SV, REF, DM, MisM, RO, CS, Dead, or Verb.

1. The archaeologists recovering the sunken Greek ship kept a rabbit in the darkroom to whom they fed watermelon rinds. . . . . .
2. It don't pay to talk politics to some people. . . . .
3. To make his mash ferment more quickly, the blockader added Red Devil Lye, threw in a dead cat, using horse manure, but claimed these ingredients would distill out. . . . .
4. Romanticism was a revolt against neo-classicism, which they felt was too logical and unemotional. . . . .
5. Dr. and Mrs. Leakey found in Tanganyika a skull whom they thought was 600,000 years old but whom potassium-argon tests showed to be at least one and a half million years old. . . . .
6. There was a special training session for we new men going into the field. . . . .
7. While picking blackberries, a dozen chiggers bit me. . . . .
8. In France they admired Poe's work long before they did so in America. . . . .
9. Bongos needing room to run and breed. . . . .
10. Undiscovered for thousands of years, the rangers admired the petroglyphs. . . . .
11. The farmers protested at the railroad's refusal to ship goats. . . . .
12. Greta Garbo denied she was swimming topless-bikined in the Mediterranean in a letter reported by TV producer Bill Frye. . . . .
13. Baroque art degenerated into Rococo, which they often made vulgarly ornate. . . . .
14. Neuschwanstein looks like a medieval castle, actually it was built in the late nineteenth century. . . . .
15. All information will be sent to you free and without obligation by just completing and mailing this postage-free card. . . . .

331

16. After Melville escaped from the Typees. He was involved in a mutiny and was put in the calaboose at Tahiti.   . . . .
17. Grandmother wore a scarf around her head and a long white shawl with tasseled ends that reached almost to the ground on her shoulders.   . . . .
18. Euphemisms were so habitual in the late nineteenth century that they even spoke of roostering a rifle.   . . . .
19. Following the mistake of Leo Africanus in the early sixteenth century, the river was widely believed to flow from east to west.   . . . .
20. Audubon was another American painter who also wrote down his observations. Not necessarily about flora and fauna. . . . . .
21. Alfred E. Neuman is the candidate whom pollsters say is most likely to win.   . . . .
22. Approximately about ten percent of the voters favor Ringo Starr.   . . . .
23. Even with a tight lid a bear can knock over a garbage can and open it.   . . . .
24. The night was spent addressing letters to Bedouin chiefs.   . . . .
25. "Each step of our road to join the British was possible most; of them easy."—Lawrence of Arabia   . . . .

Exercise 43: Using the symbols from the preceding three exercises, identify the errors in the following sentences.

1. Isabella of Aragon gave her daughter an excellent education for a woman of that time. Even for a princess who later became Queen of England.   . . . .
2. I'm phoning from a phone booth about to go on the highway.   . . . .
3. In most parts of the United States, malaria have been eliminated.   . . . .
4. When you were in Rhodesia, did you see the Kariba Dam's being built across the Zambesi?   . . . .
5. In colonialism there is always two conflicting attitudes.   . . . .
6. Harry is a writer, and it nearly breaks his heart.   . . . .
7. The bear ripped off the top of the convertible, insatiable in its search for food; it found a pound of bacon inside.   . . . .
8. Names and letters three feet high were painted on the parapet of a new bridge, using a can of spray paint.   . . . .
9. Because of Wolfe's unflattering portrait of Asheville, they resented him bitterly for a long time.   . . . .
10. It is such elections as these that makes one wonder whether some communities really have democracy.   . . . .

11. Many cars brake instead of using a lower gear going down mountains, which sometimes burns out or crystallizes the brakes. . . . .
12. Will you pick up the other library books that's at home? . . . .
13. A kola nut was broken and passed to Livingstone and I. . . . .
14. Although the LP record was expensive when it first came out, they are one of the few items that has gone down in price. . . . .
15. When Segovia was playing at Miami University. One of his guitar strings broke. . . . .
16. Oedipus's killing his father and marrying his mother are the theme of the play. . . . .
17. We may meet the bear coming back from the garage. . . . .
18. Marcello Maistroianni is the Italian actor who is the most popular today. . . . .
19. I saw a Sinclair dinosaur driving through town. . . . .
20. Even though Sinclair Lewis gave a scathing portrait of Sauk Center in *Main Street,* they renamed their main street Main Street. . . . .
21. We watched TV riding through the desert. . . . .
22. Because Thomas Paine was a Deist. He became anathema to the orthodox Americans whom he had helped win the Revolution. . . . .
23. The short-winded young man or the awkward young woman do not usually take up long distance running. . . . .
24. In Texas they drink warm deer blood. . . . .
25. Melville wrote that Washington Irving imitated English writers too much, according to Melville we did not need an American Goldsmith. . . . .

Exercise 44: In the following sentences correct any grammatically inaccurate words and constructions.

1. Though William Faulkner is Mississippi's greatest writer, they often denounce his books there.
2. Drivers often blow their horns in tunnels, which disconcerts me.
3. You should not of lost your temper that way.
4. You don't got to talk too long on the phone.
5. Hickory nuts be very difficult to process.
6. This rain is the worstest toad-strangler I ever seen.
7. *The Grapes of Wrath* were made into an Academy Award-winning movie.
8. It looks like millionaires can marry just about whoever they wish.
9. How are the dishes scrubbing theirselves in the cartoon?
10. I could of swum the English Channel while you were taking your bath.

11. Them pizzas looks differently tonight.
12. Hold the lid when you shake the salad dressing, so's you won't spill none.
13. There were three ravens sat up in a tree.
14. There is not so great a gulf between the *B Minor Mass* and *The Gospel Boogie* as you may think there is.
15. "I get awfully sick of sitting down here at the end of the table and having whomever wants to interrupt in the middle of a sentence."— Senator Joseph McCarthy.
16. They probable packed a picnic lunch.
17. The movie condenses the story of Lawrence and the Arab revolt considerable.
18. *Like* as a conjunction is not confined nor particularly characteristic of any region.
19. Be sure and go get the rifle Paw took and threw in the branch.
20. If you think one wife can nag, you should imagine what three polygamous wives can do together in unison.
21. African tribesmen were and are not deprived.
22. Edward G. Robinson acted toughly in *Little Caesar*.
23. Though he was hurt fatal at the battle of Zutphen, Sir Philip Sydney asked that others be taken care of first.
24. It doesn't look as if this rain will never stop.
25. Legend says that when Shakespeare first went to London he held horses, he was an Elizabethan parking lot attendant.

Notes

1. COMMON SENSE AND THE PSYCHOLOGY OF GRAMMAR

1. ALAN JAY LERNER, *My Fair Lady; A Musical Play in Two Acts,* adaptation and lyrics by [the author], music by Frederick Loewe (Coward-McCann, Inc., New York, 1957), p. 28.
2. CHARLES M. SCHULZ, "Peanuts," February 28, 1964.
3. HENRY NASH SMITH, *Virgin Land: The American West as Symbol and Myth* (Harvard University Press, Cambridge, 1956), p. 98.
4. EDGAR RICE BURROUGHS, *Tarzan, Lord of the Jungle* (Ballantine Books, New York, 1963), pp. 66–67.
5. HORTON COOPER, *The State,* North Carolina, March 21, 1959, p. 10.
6. JOHN STEINBECK, *In Dubious Battle* (Modern Library, New York, 1936), p. 142.
7. BERGEN EVANS, "Grammar for Today," *The Atlantic Monthly,* CCV, March, 1960.
8. LIONEL TRILLING, "Introduction," *The Adventures of Huckleberry Finn* (Rinehart Editions, New York, 1948), p. xvi.
9. T. E. LAWRENCE, *Seven Pillars of Wisdom* (London, 1955), p. 63.
10. HARPER LEE, *To Kill a Mockingbird* (J. B. Lippincott Company, Philadelphia, 1960), p. 118.
11. ALAN JAY LERNER, *op. cit.,* p. 78.
12. JAMES THURBER, *The Years with Ross* (Little, Brown and Company, Boston, 1959), p. 271.
13. LOUIS B. SALOMON, *Bulletin of the American Association of University Professors,* Vol. 38, Autumn, 1952, p. 449.
14. ERNEST HEMINGWAY, *The Fifth Column and the First Forty-nine Stories* (Charles Scribner's Sons, New York, 1938), p. 368.

3. YOU NAME IT

1. *Esquire,* Vol. 60, December, 1963, p. 16.
2. GEORGE ORWELL, *1984* (Harcourt, Brace and Company, New York, 1949), p. 310.
3. ROBERT E. MORSBERGER, *How to Improve Your Verbal Skills* (Thomas Y. Crowell Company, New York, 1962), pp. 98–100.
4. *Vogue,* Vol. 141, June, 1963, p. 18.

5. RODERICK PEATTIE, ed., *The Great Smokies and the Blue Ridge* (The Vanguard Press, New York, 1953), pp. 147–148.

4. THE PERPLEXING PRONOUN

1. EDGAR RICE BURROUGHS, *Tarzan, Lord of the Jungle* (Ballatine Books, New York, 1963), p. 85.
2. JOHN P. MARQUAND, *Sincerely, Willis Wayde* (Little, Brown and Company, Boston, 1955), p. 36.

5. WHO'S ON FIRST? RIDDLES OF REFERENCE

1. AP News, December 7, 1962.
2. JAMES THURBER, *Let Your Mind Alone!* (Harper & Brothers, New York, 1937), p. 172.
3. TRUMAN CAPOTE, *Breakfast at Tiffany's* (Random House, New York, 1958), p. 35.
4. JOSEPH HELLER, *Catch-22* (Simon and Schuster, New York, 1962), p. 56.
5. JAMES THURBER, *The Years with Ross* (Little, Brown and Company, Boston, 1959), p. 242.
6. ALFRED DUGGAN, *The Cunning of the Dove* (Pantheon Books, Inc., New York, 1960), p. 41.
7. *Life,* Vol. LIV, January 18, 1963, p. 4.

6. PRONOUN-ANTECEDENT AGREEMENT

1. "Outrage over the Death Business," *Life,* Vol. LV, September 20, 1963, p. 98 B.
2. RAYMOND SCHUESSLER, "Blowing Rock, N.C.," *AAA Motor News,* September, 1962, p. 33.
3. *Mad,* June, 1963, p. 44.
4. TRUMAN CAPOTE, *Breakfast at Tiffany's* (Random House, New York, 1958), p. 20.
5. CHARLES M. SCHULZ, "Peanuts," February 28, 1963.
6. JAMES THURBER, *Thurber Country* (Simon and Schuster, New York, 1953), p. 60.
7. JOHN P. MARQUAND, *Sincerely, Willis Wayde* (Little, Brown and Company, Boston, 1955), p. 282.
8. NORMAN MAILER, "Ten Thousand Words a Minute," *Esquire,* Vol. LIX, February, 1963, p. 120.

336

9. NORMAN MAILER, "Norman Mailer Versus Nine Writers," *Esquire*, Vol. LX, July, 1963, p. 65.
10. *Time*, Vol. LXXX, December 2, 1962, p. 22.
11. *U.S. News and World Report*, Vol. 55, September 2, 1963, p. 54.
12. "Pork Barrel," *Life*, Vol. LV, August 16, 1963, p. 26.
13. EDMUND WILSON, *Patriotic Gore* (Oxford University Press, New York, 1962), p. x.
14. ANN BRIDGE, *The Portuguese Escape* (The Macmillan Company, New York, 1958), p. 215.
15. MARGARET BOURKE-WHITE, *Portrait of Myself* (Simon and Schuster, New York, 1963), p. 158.
16. *Mad*, June, 1963, p. 45.
17. NORMAN MAILER, "The Big Bite," *Esquire*, Vol. LX, December, 1963, p. 24.
18. *Op. cit.*, November, 1963, p. 30.
19. JOSEPH HENRY STEELE, *Ingrid Bergman: An Intimate Portrait* (David McKay Company, New York, 1960), p. 39.

7. CASE AND ITS CURIOSITIES

1. JOHN P. MARQUAND, *Sincerely, Willis Wayde* (Little, Brown and Company, Boston, 1955), p. 34.
2. JAMES THURBER, *A Thurber Carnival* (Samuel French, Inc., New York, 1962), p. 10.
3. JAMES THURBER, *The Owl in the Attic* (Harper & Brothers, New York, 1931), p. 97.
4. JOSEPH HELLER, *Catch-22* (Simon and Schuster, New York, 1961), p. 61.
5. NORMAN MAILER, "The Big Bite," *Esquire*, Vol. LX, November, 1963, pp. 28–30.
6. JAMES THURBER, *Credos and Curios* (Harper & Row, New York, 1962), p. 34.
7. *Life*, Vol. LIV, January 18, 1963, p. 13.
8. GLENDON SWARTHOUT, *The Cadillac Cowboys* (Random House, New York, 1964), p. 65.
9. TRUMAN CAPOTE, *Breakfast at Tiffany's* (Random House, New York, 1958).
10. JOSEPH HELLER, *op. cit.*, pp. 210–211.
11. JOHN OSBORNE, *Luther* (Criterion Books, New York, 1962), p. 38.

8. THE WAYWARD VERB

1. WILLIAM T. POLK, "Folkways and Folklore," *The North Carolina Guide* (ed., Blackwell P. Robinson, University of North Carolina Press, Chapel Hill, 1955), p. 13.

2. JAMES THURBER, *The Owl in the Attic* (Harper & Brothers, New York, 1931), pp. 132–133.

3. ANN CHAMBERLIN, "Two Cheers for the National Geographic," *Esquire*, Vol. LX, December, 1963, p. 300.

4. C. VANN WOODWARD, *The Strange Case of Jim Crow* (Galaxy edition, Oxford University Press, New York, 1957), p. 8.

5. RODERICK PEATTIE, ed., *The Great Smokies and the Blue Ridge* (The Vanguard Press, New York, 1953), pp. 109–110.

9. "IS YOU IS OR IS YOU AIN'T MY BABY?"

1. RODERICK PEATTIE, ed., *The Great Smokies and the Blue Ridge* (The Vanguard Press, New York, 1953), pp. 109–110.

2. HORTON COOPER, *The State,* North Carolina, March 21, 1959, p. 10.

3. ELIZABETH SKEGGS BOWMAN, *Land of High Horizons* (Southern Publishers, Inc., Kingsport, Tenn., 1948), p. 158.

4. *Ibid.,* p. 41.

5. *Ibid.,* p. 53.

6. JOSEPH HELLER, *Catch-22* (Simon and Schuster, New York, 1961), p. 170.

7. ERNEST HEMINGWAY, *To Have and Have Not* (Charles Scribner's Sons, New York, 1937), p. 193.

8. JOHN OSBORNE, *Luther* (Criterion Books, New York, 1962), p. 75.

9. *Ibid.,* p. 89.

10. ADJECTIVES AND ADVERBS

1. RODERICK PEATTIE, ed., *The Great Smokies and the Blue Ridge* (The Vanguard Press, New York, 1953), p. 148.

2. JOSEPH HELLER, *Catch-22* (Simon and Schuster, New York, 1961), p. 212.

3. *Vogue Pattern Book,* Vol. 38, February–March, 1964, p. 91.

4. LILLIAN ROSS, *Portrait of Hemingway* (Simon and Schuster, New York, 1962), p. 37.

5. NORMAN MAILER, "Norman Mailer Versus Nine Writers," *Esquire,* Vol. LX, July, 1963, p. 63.

6. ROBERT ADAMS, "Books," *Esquire,* Vol. LX, July, 1963, p. 63.

7. RUTH KRAUSS, *Open House for Butterflies* (Harper & Brothers, New York, 1960).

8. JOSEPH HELLER, *op. cit.,* p. 258.

9. *Ibid.,* pp. 259–260.

10. JAMES THURBER, *The Years with Ross* (Little, Brown and Company, Boston, 1959), pp. 129–130.

11. JAMES THURBER, *Credos and Curios* (Harper & Row, New York, 1962),
p. 92.

11. AMBIGUOUS MODIFIERS

1. JAMES THURBER, *Let Your Mind Alone!* (Harper & Brothers, New York,
1937), p. 185.
2. ANTHONY NUTTING, *Lawrence of Arabia* (Signet Books, New York, 1962),
p. 15.
3. MARK RASCOVITCH, *The Flight of the Dancing Bear* (Popular Library,
New York, 1962), p. 15.
4. IRVING STONE, *Clarence Darrow for the Defense* (Bantam Books, New
York, 1958), p. 6.
5. STEWART HOLBROOK, *The Age of the Moguls* (Doubleday & Company,
Inc., New York, 1953), p. 192.
6. NORMAN MAILER, "The Big Bite," *Esquire,* Vol. LX, November, 1963,
p. 28.
7. "Pork Barrel," *Life,* Vol. LV, August 16, 1963, p. 56.
8. *Lansing State Journal,* January 9, 1964, p. A–10.
9. JOSEPH HELLER, *Catch-22* (Simon and Schuster, New York, 1961), p.
154.
10. IRVING WALLACE, *Fabulous Showman: The Life and Times of P. T.
Barnum* (Alfred A. Knopf, Inc., New York, 1959), p. 167.
11. PETER BART, "The Money Managers," *Esquire,* Vol. LX, December,
1963, p. 204.

12. CONFUSED CONJUNCTIONS AND PREPOSITIONAL PUZZLES

1. LILLIAN ROSS, *Portrait of Hemingway* (Simon and Schuster, New York,
1962), p. 60.
2. TYRONE GUTHRIE, "So Long as the Theater Can Do Miracles," *The New
York Times Magazine,* April 28, 1963, p. 34.
3. MAURICE DRUON, *The Lion and the Lily,* trans. Humphrey Hare
(Charles Scribner's Sons, New York, 1961), p. 137.
4. LAWRENCE DURRELL, *White Eagles over Serbia* (Criterion Books, New
York, 1958), p. 94.
5. WILSON FOLLETT, "Sabotage in Springfield," *The Atlantic,* January,
1962, p. 75.
6. LILLIAN ROSS, *op. cit.,* p. 31.
7. EDMUND WILSON, *Patriotic Gore* (Oxford University Press, New York,
1962), p. xxviii.
8. GEORGE BERNARD SHAW, *Pygmalion* (Penguin Books, Inc., Baltimore),
p. 206.

9. JOSEPH HELLER, *Catch-22* (Simon and Schuster, New York, 1961), p. 70.
10. *Ibid.*, p. 219.
11. NORMAN MAILER, *The Naked and the Dead* (The Modern Library, New York, 1961), p. 270.
12. LILLIAN ROSS, *op. cit.*, p. 24.

13. NEGATIVE NEGATIVES

1. GEORGE ORWELL, *1984* (Harcourt, Brace and Company, 1949), p. 305.

14. SENTENCE STRUCTURE

1. *Time,* Vol. LXXX, December 21, 1962, p. 22.
2. RUTH KRAUSS, *Open House for Butterflies* (Harper & Row, New York, 1960).
3. *Ibid.*
4. EDGAR RICE BURROUGHS, *The Son of Tarzan* (Ballantine Books, New York, 1963), p. 124.
5. JAMES THURBER, *The Owl in the Attic* (Harper & Brothers, New York, 1931), p. 106.
6. EDGAR RICE BURROUGHS, *Tarzan of the Apes* (Ballantine Books, New York, 1963), p. 138.
7. EDGAR RICE BURROUGHS, *Tarzan, Lord of the Jungle* (Ballantine Books, New York, 1963), p. 60.
8. JAMES BALDWIN, *The Fire Next Time* (Dial Press, New York, 1963), p. 44.

15. THE PITFALLS AND PRATFALLS OF PUNCTUATION

1. JAMES THURBER, *The Years with Ross* (Little, Brown and Company, Boston, 1959), p. 267.
2. EDGAR RICE BURROUGHS, *Tarzan of the Apes* (Ballantine Books, New York, 1963), p. 176.
3. HENRY JAMES, *The American* (New York Edition, Charles Scribner's Sons, New York, 1907).
4. *Ibid.*
5. *Ibid.*
6. JAMES THURBER, *Thurber's Dogs* (Simon and Schuster, New York, 1955), p. 8.
7. *Ibid.*, p. 29.
8. *Ibid.*, p. 80.
9. *Ibid.*, p. 263.
10. *Ibid.*, p. 275.

17. GRAMMAR IS NOT ENOUGH

1. ALAN JAY LERNER, *My Fair Lady, A Musical Play in Two Acts,* adaptation and lyrics [by the author], music by Frederick Loewe (Coward-McCann, Inc., New York, 1957), p. 108.
2. KENNETH ROBERTS, *I Wanted to Write* (Doubleday & Company, Inc., New York, 1949), p. 400–402.
3. HERBERT BREAN, "The Man of More than 400 Mysteries," *Life,* Vol. LII, April 27, 1962, p. 22.
4. *The New York Times,* December 14, 1942, p. 16.
5. HAROLD WENTWORTH and STUART BERG FLEXNER, *Dictionary of American Slang* (Thomas Y. Crowell Company, New York, 1960), pp. xi–xii.
6. RICHARD CHASE, *Herman Melville: A Critical Study* (The Macmillan Company, New York, 1949), p. 270.
7. ROBERT BOLT, *A Man for All Seasons* (Random House, New York, 1962), p. 116.
8. JAMES D. KOERNER, *The Miseducation of American Teachers* (Houghton Mifflin Company, Boston, 1963), pp. 283–294.
9. NORMAN MAILER, "Norman Mailer Versus Nine Writers," *Esquire,* Vol. LX, July, 1963, p. 105.
10. "The Jargon that Jars," *Time,* Vol. LXXXII, November 8, 1963, p. 57.
11. DWIGHT MACDONALD, "Films," *Esquire,* Vol. LX, November, 1963, p. 70.
12. GEORGE REAVEY, ed. and trans., *The Poetry of Boris Pasternak* (G. P. Putnam's Sons, New York, 1959), p. 70.
13. EDGAR RICE BURROUGHS, *Tarzan of the Apes* (Ballantine Books, New York, 1963), p. 114.
14. EDITH WHARTON, *A Backward Glance* (Appleton-Century-Croft, Inc., New York, 1934), pp. 242–243.
15. RICHARD WILSON, "Friend of the Family," *Star Science Fiction Stories No. 2* (Ballantine Books, New York, 1962), p. 182.
16. JOHN STEINBECK, *The Grapes of Wrath* (The Viking Press, New York, 1939), p. 32.
17. JAMES THURBER, *The Years with Ross* (Little, Brown and Company, Boston, 1959), p. 6.
18. *The Readers Digest,* Vol. LXXXIII, August, 1963, p. 113.
19. STUART FLEXNER, "The Man Who Corrupted California," *Esquire,* Vol. LXI, March, 1964, p. 83.
20. *Ibid.,* p. 152.
21. *Ibid.,* p. 153.

18. THE GRAMMAR OF MARS

1. *Atlas,* Vol. III, June, 1962, p. 482.
2. ARTHUR MILLER, *Show,* Vol. IV, January, 1964, p. 98.

Index

347